KV-638-543

FORD MADOX FORD

Critical Essays

Selected, edited and introduced by
Max Saunders and Richard Stang

1453208
CHESTER COLLEGE
ACC No. 01090036 DEPT
CLASS No.
824.912 FOR
LIBRARY
WITHDRAWN

CARCANET

Published in Great Britain in 2002 by
Carcanet Press Limited
4th Floor, Conavon Court
12-16 Blackfriars Street
Manchester M3 5BQ

Copyright © 2002 Michael Schmidt

Introduction, notes and selection copyright
© 2002 Max Saunders and Richard Stang

The right of Max Saunders and Richard Stang to be identified as the editors of this book has been asserted by them in accordance with the Copyright, Designs and Patents Act of 1988.

All rights reserved.

A CIP catalogue record for this book is available from the British Library.

ISBN 1 85754 546 X

The publisher acknowledges financial assistance from the Arts Council of England.

Funded by THE ARTS COUNCIL OF ENGLAND

Set in Monotype Bembo by XL Publishing Services, Tiverton
Printed and bound in England by SRP Ltd, Exeter

Accession no.
01090036

WITHDRAWN

LIBRARY

Tel: 01244 375444 Ext: 3301

This book is to be returned on or before the last date stamped below. Overdue charges will be incurred by the late return of books.

Chester
A College of the University of Liverpool

UCC LIBRARY
4 DEC 2002

CANCELLED

UCC LIBRARY
11 DEC 2002

CANCELLED

WITHDRAWN

e
d
d
's
n

St
Louis. His previous publications include *The Theory of the Novel in England 1850–1870* (Columbia University Press) and *Discussions of George Eliot* (Boston).

Also by Ford Madox Ford from Carcanet

The Rash Act
Ladies Whose Bright Eyes
The Good Soldier
Parade's End
Selected Poems
The Ford Reader
A History of Our Own Times
The English Novel
Return to Yesterday
War Prose

Contents

Introduction by Richard Stang and Max Saunders ix
Note on the text xiv
Acknowledgements xiv

The Evolution of a Lyric (1899) 1
Creative History and the Historic Sense (1903–4) 4
The Collected Poems of Christina Rossetti (1904) 15
A Literary Causerie: On Some Tendencies of Modern Verse (1905; on Sturge Moore) 28
Literary Portraits from *The Tribune*
III. Mr John Galsworthy (1907) 33
VIII. Mr Joseph Conrad (1907) 36
[X, but says VIII]. Maxim Gorky (1907) 39
IX [*sic*: should be XI]. Mr Dion Clayton Calthrop (1907) 43
XIV. Mr Maurice Hewlett (1907) 46
From XXIII. The Year 1907 49
XXIV. The Year 1908 49
XXVII. Mr Charles Doughty (1908) 52
Shylock as Mr Tree (1908) 56
Essays from *The English Review*
The Unemployed (1908) 59
Review of George Saintsbury, *A History of English Prosody* (1909) 62
The Work of W.H. Hudson (1909) 65
Algernon Charles Swinburne (1909) 71
George Meredith OM (1909) 72
Review of C.F.G. Masterman, *The Condition of England* (1909) 73
Joseph Conrad (1911) 76
D.G.R. (1911) 91
Essays from *The Bystander*
A Tory Plea for Home Rule (2 articles; 1911) 98
Pan and the Pantomime (on Shaw; 1912) 106
Literary Portraits and Other Essays from *The Outlook*
I. Mr Compton Mackenzie and *Sinister Street* (1913) 110
VI. Mr John Galsworthy and *The Dark Flower* (1913) 114
VII. Mr Percival Gibbon and *The Second-Class Passenger* (1913) 118
XII. Herr Arthur Schnitzler and *Bertha Garlan* (1913) 122

XXIII. Fydor Dostoevsky and *The Idiot* (1914) 126
XXV. Monsignor Benson and *Initiation* (1914) 129
XXVI. Miss Amber Reeves and *A Lady and her Husband* (1914) 133
XXVIII. Mr Morley Roberts and *Time and Thomas Waring* (1914) 137
XXXI. Lord Dunsany and *Five Plays* (1914) 142
XXXIV. Miss May Sinclair and *The Judgment of Eve* (1914) 146
XXXV. Les Jeunes and *Des Imagistes* (1914) 150
XXXVI. Les Jeunes and *Des Imagistes* (Second Notice) (1914) 154
XXXVIII. Mr W.H. Mallock and *Social Reform* (1914) 159
XXXIX. Mr W.B. Yeats and his New Poems (1914) 163
XLII. Mr Robert Frost and *North of Boston* (1914) 167
France, 1915 (continued) (1915) 170
Sologub and Artzibashef (1915) 173
A Jubilee (review of *Some Imagist Poets*) (1915) 178
On a Notice of *Blast* (1915) 182
'Thus to Revisit', *Piccadilly Review* (1919)
I. The Novel 186
(Gilbert Cannan, *Time and Eternity*; Virginia Woolf, *Night and Day*)
II. The Realistic Novel 190
(Dostoevsky, *An Honest Thief*; George Stevenson, *Bengy*)
III. The Serious Books 192
(Max Beerbohm, *Seven Men*; W.H. Hudson, *Birds in Town and Village*)
V. Biography and Criticism 197
(Henry Festing Jones, *Samuel Butler*; Wyndham Lewis, *The Caliph's Design*)
Letter to the Editor of *The Athenaeum* (1920) 203
An Answer to 'Three Questions' (1922) 206
A Haughty and Proud Generation (1922) 208
Ulysses and the Handling of Indecencies (1922) 218
Mr Conrad's Writing (1923) 228
Literary Causeries from the *Chicago Tribune Sunday Magazine*
II. Vill Loomyare (1924) 232
III. And the French (1924) 233
VIII. So She Went into The Garden … (on Joyce; 1924) 235
Essays from *the transatlantic review* (1924)
Stocktaking: Towards a Revaluation of English Literature
II. Axioms and Internationalisms 241
[III. but headed] II. (continued) 243
IV. Intelligentsia 248
IX. The Serious Book (continued) 254

X. The Reader 261
From a Paris Quay (II) (1925) 269
The Other House (review of Jean-Aubry's *Joseph Conrad*; 1927) 272
Cambridge on the Caboodle (on Forster; 1927) 276
Thomas Hardy, OM Obiit 11 January 1928 282
Elizabeth Madox Roberts by Ford Madox Ford (1928) 285
On Conrad's Vocabulary (1928) 288
Review of Josephine Herbst, *Nothing is Sacred* (1928) 292
Review of Sinclair Lewis, *Dodsworth* (1929) 294
Mediterranean Reverie (on Pound; 1933) 296
Hands Off the Arts (1935) 300
Men and Books (on Conrad; 1936) 309
Observations on Technique (1937) 312
Ralston Crawford's Pictures (1937) 314
The Flame in Stone (on Louise Bogan; 1937) 316
None Shall Look Back (on Caroline Gordon; 1937) 319
Statement on the Spanish War (1937) 321

Index 323

Introduction

The purpose of this volume is to bring together essays very few of which have been republished in books before. Because Ford wrote critical essays all his writing life – well over five hundred periodical contributions have been discovered – it seemed to the present editors that it would make sense to allow the general reader access to the best of them, especially now that Ford enjoys a rather general recognition as a major twentieth-century author.

Perhaps these essays will send the reader to Ford's many books of criticism, such as *Thus to Revisit, Portraits from Life, Henry James, Joseph Conrad, The English Novel*, and *The March of Literature*; and to the essays in collections such as Sondra Stang's *A Ford Madox Ford Reader*, Frank MacShane's *Critical Writings of Ford Madox Ford*, Brita Lindberg-Seyested's *Pound/Ford*, Martin Stannard's Norton Critical Edition of *The Good Soldier*. Work now in print was not included in the present volume since it seemed wasteful to use the limited space available to us reprinting material easily accessible.

The essays are arranged chronologically. They span nearly forty years, covering most of Ford's publishing life, from his formative collaboration with Conrad to his last years. Three phases predominate, however, and they correspond to the three phases of his greatest creative intensity, when he was not only prolific, and at his best, as a critic, but was also writing his best fiction. From 1907 to 1910, when completing the *Fifth Queen* trilogy and writing *A Call*, Ford was producing weekly reviews for the *Daily Mail* and *The Tribune*, then writing for the magazine he founded and edited, *The English Review*. From 1913–14, while writing his best pre-war novel, *The Good Soldier*, and into 1915, he contributed weekly essays to *The Outlook*. Then in the mid-1920s, while working on his post-war masterpiece *Parade's End*, he founded and wrote for a new magazine, *the transatlantic review*, as well as writing for other periodicals, and producing one of his best books of critical reminiscence, *Joseph Conrad*.

These essays, most of which give us Ford's response as a reader to work just published, will perhaps help us to understand why Pound claimed in 1914 that Ford was 'the best critic in England, one might say the only critic of any importance', and Marianne Moore that Ford's reviews 'were of inestimable value to me, as method'.[1] Few people today have heard of

1 Pound, 'Mr Hueffer and the Prose Tradition in Verse', *Poetry*, 4 (June 1914), 111–20; *The Complete Prose of Marianne Moore*, Patricia C. Willis (London, 1987), p. 593.

most of the books Ford reviewed in the pages of *The Tribune, The Outlook, The Daily Mail* and other newspapers and magazines. His portraits included writers we no longer read or whose names are only familiar to us from literary histories: Hall Caine, Mrs Mary E. Mann, Maurice Hewlett, Charles Doughty, Lord Dunsany, W.H. Mallock. Many of the books are clearly period pieces not likely to be exhumed. But because Ford asks the right questions when confronting a new work by a contemporary, these reviews of now forgotten books and the larger questions about writing they raise make them worth rescuing.

Interspersed with these are a large number of reviews of more significant figures: Shaw, Pound, Anatole France, Joyce, Wells, Bennett, Galsworthy, Conrad, Hardy, Schnitzler, Gorky, Dostoevsky, Yeats, Frost. In both categories, one reads Ford's reviews for what he tells us about literature and its relation to a given time, and in doing that he communicates to us his distinctive note – genial and serious, civilized; if sometimes quirky, wrong-headed, and mildly outrageous. Clearly, it is immensely valuable to have the immediate response of an intelligent contemporary, especially one like Ford, who was at the same time reshaping the literary landscape.

Indeed, if all the literary portraits from *The Daily Mail, The Tribune*, and *The Outlook* were published as a group, it would provide a great source for understanding the literary situation of that time: the literary diary of one of the great minds of modern literature, showing how the modern movements (Impressionism, Imagism, Vorticism, Modernism) appeared in the cultural milieu of early twentieth-century London.

He was not necessarily interested in 'judicious' criticism. Rather, his instinct as a critic was bold and excessive – to follow wherever the friction between the work and his temperament might take him. Always deeply engaged, always vital, his writing tended to proceed by leaps, even overstatement, never to provide a final judgement on the work he was discussing, but to arouse a response in his reader, to provoke thought rather than foreclose it. His deliberately sweeping statements were not meant to be taken literally, but he did want to be taken seriously. Hence, he was never cautious and did not mind being shocking. As he said in *The English Novel*,

> what I am about to write is highly controversial and [... the reader] must take none of it too much *au pied de la lettre*. I don't mean to say that it will not be written with almost ferocious seriousness. But what follows are suggestions not dictates, for in perusing this sort of book the reader must be prepared to do a good deal of the work for himself – within his own mind.

On some of the sweeping statements of that book, he said the reader must object 'as violently as possible: then, in reaction, thinking it over he will probably find there is something in what I say'.[2]

For Ford, the purpose of his criticism was to force the reader to be open to new impressions. The great enemy of art, as he saw it, was received opinion, stock responses, following conventions for conventions' sake. To lose touch with reality – with the world outside of one's self – would be to forestall the kind of reaction he had to reading for the first time the first Lawrence story he saw, 'Odour of Chrysanthemums'. In *Portraits from Life* he gives a marvellous vignette of that exemplary close-reading.[3]

His criticism is never systematic, theoretical, abstract, academic. He hated systems and the systematizing mind, the kind of mind he thought of as Prussian, resulting in the kind of work then emanating from German universities, as he hated language which loses touch with the spoken word, poetic diction, conventional language, academic jargon. (The parallels with Wordsworth's famous preface to *Lyrical Ballads* are striking.) For him all writing had to be an individual rendering of what an individual really perceived. Even though he claimed to have hated Ruskin as one of the bearded Victorian greats who made his childhood miserable, Ruskin stated Ford's credo as clearly as anyone:

> ... the greatest thing the human soul does in this world is to *SEE* something, and tell what it *SAW* in a plain way. Hundreds of people can talk for one who can think, but thousands can think for one who can see. To see clearly is poetry, prophecy, and religion – all in one.[4]

Seeing clearly is what most of us do not do most of the time. It follows that when an artist sees clearly, and communicates to us his vision, something in our world has altered: our world has been transformed. According to Ford, in *Provence*, 'the authentic note of the great poet is to modify for you the aspect of the world and of your relationship to the world', and in his introduction to Hemingway's *A Farewell to Arms*, he develops this idea:

> a writer holds a reader by his temperament. That is his true 'gift' – what he receives from whoever sends him into the world. It arises from how you look at things. If you look at and render things so that they appear new to the reader you will hold his attention [....] You

2 *The English Novel* (London, 1930), pp. 24–5, 26–7.
3 *Portraits from Life* (Boston, 1937), pp. 70–74. Published in Britain as *Mightier Than the Sword* (London, 1938); see pp. 98–103.
4 *Modern Painters* , Vol. III, part 4, chapter 16.

> have had a moment of surprise and then your knowledge is added to. The word 'author' means 'someone who adds to your consciousness'.[5]

Thus the artist must be an individual with an individual manner of seeing, an individual temperament, yet he is also part of a larger whole, which Ford liked to call 'the Republic of letters', which with the other arts is 'the only real civilizing agency at work today'. After the First World War, which ushered in an increasingly bleak world marked by nationalism, militarism, mindless technology and 'technocrats', and totalitarianism, he wrote: 'beautiful talents are the desperate need of these sad months and years when we tremble on the verge of a return to barbarism…'[6] In the *transatlantic review* he explained why, in a passage reminiscent of Matthew Arnold's definition of culture as the humanization of man in society:

> the Arts […] make you understand your fellow human being: they may indeed make you understand your fellow brute beast. In either case in the train of comprehension come sympathy and tolerance and after subjecting yourself for some time to the influence of the arts you become less of a brute beast yourself.
>
> This is the only humanising process that has no deleterious sides since all systems of morality tend to develop specific sides of a character at the expense of all other sides.[7]

Ford was clearly influenced by the aestheticism of the 1880s and 1890s. He writes of 'that high, fine pleasure' of poetry; and his great pleasure in reading comes across powerfully.[8] Yet at the same time he always thought of art as communication. 'An art is the highest form of communication between person and person'[9] – again a Wordsworthian ideal, that of the poet as 'a man speaking to men'. He is at his best as a reader of other writers – responding to their temperaments, their perceptions, their language, their art – rather than as a theorizer.

Sondra Stang, who sadly did not live to finish this project which she began, should have the last words. She wrote of Ford's unusual preference for Christina Rossetti's verse over that of her brother Dante Gabriel:

> Her achievement was that, looking at life around her, she wrote in the 'clear pure language of our own day', unlike her brother Dante Gabriel, who had given the 'numbing blow of a sandbag' to the art of

5 *Ford Madox Ford Reader*, ed. Sondra J. Stang (Manchester, 1986), p. 252. Ford reiterates this idea in *It Was the Nightingale* (London, 1934), p. 69, when he defines the artist as 'the man who added to the thought and emotions of mankind'.

6 *Thus to Revisit* (London, 1921), p. 15.

7 'Stocktaking. IV', *transatlantic review*, 1:4 (April 1924), 169–70.

8 *Thus to Revisit*, p. 129.

9 *The March of Literature* (London, 1939), p. 4.

> writing in English, 'digging for obsolete words with which to express ideas forever dead and gone'.
>
> Whether or not Ford was fair to either of the Rossettis, and whether or not Christina's poetry was significant for the twentieth century, Ford's preference should be understood as a moment in the gradual clarification of his own aesthetic. Readers looking for a judicious and disengaged point of view, that of an ideal literary historian, perpetually contemporary with them, have of course found Ford's criticism disturbing, and his attack on the nineteenth-century English novel (or 'nuvvle', as he called it to distinguish it from what he considered was the genuine article, the Continental novel) has probably done its share in alienating readers. Ford's judgements were highly personal, often overstated, and deliberately outrageous, but behind them was an unwillingness to corroborate an aesthetic that had already had its day. How he read other writers and how he theorized about his own writing all had to do with his forward-looking momentum: the writer must represent and interpret his own age and look toward the future.[10]

She also explained (in the notes she left for her selection, some of which have been incorporated into this introduction) how Ford's criticism can give us a most refined – and at the same time realistic – sense of what art is, what it can do for human life:

> Beyond their generosity and their grace, the pieces collected here contain the just pronouncements of a serious writer practising his craft and passing on to other [readers and] writers what he has clarified for himself, passing on to his readers what the work before them reveals to him. In these modest and often trenchant statements, Ford writes about the relation between language and literature, between temperament and writing; he defines for us what style is; and finally, he reminds us, if we are in any danger of forgetting, why we go to fiction, to poetry, to painting.

10 Sondra J. Stang, *Ford Madox Ford* (New York, 1977), pp. 20–1.

A Note on the Text

The essays in this volume come from a wide range of periodicals, all using different conventions of layout and punctuation. These have been converted to the Carcanet house style. Topical information (such as details of publishers and prices) have been removed. However, journalistic sub-headings have been retained. Typographical and other obvious errors have been silently corrected. Spelling and transliterations have been standardized. Ellipses of three or four dots represent Ford's own. Editorial ellipses are indicated by three asterisks. Editorial footnotes are given in square brackets.

Acknowledgements

The editors would like to thank the following for their help in the preparation of this volume: the late Janice Biala; the Centre for Computing in the Humanities at King's College London, and in particular Harold Short and Pam Jones; Susan Fox of New York City; the staff of the Washington University Library; Will Harris; Elena Lamberti; Leslie Verth; Hamish Whyte; Joseph Wiesenfarth; and Susan Hacker Stang. The greatest debt we owe is to Sondra Stang, who began this project and was working on it at the time of her death in 1990.

The Evolution of a Lyric

The baby was being put to bed in the room over the head of the writer of lyrics. He was pacing up and down the border of his carpet. He could hear the nurse crooning a lullaby that had hushed to sleep little negroes out in Louisiana.

'Hang it all!' he said; 'the kiddy ought to have a lullaby of her own.' One's own baby is something precious to one; so are one's own lyrics; and 'Sweets to the sweet,' they say; therefore, things precious to the precious.[1]

He went to the window and looked out. It was falling dusk. Shadows were creeping up the hedgerows, the red rays of the sun fell aslant along the downs that closed round the farm. On the terrace above the stockyard the flowers were passively awaiting the oncoming of the night. The great white poppies were folding their petals together. High overhead the pigeons were circling round and round, the flush of the sunset irradiating their breasts and the inner sides of their wings. The writer of lyrics sat down at his desk, and began to scrawl upon a scrap of notepaper. The negro melody was running in his head.

'*Poppy heads are closing fast*,' he wrote, and then paused. What next? Ah! the pigeons – the child liked the pigeons, and the word began with a 'p'. A little alliteration does no harm.

'*Pigeons wing their* –' No; that was no good. 'Pigeons wing' is wretched. Pigeons – pigeons – what do pigeons do? Ah! –

'*Pigeons circle home at last*' – the line wrote itself almost. So did the next three words, with the tune to help them:

'*Sleep, baby, sleep.*' Anything will do here – anything. But what is it to be? A bat cried outside. Yes – yes – the bats – '*The bats are calling.*'…

He looked out of the window again. The round beds on the terrace were bordered with hearts-ease – blue and yellow hearts-ease, and hearts-ease so dark that they were almost black—so black that the darkness could make very little difference to them.

'*Pansies*' he wrote – another 'p'. He was rather doubtful about so much alliteration, but still 'pansies' is pretty, and then … '*Never miss the light.*' The next line suggested itself, because, even if pansies can do without

1 [The lyric in question was later re-published as 'Lullaby' in *From Inland* (1907) and *Collected Poems* [1913], p. 99.]

light, babies can't. 'But sweet babes must sleep at night.' A glance out of the window had caught the settling down of the white shrouds of mist:–

'sleep, baby, sleep, the dew is falling.'

That was a whole verse. But this only stood for the chorus of the tune. There was the body of the melody to be attended to. It was a terrible task, and cost a week's wrestling. To begin with, the melody opened on the second note of a bar and ended on a slur that called for a 'female rhyme'. At last he got as far as: 'We've wandered all about the downs together', but the rhymes to 'together' are all hopelessly hackneyed and necessitated for the third line: 'But now, good-bye, good-bye, dear summer weather', a line that might be good enough for a song translator. Besides, it was the beginning, not the end of summer. At last, for 'downs together' 'upland fallows' suggested itself, and, after that, the verse wrote itself. That made: one four-line verse and one sestet. There was as much again to do. Curiously enough, this time it was not the four-line, but the chorus verse, that gave the trouble. Before it was finished it looked like this:

'You may slumber in your cot' (*scratched out*).
'Ducks' heads underneath each wing' (*scratched out*).
'Warm beneath their mother's breast' }
'Little chicks have gone to rest' } (*vigorously erased*)
'Sleep, baby, sleep, the moon is rising, risen' (*erased*).
'Little mice have stolen out, on the sea the lights shine out'
(*erased*)
'Hoping pussy's not about' (*scratched out*).

But at last – after fourteen days' work – the thing was done. You will observe that each line cost nearly a whole day. On the morrow, a fellow-writer – a prose man – but one of the great ones of the earth, one of those who receive fifteen guineas per 1,000 words, looked in and picked up the fair copy.

'Ah,' he said, 'if I could reel off little things like that and get half a guinea apiece – as you do – I'd soon be a millionaire.' The writer of lyrics looked at his finished production. It ran:

We've wandered all about the upland fallows.
We've watched the rabbits at their play,
But now good-night, good-bye to soaring swallows,
Now, good-night, good-bye, dear day.
Poppy heads are closing fast, pigeons circle home at last;
Sleep, baby, sleep, the bats are calling;
Pansies never miss the light, but sweet babes must sleep at
night:

Sleep, baby, sleep, the dew is falling.

Even the wind among the whisp'ring willows
Rests, and the waves are resting too.
See, soft white linen; cool, such cool white pillows
Wait in the darkling room for you.
All the little lambs are still, now the moon peeps down the hill;
Sleep, Liebchen, sleep, the owls are hooting;
Ships have hung their lanthorns out, little mice dare creep about:
Sleep, Liebchen, sleep, the stars are shooting.

He groaned: '"Ships have hung their lanthorns out" is the only line that doesn't make me feel ill – all the rest is rubbish.' And he sat down to rewrite the lyric from end to end.

Outlook, 3 (22 April 1899), 387–8.

Creative History and the Historic Sense

Mr A. F. Pollard has written a book on Henry VIII[1] & Professor Goldwin Smith reviews it in the *North American Review*.[2] Professor Smith's article is mainly an attack on Henry & the late Mr Froude: immediately afterwards there appears in the *Fortnightly Review* Mr W.S. Lilly's article on the last named historian.

Froude thought Henry was a marvellous instrument of Providence in the evolution of the Church of England, Professor Smith thinks that Henry was not a 'high bred gentleman', Mr Lilly thinks that the late Mr Froude was congenitally incapable of speaking the truth. (Mr Lilly is secretary to the Catholic Association of Great Britain.) Someone else says that 'The proper place among the diseases of the mind for this wanton insolence may be found by anybody who has the patience & the spare time to read the works of Mr Lilly'.[3] On such lines & in such tempers do we approach creative history & its heroes.

MM. Bouvard & Pécuchet, before they began their never finished Dictionary of Accepted Ideas, studied the works of Professors to find Truth. They attacked for instance the subject of literary style; they discovered Marmontel groaning over the licence that Homer allowed himself & Blair, an Englishman, lamenting the violence of Shakespeare. Bouvard found the disagreements of Professors so confusing & so distracting... 'ces questions le travaillèrent tellement qu'il y gagnait une jaunisse'. After much reading the works of Professors & others on the question of the personality & the Times of Henry VIII it is difficult to escape the fate of Bouvard. It is at least refreshing to consider the point of view of one simple minded & aloof. A question was set in an examination paper: 'Who was your favourite historical character & why?' A schoolboy answered: 'Henry VIII, because he was the only one that had more wives than children'.

This has a frivolous sound but actually that answer is a symptom serious

1 *Henry VIII* by A.F. Pollard, London, Goupil & Co.
2 'A Gallery of Portraits,' by Goldwin Smith, DCL.
3 *Daily Chronicle*, 1 June 1903.

enough: it represents the net value of History as it is taught today, in so far as it touches the time of Henry VIII.

That schoolboy, seriously considered, voiced practically the general view. The matter of the wives is a very insignificant detail of a whole reign, long, tortuous in its intrigues, extremely difficult to follow in its very broadest outlines: before ever one is able to descend to the king's psychology & motives. Yet that matter has obsessed all our historians: it obsessed Mr Froude; no doubt it obsessed the first Defender of the Faith himself. It obsesses Professor Goldwin Smith to the point of hysteria; it 'intrigues' to this day the whole of Catholic Europe & as much of Protestant England as thinks of sixteenth-century history. It can not, apparently, be got away from.

Immediately after reading Professor Smith's article I discussed the whole personality of Henry with three *ex officio* leaders of public opinion of today. Their joint, net, opinion was that he was a 'lover'. Professor Smith however calls Henry a 'human tiger' who could not feel love. Yet Marillac the French Ambassador says (*Letters & Papers*, vol. xvi, 12) that Henry was 'so amourous of the Queen, Katharine Howard, that he could not do enough for her' & Chapuys, Charles V's ambassador, says (Ibid, vol. xvii) that he thought Henry had his death at her execution he looked so ill after. Froude says that it was a pity Henry could not have lived in a world without women, to which Professor Smith gallantly but quite inconsequently retorts: 'Would Mr Froude have found it a pleasant world?' But Jerome Cardan, a professor with his eyes on the stars, accounts for the poor king's matrimonial misfortunes which he had witnessed & lamented, thus: 'Venus being in conjunction with Cauda, Lampas partook of the nature of Mars: Luna in occiduo cardine was among the dependencies of Mars & Mars himself was in the illstarred constellation Virgo & in the quadrant of Jupiter Infelix'. Mr Froude calls this 'abominable nonsense' whilst Henry himself remarked: 'Happy those who never saw a King & whom a King never saw'.

Cardinal Pole in the revised version of *De Unitate Ecclesiae* accuses Henry of having debauched the sister of Anne Boleyn before divorcing Katharine of Aragon. Froude calls Cardinal Pole an arrogant, loquacious & ineffectual traitor. But Professor Smith says he was broadminded & exactly the reverse of everything that Froude called him. Pole says of himself that at the age of thirty-six he had long been conversant with old men & had long judged the oldest men too young for him to learn wisdom from. On the other hand he freely acknowledges that this remarkable wisdom was the gift of the king who had specially fostered his education. He wrote a book for the king's private reading intended to turn the king back to the Old Faith & away from Anne. He swore to the king that no one had seen it after he had submitted it for the approval of the Vatican authorities. It contained such passages as: 'Your flatterers have filled your heart with folly, you have made yourself abhorred amongst the rulers of Xtendom.... Rex est partus Naturae laborantis, populus enim regem procreat'. It astonished him that this failed to convert Henry & he travelled all Europe over seeking to raise a crusade against his king.

Froude accordingly calls Pole a fool, an evil genius, a narrow & odious fanatic, & a traitor to the Instrument of Providence. But Professor Smith excuses this treachery with: 'surely without any religious fanaticism any man might well object to seeing the Church, the unity of which all Xtians prized, rent in twain in order to satisfy a tyrant's lust'.

Henry however had been able to satisfy his lust with Anne, not to mention her sister, without rending the church in twain, for according to both Pole & Professor Smith Anne had been his mistress for years before the divorce. (Professor Smith speaks of Henry's 'brutal behaviour in openly installing his mistress as Queen designate at her side'.) The king had also, according to them both, 'certainly' enjoyed her sister. Mr Froude however thinks it unlikely that in that case Henry, his people & his Parliament could have been so 'cynically heartless' as to demand his separation from Katharine on the ground of incest. Professor Smith however considers the charge 'certainly proved': for, in the Act of Parliament, 28 Hen. VIII cap. 27, illegitimate unions are decreed to bring persons within the degree of consanguinity of marriage. Charles V's view of the matter was (he was telling Wyatt, Henry's ambassador, that he could not prevent Spanish preachers uttering these slanders against Henry): 'Preachers will preach against myself whenever there is cause; that cannot be hindered; kings be not kings of tongues. And if men give cause to be spoken of they will be spoken of'. Thus Charles supported freedom of speech. On the other hand, the Queen of Navarre said to the Papal Nuncio at about the same time: 'Say you that the King of England is a man lost & cast away? I would to God that your master the Pope, & the Emperor, & we here did live after so good & godly a sort as he & his doth.'

Thomas Cromwell's portrait by Holbein, says Professor Smith, 'is a softened version of the subject'! It is not ugly enough. His authority for this is Mr Merriman, who wrote in 1902. And: 'For thorough paced villainy Cromwell had no peers. Who besides him has ever deliberately set down his criminal intentions in a memorandum book: "*Item*, The Abbot of Glaston to be tried at Glaston & also to be executed there with his accomplices. *Item*, to see that the evidence be well sorted & the indictment well drawn.... *Item* to send Gendon to the Tower to be racked. *Item* to appoint preachers to go through the realm to preach the gospel & the true word of God".' Yet Cardinal Pole, whom Professor Smith so much admires, was setting down in memoranda in books, & crying to all the princes in Europe, that his own king must be taken upon the field of battle & his entrails torn out & burnt before his face. And Pole too would have sent preachers with the true word of God throughout this realm.

The late Mr Froude found Cromwell a mighty minister & a consummate diplomatist, skilfully balancing the Powers one against another & crushing out seditions with a strong but necessary & beneficent hand... until Henry began to frown on him. Then immediately, Cromwell's bringing about the diplomatic marriage with Anne of Cleves becomes 'stooping to dabble in the muddy waters of intrigue'. When he was in the Tower Cromwell wrote: 'Most Gracious Lord, I never spoke with the Chancellor of the Augmentation & Throgmorton at one time. But if I did I am sure I never spoke of any such matter & your Grace knows what matter of man Throgmorton is.' But Froude says this denial 'was faint, indirect, not like the broad, absolute repudiation of a man who was consciously clear of offience'. Cromwell was accused of having said before the Chancellor & Throgmorton that he would fight against the king sword in hand if the king reversed his policy. Cromwell of course had hanged many men on hearsay evidence of informers like Throgmorton, & Marillac puts the matter: 'Words idly spoken he had aforetime twisted into treason: the measure which he had dealt out to others shall now be meted out to him.' And this was practically the view of the Council that condemned him. Froude however says that Henry was forced to execute Cromwell because 'the illegal acts of a minister who had been trusted with extraordinary powers were too patent to be denied'. Professor Smith accounts for it all by: 'The king feared those under whose influence he had been & could not bear to let them live.' The King of France & Cardinal 'Du Bellay' were of opinion that Cromwell fell because he wanted to marry the Princess Mary, no doubt with a view to the succession: 'insomuch as at all times when any marriage was treated of for the Lady Mary he did always his best to break the same'. It should be remembered that the fondest desire of the Cardinal & Francis had been a French marriage for Mary.

Thus each man may see in the case of Henry VIII what he most desires to see, Professor Smith seeing that it is almost needless to add Cromwell was corrupt, & 'accumulated wealth by foul means'. Yet in the nature of the case the only proof of this is the accusations of his enemies, for Cromwell was not even tried. The case against Anne Boleyn rests perhaps on no better evidence. She was at least tried & – Froude urges – found guilty by the greatest peers of the Realm, her own father being amongst them. Yet in her case, tho' not in Cromwell's, Professor Smith can see that nothing was proved against her... because he desires to prove that Henry was a human tiger.

I propose to sum up very briefly my views of Henry, to add one more to the small collection of bizarreries of judgements here adduced. (I had studied the matter for some years & had got together all the materials for a life of this king & I had written my first chapter when Mr Pollard forestalled me with his book, which for that reason I refrain from commenting upon.) Henry to me was a man very much of his age. He was of course a Tudor & a king: this made him unreasonable, ungovernable, with the horrible suspicions of a high solitude & a great craving for a companion he could trust. But it was in the nature of the policies of that day to be tortuous & in their very basis unscrupulous. Deceit was a recognized factor in public life & Henry employed all his trusted companions in endless intrigues that were based on sheer deceit. Taking this king & these things together it needs very little knowledge of psychology to see that his career must be one of passionate attachments reacting towards still more passionate suspicions. He employed these persons to deceive, he trusted them; sooner or later he must have the thought in his mind: These persons are deceiving me. And, that being the case in a Court circle, grounds for that belief could never be long wanting. Anne Boleyn & Katharine were as inevitably doomed to suspicion as Wolsey & Cromwell. He was a king & by every scheme of ethics of his contemporaries the fitting penalty for deceiving him was death. If we accept Professor Smith's view of Henry as an insensate human tiger there were certainly no high-bred gentlemen in Europe of that day. It was a world of tigers.

It naturally was not, being only a world with other ideals from those of XXth century England & North America. 'Tue la' is still the hardly ethically or legally condemned remedy for matrimonial infidelity of the great Latin races & of by far the greater portion of the population of the globe. Very possibly Henry 'lusted' after other women as soon as he tired of one & very possibly too that helped him to desire the divorce of Katharine. But very possibly it did not. It must be remembered too that in those days what Schopenhauer called 'Christo-Germanisch Dummheit', the idea that women were to be more tenderly treated than men, had hardly been evolved & Henry was quite within his ethical scheme & the scheme of his contemporaries when he swept women as well as men out of his way by execution. The legal penalty for high treason was burning in the case of women & Henry was very essentially a child of his age. *Populus enim regem procreat*, as Pole said.

He was in fact not much more monstrous than his people but his people had given him more scope. And monstrous as we may account his treatment of Katharine of Aragon, judged by our own standards, it was as nothing to the treatment of that very unfortunate lady by Henry VII, the king whom so humanitarian a person as More eulogized.

But if it be Pharisaism to call Henry a human tiger it is blind Hero Worship to call him an instrument of providence or even a particularly great king. He was certainly a very hard worker but otherwise he was little more than a very obstinate opportunist. If he escaped ultimate disaster it was only on account of the utter incapacity & irresoluteness of his fellow rulers in Christendom. To a person with any imagination it is little less than maddening to follow the proceedings of Charles V during the great rising in the North when Henry was absolutely at his last gasp before the Catholic rebels. Of policy he had none & his mind was always fixed on the most meticulous details of his day's chicanery. He detested Protestantism & he forced it upon the world, he held public debates with heretics & when he failed to convince them he had no better remedy than to let them be burnt for beliefs which, two years later, his opportunism forced him to tolerate. Upon the whole he increased the prestige of the Crown very materially but he did it in such a way that as soon as the personal power of the Tudors went from the Throne the Throne lost that power of packing juries & parliaments which was essentially the secret of his government.

Heavy, threatening, jealous & craving for that sympathy that is admiration, he made an immense splutter in Christendom. But he did not direct any tendencies: he merely changed them in a time when change was in the air.

If we regard him personally he seems, I think, a tragic figure as every suspicious man born to great power must be. Temperamental jealousy & suspicion are the greatest of all the plagues of the flesh, since jealous man is incapable of believing the most material proofs of innocence and perpetually torments himself very horribly for reasons that come out of his own being, & I am strongly inclined to believe that he must have been what today we call a neurotic subject, at any rate in his later years. The times were very complicated & the daily work that he had to get through was very great. Merely to read today & to keep in mind all the separate threads of events in the *Calendars of Letters & State Papers*, merely to follow them very much at one's leisure is a sufficiently great undertaking. But to have been buried deep in the very belly of the events, to have trembled for one's throne, for one's dynasty, one's land, one's personal honour & very certainly for one's soul, to have been certain of only one thing… that there was no man one could trust: all that must have meant a strain constant, increasing & maddening. I am not in the least inclined to doubt that Henry may really have believed his marriage with Katharine cursed by God. He was a superstitious man in a superstitious age & all her sons died at birth. It is possible even that he believed the adulteries of Anne & Katharine Howard were the successive revenges of Providence for his breaking up the Church & that this rivetted in his mind the belief in their adulteries. His precautions for keeping his son alive were those of a man in a panic & there is no doubt that, had he lived, he would have sought reconciliation with the Pope. A letter to Charles V asking for his intercession was actually drafted but never sent. You have only to look at his portrait to see that his life was not very merry.

The fact is that any study of Henry & his times must be a pathologic one. To approach them in any *ex parte* spirit... to approach any period of revolution, any revolutionary figure, or indeed to approach any figure or any period in a partisan spirit, is to do no more than to convince men who already agree with you or to give a picture of yourself to anyone who may happen to be disinterested. One or two foreign historians of distinction have assured me that the distinguishing defect of their English confrères is their insularity... their being exclusively preoccupied with the affairs of England. And when we look at the wideness of research of German professors the charge seems comparatively correct, though I suppose we may point to Robertson & Gibbon, not to mention the researches of Mr Martin Hume in the archives of Simancas or the delightful South American studies of Mr Cunninghame Graham. But the insular tendency is traceable to our inborn habit of regarding History as a branch of polemics. It is obvious that in that case our polemics will bear upon points that most nearly touch ourselves & that we shall find those points in our own history.

And the English public does not want impartial history. It asks for ethical points of view, ethical 'leads'; just as it can not understand 'the use' of impersonal fiction. Consequently only the political tract 'pays' & we have phenomena like the histories of Hume, Macaulay & Froude; that amusing skit, Professor Smith's article, & articles of similar, less exaggerated, but less amusing types.

The polemic is of course very stimulating & very exhilarating when it is well done: at its best it promotes thought, at its worst it provides a human document, casting light upon the workings of its writer's mind. But it reduces History to a battlefield, rejoinder following rejoinder, so that the course of historic study remains perpetually in the same groove until it vanishes altogether in mere meticulousness or personal abuse.[4]

On the other hand the writing of impersonal history is a difficult matter, because the suppression of self is difficult. Yet in spite of the fact that the public does not want impartial writing & of the race habit of regarding History as polemics we have a powerful & industrious school of 'scientific' historians, a comparatively new growth in England. The State subsidizes great historical works & Lord Acton has left behind him as a memorial a gigantic enterprise of historical projection. Thus as far as research goes impersonal History is practicable in England. Unfortunately for the projection of these researches, meticulousness & the habit of rejoinder distinguish the Scientific Historian as well as the Polemical. And these things tend to destroy the sense of proportion which is really the Historic Sense. If one reads works of the type of Mr Round's *Commune of London* one discovers that the greater part of them is given up to the

4 Cf. Mr Lilly or Mr Froude.

battleaxing of opponents over matters that, relatively speaking, are not of much more importance than the authenticity of a disused postage stamp. It is almost nothing more than a manifestation of the collector's habit.

This phrase is of course too violent & is hitting below the belt, for very obviously it is Mr Round's business, as it is one of his supreme qualities, to strengthen the minutest links of his chains as he goes along. But to devote too much space to mere controversy & to leave selection entirely out of a work is to make one's work comparatively useless as projection, though as research it may be supremely useful. Lord Acton on the other hand made little use of the controversial battleaxe, his habit of research was almost incredible, but he was so essentially rather the reader than the writer that he left practically nothing behind him except his tradition. It is in the spirit of this tradition that the committee of Scientific Historians to which I have referred is now engaged in putting pens to paper.

But as soon as they have begun to write – as soon as they have begun that projection of materials which is Creative History – they have, according to their own earlier ideals, slipped down hill and they confess that it is impossible to write without 'points of view'. In the journal which to the public at large represents the Scientific Historian this reaction is marked enough. Thus today one may read in its columns the query whether Mazarin is not more vividly portrayed in Dumas' *Vingt Ans Après*, than in what purports to be a serious historical work under review &, on the same page, in a review of Mr Roby's *Roman Private Law* there appears: 'Certainly an author who does not reverence the functions of imagination in history is not likely to make much of the origins of ancient institutions'. Thus we have the pendulum shewn in its swing back towards the Historical Novel. It is in fact quite possible to be impersonal in research; it is frankly impossible as soon as it comes to projection. Even in his prefaces to the *Calendars of Letters & Papers* (I remain for purposes of unity within the reign of Henry VIII) Dr Gairdner commits himself to such a sentence as: 'Sane men it would seem, did not covet martyrdom.' And later on he has a paragraph commencing in the old polemic way: 'We have heard it said in times past & sometimes in our own day, that…' & going on to combat what he had heard said. (*Letters & Papers*, Hen. VIII, vol. xvi).

I do not of course condemn Dr Gairdner as intemperate, but it seems to me that, if counsels of perfection prevailed at the Record Office, the Master of the Rolls should reprove Dr Gairdner… which would be absurd. Yet that *reductio ad absurdum* should add one more to the proofs that absolute detachment in historic writing is an impossibility. And it gives the pendulum one kick further back towards the Historical Novel of the type of *Salammbô* or the *Education sentimentale*. Or even, horrible to think, it may swing once more towards works like *Vingt Ans Après*, or *Windsor Castle*.

History conceived as an exact Science is an impossibility because even the minutest of financial accounts is made by human means, coloured by human views or liable to the slips of human pens, & as soon as your historian has gathered his materials together the devil of theorizing enters into him. One might say, a priori, that to get to know history one is safe in studying the accumulations at the various Record Offices of the world, yet Froude did this with fatal results. He went there with preconceived notions & preconceived notions are the death of the historic sense. Without that last the writing of history becomes as worthless as the writing of advertisements. For, in essence, such an article as Professor Smith's is a form of self advertisement ... not an odious one or in any way a reprehensible one, but still a form. When Professor Smith looks at the portraits of Henry's queens he says at once that these 'do not indicate that His Majesty's sense of beauty was very keen'. This 'advertises' Prof. Smith's taste at the expense of Henry's, leaving quite out of account the fact that the aesthetic sense is a matter of associations & that ideals of beauty can never be fixed. It is in fact an attempt to force the writer's personality & standards upon the world. The possession of the historic sense would make this impossible: it may drive the writer to want to know what type of beauty was then dominant, it might even drive him to ask why; it would at any rate cause him either to attempt to understand these matters or to leave them alone. But it would certainly prevent his ever trying to force his private preferences upon the world at the expense of his subject. It would do this in ethical matters as in aesthetic, in the domain of religious as of national feelings. For the possession of the historic sense makes first of all for comprehension. It implies an immense tolerance, an immense understanding, possibly an immense pity or possibly an immense contempt for one's kind.

One of these last will be the writer's 'point of view', essentially true or essentially false according to the standard of the reader. But it will be innocuous because it will be the product not of a doctrinaire spirit but of temperament. It will warp the presentations of character all one way or all another way, it will select no one type for praise & no other for blame. It will be honest.

In the domain of History there is no such thing as Time. She deals either with those who are dead or those who will soon be as dead as the men who fought before Troy. *De mortuis nil nisi bonum*[5] is an idiotic & harmful motto, but it recurs with a pleasant ring when one is reading Froude's blackening of Pole or Professor Smith on Thomas Cromwell. For these men, if one thinks of them at all, become alive once more, once

5 [Speak nothing but good of the dead.]

more strive, once more err, die & enlist one's feelings in their opposing struggles, failures & inevitably tragic deaths.

The Scientific Historian is a private worker, he collects matter as another man collects mezzotints, he may annotate texts or refute errors. But the moment he emerges from these retreats it is his duty to be a creative artist, it is his business to evolve from his dry bones a picture of an era, of an individual, or of a type. And being thus a creator, he should be above his creations to the extent of checking both his preferences & his dislikes. Let him set his Henry on his feet & put into his mouth the words he really did utter; let him make Charles move once more & once more speak to Wyatt; the cry of the common people may sound through their voluminous protests to the Privy Council. Let the gossip of Marillac be set against the gossip of Chapuys: the most outrageous of Henry's dialectical outpourings against the most outrageous of Luther, of Bucer, of Pole, of Latimer, of Shaxton, of Jerome & of the Anabaptists, let the Creative Historian set their most noble utterances & deeds against their most noble. Let his writing be 'documented' down to the bottom, colloquial of the vernacular, & above all let it be interesting. He may leave his readers to draw their own morals.

It may be objected that such a work of art would be in technique a work of fiction. One replies: 'Why not?' For in their really higher manifestations History & Fiction are one: they are documented, tolerant, vivid; their characters live & answer & react one upon another each after his own sort. Fiction indeed, so long as it is not written with a purpose, is Contemporary History & History is the same thing as the Historic Novel, as long as it is inspired with the Historic Sense… the Historic Novel with a wide outlook upon peoples & upon kings. What was Tacitus but a novelist (Mr Tarver would say a novelist with a purpose) or what is the following passage but incomparable History:

> Il connut la faim, la soif, les fièvres et la vermine.
>
> Il s'accoutuma au fracas des mêlées, à l'aspect des moribonds. Le vent tanna sa peau. Ses membres se durcirent par le contact des armures; et comme il était très fort, courageux, tempérant, avisé, il obtint sans peine le commandement d'une compagnie.
>
> Au début des batailles, il enlevait ses soldats d'un grand geste de son épée. Avec une corde à noeuds, il grimpait aux murs des citadelles, la nuit, balancé par l'ouragan, pendant que les flammèches du feu grégeois se collaient à sa cuirasse, et que la résine bouillante et le plomb fondu ruisselaient des créneaux. Souvent le heurt d'une pierre fracassa son bouclier. Des ponts trop chargés d'hommes croulèrent sous lui. En

tournant sa masse d'armes, il se débarassa de quatorze cavaliers. Il défit, en champs clos; tous ceux qui se proposèrent. Plus de vingt fois on le crut mort.[6]

[1903–4], ed. Sondra J. Stang and Richard Stang, *Yale Review*, 78:4 (Summer 1989), [511]–524.

6 'La Légende de Saint Julien l'Hospitalier'. ['He knew hunger, thirst, fevers, and vermin. He became inured to the din of battle, to the sight of the dying. The wind tanned his skin. His limbs were hardened by their contact with armour; and hecause he was very strong, brave, temperate, shrewd, he easily obtained the command of a company.

When the battle started, he would spur his soldiers on by brandishing his sword. With the help of a knotted rope, he would climb over the walls of citadels at night, swinging in the gales, while sparks of Greek fire stuck to his armour, and boiling oil and molten lead poured from the battlements. Often the blow of a stone shattered his shield. Bridges, overloaded with men, crumbled under him. By swinging his mace he got rid of fourteen horsemen. In single combat he defeated all who challenged him. More than twenty times he was presumed dead.']

The Collected Poems of Christina Rossetti

To appear in the familiar livery of the Standard Edition, if it isn't a canonization for a poet, is as nearly as possible to be beatified.[1] It is to be singled out and given, as it were, the chance to show what miracles may be worked by invoking him, what cures wrought in his name – how, long, in fact, his 'bell' will ring. It is a step upwards in the hagiology, but it is, also, to be put very decidedly on trial. It gives us, I mean, something to think of when the best work of a newly 'collected' poet is presented to us suddenly in a type, and on a page, where most plain men are accustomed to find *The Tempest*.

It is like seeing a wall-painting taken from the painter's studio and set into its niche in a great hall. 'Values' readjust themselves, details drop into place or stick out, and you are set thinking: Will this last and be reverently taken care of, or will the dust finally settle on to a thing grown dull, until it flakes from the wall and is forgotten?

In the case of Christina Rossetti, the image is that of a mosaic rather than of a fresco, since hitherto the tendency has been to regard her as the poet of what some one has called small-gemmedness. Ever since the appearance of 'Uphill', in 1861, small fragments of her verse have been floating in the air, as it were. Almost every person at all lettered has carried about with him some little piece. You will find one man who retains with intimate pleasure some small phrase, like, 'Beneath the moon's most shadowy beam'; others have not forgotten a stanza or so of, 'When I am dead, my dearest'; some have by heart nearly the whole of:

> Does the road wind uphill all the way?
>   Yes, to the very end.
> Will the day's journey take the whole long day?
>   From morn to night, my friend.

And I know that a great many more, not literate at all, do constantly read favourite verses of her religious poems. At any rate, up and down the land

1 *The Poetical Works of Christina Georgina Rossetti*. Preface, Notes, &c. by William Michael Rossetti.

there have been treasured for many years these small and gem-like fragments. Now, at last, the mosaic fits back to the wall, and the whole figure can be seen.

She lived her whole life behind a veil. She had not any literary contacts that counted very much. Upon the whole, in early days, she was a dark horse, not very much valued, if well loved, in a circle brilliant, buoyant, and, as youth will be, noisy in a fine way. She must have been often enough in the room with several great personages at one time. But it was natural that in such a roomful she should not make much noise. Her brothers and their distinguished companions troubled mostly about abstract ideas, they made movements, and such large things. In abstract matters she was not singularly intellectual: indeed, we may say that she was not intellectual at all. She had strong and settled faiths that simply could not be talked about, and she had above all a gift that was priceless; a faculty for picking up, like a tiny and dainty mouse, little precious crumbs of observation that were dropped unnoticed by people who, in argument, assailed each other with tremendous words. Mr Ruskin, for instance, considered that her verse was hardly worth publishing.

In those tremendous contests of young lungs of genius, whilst Ingres' works were being called filthy slosh, Van Eyck's tremendous, Michael Angelo's *Last Judgment* simply comic, and Delacroix a perfect beast; whilst Academicians were being damned, and Primitives belauded; whilst, in fact, the P.R.B. was still, as is the way with romantic youth, hammering the Universe to its pattern, Christina's voice simply did not carry. No doubt she learnt lessons, But you may imagine her sitting still, bright-eyed, smiling in the least, observing very much, and quite content to write one of her little poems next morning on the corner of her wash-stand.

The least considerable of the Pre-Raphaelites ruined the youth of her life. She was a person of rigid principle, and a wavering human being. (I imagine that the story is well enough known.) She was a convinced Anglican: Mr Collinson had been one. He had become a Roman Catholic when he fell in love with her. She refused him on account of his religion, and he shortly afterwards reverted to Anglicanism. She accepted him then, and after a time he once more became a Roman Catholic. It isn't one's business to reprehend Mr Collinson; he was obviously concerned for his soul. 'He had none the less,' says her brother, 'struck a staggering blow at Christina Rossetti's peace of mind on the very threshold of womanly life – a blow from which she did not recover for years. He died in 1881.'

And, indeed the tinge of sadness, of resignation, the attitude of hands folded in the lap is the suggestion of a great part of her verse. But there are other tones:–

My heart is like a singing bird,
Whose nest is in a watered shoot,
My heart is like an apple tree,
Whose boughs are bent with thickset fruit.

⋆ ⋆ ⋆ ⋆ ⋆

Raise me a daïs of silk and down,
Hang it with vair and purple dyes,
Carve it in doves and pomegranates,
And peacocks with a hundred eyes.

⋆ ⋆ ⋆ ⋆ ⋆

Because the birthday of my life
Is come, my love is come to me.

And this may be cited not as evidence of any historic event, not for instance as a paean for Mr Collinson, but simply to show that she had in her a strain of pagan feeling and a capacity for pure joy. And even if you put, as the other end of the scale:

The hope I dreamed of was a dream,
    Was but a dream, and now I wake
Exceeding comfortless and worn and old,
    For a dream's sake.

it will stand as much for desire as for resignation.

Her union with her family was very close. For her mother she had a love which was an adoration. These two lived together with nothing to disturb their ties, with no events save deaths and bereavements, maintaining thus apart a life so tranquil that the rumour of events in the outer world penetrated through the mists and shadows of the regions round Bloomsbury into their warm home like sounds heard faintly and from a distance through closed doors – until her mother too died. She knew, later on, a period of tranquil and deep love for a very charming and unworldly scholar. Him, too, she could not marry because of his religious belief, or because of his latitude. Says Mr Rossetti: 'She declined his suit without ceasing to see him, and to cherish him as a friend. Knowing the state of her heart at the time the offer was made, I urged her to marry, and offered that they should both, if money difficulties stood in the way, share my home. But she had made up her mind.... and she remained immovable. Years passed; she became an elderly and an old woman, and she loved the scholarly recluse to the last day of his life, December 5th, 1883, and to the last day of her own, his memory.'

And it is pleasant and instructive to transcribe this note to one of her poems: '"My Mouse". This was not a mouse in the ordinary sense, but a "sea-mouse". Mr Cayley had picked it up on the sea-shore, and presented it to my sister, preserved in spirits. The sea-mouse was with her to the end, and may remain with me to the end; its brilliant hues are still vivid.' Towards the close of her life she became almost a recluse; her mind dwelt solely upon her religion, her verses became exclusively devotional, and her time was given up to acts of charity. She was then very brown in complexion, and somewhat startling in aspect, because a disease caused her eyes to protrude. She dressed in deep black, and spoke with precision, pausing for words with her head a little on one side. A half-humorous, half-introspective smile was never far from her lips. In an atmosphere of shadow, in a house over-shadowed by the tall trees of a London square, she was a figure not so much striking as penetrating, and, in face of her self-possession, her deliberate and rare movements, her clear and bell-like enunciation – it was difficult to realize that one had in front of one either a great poet or a woman suffering from more than one painful and lingering disease, from great bereavements, and, above all, from very terrible religious fears.

But if she were a recluse, she was not shut out from personal contacts; if she did not 'go out' much, she did not shut her doors. She had her reservations: in matters of her faith her mind was simply closed. She neither debated nor, as far as I know, did she ever attempt to convert any one who differed. But very decidedly she was not unable to be vigorous if she considered herself attacked. A young poet of an ingenuous and seraphic appearance once went to see her. He wanted to offer homage, and he had the top of a thin volume peeping out of his jacket pocket. He belonged to a school that in those days was called *fin-de-siècle*, his verse was rather aggressively decadent, and he was in a small way well known. I suppose she considered that his coming was in the nature of an aggression, and, almost before one had realized that conversation had begun, she was talking about modern verse – deploring its tendencies, deriding its powers of expression, and attacking it in a gentle voice with words keen, sharp, and precise, like a scalpel. It was an uncomfortable twenty minutes, and the young poet went away with his volume still in his pocket. So that, as a general rule, if she never obtruded her beliefs, she was, upon occasion, perfectly able to keep her own end rather more than 'up'.

No other biographic details seem to tell anything about the main tendencies of her verses. Many of her poems may have been suggested by events, but they were inspired psychologically. They were renderings of emotions she had felt. She did not, I mean, sit down to 'poetize' on her vicissitudes.

It is convenient to call her verse lyric, but the term is not strictly correct, as I shall attempt to explain later. It is assuredly not Epic; it is never exactly Elegiac, nor is it ever really Narrative verse. Most particularly it is not philosophic, hortatory, or improving. Even her devotional poetry is seldom other than the expression of a mood. It is a prayer, an adoration of the Saviour, a fear of the Almighty, a craving for pardon and for rest. 'Passing away, saith the World, Passing away' is the presentation of a Christian mood; her devotional poem on the largest scale, the 'Processional', is a presentation of the whole of Creation defiling before God the Father, and uttering a Doxology. But her verse is never a sermon; it never preaches, and that, no doubt, is why it lives. In that matter she had the Latin temperament, the instinct that makes you see that if you want to convince you must interest, and if you want to interest you must draw concrete pictures, leaving your hearer to draw the morals. That too, as far as the presentation of her matter goes, is the 'technique' of her secular poetry; she had the gift of just, simple, and touching words, and with them she drew pictures that expressed her moods.

The expression of moods – that after all is the only business of the lyric poet. And when he has conveyed those moods to others he has succeeded. It is very decidedly not his business to look at things on the large scale, to 'write poetic', to be more impracticable, frenzied, or romantic than Nature has made him. He has to appeal rather than to overwhelm, to hang in the ear rather than to sweep you away with organ peals. It is for these reasons that Christina Rossetti deserves to live.

This new edition challenges a readjustment of our views of her. It emphasizes her other sides; it brings forward her larger flights. It groups together in a prominent place works in which, if the modelling is not broader, the outlines at least contain more canvas. This does not much affect one's view of her technique; she remains still the poet of lines, of stanzas, of phrases, and of cadences that are intimately right. But, with the grouping together of her longer verse, there stands out a buoyancy of temperament, a profuseness, a life, and, as far as the metre of the verse is concerned, an infectious gaiety. There appears too, more strongly defined, her little humour, her delicate playfulness, her major key.

'Goblin Market', with which the volume opens, moves breathlessly. Its metre is short, its rhymes are concealed enough not to hinder you with a jingle of assonances, and accurate enough to keep the stanzas together.

> At last the evil people,
> Worn out by her resistance,
> Flung back her penny, kicked their fruit,
> Along whichever road they took,
> Not leaving shoot or stone or root;
> Some writhed into the ground,
> Some dived into the brook,
> With ring and ripple,
> Some scudded on the gale without a sound,
> Some vanished in the distance.

The whole poem goes in one breath. Yet it is treated with so much detail as to give the impression of profusion and of value. It is succeeded in the volume by three earlier poems of some length. 'Repining' and the 'Three Nuns' are juvenile efforts, rather dry in tone, and a little formal, but austerely worded. They show interestingly how, in the girl, the organ, the vehicle of expression, was already formed and waiting for the afflatus. Or, perhaps, it was only for the subject that she was waiting, since between the two poems she had already written: 'When I am Dead, my Dearest' (and, indeed, it is no small boast for a family to be able to make that one member should have written this poem when she was eighteen, and another, ' The Blessed Damosel', before he was twenty).

'The Lowest Room' and 'From House to Home' were both written before 'Goblin Market' and both after she had attained to maturity, the one in 1856, the other two years later. They indicate change of temperament, a hardening of point of view as well as of technical attainment. The first is a sort of commentary on the Homeric combatants, and, if at the end it strikes the note of resignation, and utters the words: These things are not for me, it certainly shows that the poet enjoyed describing the combats whilst they lasted. This note of life as a thing enjoyable and exciting is also the note of the opening of 'From House to Home', but the recoil from that idea is here not towards resignation. It announces definitely – and in more set terms than she employed anywhere else – that earthly joy is a snare and a lure:

> The first was like a dream through summer heat,
>
> * * * * *
>
> It was a pleasure place within my soul,
>
> * * * * *
>
> That lured me from my goal.

She draws a picture of her royal estate: a castle, a pleasaunce, pastures, parks, and forests peopled with the quaint and sprightly beasts that she loved:

> My heath lay further off where lizards lived,
>   In strange metallic mail, just spied and gone,
> Like darted lightnings here and there perceived,
>   But nowhere dwelt upon.

And there she delighted harmlessly enough walking with a being like an angel:

> And sometimes like a snowdrift he was fair,
>   And sometimes like a sunset glorious red,
> And sometimes he had wings to scale the air,
>   An aureole round his head.

* * * * *

'To-morrow', once I said to him with smiles,
    'To-night', he answered gravely and was dumb,
But pointed out the stones that numbered miles,
    And miles and miles to come.
'Not so,' I said, 'to-morrow shall be sweet.
    To-night is not so sweet as coming days.'
Then first I saw that he had turned his feet,
    Had turned from me his face.

The angel left her; her earth turned to winter, and the poem becomes one long apocalypse of pictures seen by a soul that is tortured by the remorse of having lived. It contains magnificent verses, but it falls off. It has poignant lines like this, from a description of souls before the throne: 'Each face looked one way like a moon new lit', but the impetus of the verse disappears. This may be because it is didactic, or derivative, or because the poet simply had not yet the strength to keep up – or because it was written with more emotion, and in consequence with more inflation.

But 'Goblin Market' was written next year, and from that time onward all her longer verse kept its level of inspiration. It has a profusion of imagination, a power of painting pictures; here and there it has dramatic places, and always a level austerity and restraint in the wording. The longer poems range from a 'Royal Princess', which is dramatic, vigorous, and bitter, to a charming ballad of three maidens with happy loves, and from that to the fine 'Proccesional of Creation'.

The last of the longer poems here given is 'Later Life, a double Sonnet of Sonnets', and this suggests, after all, the clue to all her longer pieces. The throwing these thus together challenges, as I have said, a readjustment in our minds, a revision of our mental image of Christina Rossetti's structural technique. It holds out, as it were, this rearrangement, the idea that here was a writer of 'sustained' verse, who had, at least potentially, epic as well as lyric gifts, But 'Later Life' is a sequence of sonnets and careful examination will reveal that the 'Processional of Creation' is a sequence of pictures, and so, too, the 'Prince's Progress' and 'Goblin Market' are sequences – as you might say, strings of beads. They prove, if proof be needed, that, by very careful handling, the lyrical method may be applied to make long poems that are readable and entrancing. But there is not the sweep of pinions; the flight is that of the fieldfare that now and then crosses a sea.

That is, of course, a method like another, and it is no condemnation to say that a writer's method is not the Epic; it is mostly a matter of temperament, the Epic's being the temperament of action, the other's that of observation. For if each of these longer poems is a chain of delicate and intimate 'places', beads of pure beauty, the links between are little quaintnesses, little pieces of observation so humanly rendered that they make you read on to the next 'place'. And each whole poem has its key, its level of individuality. That is, so to speak, the string on which the beads, little and big, are strung. Here the method and temperament are generally lucky. Delicate humour, as a rule, counteracts that tendency to 'write poetic', which is the bane of so many poets; it does away with any danger that the writer will try to get the 'poetic point of view', it leaves her simple and natural. It lets her be human and interesting, when for the moment the theme is not grandiose, and it does not hinder soaring when the time comes.

'Goblin Market', for instance, is a poem concerned with human beings exposed to temptations. The human beings and their cravings are the subject, the tempters are subordinate. If, then, Christina Rossetti had made the tempters evil demi-gods, they must have been either well done, and too large for the frame, or ill done and not alive. Here they are:

> Curious Laura chose to linger,
> Wondering at each merchant man;
> One had a cat's face,
> One whisked a tail,
> One tramped at a rat's pace,
> One crawled like a snail,
> One like a wombat, prowled obtuse and furry.

These, if you like, are unconventional and not dignified, but they are – and that is the main thing – in tone with the piece. And the passages in higher notes have not need to strain in order to rise from that level. This is a note of craving:

> One day, remembering her kernel stone,
> She set it by a wall that faced the south,
> Dewed it with tears, hoped for a root;
> But there came none.
> It never saw the sun,
> It never felt the trickling moisture run,
> While with sunk eyes and faded mouth,
> She pined for melons…

Most of the strong effects of the poem are no more forced than this – they are poignant and human rather than aloof and poetic. (This stanza, by the by, is a very good instance of what, for lack of a more precise word, I have called her Latin technique of presentation. The longing is not written about, but the actions of one longing are rendered and her picture drawn: 'With sunk eyes and faded mouth, she dreamed of melons.' It is not stated that she 'craved very much', or that 'her sufferings were intense'.)

Christina Rossetti arrayed herself very little in the panoply of poetic phrases; she wrote as she spoke. And, indeed, when she was in the mood, she wrote nearly as easily as she spoke. Thus, on one day, she produced three of her best poems: 'Uphill', 'At Home', and 'Today and To-morrow', on 29 June 1858. And it is the distinguishing characteristic of her best poems that they open always with a line that is just a remark, not the 'strong first line' of a song. She seems to utter a little sentence like, 'I wonder if the sap is stirring yet', and the spring is presented. For the most part she kept to that conversational key. Her vocabulary was not that of the first man you might meet, because she lived among exceptional people, and thought of exceptional things. Indeed, her choice of words was rather limited, and, along with it, her choice of images. She used words like 'rest' and 'rain' over and over again, without troubling to find synonyms. Verses as similar as:

> Rest, rest, a perfect rest,
> Shed over brow and breast,
> Her face is towards the west,
> The peaceful land.
> She cannot see the grain
> Ripen on hill and plain,
> She cannot feel the rain
> Upon her hand.

And

> I shall not see the shadows,
> I shall not feel the rain,
> I shall not hear the nightingale
> Sing on as if in pain.
> But dreaming thro' the twilight
> That does not rise or set,
> Haply I may remember,
> And haply may forget,

are moderately common to each of her small volumes. This implies of course, limitations, both of vocabulary and of temperament. It means, too, that every word that she used was her own; it means, perhaps, an overscrupulousness.

Scrupulous she was to a degree beyond that of common humanity. She suppressed her work for fear of repeating herself, she suppressed still more of it for fear it was too pagan or too sensual. And how much of herself she suppressed in that fear we cannot do more than guess. But it is obvious that a person who could write:

> Raise me a daïs of silk and down,
> Hang it with vair and purple dyes –

that a person who had in her at once that pagan strain, and that other scourge of delights, the ascetic fear of eternal penalties, cannot in this world have done other than crave for rest between these warring components of her being. She was in the Christian Commonwealth the very antithesis of that other poetess, the nun Hroswitha, who, in the days of Otho the Great, wrote medieval Latin comedies to deride the carnal spirit. Hroswitha showed to her fellow nuns the Roman governor, intent on overcoming the virtue of Christian maids, and going, muddled, into a cellar in mistake for their room, to embrace pots and amphorae, and to be derided by the virgins. I am driven, indeed, to wonder whether Christina

Rossetti were not better adapted for life in the other Communion. For her Southern nature the Northern cult was too stern, or was, perhaps, not adapted. Possibly in a convent with its petty detail of devotion, its spiritual direction which forbids too deep introspection, and enjoins a certain cheerfulness as a duty, she might have escaped many terrible moments, and have written verse with a wider range. It is possible that she would not, for the perils of the other system are great too – but the speculation is worth making. It is certain, at least, that a greater stability of mind, wherever she found it, would have been beneficial to her verse because she would have dealt less in suppressions. Suppressions, of course, are legitimate enough aesthetically, when they are made for aesthetic reasons. But it is a loss to both humanity and to art when they are made for reasons so personal – out of a fear for one's soul, that if it is not purely pagan, is at least in essence a survival of devil worship and of the dark ages of the soul.

But if Christina Rossetti suppressed, as far as she was able, whatever was sensual and joyous in the matter and in the temperament of her poems, her faculty for pure delight and for aesthetic enjoyment was expressed all the more strongly in her metre. For her verse is neither musical nor lyrical, it has not the unconscious quality of 'lilt', or of the song that merely bubbles. It is rhythmical and even intricate; it is a faculty that, coming from very deep in the sources of enjoyment, moves us for deep and unexplained reasons just as the rhythms of music do. If it has not the quality of lilt it has not the defect; it is never mechanical with numbered syllables. A distinguished French critic has lately discovered that the distinguishing quality of English metre is its (musical rhythmical) rests, not its (metrical-stressed) accents. It is exciting as much on account of the accents it misses as of those it meets. If, for instance, you listen to a pulsing rhythm, which, in an orchestra, is emphasized by drum strokes, you will find that when the drum misses a beat or comes in on a half-beat, the rhythm is actually accentuated because your ear unconsciously supplies a sound. Christina Rossetti probably never knew of this fact, or of the theory that is founded upon it, but she wrote as if she knew them at a time when English verse, if it ever was governed, was governed by a hazy idea of Latin principles of prosody. A man, who as a child was brought up on Christina Rossetti's 'Sing Song', tells me that the quality of the metre was one of the great delights of his ear. (And it should be remembered that children, like barbarians, and young peoples, take a most sensuous pleasure in rhythms of words. They are the real connoisseurs.)

> Dead in the cold a song-singing thrush,
> Dead at the foot of a snowberry bush,
> Weave him a coffin of rush,
> Dig him a grave where the soft breezes blow,
> Raise him a tombstone of snow.

The sense of such a verse does not matter to a child. He will sing 'London Bridge is broken down' without thinking of the meaning. But that verse was to the child profoundly affecting and delightful. It is so still. But I imagine that had it run:

> Dead in the cold (*here's a*) song-singing thrush,
> Dead at the foot of a snowberry bush.
> Weave him a coffin of (*straw and of*) rush,
> Dig him a grave where the soft breezes blow,
> Raise him a tombstone of (*soft-driven*) snow,

had, in fact, the metre been regularized with dactyls into the expected decasyllabic lines, he would simply not have listened to it.

In Christina Rossetti's verse it is this quality of the unexpected, the avoidance of the cliché in metre, the fact that here and there you must beat time in a rest of the melody, that gives it its fascination and its music. And it is that, after all, that is the supreme quality of English metricists – the quality that, when it is used in a masterly way, sets them apart, and differentiates them from poets in other tongues. (I am not, of course, talking of the sonnet line which isn't an indigenous thing, or of the Alexandrine. But it applies to blank verse with its lines, when it is good, always linking together, and so overlapping that the ten or eleven-syllabled character is constantly eluded.)

She, as I have said, was unacquainted with these principles. Probably, too, she had never heard of Chromatics, or of Phonetic Syzygy. Yet when it was appropriate, her verse contrived to be quite sufficiently close in its assonances, its vowel effects, and its chromatic texture. Her skill in true rhymes was only equalled by her delicacy in using false ones – those delicious things that there are still miscreants hardhearted enough to reprehend.

She wrote, in fact, without any professional equipments – on the corners of washstands, as it were. Sometimes her verses came with ease – three masterpieces in a day; sometimes her difficulties with rhymes, metres, and ideas, were such that her little scraps of paper resembled palimpsests, lines in pencil and in pen crossing and recrossing as they used to do in old letters, as if she did not value her poems at the paper they cost. But practically her last and one of her best short poems, only shows four changes of ten words in all on the first pencilled draft.[2] Her 'manuscripts'

2 I reproduce here from the *Academy* a version in print of this poem which I used some years ago to illustrate an article on another subject. It would seem to show that her gift attended her to her deathbed, and that at times, at least, she found comfort in her faith:

> Heaven overarches earth and sea,
> Earth sadness and sea bitterness.
> Heaven overarches you and me,
> Heaven overarches you and me,
> And all earth's gardens and her graves
> Look up with me {until we see

will be found on the backs of used envelopes; in the little notebooks which she made herself out of scraps of notepaper poems alternate with accounts, with the addresses of charitable ladies, and with the dates of favourite preachers. It might have been better had she valued her talent more highly, or perhaps that would only have led her into over-elaboration and 'writing poetic'.

She wrote a great deal of verse that to one taste or another is comparatively poor, and many of Mr Rossetti's inclusions she herself did not publish. But nearly all her poems are 'authentic' in tone; they yield generally a touch of her flavour here and there, even if the general quality be thin. The very quantity will probably help her fame to stand in the long run. For the saying of Goethe's: 'Who brings a lot of many kinds, brings something to many' holds good in verse as in merchandise; A. liking one stanza which B. despises, and laughing at another which B. loves. In this edition there are 458 double-columned pages awaiting the selector and the anthologist. That, perhaps, is the function of collected editions. And there are Mr Rossetti's helpful and restrained memoirs, a bibliography and notes which, with their occasional quaintness of phrase and observation, prove him to have the humorous seriousness that so distinguished his sister.

It is seldom safe to prophesy how an artist will stand with the Future, and it is always dangerous to attempt to place him in relation to his great contemporaries. As far as Posterity is concerned, I have tried to indicate those technical qualities in her verse which should – if technical qualities ever do make for delight – render Christina Rossetti's poems a source of pleasure for several generations to come. My personal pleasure in her work is so great that I will not approach the 'placing'. But she had one characteristic which should make her gain upon all her distinguished contemporaries – she held aloof from all the problems of her day. She was not greatly esteemed as a teacher in the nineteenth century, because she had not any lessons for that strenuous age. She did not evoke national enthusiasms, nor strive to redress the wrongs of martyred children; she was the poet neither of the Democracy nor of the County Family. She had not that boundless faith or love for her kind that makes writers become influences or social reformers; she did not help forward towards its unseen and mysterious goal the human destiny that follows blindly the calls of leaders, who cry from so many directions in the wilderness. This

A little while and we shall be
(Please God) where there is no more sea
Nor { barren wilderness.
{ parting nor distress [**deleted**]

{we both shall see [**deleted**]
The day break and the shadows flee;
What { tho tonight
{ if today [**deleted**]wrecks you and me
{ If so
{ so that [**deleted**] tomorrow saves?

makes her less of a human figure, and less of a benefactress to her day and hour.

She was comparatively self-centred, but, inasmuch as the succeeding centuries will cease to be interested in the problems of yesterday, she escapes a danger if she missed some love. For the man, poet, or tailor, who identifies himself with the spirit of his time, is apt to take on the fashion of his age, and to become old-fashioned. This for either's survival is disaster, for it renders him uninteresting.

Christina Rossetti, with her introspection, studied her soul; with her talent she rendered it until she became the poet of the suffering – and suffering is a thing of all the ages. It is the defect of this quality that it only consoles by saying to others in misfortune: 'I, too, suffer, I am a comrade.' It teaches no one how to find new heart, it is not obstinate towards optimism. (It is hardly necessary to say that to call this temperament morbid is to be unreflecting. Morbidness is a dwelling on suffering for wantonness' sake; it is to find a joy in gloating on sorrows, and is a sensual pursuit like any other self-indulgence.) Christina Rossetti had great sorrows, and her work reflected her life. To have affected cheerfulness would have been harmful to the republic.

For the man who says: 'There is no sorrow' harms the young, the weak, and the inexperienced, making their disillusionment when experience brings it the more bitter. After all, there is demanded of each poet after his kind, only the true image of himself as he mirrors life, only his individual truth. And if it is good that there should be poets to teach the eternal child, which is man, to greet the unseen with a cheer, it is good also to leave him not too open to the miseries of defeat, to let him know that others, too, have fallen and found life bitter. That child is happy in his master who has been taught to say, along with Psalms of Life:

> What are heavy? Sea sand and sorrow.
> What are brief? Today and tomorrow.
> What are frail? Spring blossoms and youth.
> What are deep? The ocean and truth.

Fortnightly, 75 (March 1904), 393–405.

A Literary Causerie: On Some Tendencies of Modern Verse

The state of the present world of poetry is curious and worthy of attention. On the one hand poets and publishers declare that there are no readers: poets and readers declare that there are no publishers: and publishers and readers declare that there are no poets. Here we have, reproduced, the celebrated triangular duel of Mr Midshipman Easy. That readers exist, even as they did in the days of Satan Montgomery or of Festus Bailey, may be doubted: that they exist in sufficient numbers to form a Public is, however, indubitable. What one is left to wonder at is: Why they are not 'reached'. Is it lack of enterprise on the part of the publisher or lack of attractiveness in the poet? Is the answer to the riddle simply that the 'Fifteen Hundred Market' is overlooked or despised by the publisher whose eyes are fixed on the shining glories of the boomed novelist? Or is it simply that the verse that sees the light in the waste corners of the magazines is too good, in the sense of being too 'literary'? Let an example be made of one of the more excellent of the body of poets.

There has been appearing lately, in a humble, almost periodical form – in 'parts' as it were – a series of shilling volumes of the poems of Mr T. Sturge Moore. That this enterprise has been completed may be taken as evidence that it has found a public to the extent of paying its way. That it has not overlapped the Fifteen Hundred connoisseurs we may take for granted. I first came across the work of Mr Sturge Moore at the house of a friend – a connoisseur of the connoisseurs – where, lying amongst a heap upon a table, I saw what appeared to be a pamphlet, called *The Gazelles*. One does not know what these things may not prove: a pamphlet called *The Gazelles* might be anything; most probably a tract of some society for the prevention of one form or other of vice or cruelty. But, opening it because I was too uninterested to lay it down, I read:

> When the sheen on tall summer grass is pale,
> Across blue skies white clouds float on
> In shoals, or disperse and singly sail,
> Till, the sun being set, they all are gone:

Yet, as long as they may shine bright in the sun,
They flock or stray through the daylight bland,
While their stealthy shadows like foxes run
Beneath where the grass is dry and tanned:

And the waste, in hills that swell and fall,
Goes heaving into yet dreamier haze;
And a wonder of silence is over all
Where the eye feeds long like a lover's gaze:

Then, cleaving the grass, gazelles appear....

Now here is the opening of a rather long poem. And it is, essentially, the right opening – the wording not too close, the frame of the picture, the landscape, put in with simple words, the phrasing not intricate, the rhythm running easily. And, at the right moment, the heroes – the gazelles – appear. It reminds me, in fact, of the opening of the best of Maupassant's long *contes* – 'The Field of Olives'. And, in all these respects, the poem maintains its level to the end.

The other verses of the same fascicule were not so interesting to me. The wording of them was, precisely, too close: the rhythms intricate and rather crabbed: the ideas not very arresting to an unaroused mind. And it must be remembered that verse, suffering under those shackles of metre and form that later so greatly help it, *must* make an appeal sufficiently strong to arrest unaroused minds. I am glad therefore that I made the acquaintance of Mr Sturge Moore through his 'Gazelles' and not through, say: 'Desire Sings'; 'Desire Pleads'; and 'Desire Muses' – verses which are, as the titles indicate, derivative, allegorical, rather cold and rather crabbedly expressed.

Accidentally and desultorily I came across others of these little pamphlets – (I have them all now in a brown cardboard case) – and gradually there arose in my mind the figure of a poet who interested me – who came back to me at odd moments and set me wondering vaguely. They set me, in fact, wondering what he could be like – using the words in no personal sense – what could be his *provenance*, who his literary fathers and sponsors. I could not 'place' him anywhere. In a sense much of his verse was derivative, much of his vocabulary irritating because of a certain preciousness. Thus the prose introduction to *Pan's Prophecy* is in a sort of Wardour Street English, and frequent use of alliteration such as '... she sits and works / As women work weaving in wall-cloths wide;' renders whole passages uninteresting because of their artificiality. But one pardons – or rather one forgets – these things for the sake of a personality that interests one or because of a point of view novel and well worked out.

All the poems contained good things, if all tasted a little too strongly of the honeycomb. On the other hand, if most of the subjects were derivative – classical and not significant to a workaday world – the approach to the subject was new and individual. Thus the *Rout of the Amazons* is related by a Faun, appalled at the sight of so much beauty, feminine and shining, crushed by the hoofs of horses or emptied of its bright blood by men's spears. That, too, was the root idea of the 'Gazelles'.

I know now, because I have heard critics say so, that Mr Sturge Moore is by descent one of the Pre-Raphaelite poets; that he has worked at woodcutting; has made designs; is a thoughtful critic of the plastic arts – that in all probability he is, temperamentally or by accident, an aesthete. I am glad upon the whole that I did not know this until comparatively recently, since the ignorance had let me approach his work with a quite clear mind. But, of course, every man must have a parentage and a jumping-off place; and the question is how far Mr Moore will jump. It is for that that one examines his verse anxiously – for that and because he represents, typifies, and stands for most of the tendencies of the Modern Poet. One may, I mean, see in his verse at its least good pretty clearly, why Modern Poetry makes so little appeal to the modern world; and, in his verse at its really best, one may see some hope for an approaching renascence of appeal.

The Pre-Raphaelite poets – from whom nearly all the poets of today, including Mr William Watson and Mr Rudyard Kipling, in one way or another descend — put back the clock of British verse so woefully not because they sought their 'subjects' in the medieval world but because they tried to identify themselves with the medieval point of view. They could not, I mean, see that *per se* a sewing-machine is as romantic an object, or as poetic a symbol of human destinies, as an embroidery frame. But all the really great poems of the world have been expressed in terms of thought modern to them. It has never been the 'documenting' of a poem that has been the important matter. *Paradise Lost* made its appeal because of its reading of life in terms of the seventeenth century; because it voiced the thought of its time and not because it was a fine projection of the mental state of the Garden of Eden. But the verse of the present day is almost entirely derived from the thought of the present day. It goes searching, as it were, the hidden graves, ruined temples, or golden closets of forgotten worlds. In consequence it deals almost entirely in 'pictures'; and, at the best, the appeal of the 'picture-poem' must be limited.

To a large extent it is a matter of the very bed-rock of all verse – of vocabulary. Imagine a modern poet lying on the beach at, say, Hastings. There is the hot shingle, a dove-coloured sea, a sky half silver half gold, and that most pathetic, suggestive and bewildering of all modern objects – the immense crowd. If we can imagine our modern poet being there at all and not hiding in an Italian cloister, what words will he have to describe the scene, what 'tone' will he get into his poem? How will he avoid making it wholly vulgar, or how will he avoid sudden contrasts of 'poetic' words with everyday objects? Yet assuredly such a 'subject', poetically viewed – the great crowds pouring out of the vast towns in search of *some* sort of Island of the Blest, in search of some sort of Ideal, Joy, Love, Health, New Youth, or whatever it be they seek – such a subject is worthy of treatment. Are there no classical Idylls that treat of lower middle-class people waiting to view the opening of temples? And are these Idylls not Poetry?

Such subjects are almost barred to the modern poet – by his 'poetic' dialect. He finds it, in fact, easier to ransack Chaucer or Spenser for archaic words that gain a certain glamour from their remoteness; he shirks the labour of selecting such modern words as should give his page aloofness from mere colloquialism, and instead of trying to form a modern language that shall be at once vivid and delicate as an instrument he goes further and further in the direction of evoking a literary dialect from dead languages. And the difficulty of understanding him, however slight, induces a weariness in his reader and a general distaste for attacking new verse, since the appreciation of each new poet means for the reader learning a new dialect in addition to getting into touch with a new personality. We wait, in fact, for the poet who, in limpid words, with clear enunciation and, without inverted phrases, shall give the mind of the time sincere frame and utterance.

It is not, let it be repeated, the choice of subject that is at fault. There is no reason why the poet should write solely of the Housing Question, the Sex Problem, or the new forms of locomotion, nor is there any reason why he should not set his story in Persia or in Verona before the Renaissance. There was no reason why Webster should not write of Amalfi or Shakespeare of Elsinore – a dim antiquity; the point is that the mind of the poet should be modern. The appeal of Webster's *Dance of Madmen*[1] was Cockney of the sixteenth century; and the soliloquy commencing 'To be or not to be…' was written by a man alive to the problems of his fellow men of the day. And, too, it is not necessary that the poet should regard himself as a teacher. But, whether he write lyric or epic, drama or *contes* in verse, it *is* necessary, if he is to appeal, that he should promote vital thought. He must rouse ideas in the minds of his fellow mortals; and, to that extent, he must voice his time.

It is for that reason that we see cause for hope in the works of Mr Sturge Moore and of some of his fellows. For the 'problem' – the query – of his 'Gazelles', as of *The Rout of the Amazons*, is simply: Why was so much beauty, of delicate beasts, of fair women, created to be so senselessly marred? Why are the gods so profuse of beautiful living organisms which are destined to be put to so little apparent use? And that is one of the 'questions' of today – one of the things that we are all asking, of our souls

1 [Ford refers to Act IV, scene 2 of *The Duchess of Malfi*, which was written in the seventeenth century. Cf. p. 77.]

as of our neighbours, of our poets as of our preachers – a question that we may ask, lying on the beach at Hastings too. For why does the immense crowd exist? Merely to fill graveyards? It is, too, like the problem set in Hamlet's soliloquy, one of the eternal questions – one that has been asked by Roman emperors, and one that will be asked, no doubt, by the commanders of the great Trusts of the dim future.

So that, given a vital and expressive vocabulary and a clear use of phrase, there is not much reason why Mr Sturge Moore or one of his fellows should not pass into history – into the history of human thought. But they must put aside – or at least they must digest – their derivations: they must forget that they are literary men. If, given the fact that they possess poetic personalities, they will give up the forcing of their own notes; if they will abandon the attempt to 'write poetic' and express themselves – not themselves in the mantles of the dead Elijahs that they variously affect, if they will forget that they are men of letters and discover that they are human beings they will come at last to that psychical suckling of fools, and metaphysical chronicling of small beer that, rightly understood, is the function of the poet. But of course they must first be poets.

Academy, 69 (23 September 1905), 982–4.

Literary Portraits from *The Tribune*

III. Mr John Galsworthy

The novel in England occupies, rightly or wrongly, the position of a suspect – as it were a thing from which nothing can be learned and over which much time may be wasted. And time, of course is money. But it is possible to imagine a novel so true to life that it may have a certain sociological value, and yet so well written and constructed that it may make pleasurable reading. Thus, theoretically at least, you might combine that deleterious thing, amusement with that highly desirable factor in the life of an ordered State – with instruction. Consider, for instance, the work of Mr Galsworthy.

Mr Galsworthy is all the better as a subject for examination in that he is so typically – I had almost said so bewilderingly – English. There is not the least strain of foreign blood or appearance in him. You may be certain that the lessons he will give will be such as England needs. It is not only that you could not mistake him, anywhere, in any crowd, for anything but an English gentleman. It is that he is so representative as not to be noticeable at all. There are men with whom you may claim a very long acquaintanceship, yet with whom you never feel any intimacy. These men are always the fine flowers of English society, and one of them is Mr Galsworthy. I do not know the colour of his hair; I do not know the colour of his eyes; I am not certain that he is tall; I think he is slight, upright and rather athletic; I imagine him to be blond, possibly he is a little darkish. But – and that is the point – he does not in the least stand out; he is just an Englishman. His voice is probably low, his air unassuming. And, with this type of Englishman, you feel that – if his manner is a little cold and reserved – his heart is probably quite in the right place. He looks down upon you a little, as the Englishman does with foreigners or persons outside his set, but he is always quite polite.

There, in fact, is the typical Englishman from whom nothing 'sticks out'. But stay. There is just one thing: I remember that at times Mr Galsworthy has an odd, rapt expression. He appears to think – slowly, coldly, tenaciously. He seems to take hold of something with the remorseless grip of a pike. He does not let go.

THE ENGLISHMAN

In one of his books Mr Galsworthy has described a man who was not 'sound' – a man who behaved, looked, acted, and dressed like every other man at a good club. But he had a something odd about him. What Mr Galsworthy meant was that this man – at some period of his career – had begun to think. The Englishman must never think; once he does that he is lost, socially speaking. And he is lost mentally too. He never reacquires an equilibrium – for the mental strain needed for breaking away, the impetus acquired, is so huge, that for the rest of his career he will be always, romantically, seeking for abuses to conquer or windmills against which to tilt. The Englishman – and Mr Galsworthy with him – is never content to be physically within the pale and mentally without it. The English education is directed towards giving a man settled manners, settled ideas, settled beliefs, and a standard of probity. It is directed remorselessly against his developing any independent thought. His business is to act in conformity with his standard that he learnt at Harrow and Oxford – or at Stepney Board School and a coal mine. It is all one, so he acquires a settled habit of thought and knows what he wants.

Mr Galsworthy's 'unsound man' – Mr Galsworthy himself – is a striking instance of the dangers of individual thought. Heaven knows where they will not – the two of them – end! Heaven knows why Mr Galsworthy started to write! Is the odd, thinking look in the eye a product of the writing habit? Or is it that, he having given in to that literary temptation that besets all of us – for there is no man who has not tried to write at least one book – having given in to that temptation, the writing habit produced the thinking look? I do not feel certain.

HOW THE NOVELIST DEVELOPED

But the fact remains that Mr Galsworthy for many years enjoyed every social advantage of a public school-University-country-house-good-people-and-pleasant-affluence type. He had time enough and leisure enough to look around him and to get his material together. Then he took to writing. He devoted himself with cold and single-minded tenacity to a heavy apprenticeship. He followed French models for many years; he forsook them, as one might expect, in favour of Russian, turning from Flaubert, who is too cold-blooded, to Turgenev, who is so amiable and touching. His literary career is a most interesting object-lesson. His first books are purely amateurish in the English way; then he begins to show signs of trying to learn from one master and another until his *Villa Rubein* appears to be a simple, sweet essay in the manner of Turgenev. In it he begins to show signs of having achieved method, style, construction – Art, in fact.

But the English reader need not be alarmed. Mr Galsworthy is English; he is not the man to stop at Art; he will go on to being useful to the

Republic. That malaise, that restlessness which drove him to writing as a refuge from social boredom – that restlessness has developed far beyond the mere stage of desiring to be an artist. It has taught Mr Galsworthy to become a splendid champion of the oppressed, the needy, and the down-trodden – a generous and romantic literary figure. The artist is a simple collector, collecting effects as another man collects cigar labels. Mr Galsworthy is a man of enthusiasms and indignations. Since the days of the *Villa Rubein* he has attacked many things. *The Island Pharisees* attacks English want of imagination; *The Man of Property* attacks English self-sufficiency and materialism; *The Country House* attacks English sexual relations and the law of divorce. At present Mr Galsworthy is conducting a series of attacks on the rich in the interests of the poor; and his attacks are all the more skilful and worthy of attention because of his fine literary training, his delicate sense of the value of words, his power of character-drawing, and his really noteworthy skill in selection.

HIS METHODS

He has become a dramatist. *The Silver Box* having been received with such marked attention at the Court Theatre, he is understood to be devoting the greater part of his attention to the drama, whilst a series of sketches from his pen which have been appearing in *The Nation* show that his mind is still engaged with the problem of poor versus rich.

Mr Galsworthy is probably quite right in turning his attention to the drama. For his method of projection, excellent and even beautiful as it is, is almost entirely that of setting what in law are called 'hard cases' one against the other. He shows us imbecile but respectable people taking tea on the lawns, whilst just outside the hedge a divorced lady will fall off her horse and exhibit courage, wit, temperament, and that indefinable quality called attraction: he shows us overfed City merchants contrasted with bright, winsome, and attractive prodigals; he shows us little rabbits dying after gross battues of game, and the shooter gorging on semi-putrid pheasants.

It is, in fact, the dramatic method – and it is therefore better suited for the drama than for the novel over which the audience can reflect. It is a method rather of artifice than of inspiration. When, in *The Silver Box*, the curtain divides a scene of middle-class over-eating from another of pauper starvation, a terrific and quite legitimate sensation is caused. The effects of a drama require to be quick: the mind accepts the situations as part of an individual story, and believes them.

But it is a little different with his novels. *The Country House* presents itself definitely as a typical country house. Yet one does not quite 'believe in' the patness of contrast to contrast; one's innate fairness of mind resents the labelling of a well-hung pheasant as a semi-putrid viand. For after all, the reader instinctively reflects, what moral difference does it make at what stage you eat meat which is destined at one stage or other to pass into the human frame?

In the novel, in fact, Mr Galsworthy's indignation and his tremendous literary adroitness lead him into a little want of fineness. He wants to beat a dog, and so he uses a singular ingenuity in finding sticks. Thus the general effect is one of a slight crudeness that militates against the reader's power to believe, and so to be lost, in the projection. But this, if it militates against the Art of Mr Galsworthy's books, does tremendously help his plays. And if it militates a little against the value of his novels as Art, it does tremendously help them as sociological sidelights. Hence our great pleasure at finding that an artist so careful as Mr Galsworthy can yet find such a very considerable public.

Tribune, 10 August 1907, 2.

VIII. Mr Joseph Conrad

I have spoken rather freely in these papers of the novelist as an exact – and more particularly as an aloof – scientist. But, as far as I can remember, I have not yet quite defined what I mean by 'an exact scientist', and I have not – except, perhaps, in the case of M. Anatole France – yet analysed the work of any imaginative writer who could come under this heading

For me, the first essential of a scientist is that he should be as far as possible passionless when he is at work. He should, that is to say, close up that portion of his brain in which labelled and docketed, there repose his cranks, his fads, or his great and overwhelming social ideals. The night before last, upon a platform of the Underground, I heard a gentleman exclaim – he was not quite steady upon his legs – '… So we finished up all the beer in the club. Fourteen dozen bottles. It's this teetotalism that is the curse of the land!'

This is a point of view like another. An excellent pamphlet ornamented with quotations from Fielding, Shakespeare, and the Bible might be written on that text. But imagine our friend writing a novel in which the only virtuous characters were these who staggered! It would not be a good novel.

It would not be a good novel – because it would not carry conviction. It would not carry conviction because it forced the note. We may believe in Tom Jones; though Tom Jones believed it was quite proper to be drunk upon occasion. (And I know a young man who was cut out of an uncle's will because he refused to get drunk.) But we should not believe in Tom

Jones if Fielding made his drunkenness the chief virtue of his character.

And the object of a work of art is to carry conviction – as a work of art it must have no other object. Its mission is to soothe, to solace, to excite, to move – to do anything that will make us forget our squalid lives, our daily toils, the miseries of our friends, or our intolerable futures. What the artist wishes to do – as far as you are concerned – is to take you out of yourself. As far as *he* is concerned, he wishes to express himself

Personally, I take an extremely gloomy view of Literature in England at the present day – of Literature judged from this standpoint. I can find very few books that will carry me out of myself. I can find still fewer in which the writer seems to think only of expressing his real personality.

MR CONRAD'S SELF-EXPRESSION

Of these few writers one is Mr Conrad. In his person he has the two absolutely necessary qualifications of the writer: he has lived a real life, and he has a passion for self-expression. Most writers of today have never lived at all, and most of us have a passion for representing ourselves as some sort of moralist. Practically the passion of Mr Conrad is to see things done in a ship-shape way – not because of any thought-out point of view which he parades on every occasion, but because it irritates him to come in contact with slovenliness in action and with inexact thought. And along with this passion for that which is ship-shape, with this passion which fatally predestined him to 'follow the sea', he has the passion for self-expression. It is not only that in his books almost magically he expresses the seas, the skies, and the faces of the men that he has seen. It is that personally he is a whole-souled raconteur. He tells stories with his hands, his eyes, his shoulders, his attitudes – or, in the darkness of a midnight verandah, with nothing visible but the glowing end of his cigarette, he uses every cadence of a voice to which a life at sea has given an extraordinary command of loudness, to which a life in many romantic drawing-rooms has given a singular touch of softness. But the point is that he tells his tale with every kind of aid to expression.

On the surface his life has been fabulous – that is the precise word. To have been born in Poland, to have arrived at the first rank of writers of a foreign tongue, to have suffered and contrived, in between an absolute odyssey of travel and of vicissitudes – these are the sort of thing, that, in skeleton, one hardly believes. But there they are, and it is from these strenuousnesses that he has drawn his knowledge of the sort of thing that can happen to man, of the sort of passions with which man can be beset.

And, having seen so much, it is hardly to be wondered at if he philosophizes little. What he desires to get into his books is not his views of life, it is his knowledge. He presents us with facts, not theories. That is why, though his literary standard, his mere standard of writing is so high, he has so wide an appeal.

Literature in England has lost touch with the People because the People – I, you, and the man selling papers at the corner – do not really want to hear the views of Mr X or of the Archbishop of Canterbury; we want to hear their experiences sincerely related. From these we can form our views for ourselves. Mr Conrad hardly ever expresses his views – unless he writes a letter to *The Times* about the merchant service. But lavish and extraordinarily well projected his experiences are at our service. In that he is the exact scientist – the real servant of the Republic.

For what we need – apart from Art – is true details to go upon. What we do not need is details falsified to fall in with the theories of Mr Y. or of Father Bernard Vaughan. In this way, quite apart from his Art, Mr Conrad is a valuable man.

HIS LATEST BOOK

When it comes to his Art, the broad outlines of Mr Conrad's method are easy to define. He differs from the typical Englishman of letters in this, that he is considering, always and before everything, the carrying of conviction to his reader. The ordinary English writer – the high-class writer – writes to please himself, sometimes, or more often to please a small circle who have read Dante or Ibsen or the writers of early Irish verse. But Mr Conrad writes as if for men who have acquired no literary jargon. He writes to give the unprovincial man the impression of having had a real experience. He writes, that is to say, as nearly as possible, such a book as would convince himself.

These facts account for all his excellences and most of his defects. His excellences are the reality and force with which he makes his characters live and react one on another; his principal defect is that he over-elaborates because he is profoundly sceptical. His latest book, *The Secret Agent*, is less over-elaborated than most of his former works; in comparison, indeed, it is singularly clear and direct in the way the story is told. The story is that of the poor imbecile who was induced by a foreign police spy to throw a bomb at Greenwich Observatory some years ago. A less scrupulous writer than Mr Conrad would have been content to state the fact – it is historic – and arising from that fact would have provided us with a 'spirited' detective story. Mr Conrad, on the other hand, must account at once for the motives of the pseudo-Anarchist, of the poor wretch who threw the bomb, of the Secretary of the Embassy that caused the outrage, and of the Assistant Commissioner of Police who detected the plot. All these people are made so singularly real that as you read the book you have the impression of undergoing actual experiences. You really seem to have been present, say, at the singular and exciting conversation between Chief-Inspector Heat and the Perfect Anarchist, the ancient scientist who carries always in his pocket a perfected infernal machine. And if at times the experiences with which you are provided seem a little long-drawn out, that is simply the defect of Mr Conrad's method – and every method must have a defect.

But, as I have said, *The Secret Agent* is a much more direct story than any that Mr Conrad has yet given us. For that reason it takes a very high place as a work of art. And those who are not interested in works of art – those who seek to make Art the servant of the Republic – will find it a work of great informative value. It casts a great deal of light upon a very obscure problem, since it is the work of a novelist who is a very exact scientist – of an imaginative writer who, having been given by the gods the gift of seeing life, has, with tremendous effort, evolved a method of rendering it. It is over such work that the Artist and the Moralist find in astonishment their hands meeting and then is made clear the obscure saying that 'Every work of Art has a profound moral significance'. It has. Because every work of art is a true rendering of a human instance, and every human instance has a profound moral significance for you, me, and the man selling papers at the corner.

Tribune, 14 September 1907, 2.

[X, but says VIII]. Maxim Gorky

The eloquent and generous rhetoric of the article by Count Tolstoy published last week in *The Tribune* naturally turns one's thoughts back to the day when Count Tolstoy had not developed into the splendid pamphleteer, but was still an imaginative – and how very exact a – renderer of human passions and vicissitudes. Considering how terrible are the necessities of the Russian nation in these days, it would, perhaps, be wanting in imagination to bewail this change, however little we may or may not think that the lesson of Tolstoy is the lesson that Russia needs. Of that, it is obvious, we cannot be the judges. A nation works out its own salvation along its own lines, and, without doubt, Tolstoy, with his doctrine of renunciation, non-resistance, and quietism, voices a great body of souls – an innumerable host that to more Occidental, and possibly cold, eyes appears to typify in Central Europe the whole East, with its patience, its introspection, its eternal 'Kismet! – it is fated'.

But apart from its national necessities, Russia has given to Europe three or four writers. One of them seems to take up, for the Western world, more and more the position of one of the unapproachably great. Young Russia herself has 'gone back on' Turgenev. That is because – surely only for a time – Russia has immense physical and material needs that obscure the demand for the humaner letters. We cannot object to Rome's disliking Nero, the artist who fiddled whilst the august city was burning. The heart of another is a dark forest, and young Russia craves for something harsh, virile, practical, non-contemplative. But for us who are the Western nations it is Turgenev who makes us most thankful that Russia has existed. It has given to our culture very little else.

Tolstoy the novelist gave us exact and very wonderful observations of life: Dostoevsky gave us the most wonderful registrations of mental abysms, of darkness, of profound and irremediable gloom. But Turgenev gave the world a tender, exact, and poetic rendering of human life. There is nothing in the world more poetic than some of the sketches in *A Sportsman's Letters*, there is nothing in the world that more pitifully sums up the enigmas of human lives than *Fathers and Children*, nothing that puts more piteously the case of humanity bound down by and bowing down to the conventions of humanity itself than the story of Lisa in the *House of Gentlefolk*.

TURGENEV AND SHAKESPEARE

It is useless to say that he is greater than Shakespeare, but he has, in common with Shakespeare, the quality of being unapproachable, and he lacks some of Shakespeare's faults. He is so unapproachable, because, as a writer, you can learn nothing of him. His methods are undiscoverable; you might imitate him, but you would never get any further. And, inasmuch as the figures that he draws are more actual, less typical, than those that Shakespeare drew, and inasmuch as the human vicissitudes that he narrates are less legendary, he is a writer more humane. Lisa is a more womanly figure than are Cordelia, or Portia, or Anne Page, just because the mental struggles through which she went are the struggles through which we all have to go at one time or another and in one form or another.

And if we go to a novelist to learn what life is, to whom can we go with a surer faith than Turgenev? That makes him, of course, have less significance for Russia, since Russia desires first to hear what to do as a nation. But we whose national problems are solved pretty well and in a rule-of-thumb way have leisure to set before us the problem of how to live tolerantly, and, in a high sense, gently, with our individual fellow-men.

But Turgenev is dead, and Dostoevsky is dead, and, as a novelist, so is Tolstoy. There is alive today only one Russian imaginative writer whose appeal to the world is widespread. He is, of course Aleksei Maksimovich Peshkov, a man of 38, who uses the pseudonym of Maximus the Bitter – Maxim Gorky. Broad-faced, with a set frown, high-cheek-boned, rather harsh voiced, rhapsodizing and a little overbearing, you cannot imagine a greater contrast with the gently wise, smiling, civilized, and sad face of Turgenev. If, as it were, Maxim Gorky sits by the roadside violently breaking stones for the onward march of humanity, Turgenev with a resigned irony destroys the boulders that beset us, as did Hannibal the rocks of the Alps, aceto infuso.

Turgenev is, as it were again, a duellist turning a light steel against human weakness that he accepts. But there is singularly little of the 'Kismet' that we attribute to the Russian psychology to be found in Gorky's utterance. He accepts with a sort of fierce gusto starvation, sickness, chilly rains, the black mud of the Steppes, the bitter cold of the seas. But he rages against human nature. In that he is the poorer workman.

He has had the advantage of a life in which he has sounded the bitterest depths. He has been a biscuit baker, a road mender, a tramp, a dock rat. He tells us of murderers, of dossers, of wharf thieves, of prostitutes. He has rubbed up against thousands of men; he has seen thousands of faces. But, perhaps because he has thought little, his stories affect us as having less of truth than we need in the works of great writers.

He is intensely dramatic; he has a store of excellent stories. We can believe in most of the things that he describes, but we do not feel that they happened just as he describes them. Chelkash the harbour thief is a little overdone: he is too gay, too ferocious, too sentimental, too amiable, by turns. The twenty-six biscuit bakers are too continually harping on one note in 'Twenty-six Men and a Girl'. We do not quite believe that the girl of the streets spoke as Gorky says she did in 'An Autumn Night'. We are willing, however, to believe that she shared her last crust with the starving boy beneath the boat.

THE REALISTIC ELEMENT

Gorky has, of course, a singular power of giving realistic details: we *do* believe in his rags, his mud, his seas at night, his priests, his dosshouses. But, most of his human beings appear to be what the French call 'chargés' – overdrawn.

It is as if Gorky at some time or other had read Bret Harte. His outcasts are not as sentimentalized as those of Poker Flat. But they have that suggestion about them. And indeed he has told us that he has read a great deal of foreign work. 'It is not too much to say,' says one of his biographers, 'that no other Russian writer ever uses so many foreign terms (English and French especially) or has coined so many new words from extraneous Western sources.' I do not think that that is exactly a commendation.

We seem, in fact, to see in M. Gorky a writer with tremendous aspiration to change the Russian nature. Just as at one time Russian landed proprietors had a mania for English farming, so many Russians of today desire to give their countrymen the English – or more particularly the American – point of view. Perhaps they are right, perhaps wrong; we cannot ever say whether the in-grafting of a foreign point of view is good for a nation or whether the working out of salvation along national lines is better and saner.

It might be fanciful to say that M. Gorky, in his desire to Americanize Holy Russia, has made his outcasts like those of Bret Harte in order to prove that the Russian man has American capabilities. But brilliant and impressive as his sketches are, they do give the impression of being hybrid things. For that reason they seem to lack conviction, which, as it were, he seeks to atone for by using a tremendously loud voice.

This may for these reasons be useful to the Russian republic; but just because we have our own Bret Hartes and Dickenses it renders him less useful to us. We cannot, that is to say, learn more of him than how pitiable is the condition of the lower classes in Russia. If, however, that moves us to human sympathy that may be good for us: if it moves us to make what efforts we may on their behalf that is probably what M. Gorky most desires. Perhaps for that reason he is right to paint with a rather coarse brush.

HIS LATEST BOOK

These words may well apply to Gorky's latest book (*Comrades*, Hodder). We believe – perfectly and with a sure faith – that the circumstances, pitiable, horrible, or merely soul-numbing, of the life of the Russian proletariat are just as M. Gorky describes them. We believe that the Russian police make domiciliary visits just such as M. Gorky describes them. The circumstances are so put before us as to stir some of us, or to open the purse-strings of others. But the characters leave us a little unmoved. As a matter of fact the hero, Pavel, is dull and wooden. Only his mother lives – and she lives so well and so really that we can pardon a good deal of the rest. If we do not see why she should love her son, we know nevertheless that mothers do love the dullest of sons. But in another sense she is a misfortune for the book, since as an old mother would be, she is a little stupid, unreceptive, and unawakened, and by enlisting our sympathies for her M. Gorky enlists them for the stupid, the unreceptive and the unawakened that is in humanity. He runs the risk of making his reader say: 'Oh, well, the unawakened soul is the best of the bunch!'

That is always the penalty of faulty art; it defeats itself. And M. Gorky, unthinking and natural genius as he is, has serious defects as an artist. Nevertheless, even as an artist he has his great moments, whilst, for those whose chief interest is in ideas – of liberty, revolution, and of the advance of mankind towards a perfect social system – M. Gorky brings a sombre and glowing passion. His ends are not in any particular sense literary, but, as a peasant of genius telling impassioned tales of injustice and heroism, he certainly achieves his own ends.

Tribune, 28 September 1907, 2.

IX [*sic*: should be XI]. Mr Dion Clayton Calthrop

M. Gorky, then, is an excellent specimen of the writer who is needed by a nation in its birth-throes. But, as I said last week, roughly and in a rule-of-thumb way we have settled most of our constitutional and most of our social problems. We have settled them, that is to say, all but the details, and those details the writer, the imaginative writer, cannot, in the nature of things, very well approach. For, roughly speaking, it is the function of the imaginative writer to state things as they are, to voice the people as it is, to see, to feel. Only very rarely, is he a fitting man to suggest remedies. His intellect, as a rule, is of a different order; his province is to present life for the consideration of the law-giver, not to make laws. We might, that is to say, very well trust ourselves to a statesman deeply read in Shakespeare; we should hardly like to trust ourselves to Shakespeare for the framing of our housing regulations.

In a State whose conditions, economic, constitutional, legal, and social, are fairly settled, what then remains the public function of the imaginative writer? At first sight you would answer, 'Nothing.' But, though roughly speaking the laws of a nation may form, as it were, an easy cloak, there remains always the question: how do the individuals of the nation bear themselves in the extra-legal sphere? How, in fact, is it with their manners? Or, again, when the workers of a nation have secured a machinery that upon the whole renders them able to exact a reasonable wage, the question always remains: How do these workers spend that wage? Or yet again: when a nation has settled how the families of a nation may, upon the whole, live pleasantly side by side, the question always remains: How do the units of these families live one beside another?

It is, upon the whole, to that stage that we have attained, and it is to these questions that, as a public functionary, the imaginative writer has to turn his attention. For, though we may well be fairly satisfied with the public aspects of our nation, we can hardly be satisfied that our private contracts are all that they should be. Our laws are good, our manners – our powers of understanding, sympathizing with or aiding one another – might be so very much better. Our families have each one a little castle at peace with each other little castle; but in so many of them the peace within might be so very much deeper. And though upon the whole we earn fair wages, how very much more full of amenities life might be if we had better things upon which to spend them.

THE NEED FOR ROMANCERS

It is this aspect of our life today that is the most dismal. For when we have satisfied the cravings of our hunger, the needs of covering and shelter, and the just dues of the Republic, what remains for us to do with our surpluses? So very little that satisfies a man of reasonable refinement. And this implies a huge body of uncultured members of the Republic; a huge need for these imaginative writers whose function it is to spread a power of rationalized appreciation which is called culture.

It is said that the English take their joys sadly. It would be almost more just to say that they take no joys at all. When we set out in pursuit of pleasure we are almost always a little 'on the make'. We play games to improve our physique; we read books to make us better money makers or moralists. We dress ourselves with a view to health, use, or the avoidance of dirt, never with a view to beauty and the pleasure that comes of beauty. We go to theatres.... Well, I cannot imagine why we go to our theatres. Perhaps it is because we are told that we ought not to.

But the point is that we never abandon ourselves – never let ourselves go. We are always self-conscious. And that is dismal. When I sit down at the end of my day's work I bethink me: Where can I go to get a little simple enjoyment that will rest my mind? And, upon my word, now that I have been to see Miss Genée in her new ballet I have nothing left that calls me out of doors. I sit still in my chair and consider. I might re-read the *Pseudolus* of Plautus. I might reread the lyrics of Heine or the *Rape of the Lock*. But if I am in the mood for something new, what is there that is irresponsible, delicate, that would not improve me, that will whimsically take me out of myself? I cannot think of very much.

MR CALTHROP'S RECORD

It is when I am in this vein that I wish that Mr Calthrop had a great following; for if Mr Calthrop had a great following he might do much better work – and if his work were just a little better it would be exquisite. At present it just falls short of being exquisite because, spreading himself over too many fields, probably in the search for success, he lacks the time to think about his work. Keen, responsive, with reservations, with a little of the actor's manner and a taste for the picturesque in dress, he is full of quips and cranks of personality. Those are the attributes that come out in his work.

He has written a *Guide to Fairy Land* that lets us half believe that he believes in his own fancies: he has illustrated it with just the quaint, pretty, whimsical pictures to make us half believe that he has seen those places. He has written a history of English costume that makes us half believe that he knows all about English costume. He has written a book called *King Peter* that is a dreamy, quaint, and delightful chronicle of the Court of a King of Yvetôt. It is so quaint, so delightful, and so dreamy that we can more than half – we can very nearly quite – almost altogether – believe that he lives in a little precious realm of his own. It is one of the things that makes me believe our Public is gross and vulgar, that our Public took so little notice of *King Peter*. (But, after all, Miss Genée had been dancing for years before she was divorced.)

If, however, the Great Public *had* discovered *King Peter*, it would have left Mr Calthrop no excuse. He would have *had* to go on to making us really quite believe. He would have gone on to working out a method. His fault is that he has never mastered his own personality. He is a little French, a little Irish, a little stage-born, and, to complete the Romantic touch, he is, I believe, descended from the sister of Queen Anne Boleyn. Thus he has several excuses for running away with himself.

HIS LATEST WORK

But if the Great Public had discovered *King Peter*, Mr Calthrop might not have given months of time to designing the costumes of the Oxford Pageant. In that case his latest book might have been his masterpiece. As it is, it is a little more coloured than the book that preceded it. It is a little gayer; a little noisier; a little more restless. It purports to be the adventures of a medieval knight's son in search of a Perfect Love. He travels all Europe over, on foot, with tramps on horseback, with a dancing bear. He travels east, he travels west; he is robbed in green shaws; he is sad on the sea and in taverns; he rejoices on highroads; up hill, down dale, he tests the natures – and sometimes the lips – of Yolande, Clare, Phillipa, Anne, Gabrielle, and just under a score of other maidens. He returns home at last to find in his own parish the Perfect Love that he had sought half the world over. And, in a sense, he exhibits the gay resource of Pseudolus, the lyrical mood of Heine's knights, and the taste for costume of the *Rape of the Lock*.

Mr Calthrop's medieval Europe is no more medieval Europe than his Court of King Peter is at Yvetôt or Brentford. It is a broad, sunlit, coloured, ruffled world of hills and roads tucked somewhere away in a plane, a Fourth Dimension, known to Mr Calthrop alone. And with just a little more work how absolutely exquisite a book the *Dance of Love* might have been!

As it is it rings in places just a little false. The hero is a little theatrical – or let us say he is a figure of a Pageant; the book is a little long in opening; it is a little long in passages. That is because, in passages, Mr Calthrop is apt to be too pleased with himself. And it is a fairly safe thing to say that when you are pleased with yourself you are apt to dwell – and when you dwell you give your friends what the French call 'longueurs'. An excellent and empirical rule for doing away with these blemishes in one's work is to eat a very indigestible supper and read one's proofs next morning.

But, in spite of what I have said against the *Dance of Love*, it remains one of the few books of its genre that this season will bring us. It is so gay, so ingenuous, so unusual in these uniform days, that if the few tens of thousands of the nation who delight in the gay, the ingenuous, and the unusual can only be got to read it they will get a great deal of delight from it. I wish they would; for then Mr Calthrop would have no more excuse

CHESTER COLLEGE LIBRARY

to be spendthrift with a rare talent. For the talent of conveying irresponsible joy is a rare one, and to any Republic it is very valuable.

Tribune, 5 October 1907, 2.

XIV. Mr Maurice Hewlett

The novelist to whom I referred last week as acting very efficiently the part of lightning-conductor, letting a dangerous stream of electricity run to earth, was Mr Maurice Hewlett. And it may be taken as a sign of his quick appreciation of minute tokens that he so subtly apprehended the not very obvious indications of tension that there were in the air. A quick appreciation, a power of observing, or perhaps of feeling, are patent in all his works, just as they are obvious in his person. It is the sort of vibrating nervousness of a man who, having had many sensations, has lived much. It is, in fact, modernity – for what separates the life we live today from the lives that all former men have lived is the fact that we are surrounded by such an infinite number of little and transitory facts – the tram-tickets of life, as it were – and of little transitory objects. If we fail in quickness of apprehension we fall short of being modern.

But Mr Hewlett has all the quickness, the quality of vibrating like a stretched string, the power, as it were, to do without leisure, the openness to swift and passionate sensation, and the ability swiftly to savour and analyse the emotions that assail him. He has the polish, the unobtrusiveness, the manner, and the necessary slight power of self-assertion – of resistance – that are necessary to get through modern life. He gives in his books, and largely in his person, the idea of having lived and appreciated the colours of life.

I will confess to having as much misunderstood Mr Hewlett as anybody. *Earthwork Out of Tuscany* I dismissed as William Morris diluted by John Ruskin; the *Forest Lovers*, I remember saying, succeeded because it was William Morris and water. But the *New Canterbury Pilgrims' Tales* delighted me. They delighted me in a way that, I felt at the time, was immoral, aesthetically speaking. I tried to convince myself, intellectually, that here was the real medievalism – Chaucer, Froissart, Boccaccio, the *Cent Nouvelles Nouvelles*, with a touch of Brantôme and of Straparola.[1]

1 [The *Cent nouvelles nouvelles* is a fifteenth-century collection of tales modelled on the *Decameron*. Pierre de Bourdeilles Brantôme's *Vie des dames galantes* (1665) recounts court intrigues. Giovan Francesco Straparola's *Piacevoli Notti (Pleasant Nights)*, 1550–3, contained folk-tales such as 'Beauty and the Beast'.]

But I could not feel certain: there was a something that I could not analyse, that led me to mistrust my joy, a piquant note, out of tune with the august directness of these models. I tried to assure myself that it was an improvement upon the originals, but, maugre me, as they used to say, I could not feel at ease. *Richard Yea and Nay* confirmed my doubts; the *Queen's Quair* taught me a good deal; an eighteenth-century romance made me certain that Mr Hewlett belonged to at least as late as the Late Renaissance; Mr Hewlett's latest book makes me certain that his place is in the twentieth century.

A MODERN WRITER

It is a welcome discovery, for we have too many writers who will treat modern life in terms of heaven knows what parochial, Victorian or pre-Victorian, dialects; we have hardly any that are capable of registering it as the delicate thing of little lights and trifling shadows that it is. It is, of course, a good thing – a goodish to good thing – to have treated of past life in the terms of modernity. But Mr Hewlett will come into his own quite soon now.... I am, of course, treating this writer very seriously. The reviewing of today will say – it has said – that Mr Hewlett's romances of the past are Books of the Year, of the century, or supreme masterpieces. And so they are, in the proportions of the day. But let us treat him in the terms that apply the word 'masterpiece' to, say, such novels of the one kind as *Macbeth* and *Julius Caesar*, or such masterpieces of the other kind as *Salammbô* or 'Saint Julien l'Hospitalier' – or as *Thais*. In that gallery *Richard Yea and Nay* does not stand for very much, and *The Queen's Quair*, perhaps, for less still.

Richard Yea and Nay fails, oddly enough, because it is too little documented to be convincing; *The Queen's Quair* fails because it is too overlaid with documents. In the main, the writing of historical novels is a silly business. We mostly write stories that would be a great deal better, placed in our own day; sometimes we do it because the story that possesses us cannot be placed in 1907 by reason of incidents or passions or the exigencies of time. And, of course, if a story possesses us, we must get it out, and thus we have the historical novel.

But, in Mr Hewlett's case, I fancy that he adopted the Historian's pose more or less by accident. Medievalism – a sort of legacy of the Aesthetic movement – was in the air when he began to write – and he was by his occupation brought much in contact with the Documents. And what was wrong with the Tales of his Pilgrims was not the colour, the body, or the texture – it was just the spirit. The little, quaint, regretful, inconclusive turns of his stories; the little, quaint, regretful, inconclusive passions of his figures were those of, let us say, a modern French *chanson*. It was delightful – but it was not Boccaccio. The passions of medievalism were direct and simple – in spite of the Lays of Bertrand de Born; it was only the court costumes, the castles, and the vocabulary that were quaint. It was life or death; satisfaction or death; guilt and joyous escape; or discovery and death, or worse. We cannot have these things today, apparently, and Mr Hewlett is too modern to infuse them into his medieval stories.

His eighteenth-century book was very good; it had still the demerit of being rococo and modern rococo at that. The eighteenth century, save for its dress and its address, was as direct as the eleventh in its passions.

HIS LATEST BOOK

The Stooping Lady is still better; but still the spirit is unsatisfying. Someone has said that Mr Meredith's figures are all seven feet high – and Mr Hewlett's Lady stoops, as it were, from seven feet and a half. She is too tremendous to be really believed in; she is too spirited. We can hardly credit that Rose, in the delightful *Evan Harrington*, married a snip. It is still more difficult to believe that Mr Hewlett's Lady Morfa did not recoil when her stooping brought her near to the cleaver and the block with its fragments of suet. Whereas, had she lived today! ....

She might have been a wilful, upper middle-class member of a Social-Democratic society; she might have married her butcher. And then think of how significant and sardonic and tragic the book might have been! That is what we need from Mr Hewlett – a lady five foot seven high. And now, no doubt, having served his apprenticeship, having made his *Wanderjahre* across the centuries, he will give her to us.

For what we do need today are writers, approximately of the first class, who will register modern life for us, from as many angles as may be. From one angle, of course, Mr James does this consummately, but there are so few others who have the really sensitive personality, the power to register fine shades – so that we want Mr Hewlett to write what he really believes in. For we cannot really believe that Mr Hewlett really believes that there are giants today. He forces himself into a sort of hypnotic belief that there were such giants in the old days; he has given us a colossal fresco figure of Richard I; he has brought us down to the seven feet and a half of the Stooping Lady. But all these figures are products of a sort of derivativeness, Richard I of the Aesthetic Movement, the Stooping Lady of the Romantic-Ethical myth, for which Mr Meredith is responsible. But we want Mr Hewlett to be his real self: it is a self quite good enough. We want, that is to say, Mr Hewlett's image of the possibilities of life; we do not nearly so much want to know what life might have been like had there been giants in the old days. But I am not saying that Mr Hewlett's speculations are not charming speculations or that *The Stooping Lady* is not a book out of the common run.

Tribune, 26 October 1907, 2.

From XXIII. The Year 1907

The other night I was going eastward upon the top of a bus. It was just outside the Tottenham Court Road tube station. In front of us was a tongue of deep shadow, the silhouetted forms of bus-tops, dray-tops, drivers' hats, all in a pyramidal mass of darkness, and a stimulating, comfortable, jangling confusion. Before us was a blazing haze of golden light, on each side the golden faces of innumerable people, lit up by the light that streamed from shop-windows, and up along the house fronts the great shafts of light streamed heavenwards. And the gloom, the glamour, the cheerfulness, the exhilarating cold, the suggestion of terror, of light, and of life …

It was not Romance – it was Poetry. It was the Poetry of the normal, of the usual, the poetry of the innumerable little efforts of mankind, bound together in such a great tide that, with their hopes, their fears, and their reachings out to joy they formed a something at once majestic and tenuous, at once very common and strangely pathetic.

But of that I find little in the work of living novelists, and less or nothing in the work of living poets.

Tribune, 28 December 1907, 2.

XXIV. The Year 1908

In this series of papers I have, with some few digressions, adhered pretty closely to my original design of descanting upon Literature and its functions in the Republic. This has excluded to some extent any treatment of Literature as an art. For, although it is a truism that the better a book is written the larger will be its appeal, that is a truism which the present cloistral state of the art has so obscured that – for fear of appearing nonsensical or a dealer in nothing but paradoxes – I have left it severely in the background.

The function of Literature as an art is to give joy – to give joy to the reader, not to the writer, for the art of creation is accompanied always with pain. (That, however, is another truism which is so controversial that I hesitate to make it. Having made it, however, I will venture a few words more.) For it is obvious that the writer who writes to please himself – the writer who, having written, smites his forehead and exclaims: 'By Heaven, this is Genius' – that writer already has his reward. But the writer who writes with the desire to please Humanity – to please, that is to say, as much of ordinary mankind as he may appeal to – that writer is attempting to find a technique. For technique is the science of appeal.

On the other hand, the writer may seek not solely to give joy to, but to profit the Republic. If he do that he hungers, not only after appeal, but after truth. Thus he essays a doubly difficult task. For he must put away not only all desire to write with the vine-leaves in his hair – to write 'Genius work' – but all his views. He must, in fact, stifle his desire to preach; he must forget that he is prosecuting or defending barrister; he must remember that he is not a juryman; he must sum up with as little bias as, humanly, he may. Then, for the Jury who have to deliver the verdict on this long, sometimes entrancing, sometimes appalling, sometimes dull trial that is the life we live, he will have cleared the issues.

THE OMNIPOTENT NOVELIST

To clear the issue. That is the position, in the Republic, of the imaginative writer. And the imaginative writer of today is almost always a novelist – for the serious book has become so severely factual that it presents no side at all for literary criticism. (This, of course, is a slightly sweeping statement that should be tempered with an 'as a whole'; for, on looking through a convenient summary of the Books of the Year, I see that 1907 has given us not only one, but three or four serious works of the imaginative tradition, the most prominent of which have been Mr James's *American Scene*, *Father and Son*, by an anonymous hand,[1] and the historical essays of Lord Acton. But it is significant enough that the two former works are by writers distinctly of the older tradition, and the last by a great man who was hardly a writer at all and is now dead.)

Roughly speaking we may say that the serious book has ceased to be literature, because it has fallen into the hands of the specialist. And the charm of the serious book of old was that the writer, not being a specialist, had eyes for the world around him, and could point out enlivening or enlightening analogies. So that, in portraying 1908, in forecasting what its features are likely to develop into, and in trying to point out from what few writers we may expect work which will both delight and profit the Republic, I am almost forced to fall back on the novelists alone.

The *Revue des Deux Mondes* has been publishing a series of appreciations of British novelists of today. Looking at us from afar, less concerned perhaps than we ourselves, and pushed to it, no doubt in some degree by the courtesy of his nation, the writer, M. Wyszewa, gives of us a very flourishing account. Seated as I am in what Carlyle called the 'belly of the ugly enterprise', I cannot be so cheerful. But one is prone to underrate

1 [Edmund Gosse]

one's contemporaries, if only because they are apt to be, as it were, the members of one's household. Looking through again the list that I have mentioned, I see the names of three of four novelists whom I should class as approximately of the first class, and as approximately rendering life as it is lived. There are Mr Henry James, Mr Conrad, Mr Hudson, the naturalist, and Mr Galsworthy. Of these, though they are mentioned, neither Mr James nor Mr Hudson gave us novels last year. Mr Galsworthy's *The Country House* was a very serious and, technically, a very delicate attempt to render modern life. Mr Conrad's *The Secret Agent* dealt less with the typical than with the exceptional. In that, however, it was an exception amongst Mr Conrad's works.

MORE KIPPSES WANTED

My mentor leaves out the name, however, of the novelist most useful for my purposes – Mr H.G. Wells; not the Mr H.G. Wells of Utopias and airships, but the author of *Kipps*. It is for me a cause of lamentation that this author devotes – I will not say 'wastes' – his time to Utopias and airships. It is a cause of lamentation because what we so very much need is just such a book as *Kipps*, purged of some of the defects of *Kipps* – and these defects were accidental, not inherent – and longer, weightier, dealing rather with the fortunes of groups than the vicissitudes of a single individual. I would, indeed, shake off my diffidence – I would imitate the fine courage of this author – and prophesy that Mr Wells has such a book on the way, and to be published in 1908, were I not certain that Mr Wells's airships and Utopias will delay its appearance for more than the three hundred and sixty-two days that of this Leap Year remain to us.[2]

Of other writers of modern books who appear to seek after Truth we may expect in 1908 activities from Mr de Morgan (who has revived the typical English Novel of the nineteenth century); from Miss Sinclair, who is a valiant soul, a little lacking in the scientific composure of one of His Majesty's Judges; from Mrs Wharton, who is still of the school of Mr James; from Mr Owen Wister, who writes charmingly but wavers still between the exceptional and the typical; from Mr Archibald Marshall, whose leisurely equanimity recalls the mood of that great writer, Anthony Trollope; from Mr Pett Ridge, whose last book seemed to embody the very soul of that cheerful and wonderful sparrow, the Londoner of today, and from Mr Edwin Pugh, whose *Tony Drum* gave promise of so very much....

The turn of the tide! – As I write the sea is at the turn of the tide, wearily, below my windows. – Will the turn of the tide come in 1908?

2 [Wells did indeed have such a book on the way, *Tono-Bungay*, which Ford began to serialize in *The English Review* in December 1908, though (as Ford prophesies) the novel didn't appear in book form until the following year.]

Will this year begin to show us English Literature registering and presenting in a great body, Modern Life? Will it begin to show us that Literature can still do for this Age what it has done for all that preceded it? Will it register and give to our time a form and an abiding shape and stamp? I wonder. We have, of course, the three or four writers. But are they enough to form an impulse, to found a school, to turn a tide? I wonder.

To me it seems that the answer rests with the younger group – the second group that I have mentioned. Will they sit tight? Will they keep at it? Or will they, too, find a line of less resistance, ending in the conventional Novel of Exceptions or the closed castles of Literary Preciousness and Provincialism? I wonder.

Tribune, 4 January 1908, 2.

XXVII. Mr Charles Doughty

> And now we fell into a road – a road in Arabia! I had not seen a road since Damascus. We passed by a house or two built by the wayside, and no more such as the clay beyts of Arabia, but painted and glazed houses of Turkey. We were nigh et-Tayif, and went before the villa of the late Sherif, where he had in his life-time a pleasure-ground, with flowers! (The Sherifs are commonly Stambul-bred men.) The garden was already gone to decay.

My old schoolmaster – God rest his harmless, didactic soul – had a habit. He interfered with us singularly little for a schoolmaster, but he had a few maxims, moral or of conduct, that, in a mixed jargon of English and German, he enforced upon us at every turn. One of these was: 'Schreib wie du sprichst!' We could never sit down quiet to a job of writing in our leisure hours – it might be a letter home, an article for the school magazine, or one of those glorious Novels that one writes at school – but Mr P— would poke his head round the side of the door and, having taken stock of our occupation, would ejaculate: 'Schreib wie du sprichst!'

Write as you speak! What a glorious but impracticable counsel! For if we had written as we spoke then what a queer mixture of schoolboy slang in English, what an ungrammatical, colloquial German, what queer French or Virgilian Latin it would have been! And in those days I personally – and I fancy most of the other boys – were more under the influence of a more commonplace Usher. The Usher, in setting us a Composition, would say: 'Now, H—, let us have something balanced; something Johnsonian!' And, indeed, I tried my best in those days to write Johnsonese.

But 'Schreib wie du sprichst!' How often since then have I repeated those words to neophytes; how often have I not striven after that impossible ideal!

For I speak – we all speak – a forcible, nervous, excellent, and subtle language. We express very well what we want to express. But when we take our pens in hand what a timid, literary jargon issues out in the ink. I wish I dare write: 'Chuck it!' How excellent and expressive the words are. 'Oh, chuck that gibberish' I should write if I dared. As it is, I must dilate upon 'the desirability of abandoning a derivative verbiage'.

WRONGHEADED WRITERS

England has indeed been cursed by the wrongheadedness of its great and little writers. Lily was not a supreme writer, but he infected the whole tongue of his day with euphuism. Johnson was a supreme writer: a great and virile figure; yet, having written forcible sentences in the language of his day, it was his habit to translate them into sounding Latinisms. Thus he gave us that Johnsonese from which as a boy I suffered. William Morris, again, was a fine and virile figure; yet he, too, translated his speech – into Wardour-Street Anglo-Saxon! (Even Tennyson has told us that he did this.) And there is Mr Meredith who does it – and we all do it, some more and some less. And growing thus provincial and derivative in our speech we grow more and more blind in our minds to the beauties, the problems, and the hopes of our day. So that Literature is losing all appeal – it is as it was in Alexandria. Verse is precious and dead; the prose of books is losing all its life….

I write thus energetically because this is the moral that I wish to append to this series of articles. It is the message: the 'vox clamantis'. Moreover it emphasizes the praise that I wish to lavish on Mr Doughty. I detest his style; I revel in his books.

His *Dawn in Britain* was a revelation – a revelation of life as it must have been lived in these Islands at their dawning in History. (I do not say as it *was* lived, but as it must have been since Mr Doughty made it so.) Having laboriously worked through the cacophonous verbiage of that book I have been in Britain of the Dawn. Having – not quite so laboriously – read through Mr Doughty's latest collection of pre-Spenserian epithets I have sat in the shade of tents in the desert.

But: 'Schreib wie du sprichst!'…. I wonder if Mr Doughty speaks as he writes: I wonder what his parlourmaid does, then, if he asks her to take a message to the leech. I should like to say that I consider this old work of Mr Doughty's, of which a new edition is now presented to us, one of the finest books. I read it long enough ago to have calmed down any early enthusiasms, and I am prepared to let it go at that.

Mr Doughty, who in this edition presents us with his photograph, is a hard, obstinate, sardonically-smiling bearded man. In Arabia he was not so much reckless as grimly obdurate. He encountered perils and hardships that nothing but a kind of grim mania of endurance could have carried him through – and the result of these adventures is this tremendous book. (I am tempted to say that nothing but a grim mania of endurance could have carried him through the writing of it and of the *Dawn in Britain*.)

His style is the product of wrongheadedness – of a want of logic. The virile writer of English is always apt to be appalled at the slipshod, derivative prose of his contemporaries. That is inevitable. He despises the literary language. There is the English of the Present; there is the English that is dead.

Mr Doughty had to choose between: 'cometh anon Seyd, set high on *mehtah*; javelin he brandisheth, expiring spume as lion of Atlas.'

And

'Then up comes a Pathan; he was on an old camel chucking a spear about and spitting like a cat in an area.'

One version is as attractive as the other: why does Mr Doughty choose the former? I suppose because, like every Englishman, he prefers the weight of dead authority to the transitory shockingness of his day. Yet tomorrow 'a cat in an area' will be as classical as the 'lion of Atlas', and part of a language as dead.

HIS LATEST WORK

However, this is labouring the point. The fact remains that *Wanderings in Arabia* (Duckworth, 2 vols) is a work of great value. Its value lies in the number of sensations that it conveys. When you have read it you have felt hunger, and thirst, the torrid heat of the sun; you have sat in black tents of hair; you have seen the wells of the desert. You have been alone, in these boundless sands, a starving and despised Nazarene amidst the capriciously fanatical believers. You have seen desolation, you have cried aloud at the woes of poor nomads, yourself poorer than any one of them.

The book is of this great value and interest, for it is a really projection of life; not a mere 'writing about' things. When you have read it you will know; you will have experience. And in an hour or so you will find that you can construe Mr Doughty's words quite easily; in two hours you will find yourself neglecting your proper duties to go on reading him. And, indeed, there are whole passages as little difficult as that I have quoted above. If I have attacked his language, it is on public grounds – because literature is dying, in my view, since smaller writers use dead words anaemically. But Mr Doughty is an Individualist. Probably he does not care twopence what becomes of the Republic of Letters. That is a point of view, like another. I only wish there were a few more Individualists who could let us undergo such experiences. The Letters might revive, and all be well. Was it not Herrick who gave it as his rule of life: 'To live merrily and trust to good letters'?

Tribune, 25 January 1908, 2.

Shylock as Mr Tree

Mr Tree is a gallant spirit.[1] His province in life is to keep the centre of the stage for as long as possible, to extract from audiences an infinite number of ejaculations of wonder and delight, to dominate – even to tyrannize. He exists no doubt to corrupt – from the point of view of those fastidious creatures who do not like histrionics – the taste of a whole Gentile nation and thus to avenge in part the sorrows of all the Shylocks that all the Ghettos ever saw. And very excellently he has done it. As it appears, he has hypnotized the nation, terrorized the press and rendered London a laughing-stock, since London lies beneath his feet. His triumph is all but complete. With his Shylock he has added another leaf to his laurel crown: there needs but one more.

His is a gallant spirit. Whether he takes himself seriously or not I have no quarrel with him. He follows an art with which I am not in sympathy but I can admire his skill. He is a hypnotist, almost a filibuster, a prestidigitateur. The hand, in his case, deceives the eye. He puts, as it were, the Shakespeare rabbit into the top-hat of His Majesty's Theatre, warms it over the footlights and produces a spectacular omelette. Mighty waves of sound pour out from the spectators.

And to the cynical mind, what is most delectable in the sight is the fact that the audiences believe that, still, he and they are doing homage to the ineffable name of Shakespeare.... The ineffable name of Shakespeare!

What a bad acting play *The Merchant of Venice* appears to be: how it halted: what digressions, what longueurs, it contained last Saturday night! How is it that we have for so long continued to consider Shakespeare a great dramatist? It must be, it occurred to me, between yawns and impatience audible from a dissatisfied gentleman behind me, that Shakespeare is really one of those dramatists who do no more than read well: it must be. For I have known *The Merchant of Venice* ever since I was fourteen, and on hardly an evening when I am feeling restful do I not soothe myself by repeating one or other of Portia's speeches. (I do not know why this is, for there are other plays of Shakespeare that please me better when I read them.) But nothing of the dreamy magic and ecstasy came through to me across the footlights and the palms that hid the orchestra. Perhaps that was

1 Sir Herbert Beerbohm Tree (1853–1917), great character actor, and manager of Haymarket and His Majesty's Theatres; half-brother of Sir Max Beerbohm.

because of the ejaculations, continual and disturbing, from the unknown gentleman behind me. But there were gondolas, there were masques, there were pretty pictures, refined upholstery, there was the Venice of the Ghetto … and there was Mr Tree.

But even Mr Tree with his boundless experience was not able to make *The Merchant of Venice* anything but tedious. It is true that in our midnight and voluptuous revels with the plays we do not make allowances for the interruptions, the masques, the dances, the gondolas, and the intervals when, during an episode of empty stage, a bell tolls emotionally above a synagogue. We read on, we do not remember that these things are essential to the modern stage or that Shakespeare, who was not for an age but for all time, ought to have foreseen the exigencies of His Majesty's Theatre today.

A bad play … It would not get on: it dragged over a dance: it halted for displays of erudition depicting the Ghetto and Venice of the Renaissance. It is wonderful the work that Mr Tree must have put into his production: one wonders how he ever found time to think out each of the guttural ejaculations, pauses, snorts, and the crawling motions of his fingers. He seems to have exhausted the possibilities of M. Viollet le Duc and the Jewish Encyclopaedia. The only criticism that one has to make is that he did not, as a pendant to his picture of the Jews going into the synagogue, give us an interlude representing Mass in San Marco, another with Gobbo purchasing provisions for the banquet and the Doge celebrating the marriage of the city with the Adriatic. It would have rounded off the picture and have formed, educationally, the complement to the instructive sidelights that Mr Tree has thrown upon life in the Venetian Ghetto.

It should not however be thought that Mr Tree is a special pleader for oppressed Jews. On the contrary, his Shylock is not tragic, he is not even seriously oppressed, he is so vigorous, so much the most dominant figure on the stage. Mr Tree must have felt that any expression of race feeling would have been in bad taste in a theatre whose mission is not to preach but to express to the fullest the personality of Mr Tree. No doubt he feels that Shakespeare in that particular has gone too far, so that Mr Tree makes as little as possible of, say, the speech about the ring that Leah gave him when he was a bachelor. We had come expecting to be moved by the uttering of those words. But we were not, we hardly noticed them: we were so anxiously wondering what Mr Tree would do next. And it came. Mr Tree poured something white on his head, he rent his garments, solicitously and slowly, so that we should not miss the significance of the action, he muttered incomprehensible sounds, no doubt part of a Hebrew imprecation, and thus cleverly obscured the partisan pathos of Shakespeare's words. It was all exceedingly instructive; and it was much better than Shakespeare because Shakespeare could not have given us all those details of a life with which he was unacquainted.

But what a bad play it was.... A great many of us had not the patience to sit out the last two scenes. They came as an anticlimax to the trial, since, at the end, after Mr Tree had said all the words in his part, his magnetic figure remained, for several long minutes, posturing, fainting, gasping, terrible. What was to come? What could come? There would be no more Mr Tree, and the other actors were all carefully and artistically subordinated to his figure.

Miss Dorothy Minto was adorable as Nerissa – but she was not in the picture at all. She looked as if she had dropped into it out of one of Mr Rackham's drawings for *Peter Pan*. And the rest of the tableaux were – so very fittingly – like those which we receive in the supplements to our Christmas Numbers. Miss Alexandra Carlisle seemed to have been created by Mr — R.A. for his success of the summer at Burlington House: the handsome Bassanio seemed to have stepped from the same canvas. Antonio was severe, dignified and restrained. So that, except, for Miss Minto and one or two embarrassing instants when Mr Calthrop in his recital of the Jew's agonies was actually parodying Mr Tree himself and one felt almost nervous, there was nothing that was not exactly as it should be. It was all just Mr Tree, making wonderful gestures, uttering weird cries and guttural ejaculations before an ordinary commercial picture.

Mr Tree has in fact only the one leaf of laurel to add to his crown. Let him cease handicapping himself with Shakespeare as a companion. He does not need it any longer. In earlier days, no doubt, it was prudent thus to allure an audience by appealing to the idea that in witnessing his spectacles and transformation scenes they were improving themselves. But, that is all over. Last Saturday hardly a 'quotation' came across the footlights. It was all Mr Tree, Venetian colouring, gondolas and Ghetto scenes. Let Mr Tree carry his cynical triumph just one step further. Let him give us, say *Romeo and Juliet*, by Mr Tree in a series of tableaux, arranged in a new order, after designs by Mr Frank Dicksee, without words but with four and a half hours of Mr Tree's attitudes in the foreground. Then indeed the triumph would be complete. Mr Tree would have improved Shakespeare out of existence and we should have revealed to us what really we go out for to see.

Saturday Review, 105 (11 April 1908), 461–2.

Essays from *The English Review*

The Unemployed

It is singular that in England, where any feelings of definite rank are at their least distinctive, the barriers between class and class are at the apex of rigidity. Yet they are – these barriers – singularly unsuspected. Who would suspect that a plasterer of a house in building would not eat in the same room with a bricklayer? And yet – to make the limitations most visible – who would not sympathize with a man of gentle birth whose sister insisted on marrying a railway porter? And these barriers are the causes of strange ignorances between class and class. What, for instance, do we know of the life of the poor man? He has never been voiced: he is, in the nature of the case, inarticulate. We enter his house seldom or never; if he rises in the world he forgets very soon. He may remember the material objects of his former life: he forgets how the world looked; he forgets his early views, his early knowledge.

Yet at certain times the poor man is omnipresent. He invades us, he fills us with fears, with misgivings, and he makes our hearts bleed. It is, for instance, impossible for a humane man to think of Sunderland, where firm after firm of shipbuilders has failed and shut down his work; where there is a whole town on the verge of starvation – it is impossible for a man with any heart at all to think of Sunderland without at least looking at the hedgerows with misgivings. In his garden the autumn blackbirds may be calling; the tall clumps of dahlias stand motionless and polychromatic, awaiting the first touch of frost. But his eyes will wander to the hedgerows when he thinks of the stricken town. For, if God sends a store of berries for the birds, so the saying is, the winter will be a hard one. And if this winter is a hard one – then God help the stricken towns.

And the poor are breaking in on us everywhere. They break in on us as we drive through the streets. We see them in their knots, in their bands, at street corners; the parks are full of them, the public squares. We drive past these broken knots with a touch of fear. If the winter is very hard – they may crowd together. They may sack West London. We are the men whose hearts bleed for them – but how, if passing through the streets they catch us afoot, shall we be able to escape from them? In the last unemployed riots our mothers were driving to the city. They met the unemployed; it was with great difficulty that they escaped with their lives.

They penetrate to our ears poignantly in the sounds of music. We are walking down deserted streets of a Sunday in church time and suddenly in the quiet we hear the high clear notes of a tin-whistle, bird-like, swift. A very burly navvy, white-whiskered, pink-cheeked, is walking down the middle of the road. We hear him play the 'Shaking of the Sheets', 'My Lady Greensleeves' and an eighteenth-century country dance whose name we have forgotten. He is an out-of-work from Buckingham. We sit in our restaurant, the windows open, and suddenly there rises up, in excellent voices, with perfect precision, the madrigal called the 'Pie and the Apple'; it is succeeded by 'The Five Bells of Osney', in canon. Out-of-works from Manchester are walking down the middle of the street. They are the unemployed: tramps do not sing madrigals or play those ancient tunes with such 'technique'.

With pity, with fear, or with music – in a hundred ways – the poor man is breaking in on us. Perhaps it is not worse than it used to be. We remember that as small children the most familiar song we knew was one that used to be sung by bands of dirtily clad men in the frosty days:

We've got no work to do-oo-oo,
We've got no work to do-oo-oo,
We're all froze out poor lab'rin' men
And we've got no work to do.

We were so familiar with this song we used to sing it to our toys.

But of knowledge of the lives and aspirations of the poor man how little we have. We are barred off from him by the invisible barriers: we have no records of his views in literature. It is astonishing how little literature has to show of the life of the poor. Of late years we can call to mind only the two Bettesworth books which, excellent in their way, treat the poor man objectively. Mr W.H. Davies, one of whose impressions of poverty we print in the present number, has written his autobiography. But this is the autobiography of the tramp, not of a man who makes his living by working with his hands. Otherwise, although we can lay no claim to omniscience, it may be considered a fairly safe step to say that of the thousands of books that pour upon us day by day and year by year, the percentage which gives us any insight into the inner workings of the poor man's mind is either infinitesimal or non-existent.

A serious attempt has now been made to fill in this lacuna, and since the principal aim of *The English Review* is by means of the literature which it prints and the literature to which it calls attention to ascertain where we stand and to aid in the comprehension of one kind of mind by another, we feel no hesitation in seriously commending this work to our readers. It is called *A Poor Man's House*, and is written by Mr Stephen Reynolds.[1]

1 *A Poor Man's House.* By Stephen Reynolds. (London: John Lane.)

Mr Reynolds, we understand, was in his earlier days a science student of some distinction, but circumstances forced him to abandon a career which, if any career could do it, ought to train the young men in the habit of mind to *constater* – to register, that is – not to theorize along Utopian lines. Owing apparently to some freak of his character, or to some social malaise, Mr Reynolds seems to have abandoned suddenly his contacts with what he calls contemptuously 'the cultured classes', and to have taken up his quarters in the cottage of a Devonshire fisherman. Here it seems that he has definitely supported himself for several years by acting as mate to the fisherman in question, and by rowing summer visitors for hire. Such a career, if it do not argue a disposition more romantic than that of any other boy who runs away to sea, should at least suffice to prove that Mr Reynolds' nature is no ordinary one.

His attitude, since he writes for that very cultured world he so much despises, is one of unreasonable and jaunty aggression. He flings, as it were, his cap into his reader's face at the very outset; being a scientist he utters his theory with a dogmatism that is a little distressing to ears used to a finer note, but his attitude is no doubt due to youth – though we are uncertain as to the author's age; his dogmatism is due to his scientific training, to his consciousness that he knows his subject.

He knows his subject:

> For his first marriage and towards setting up house Tony succeeded in saving twenty shillings. [Tony is the fisherman whose assistant Mr Reynolds became.]
>
> He gave it to his mother in gold to keep safely for him, and the day before the wedding he asked for it. 'Yu knows we an't got no bloody sovereigns,' said his father. It had all been spent in food and clothes for the younger children. So Tony went to sea that night and earned five shillings. A shilling of that too he gave to his mother; then started off on foot for the village where his girl was living and awaiting him. She had a little saved up: he knew that, though he feared it might have gone like his. They were married, however; they fed, rejoiced, and joked; and 'for to du the thing proper like', they hired a trap to drive them home. With what money was left they embarked on married life, and their children made no unreasonable delay about coming. 'Aye!' says Tony, 'I'd du the same again – though 'twas hard times often.'
>
> Before I left Seacombe I asked a fisherman's wife, who was expecting her sixth or seventh child, whether she had enough money in hand to go through with it all; for I knew that her husband was unlikely to earn anything just then. 'I have,' she said, 'an' p'raps I an't. It all depends. If everything goes all right, I've got enough to last out, but if I be so ill as I was wi' the last one, what us lost, then I an't. Howsbeever I don't want nort now. Us'll see how it turns out.' She

> went on setting her house in order, preparing baby-linen and making ready to 'go up over', with perfect courage and tranquillity. When one thinks of the average educated woman's fear of childbed, although she can have doctors, nurses, anaesthetics and every other alleviation, the contrast is very great, more especially as the fisherman's wife had good reason to anticipate much pain and danger, in addition to the possibility of her money giving out.
>
> Those are not extraordinary instances, chosen to show how courageous people can be sometimes; on the contrary, they are quite ordinary illustrations of a general attitude among the poor towards life. To express it in terms of a theory which in one form or another is accepted by nearly all thinkers – the poor have not only the *Will to Live*, they have the *Courage to Live*.

This passage gives a sufficient taste, both of Mr Reynolds's singular powers of observation and of his philosophic methods. His deductions we could have spared, but inasmuch as it was probably what Mr Reynolds would call his *Will to make Deductions* which buoyed him up to make his very admirable observations, to refuse to tolerate the one for the sake of the other would be an act of perversity. Mr Reynolds writes of the poor man with a comprehension that is all the more valuable because it is inspired with a great tenderness.

English Review, 1 (December 1908), 161–4.

George Saintsbury, *A History of English Prosody*

Let us – to get the statement out of the way – begin by saying that Professor Saintsbury cannot write. He cannot write so as to make himself reasonably intelligible, and this is a nuisance. For, greedy to read him, we are compelled to cast back in sentence after sentence simply to discover what he means. Thus of Drayton he says: 'In some moods I am a very little prouder of being an Englishman than I should have been if the *Polyolbion* did not exist.' Would it not have been easier to write – and how much easier to read – 'The *Polyolbion* adds little to my pride of race'?

But that is very little to the point. Professor Saintsbury is giving us a work perhaps the most valuable, certainly the most salutary, that could have been written at this period of English literature. For there was never a day when the technical side of the Art of Letters was more neglected or so jeered at. With his voice reaching so many hearers, the author of

English Prosody attempts to redress this balance. It is safe to say that the history of literature is a series of chronicles recording how great literature has risen out of technical controversies. The Elizabethans were great writers because of the technical controversies that preceded them and their works; the Cockney school of poets were great poets because of the classical traditions of the eighteenth century. The literature of today is a poor thing, because we have no trained writers who, bursting the bonds of the conventions which have trained them, have achieved an ease of phrase, a mastery of form.

Any philosophic student of the history of music will tell you that the study of counterpoint exists, not to teach counterpoint, but first to eliminate those whose sacred fire will not carry them through a period of arduous labours. Secondly, it teaches the composer how to break its own laws. The English composer of today is trained, if perfunctorily; so, too, the English artist. Even the English dramatist understands that he must learn something of stage-craft. It is only the writer who considers that all that goes to the making of a book are the pen in his hand and the vine-leaves in his hair. Professor Saintsbury is providing us with a treatise on the harmony and counterpoint of English verse.

The English language is the perfect vehicle of poets; as a medium for prose it is too vague and too rich. The ideal paragraph in French prose is a framed set of facts which move us on account of the precision of the language. The best paragraph of English prose is a rhythm of words of poetic association. Hence it arises that the most exquisite statements of fact in the English language are to be found in blank-verse speeches.

It is only with Professor Saintsbury's treatment of Elizabethan blank verse that – deferring an extended review until the issue of the third volume – we concern ourselves with for the present. English lyric verse differs from most sentimental verse – differs, that is to say, to put the distinction at its broadest, from the verse of the troubadours – mainly in that it is written for non-formal and irregular musical airs. English blank verse, on the other hand, differs radically from all other verse.

We read lately in the columns of a usually esteemed contemporary, and from the pen of a writer much looked up to, the statement that 'A speech of Shakespeare's blank verse consists of a bundle of unrhymed decasyllabic lines.' This seems almost incredible. It would be utterly incredible were we not aware that it is the prevailing impression of the practising literary world today. Yet we have professors of literature and blessed words like 'phonetic syzygy', or 'vowel colouring', and 'stopped lines'.

We wish that every Englishman would read the portions of Professor Saintsbury's book in which he deals with blank verse. There are, of course, other books, but we know of none which so hammers home the argument. For blank verse is not a bundle of lines: it is a collection of statements, whether of fact or of mood; it is expressed in rhythmic language, divisible into beats of ten or of some multiple of ten syllables. The point is that it is the statement not the line that is the unit. You could not speak of '*a* blank verse'.

We do not think that Professor Saintsbury anywhere states this theory with so much precision. In fact, as a good student of prosody rather than of poetry, he a little omits to consider that it is the sense as much as the breath that unites a 'period.' Says he, speaking of the *Two Gentlemen of Verona*: '[Fourteeners and stanzas] are nothing like so frequent as in the *Errors* and in *Love's Labour's Lost*. The blank verse itself, too, is even less run on than in either of the others – stop or no stop at the end of the line, each is formed with a single respiration.' And we take it from this that Professor Saintsbury's unit of blank verse is a respiration of whatever length.

We may, indeed, be in disagreement with our author as to small points. Of Marlowe he says: 'Yet he was not yet entirely free of the single-moulded line even here' – when he is commenting on

> He of you all that most desires my blood,
> And will be called the murderer of a king,
> Take it...

Here, indeed, if we look solely to the prosody, there is a suspicion of stoppedness. Yet as soon as we read it in conjunction with the sense of the passage we see that the 'He of you all' of the first passage is held by the mind, which awaits the completion of the statement – is held as if by a sort of capillary attraction, so that the whole passage is a single unit.

But though Professor Saintsbury ignores a little this factor in the knitting together of blank verse, we have little quarrel with him. It is, of course, his duty to overstate his case. And the wise poet will study the *History of English Prosody*. For the wise poet – like another wise man – will 'keep all his limbs very supple'. The most skilful artist in verse of the nineteenth century, Christina Rossetti, was very largely a product of metrical exercises. She was in the habit, that is to say, of writing daily a number of verses to *bouts-rimés*.[1] And to this without much doubt, she owed both her unrivalled metrical skill and her singularly large and apt vocabulary. This, indeed, is the merest common sense. For the constant practice of verse drills both the eye and the ear, and the constant swimming in the depths of metre will produce in a poet capabilities for rhythmical cadences. It will, indeed, produce such a yearning for intricate and musical forms that when the Idea comes to him – when, in fact, the Muse is paying her visit – he will satisfy them and himself.

English Review, 1 (January 1909), 374–6.

1 [A sequence of rhyme-words given to a poet to turn into a poem.]

The Work of W.H. Hudson

That saint was one of the best beloved who was called 'of the birds'. That author is one of the best beloved we have, whom we picture – don't we see him? – walking, silent, in a tranquil garden, towards evening, peering up at the families of swifts – 'never more than eight' – that career with shrill and ecstatic shrieks around the tower of the church he served, or walking, a book in his clasped hands behind his back, with softened footfalls to watch the thrushes on the lawn, running with their suddenly arrested dashes, beside the sundial that marked hours so serene. We may say that all humanity loves a lover of birds. St Francis preached to them; Gilbert White moved amongst them with softened footfalls and tranquil attention. And perhaps the image that most appeals to us of an omnipotent and a tender Creator is that of Him Who feeds the young ravens in their nests and has attention for the fall of a sparrow.

No doubt we love the lovers of birds not so much because we ourselves love the little people of heaven and earth as because for the successful watching by hedgerows certain lovable qualities are necessary – certain qualities of self-effacement, of patience, of tranquil observation, and of quiet movement. If, in fact, we do not desire, in the woods or the open, to startle little and easily frightened beings, we *must* possess those actual qualities. There must be nothing staccato in our motions; there must be nothing fugitive in our visits.

If we walk along a wood-path all the busy life around us will continue unconcerned and at no great distance – for just so long as we continue moving. But the moment that we come to a sudden halt we shall hear the rustle of fugitive wings, the sibilant and special alarm-cry of the robin will replace the conversational chatter of many small birds. Similarly, upon the ploughed downs, so long as we continue to walk upon our business the plover near at hand will run upon its own affairs or sit still in the furrows. But if we come to a sudden halt the plovers will flap all across the skies, the rooks fly away down the hill, and the partridges, with their startled skimming, brush over the nearest ridge. We shall have disturbed the rhythm of life.

To avoid causing this disturbance a man must be either a person who comes to a halt very gradually or one who comes so often that he will be accepted and be granted, as it were, the freedom of coppice or of furrow. The birds must, in fact, get used to seeing him about until they come to regard him, not as a marauder or a spy, but as one whose business it is to be abroad, motionless and silent in the solitudes. For this there are necessary a patience and a pensiveness that, in a restless age, we find attractive, and this, perhaps, is why we love bird-watchers, whether or no we love birds or have the faculties ourselves to watch successfully.

We may regard *Green Mansions* as revealing the secret of Mr Hudson's personality. It is the story of a man who goes into a forest, in beneath the huge boughs that are the mansions for so many beings. And here, in the green twilight, going often and steadfastly, he is aware of a voice, a bird-voice, that, invisible in its origin, dogs his footsteps, in the secret places of Ecuador, as here at home in a coppice the robin will accompany us, flitting from bush to bush, invisible and uttering its sweet cry, half of warning, half of companionship. The man goes often and often into the forest, and at last, shyly and capriciously, the being of the bird-voice reveals herself to him. She is a woman with the spirit of a bird, with the elusive charm, with the tender and fluttering mind, with the coloured and tenuous form, with the fluting and thrilling voice. In the soul of the man there arises an immense, an overpowering passion for this bird-creature, for this protectress of all living things of the forest, for this spirit-woman who is at one with all perching, fluttering, and creeping things. And when – since union between man and spirit is in the nature of things impossible – the man loses the wood-being he is filled for ever with a pervading, an endless regret.

That is Mr Hudson. He reveals himself: he shows us in the book the nature of the dream that he has dreamed. He is – in his being as an author – a man silent, hungry-eyed, filled with a regret and with an ideal. The ideal is to find a Being with whom he may be at one, a Being who, in return, will be at one with all the creatures of all the Green Mansions of the world. The regret is that he is born a man, since to man this union cannot ever be granted.

So we may picture him, silent, devoured by a passion, standing by a hedgerow, gazing in between the leaves, into the deep and glamorous interior, watching hungrily the little creatures who flutter about the hem of invisible garments.

This, of course, is a picture of the being who seems to look out at us from the pages of the books, not of the Mr Hudson who walks the streets of London Town, or sits watching the gulls from a rock on the Lizard. A writer reveals himself in his books as distinct from the writer in his person, the Rousseau who is shadowed in the *Nouvelle Héloïse* being different enough from the unpleasing person who abandoned his children on the doorsteps of orphanages. Nor yet is this picture of a hungry and silent man by a hedgerow any more than a partial portrait of a phase. There is the gallant and amorous horseman of the *Purple Land*, with many loves and jingling spurs, up to the eyes in South American revolutions, outwitting the bulls of the pampas, bronzed in the tropical sunlight. There is the genial and sardonic traveller who troubles with his appearance the uneasy minds of tramps on the South Downs. There is the indignant Mr Hudson of *Birds in London*, fulminating against the park vandals who condemned the tall elms in Kensington Gardens; there is the Mr Hudson who, uneasily, if gallantly, tries to make a good case for the inhabitants of Cornwall, writing, as it were, amiable compliments to the Celts with his right hand, whilst with his left he sets down instances of their cruelty, so convincingly rendered that they remain like shuddering patches in our memories.[1]

And, after all, it is the power to render convincingly circumstances observed with zest that most surely makes us know a writer and, if he be lovable, makes us love him. The admirers of Mr Hudson are, relatively speaking, a small band, but we fancy that they are a band inspired with more gratitude for pleasures received and with more affection than fall to the common lot of writers. It is very likely that the majority of Mr Hudson's champions have been roused to affection for him by this first passage from *Nature in Downland*, the introduction to the book, the passage that gives the tone, that sets the pace, that affords a taste of the personality:

> Here (where Kingston Down slopes away towards the valley of the Ouse), sitting on the dry grass with my face to the wind, I spent two or three hours in gazing at the thistledown. It is a rare thing to see as I saw it that day: the sight of it was a surprise, and I gave myself up to the pleasure of it, wishing for no better thing. It was not only that the sight was beautiful, but the scene was vividly reminiscent of long-gone summer days associated in the memory with the silvery thistledown. The wide extent of unenclosed and untilled earth, its sunburnt colour and its solitariness, where no person was in sight, the burning sun and wind, and the sight of thousands upon thousands of balls or stars of down, reminded me of old days on horseback on the open pampa – an illimitable waste of rust-red thistles, and the sky above covered with its million floating flecks of white.
>
> But the South American thistledown, both of the giant thistle and the cardoon, with its longer flower-heads, was much longer and whiter and infinitely more abundant. By day the air was full of it, and I remember that when out with my brother we often enjoyed seeing it at night. After a day or days of wind it would be found in immense masses in the sheltered hollows or among the tall-standing stalks of the dogplants. These masses gleamed with a strange whitening in the dark, and it used to please us to gallop our horses through them. Horses are nervous, unintelligent creatures, liable to take fright at the most familiar objects, and our animals would sometimes be in terror at finding themselves plunged breast-deep into this insubstantial whiteness, that moved with them and covered them as with a cloud.
>
> The smaller, more fragile English thistledown, in so few places abundant enough to appear an element in the scene is beautiful too,

1 *The Land's End.*

> and its beauty is, I am inclined to think, all the greater because of its colour.... It was as if these slight, silvery objects were springing spontaneously into existence, as the heat opened and the wind lifted and bore them away. All round me, and as far off as such slight, gauzy objects could be seen, they were springing up from the grass in this way in hundreds and thousands. Looking long and steadily at them – their birth and their flight – one could fancy that they were living things of delicate aerial form that had existed for a period hidden and unsuspected in the turf, until their time had come to rise like winged ants from the soil and float in the air.

We have transcribed perhaps a little more from this book than is exactly in proportion; but, in the first place, this is the first passage of Mr Hudson's work that we ever read, and, in the second, it is a pleasure to see flowing from the pen words written so sweetly and so well – and, indeed, we wish we had the time to transcribe, for the sheer delight of it, the whole of this book. And we think that we have not done wrong, for in this passage there is shadowed the whole of the writer – of the writer who, having galloped with young gallantry through the thistledown of early life on the pampas, comes with the fresh eyes of a stranger and the keen love of an exile into green and ancient lands, there to spend long hours in the delight of lying still, of gazing at common things, of giving himself up utterly to the spirit of the place. These are, as it were, the biographical details – and there are biographical details enough cropping up, as reminiscences, as comparisons, or as time framework of romances, throughout Mr Hudson's long tale of works.

Roughly speaking, we may guess from these that Mr Hudson was born and passed his youth and his early maturity in one or other of the South American republics. He was familiar with the Argentines, with La Plata (*A Naturalist in La Plata*), with Patagonia (*Idle Days in Patagonia*), to come, the first of his family for several generations, to settle again in England. And in England, as it were, he has sat about for years – for, say, a quarter of a century, since the earliest of his English reminiscences that we have appear to date (*Birds in London*) from, the first years of the eighties. Throughout this last quarter of a century he has seemed to saunter from one green contemplation to another, from Sussex through Hampshire[2] to Cornwall – with long and leisurely strides, keeping time, as it were, with the rhythm of his thoughts and glancing keenly from side to side at the little and real things of life, halting at a hedgerow to peer in, coming again and again to bracken patches in the bare places of which, sinuous, tawny, their backs marked as with a chain of black arrowheads, the adders sunned themselves. It is that note of sauntering and of returning again and again

2 *Hampshire Days* (1903).

that seems to distinguish all his books. And then he has his matchless style.

There is about his writing something formal and austere, something almost Spanish in its gravity, something almost naïve and childish – with the clearness of fresh phrases that a child has – in the simplicity of his verbiage. And there is nothing whatever that is literary about it: a delightful man speaks without self-consciousness, an effortless poet soliloquizes in converational tones as if he were talking to himself. He is utterly unspoiled by any literary traditions, literary provincialisms, or the literary hunger for the picturesque, for the derivative-word with associations. He has escaped alike the fatal Wardour Street influences of Pre-Raffaelism and the semi-biblical over-emphasis of Stevensonian word-jugglery. Having a clear and precise mind, he has expressed himself with clearness and precision, using simple words that are sometimes quaint, but never affected. It is for this reason that we are permitted to consider him the most valuable figure that we have in the world of writers of today – the most valuable in that we can learn of him that lesson that most of all we need – the lesson that 'style' is a matter of research, not for the striking, the telling, or the obsolescent word, but for the word most fitted to express ourselves to ourselves. No one can learn any tricks from his writing: he has none; no one can increase his vocabulary from a study of Mr Hudson, for Mr Hudson's vocabulary is quite limited. But with his limited vocabulary and his absence of tricks he has arrived at a vehicle of expression for his thought as simple as that of Christina Rossetti, as limpid as that of M. Anatole France.

With the actual value of his thoughts we are not so much concerned. He is a scientist in his rendering of facts; he is a poet when it comes to his interpretation of their spiritual aspects. We have a very intimate and somewhat cultured friend who uttered words very much as follows:

'What's the secret of this man's fascination?' – our friend was speaking, not of the man, but of the writer. 'He's the most wrong-headed fellow it's possible to imagine. He runs up against me at every turn. I detest nature books, these products of a Cockney age. He writes them. He is forever sneering at towns: I never set my foot outside London if I can help it. He has all the fads, of simple life, of anti-sporting humanitarianism. He jeers at the affecting epitaph of an ancient huntsman, one of the best and most loyal that ever crossed a saddle. He's of Colonial origin, and all Colonials are detestable. He upholds every blessed thing that's most puling in a puling and mawkish century. He gets fits of nerves because he sees an owl in a cage, and that causes him to curse a venerable and splendid city. He believes in exploded theories of race; he upholds the tomfool idea that the Celtic influence is worth a twopenny-piece. And yet I subscribe to several faddy periodicals that I detest for the mere off-chance of finding in them an article – say about *seagulls*!' – and there was an ocean of disgust in his enunciation of the word *seagulls* – 'by this addle-headed poet. It's as if I rubbed shoulders with temperance orators and Nonconformists in order to get hold of an apostle of garden cities. And why the devil do I do it?' Mr —, as will be gathered, is an obstinate Tory; but we are glad to be able, in this attempt at what may be called an apotheosis, to quote such an *advocatus diaboli*.

The fact is that he searches in these to him squalid byways because he gets so much pleasure out of Mr Hudson's manner that he forgets his matter until after the book is done. The saying Φεϊδίας ε'ἱρηνᾳ ... has a double sense, for if Phidias belongs to Peace it is part of the atmosphere of the artist who works in clear and tranquil materials, whether of marble or words, that he confers an atmosphere of restfulness upon his votaries. We are not saying that Mr Hudson's matter does not matter; but, for the great bulk of his readers, it is all one what he writes about. Who cares for all these things together: La Plata? Hampshire? a Utopia of the Crystal Age? Sussex? Patagonia? cuckoos? barrows? grasshoppers? or the sobriety of Cornish Methodists? We may care, individually, about one or other, or five or six of these matters. Some of us hate downs, a great many people hate the inhabitants of the West Country. To us the thought of South America is as a continent of boredom. Yet we read with quiet avidity *Idle Days in Patagonia*, and, concerned as we are with avalanches of new books, dreading new books, we rush helter-skelter to buy the very brand-newest of Mr Hudson, and read with engrossed insatiety *The Land's End*. Well! peace belongs to Phidias.

That, we may take it, is the secret of the matter. It is at once the secret of our enthusiasm, as of our fewness. We do not know that we regard it as a blot on the nation that Mr Hudson's name is not on all the hoardings. How could it be? With small words this poet gives us peace. You have to blare on some sort of brazen sackbut or psaltery to attract a crowd on fair-day. You will not do it by retiring into the close and meditating on the little lichens of the tombs, by explaining how they dry up and revivify, dry up and show again, minute, speckled, green and orange, as dry season succeeds to rainy and rainy to dry. We know very well that if we ask the next ten men we meet we may find that not one has heard of Mr Hudson; but we are very certain that if we put one of Mr Hudson's books into the hands of any one of the ten he will conceive a great affection for this writer. It is customary to speak of Mr Hudson as 'Mr W.H. Hudson, the naturalist'. We should prefer to speak of him as the natural writer. For he is very much more than a naturalist. It is not merely that his range of subject is very wide; that he has written pure romance, pure romantic sociology, or pure poetic imagery, as in the *Little Boy Lost*; nor is it merely that he possesses the power to observe, the patience to collect, or the delicate phraseology with which to record minute, delicate, or pretty happenings in the green chambers of this earth of many mansions. It is that he has the power – the gift – to draw comparisons; to perceive analogies; to build similes; to let his thoughts wander along delicate and touching lines. It is, in short, because he is a poet. For it is from the power to compare, to perceive the relationships of things, and to let his thoughts wander that the poet derives his attractions. To be able to perceive a relationship to the Kingdom of Heaven in the tesselated pebbles of a brook; to be able to convey how the rustle of wind in the dry, false dodder-grass of a down is at one with the thoughts that pass through the mind of a man – this is the inestimable gift, the inestimable gift of perceiving the greater truths that lurk hidden behind all the pleasant little grasses of the downs and the dry thistle-stalks of the pampas. For the poet by rendering the visible as nearly as may be to perfection, sets stirring in the dulled perceptions of humanity the minute ties that bind us always to the unseen universe. That is why we love Mr Hudson, who perceives all Heaven in the voices of the birds.

English Review, 2 (April 1909), 157–64.

Algernon Charles Swinburne

Born April 5, 1837: Died April 10, 1909

The truer poetry of the great tradition always suggests a flame: a flame of the Muse: a flame of gallant speeches, of splendid endeavour. Of the Victorian poets his was the most epic figure, the most generous, the most traditional. Of him alone it would not seem mockery to say that he smote a lyre. Of the two forms of art – that which seeks to be generous, all-inclusive, and that which is advised and selective – he chose the former, for he was daemonic. Nowadays we have swung somewhat into other courses. Swinburne represented an age of faith: and so variously and very splendidly he sang his faith, which was none the less a faith in that it came in the guise of a negation. Yet even the verse containing the line 'That no life lives for ever' must wind up with the assertion 'That even the weariest river / Winds somewhere safe to sea' so that if he did not believe in ultimate immortality he believed in an ultimate rest.

He came of an older time, of a very fine spirit; and to hear him speak was to be in touch with an old and assuredly a very fine tradition. Today we speak with the lips: if we cannot hope to achieve the broadnesses of Romance, we do at least attempt delicacies and subtleties. For these this great man – this great Figure – cared very little. He grafted on to epic volume a Berserker rage: he was a man of fine frenzies: he spoke not from the lips, but – 'with hollow mouth' – he poured out his heart. It is perhaps in the nature of the time that modern verse must be analytical. There are today so many things to see, so many to 'take stock of', that we none of us dare to generalize. We realize very fully that if today we generalize in one direction, tomorrow fresh facts will come to upset our theories. In consequence we are thrown back on ourselves: we have grown personal, intimate, subjective. Mr Swinburne was none of these. He had convictions, and the courage to utter them. Whether he were right we will not say: possibly he was wrong: at any rate he was temerarious. But what a fine temerity!

It is possible that his fame has in England suffered a little eclipse in these latter days, but he remains for the world that surrounds these islands the best-known Englishman, and the Continent, which has not forgotten Byron, will still less forget the name of Swinburne. To the Germans his splendid rhetoric appeals; he learned his art of the French Romantics; the early days of Italy and Greece inspired him. From England he took only the magic of Elizabethan verbiage: thus, if in England his work had a derivative aim, to Europe which ignores our verbal subtleties it was and remains new and very modern. And no doubt even in England a day will come when – the fashions of today being forgotten – the once splendid name of Swinburne will once again be splendid among the names of the greater poets. For of the Victorian poets he was the most generous in the outpourings of his heart, the most nobly unthinking, the bravest, the most flamelike.

English Review, 2 (May 1909), 193–4.

George Meredith, OM

Born February 12, 1828: Died May 18, 1909

Mr Meredith follows Mr Swinburne into the shadows; and now, indeed, the whole Round Table is dissolved. And this phrase seems singularly appropriate for the passing of the last great figure of the Victorian group – the Victorian group that in its literature and culture was so dominated by the Arthurian cycle. Mr Meredith, the great poet, was, perhaps, less under the influence of his age than were any other of his louder-voiced contemporaries. His was a half-comic, a half-ironic spirit. The earnestness which he certainly felt he less persistently pushed into the foreground. The child, as it were, of Dickens – and we have only to look at the pages of *All the Year Round*, where *Evan Harrington* appeared as a serial, to see how very much he was the child of Dickens – Mr Meredith achieved a lightness, a resignation that belonged in no sense to Tennyson, Carlyle, Browning, Ruskin, and all the others.

For this reason we imagine that he will survive them as a living writer, as a man whose books are read and loved. He had more of an eternal principle in his personality, his mind was less exclusively set upon the fashions and the problems of his own time. His peculiar use of words may stand in his way: but this we are inclined to doubt. Such as it is his language will not be more strange to the reader of tomorrow than is actually the language of Shakespeare or of Herrick to us today, and his thought is never obscure. So that all that the reader of tomorrow will have to do to enjoy, say, *One of our Conquerors* will be to learn his vocabulary as we have to learn the vocabulary of Shakespeare. And to read, 'Love in the Valley' he need make no effort at all. This most precious of all the poems the nineteenth century gave us is as clear, as simple, as soothing, as mysteriously moving as is the *Christina of Denmark* by Holbein that the intolerable officialdom of our nation appears to be about to permit us to lose.

And, like Mr Swinburne, Mr Meredith has not been buried in the Abbey. That, perhaps, is as well since, because it honours no great man in these days, Westminster Abbey must become the resting-place of mediocrities, amongst whom Mr Meredith would very uneasily rest, since he suffered fools badly. And Mr Meredith's dust will be at one with the Nature to whom alone he devoted none of his comic touches, in whom alone his ironic spirit discerned a perfect satisfaction.

English Review, 2 (June 1909), 409–10.

C.F.G. Masterman, *The Condition of England*

A treatise upon the condition of any people, tranquil, prosperous, and under no stress, must always be a matter of moods. It would be comparatively easy to have written, say, upon the condition of Ireland during the potato famine, or upon the condition of the Netherlands in the days of Alva. But to write about a people mixed in race, united by no common emotions, upheld by no common faith – this is a task calling for impossible qualities if the writer is at all to dogmatize with justness. These impossible qualities Mr Masterman[1] does not possess: no man could. And so Mr Masterman wavers from despondency to hope, wavers from hope

1 [Charles Masterman, Ford's contemporary and one of his closest friends, was literary editor of the *Daily News* from 1903, an MP 1906–14, and briefly a member of Asquith's Cabinet, 1914–15. He was then put in charge of a secret wartime propaganda department at Wellington House, for which Ford wrote two volumes.]

to caution and ends by saying that he cannot tell where we stand. Mr Masterman is extremely well equipped for his task. He is, we may assume, qualified by his official position to write about the social life of the upper classes: he represents a constituency of the very poor and he has lived amongst them. He has read a great many – perhaps too many – books; he has taken them seriously – perhaps too seriously. We should be the last to quarrel with Mr Masterman for taking imaginative literature seriously and it is, at least, one cheering sign of the time which, intellectually speaking, we regard even more gloomily than does Mr Masterman, that a prominent politician in a 'serious book' should quote with so much deference from so many mere novels. That is at least cheering, but for the rest it is a rather gloomy picture with which Mr Masterman presents us. In one sense Mr Masterman has made an advance on any former writer upon national characteristics that we can remember. Most of these, writing as they do from a sphere of observation purely literary, or literary and of Society, have treated only of quite a limited sphere of human life. But there is abroad – and it is a very good thing – a spirit of exploration; not a very strong spirit but still a certain motive force. We know so little of the lives of the great people: the lives of the great people are so little represented in literature. But of late years we have had the minutely photographic Bettesworth book and its sequel, which give us the chance of really studying the vicissitudes and the psychology of the agricultural labourer. We have had Mr Stephen Reynold's *A Poor Man's House* which, more coloured as it is by the author's personality, is a more vivid study of a class more suspicious, more hardy and more arrogant. We have had Mr Wells' *Kipps*, which illuminated for us the psychology of the shop assistant, and his *Tono-Bungay*, which gave us so really beautiful a rendering of the psychology of the Servants' Hall. And now we have Mr Masterman pointing out to us the fact that the immense majority of the English people are manual workers functioning in conditions sad enough – an immense crowd, unvocal, with lives quite colourless, working in circumstances frequently of extreme squalor, with joys that to us would seem no joys, with hopes that to us would seem mere hopelessness. Mr Masterman has done this very well, but he has done it a little statistically, a little coldly. For ourselves, we wish that, letting go his literary and his social side, he had given us a more emotional, a more keenly analytical picture of the great people. It is when he gives us pictures of the crowd at the Peckham Election that he is at his most valuable. For the psychology of the poor, and more particularly of the London poor, is one of the great mysteries. The feature of the London poor man that most has moved us is his singular, ironic, and fatalistic cheerfulness. It is because he takes so little account of this that Mr Galsworthy, when he has treated of the lives of the extremely poor, has always seemed to us a misleading guide. His poor are perpetually on the whine: they are perpetually folding their hands: they are perpetually giving up the game. But actually – and it is demonstrable – the poor man very wonderfully keeps on going. He has a fine energy in circumstances where none of those better placed in the world could find heart for energy: he has a fine stoicism and with his motto, 'We can't all bloody well have everything', he goes quietly on towards the workhouse or the grave, uttering by the way those Cockney witticisms which are so full of wisdom and which cast such sudden flashes upon life. Some of this psychology Mr Masterman has caught and rendered, and for this his book is the most valuable. The belabouring of Society has been done too often. Society must necessarily be vapid, aimless and of no account since it has no aims and can have no aim save that of getting through the day. Or again, Mr Masterman's analysis of the literary life of the day takes too much account of the literature of the immediate present. A despised person, finding his market almost solely in that same vapid, aimless class, the imaginative writer of today pays little attention either to his art or to the means by which he can stir the deeper emotions. If he attempt either of these last he cannot exist for there will be no market for his work. But having run through nearly all the strata of our social conditions, having uttered threats of revolution and gloomy pictures of the mental sterility of his day, Mr Masterman ends up upon a note of caution and adds a short postcript in which he casts doubt upon all that he has written.

> … The wise man will still go softly all his days; working always for greater economic equality on the one hand, for understanding between estranged peoples on the other; apprehending always how slight an effort of stupidity or violence could strike a death-blow to twentieth-century civilization, and elevate the forces of destruction triumphant over the ruins of a world….
>
> … Optimism and pessimism, in face of any civilization in a changing world, are equally untrue, equally futile. All human societies mingle selfishness and sacrifice, exultation and weariness, laughter and tears. No one age is especially wicked, especially tired, especially noble. All ages are wicked, tired, noble. Progress is always impossible and always proceeding. Preservation is always hazardous and always attained. Every class is unfit to govern; and the government of the world continues. Austerities, simplicities, and a common danger breed virtues and devotions which are the parents of prosperity. Prosperity breeds arrogance, extravagance, and class hatreds. Opulence and pride in their turn breed national disasters. And, these disasters engender the austerities and simplicities which start the cycle again anew…

This is a very proper note for the ending of a book very agreeably and sympathetically written.

English Review, 3 (August 1909), 182–4.

Joseph Conrad

I have been lately taken harshly to task for writing that the Englishman does not much respect Thought or Literature. I have been told that to write that was easy and to prove it impossible. Alas, how easy it is to prove it. Yesterday I was going through Belgium in an express train bound for Calais. In the corridor stood a lamentable little anxious being – an old, yellow, shrivelled Jew draper of Cologne. He was going to London to buy stockings; a sixty-knot gale was blowing and he was terribly afraid of seasickness. He was afraid for his life because he had a weak heart. Now I do not like Jews, I hate all shopkeepers and I particularly dislike the inhabitants of Cologne. But this poor little old man was so miserable that I had to do my best for him – to divert his mind. I talked about stockings and about whether the *Frankfurt Gazette* is a good paper to advertise in if one wants to make a profitable Israelite marriage for one's daughters. And still with his eyes of doom gazing not at my face but into the miserable future:

'*Sie sind auch Kaufmann*? You also are a shopkeeper?' he asked.

I answered with the touch of shamefacedness with which one would answer an English bagman, an English barrister, or an English baker – one of the persons who does real things and makes lots and lots of real money – I answered:

'*Nein, Ich bin Schriftsteller* – a person who produces writing.'

And, oh wonder, he answered – still with the doomed eyes:

'*Schriftsteller – das ist ein edler Beruf*! Writer! That is a noble profession.'

I laughed and said sardonically:

'*Der Herr will etlicher sagen* – The gentleman means a wretched profession – one in which there is no money to be made.' But still with the eyes of doom answered this poor little Jew:

'*Nein – ein edler! Ein edler*! – A noble profession! What does the money matter? If one of my daughters could marry a good poet I would not ask any dowry with him.'

And then I felt ashamed: he was so in earnest and so humble before me. But imagine an English linen-draper going to buy stockings with the fear of death and a weak heart and talking with reverence – snatching a moment from the fear of death to talk with reverence of the profession of letters. For suppose it was hypocrisy, or suppose it was a pious opinion, is not it a fine country the mere hypocrisy or the mere pious opinion of whose small Jew linen-drapers takes the form of such homage to virtue?

For with my inhabitant of Cologne – of peddling Cologne – to back me up I suddenly thought the great things that it is permissible to think about literature, about High Literature – the 'Noble Calling'. And then I began to think about Joseph Conrad, for Literature and Conrad are to me interchangeable terms.

★ ★ ★ ★ ★ ★

I do not know in what English criticism of the official type really consists. I think you write something about the style, by which you mean the vocabulary – the odd words that a writer uses. Then you say something – a great deal about the subject. Then you enlarge upon the philosophy – oh, you write a great deal about the philosophy and you plank, in the vulgar phrase, your bottom dollar on the moral lessons of the book under consideration. You point out how it is calculated to leave the reader a better and a wiser man. When you have written a great many exercises of that sort you are recognized as a Critic; you receive a seat at the board of the British Academy and you have the right to vote the Nobel Prize to anyone you like. I think that is the way it goes but I have no means of really knowing.

Now if I may be allowed to jumble up these headings I will try to do so much for the author of *Heart of Darkness*. I have thought very often that Conrad is an Elizabethan. That is possibly because he is a Pole – and the Poles have the virtues and the powers that served to make nations great in the sixteenth and seventeenth centuries. Roughly speaking, that was when Poland was a great Empire. They were Romantic, they were heroic, they were aristocrats – they were all the impracticable things. You could not expect their greatness to live on into the days of Mr Carnegie or the cotton spindle. It would be like Rupert of the Rhine leading a charge against all of Lord Haldane's Territorials entrenched on Primrose Hill. But, though this could no longer be done, that is not to say that it is so long ago since Poland was the beloved of the world – of all the world that was not engaged in the breaking up of the prey. And if you cannot have a fortune in the two-and-three-quarter per cents it is a very good thing to be beloved for showing a fine spirit. Thus for me Joseph Conrad is the finest of the Elizabethans.

His preoccupations are with death, destiny, an inscrutable and august force, with the cruel sea, the dark forests of strange worlds or the darker forests that are the hearts of our fellow men. It would not in the least surprise you to come upon a dance of madmen in one of his stories as in Webster's *Duchess of Malfi*; it would not in the least surprise you to come on the knocking at the gate of *Macbeth*; upon all the murders of the *Spanish Tragedy*; upon the sobbing misery of Celestina; upon the ragged knavery of Lazarillo de Tormes: why, he might have written 'The branch is cut that might have grown full straight and the laurel bough is burned that flourished once in this learned man', or he might have written 'To die is no more than a lasting sleep, a quiet resting from all jealousy, a thing we all pursue', and above all, 'It is but giving over of a game that must be lost'. And can you not imagine one of his Arab sheiks, or Marlow, that tremendous old man of the sea, or even the teacher-narrator of *Under Western Eyes*, gazing upon the face of some woman who had caused a great deal of trouble in some obscure quarter of the world and saying reflectively: 'Was that the face that launched a thousand ships and burned the palm leaf towns of Parabang?' For really there is hardly anything that was written by Marlowe or Massinger or Webster or Kyd or Heywood that would not fit into this author's works.

Of course I mean this in the sense of feeling – of what I should like to express by the word colour. For when we think of the works of the Elizabethans other than Shakespeare, we seem to see a darkness – a darkness of forests illuminated by torches, and when I think of the work of this author I always have the same image. And darkness has very curiously gone out of modern life and literature. We never see it – not the real thick blackness that seems to invade the lungs, the heart, and the very circulation of the blood. Similarly, we never think of death, of ruin, of dishonour, of chivalry, of a careless pursuing of an ideal with nothing but a thin plank between us and the fathomless sea. We never think of them – or if we do it is only for a very short moment. We switch on the electric light and turn our attentions to the evening papers.

But these things – darkness, death, honour, and a careless chivalry are the constant preoccupations of Conrad. In the one particular of honour he differs from the Elizabethans, but they were preoccupied with all the other primitive things that we have forgotten, whilst we have grown kinder. Indeed it is very curious how little space kindness occupies in the work either of Conrad or of the Elizabethans. There is of course the *Woman Killed with Kindness* – but it is a brutal sort of kindness that refrains from taking a sword to a guilty wife, and leaves her to die of despair and a decline. And of course there is kindness rendered in *Lord Jim* – that book of all others that has a vivid moral for English readers. But even here it is the kindness of old wise and sad men like Marlow or like Stein for a boy who has failed upon the point of honour. That is what they can understand, for that they can feel. In all the rest there is a desperate sort of remorselessness.

If you consider the case of the sham escape of Razumov from the police you will see very plainly what I mean. Razumov is in league with – or let us say he is under the obsession of – the Russian secret police. He has to gain the confidence of the revolutionaries, so, to add a touch of verisimilitude, as it were, to advertise his escape, he goes to a madcap boy and announces his desire to borrow money in order to pay the expenses of his escape. The boy has no money; he must rob his father in order to find it. This he does. He comes to Razumov with the money:

> Razumov nodded from the couch, and contemplated the hare-brained fellow's gravity with a feeling of malicious pleasure.

> 'I've made my little sacrifice,' sighed mad Kostia, 'and I've to thank you, Kyrilo Sidorovitch for the opportunity.'
>
> 'It has cost you something?'
>
> 'Yes, it has. You see the dear old duffer really loves me. He'll be hurt.'
>
> 'And you believe all they tell you of the new future, and the sacred will of the people?'
>
> 'Implicitly! I would give my life.... Only you see, I am like a pig at a trough. I am no good. It's my nature.'
>
> Razumov, lost in thought, had forgotten his existence till the youth's voice, entreating him to fly without loss of time, roused him unpleasantly.
>
> 'All right. Well – good-bye.'

That is just all that Razumov had to say. He had forgotten the youth's existence, though he had made the boy rob his father in order to advertise his escape to the revolutionaries....

> When dawn broke, Razumov, very still in a hot, stuffy railway car... rose quietly, lowered the glass a few inches, and flung out on the great plain of snow a small brown paper parcel.

It was the stolen money. He was too disdainfully honourable a man to use stolen money. He could not have done it.

And this same unimaginative cruelty of a man blindly pursuing his lost honour dignifies Razumov to the end. It pursues him into the room and into the presence of the sister of the man he betrayed to death – the woman with the trusting eyes who loves him, and whom he loves. He just tells her with the fewest possible words.

> 'It ends here – on this very spot.' He pressed a denunciatory finger to his breast with force and became perfectly still.

You observe those are the fewest possible words in which he could tell her that he was the traitor. Razumov is so set upon regaining his lost honour that even for the sake of the woman with the trusting eyes he cannot take the trouble to prepare her for the revelation he has to make. Then he goes to the revolutionaries in council; denounces himself to them as a police spy, receives his terrible punishment, and his soul is at peace.

It is here that Conrad differentiates himself from the Elizabethans, for they could never have worked themselves up to the pitch of subtlety. They could, as it were, have conceived a Judas, and even the remorse of such an Iscariot. They had very certainly the conception of an avenging providence. But they could not prize honour quite so high. For here is the comment of the wise woman revolutionist on the case of Razumov.

'There are evil moments in every life. A false suggestion enters one's brain and then fear is born – fear of oneself, fear for oneself. Or else a false courage – who knows? Well, call it what you like; but tell me how many of them would deliver themselves up deliberately to perdition (as he himself says in that book) rather than go on living, secretly debased in his own eyes? How many?... And please mark this – he was safe when he did it. It was just when he believed himself safe and more – infinitely more – when the possibility of being loved by that admirable girl first dawned upon him, that he discovered that his bitterest railings, the devil work of his hate and pride, could never cover up the ignominy of the existence before him. There's character in such a discovery.'

Of course this labouring of, this preoccupation with the idea of the point of honour is very foreign – so foreign that it has obviously come to this author with his foreign blood. It is a thing wholly individualistic and wholly of the aristocrat. And that is what the Poles are – aristocrats and individualists; that is why their land is harried and held down in this age of limited companies and democracy.

For the honour that obsesses all the chief characters of this author is hardly ever a question of public polity – or it might be more just to say that their souls do not treat it as a question of public polity. Lord Jim commits of course a public misdemeanour in deserting his ship because it is full of Mohammedan pilgrims; but for the rest of his life he is haunted not by the thought of thousands of drowned brown men, but by his own honour: Captain Whalley falls from honour, but it is his private soul that is harrowed, so it is with Falk the cannibal – so it is with Razumov, and in an extraordinarily imaginative degree. For the problem of Razumov is hardly to be solved by anyone but the hardest of partisans, and hardly by them. Supposing that you are the most hardened of Tories; supposing that your party is ruling the land as no land has ever been ruled for harshness and repression. On coming home one evening you find Mr Lloyd George, who has mistaken you for an advanced thinker, and he announces that he has murdered Mr Balfour, and calls on you to save him? What exactly would you do? I suppose you would compromise somehow – give the fellow ten minutes' grace before denouncing him to the police. That would be the sort of rough honour of the hunting field that gives vermin so much law – but to a man with a nice sense of the point of honour it would not be very satisfactory as a solution.

The problem of Razumov was much more terrifying. I have softened it down out of regard to the reader's feeling, when asking him to put himself in Razumov's place. And Razumov had never gone fox hunting. But at any rate that is the ceaseless moral of all this author's work – the being true to your own sense of personal honour. For my honour is not yours – you may with a good conscience commit crimes that would make me sick – you may split infinitives and praise bad books. Your honour is not mine – the other day I shot a fox, and I feel none the worse though truly the fox was among vineyards and in no English hen-roost. But there the moral of all Conrad's work just is – follow the lines of your private honour, and you will probably starve. But you will never have to confess to the woman you love that you have desecrated her ideals – you will never have to give the woman you love the pain of attending at your dishonoured deathbed, or you will never give the woman you love the infinitely greater pain of having to wait while you go to your death to satisfy the avenging providence that watches over personal honour.

Destiny! The woman you love! Deathbeds and death! How extraordinarily old-fashioned it all sounds! And for the matter of that how singular is Conrad's theory of the mysticism and awe of a man's private honour – for, as we see in the case of Razumov, that unfortunate's private honour was affected without so much as his will coming in question. He did his best to save the Revolutionist, and however much we may dislike Revolutionists or murderers I think it would be a bad world in which the majority of us would not do as much. But to save Haldin was impossible – impossible! The man who was to have driven him away in a sledge was drunk. So that all that Razumov did was to bow to what appeared to him an august and inscrutable destiny. And then the august and inscrutable destiny pursued him to the journey's end, so that he presents the picture of a flying wretch in the night, to the light of sparse torches, hiding in his arms his face averted from the strokes of pursuing Furies!

I do not know that it is the moral of this author's whole work, but so it presents itself to me, and with an extraordinary vividness – that when our private and intimate honour is in conflict with the law, we must break the law. For the law is a conventional arrangement of the relations between man and man. But a man's heart knows! I think that that is what it comes to.

I am aware that to English minds such a moral would appear shocking. We should dismiss Razumov with the trite saying that hard cases make bad law. But I am not sure that such a lesson is not good for this country at this day. I think that we have too much law; I think we think too much about lawmaking. There must come a time when the State can go no further, for the State is a clumsy and blind engine that can do no more than rough-square the material of human lives! We have our fingers too much on our moral pulse when it comes to enacting regulations for the relief of the Unfortunate in the mass: we have too little thought for what is called imagination – for our personal dealings with individuals whom destiny throws in our way.

But in the end I may be representing wrongly Mr Conrad the private gentleman, for I do not on these subjects know in the least what he thinks.

Let me hasten to say that, except for his high sense of honour, the author Conrad's morals are of a limpid correctitude, according to the very best of English standards. He is a deeply religious writer – for the figure of an avenging deity pursues a fearful course through all his pages. If you sin, he says, you must pay for it. Thus, illicit passions and theft, the breach of trust, are punished with death in the case of Nostromo. Thus a breach of the mercantile marine regulation that an officer must stick to his ship until all the passengers have left is punished with a life of penury and dishonour, with death at the end (*Lord Jim*). Falk the cannibal is punished as a cannibal should be punished, though the crew drop off his ship in Southern latitudes. Spying is punished with endless cares and a certain death (*The Secret Agent*). In the same work the Police Inspector, that symbol of rectitude and the law, is rewarded with the commendation of his superiors and a career of tranquil success. It is all as it should be – and it is all as it is in life. That is the wonderful thing about it. If there is any pitying of sinners it is not the author who writes the words, it is one of the characters who utters them. The writer, providing only the framework of the story, seems for ever to be enforcing the moral: 'Be sure your sin shall find you out.'

This is a sombre conviction, and it is all the more odd to find it in a writer of Conrad's class – for Conrad is one of the two – is one of the three – or let me say one of the two or three English writers who uphold the despised standard of Art for Art's sake. And of course when I say odd I do not in the least mean that it is odd. For every work of true art must have a profound moral significance. And I will add, that nothing that is not a work of High Art can have any moral significance at all. A work of art is passionless, a work of art is a record, a work of art is above all a symbol and the highest expression of an individual's struggle for survival. Now all Law, all Morals are the symbol of the struggle for existence of a type. English Law and English Morals are designed to perpetuate the English type; Chinese morals are an attempt to mould a world such as shall be easy for the support of the typical Chinaman. And so it is all the world over. Morals are life; sin is death. The very household laws that a mother frames for her children are intended to lengthen their lives towards that immortality that every mother wishes for her child. And the artist looking upon life and rendering only the results of his considerations produces always for his own type the one lesson – morals stand for life, sin for death.

Of course the type changes; the Universe is very large, and in it there is room for an infinite number of moral cosmogonies. The legendary Chinaman murders his daughters and, in view of the terrible over-population of China he is right in so doing. Razumov – who was probably more a Pole than a Russian – was so [ticklish] upon the point of honour that, although he gave the law its own, his conscience drove him to a death that was worse than a death. For the Poles are a nation of aristocrats, and for their survival it is necessary that the law should not be everything. Of course, if we had a great artist upon Campden Hill[1] he would not draw from Life the moral that honour is all important; or that many female subscribers to libraries should be drowned. But he would – he must in one form or the other – so project his view of life that sin should appear like death and the morals of Campden Hill the fount of Honour.

So that the artist drawing life, sombre more or less according to its latitude, is the true, is the only moralist. All the rest are only moralizers: they say what they like, not what is. Let me illustrate what I mean. I, sitting upon Campden Hill, think that there is no law that I will not break if my sympathies are sufficiently appealed to or my passions sufficiently aroused. That is necessary for the survival of my type. I will break any law I want to – but I shall end in dishonour or disgrace. I shall be immured between the stone walls of prisons; I shall be given cocoa in a filthy tin; my prison cell will be next to a drain; I shall sicken and die. Or I shall come to beggary and fade out under Charing Cross railway bridge of a deadly cough. Or I shall die upon the gallows for complicity in the escape of some murderer.

Now the passionless artist of this peaceful district would say I died as the unpitied wreckage of a sinning and immoral life. And he would be perfectly right. In Campden Hill, a tranquil and law-abiding neighbourhood, the Law so nearly approaches the moral attitude of the population that Law and Morals fade into one another. So the Artist of Kensington, W., will render Life.

But that is enough of morals; let us consider Conrad's methods. It has been said, and I think with truth, that this author is without an equal for getting an atmosphere; I will add that he is without an equal for describing action. Let us see how these results are arrived at. There is one technical maxim that jumps at the eye all through his work. It is this: *Never state: present*. And again: *Never state: present*. I am aware that these words will not be understood by the majority of my readers; I will try to make the meaning plain. The self-appointed work of an artist of Conrad's type is to make each of his stories an experience for his reader. That is his preoccupation; it is for that that an august and inscrutable providence has set him in the world; if he do anything else he offends against his personal honour.

Now in order to make a narration of events strike the hearer as an experience, the author must make the events narrated strike the senses as nearly as possible as they would be presented by nature herself. Supposing that your name is John, and that you have a friend called James, and for private reasons of his own James takes you into his billiard room and tries to shoot you with a rifle.

1 [Ford lived with Violet Hunt at her Kensington house, South Lodge, on Campden Hill Road, from 1910 to 1915.]

Now when that happens to you nothing in the outside world says to you, in so many words, '*That man is going to shoot me.*' What happens to you roughly is this. You are taken by your friend into a room. You perceive the greenish light thrown upwards from the billiard table by the shaded lamps. You perceive the billiard table. Your friend talks. You answer. You are thinking of what he says; of what you are to answer. You perceive other objects; you perceive that some of the cues are not in the rack, and that the last game marked ended at 100 to 64. James says something else. You notice that his voice is rather high. You answer. You notice that you are saying to yourself, 'I must keep my temper!' You also notice that the clock has stopped at 3.17... So it goes on, the whole way through the incident – it is a mixture of things that appear insignificant and of real action.

And the problem of a writer of the school of Conrad is to present to his readers' senses exactly that train of events. To say that James took John into the billiard room would be statement for such a writer; to present the train of action would be art.

And yet this does not really exhaust the matter – for, of course, statements must be used; indeed, paradoxically, the author of this school has nothing to use but statements. And perhaps, more exact statement of the maxim (for the words '*Never state: present*!' are a sort of slang of technical phraseology), perhaps an exact lay rendering of the maxim would be '*Never comment: state.*' For the point that has to be made is that what this type of artist has to avoid is an intrusion of his own personality into the current of his work. He has to be persuasive; he is like a man trying to catch a horse in a field. Before him he stretches out a sieve containing corn; behind his back he conceals a halter. The story is the corn in the sieve; the halter is the author's comment. If the horse-reader perceives merely the end of it his mind is away up the field.

The following illustration will make plain what I mean. There is a great writer of another school – W.M. Thackeray. Thackeray is the Prince of Comment. Now the effect of his books is very curious. There is a matchless character called Becky Sharp. In Brussels, Miss Sharp takes the bit between her teeth. She gets away from Mr Thackeray. For pages and pages the author just lets his character go on acting. He presents, in fact. We keep on saying again and again: *How wonderful she is! How wonderful she is!* And then, suddenly, when she is at the height of her achievement, there is a crack like the backfire of an automobile. Mr Thackeray has come into it. It is positively true. He bursts into Brussels to say that he is a very moral gentleman who disapproves of his puppet. And then, instead of seeing Miss Sharp's red hair any more, we see a tall gentleman with a leonine head, a broken nose, and an odd smile. And we say politely, '*How clever you are Mr Thackeray.*'

That without doubt was what Thackeray wanted. It is an aim like another; it is very nice to extort from thousands of readers ejaculations as to one's cleverness and sound morality, and thousands and thousands of readers want that sort of thing. But the problem before Conrad when he wrote *Lord Jim* was to present to us a fair-haired capable son of an English parsonage, waiting in his white canvas tennis shoes upon a boat stage in the sun for the approach of the boat – and of inscrutable and august Destiny.

And never once, never once, during the whole book do we say – if we are unsophisticated readers – '*How clever Mr Conrad is!*' We say, '*Oh, poor devil! Oh, poor devil!*' and we hope that God will be kinder to us poor Englishmen!

That is the great achievement of this type of art, and I confess that it is the only type of art that I care for. I don't mean to say that I cannot read any other kind of book with pleasure. I can get amusement from the works of Mr Nat Gould, or from any kind of book about horses. I can really revel in the adventures of the Irish M. F.H.[2] I will read Mr Sponge's adventures[3] until far, far into the night, and a detective story as long as it does not contain Sherlock Holmes I can read on any train journey. But these things are just agreeable complications – I ought, perhaps, to except Mr Sponge. I pass my time with them as I might, not being at all a superior person, at bridge, or any other round game. But when it comes to *Lord Jim* – why, it is a part of me. Yes, it is a part of my soul, of my life. It has entered into me like the blood in my veins; it has given me my English outlook, though I am a foreigner and have every kind of intellectual contempt for the countrymen of Tuan Jim. But it has made me understand the English-English with such a perfect comprehension – and what one perfectly comprehends one loves!

Now that is a great achievement – for it is a great achievement to have overwhelmed any one soul, and there are few men's souls that can resist *Lord Jim* once they have found him out. The egotism of this personal confession is not meant to display myself. It is the best way of showing what this author's work can do, and as I am perfectly sincere in every word I have written, I hope I may make the impression that I want. It is a question of the public usefulness of this author, of his functions in the Republic, of the service he has done the State. Well, he has made many men better Englishmen.

For he has taken us into wide regions of the earth; he has shown us the sea that is ours and the sparkle of the sun that we desire upon the little waves. He has given us a sense of responsibilities. He has made us desire more sedulously to do our duties. He has taught us above all to desire to be shipshape – to be shipshape on our decks, on our drawing-room carpets, and in the thoughts that we think in our minds.

2 [Master of Foxhounds]
3 [R.S. Surtees, *Mr Sponge's Sporting Tour,* 1853.]

I am aware that the great protagonist of Thackeray, in the imaginative letters of today, has written:

> There are five-and-forty ways of inditing tribal lays
> And every single one of them is right![4]

But are there? Would there be two ways of writing 'The Man Who Would be King', or 'My Lord the Elephant', or 'On the Road to Mandalay', or even *Stalky* – would there be any other way of writing them? There are other ways of writing other stories; there are other ways of treating other subjects; but, and this is the great truth that is forgotten – just as there is only one way in which a woman can dress and look her level best, so there is only one way in which every given subject, and every given story, can be treated to be at its best.

That is why there is such, tremendous pother about literature in some countries. Immense numbers of foreigners are always getting hold of immense numbers of stories and trying to find out what is the only one way of treating them.

We have seen that Conrad's method of treatment is to render. Now what about his powers of selection and what about the defects of his merits? He is, we know, concerned before everything else with getting an atmosphere. But is he? I knew at one time very well a writer who collaborated with Conrad in one or two books,[5] and has very kindly presented me with the manuscript of these works. I transcribe two passages, underlining the words that are by Conrad:

> To yesterday and to-day I say my *polite* 'vaya usted con Dios'. What are these days to me? *But that far-off day of my romance when* from between the blue and white bales in Don Ramon's darkened store room, at Kingston, *I saw the door open before* the figure of an old man with the tired, long white face, *that day I am not likely to forget. I remember* the chilly smell of the typical West Indian store, the indescribable smell of damp gloom, of locos, of pimento, of olive oil, of new sugar, of rum; the glassy double sheen of Ramon's great spectacles, the mahogany face, *while the tap tap, tap, of a cane on the flags went on behind the inner door; the click of the latch; the stream of light.* The door, *petulantly thrust inwards, struck against some barrels. I remember the rattling of the bolts on that door,* and the tall figure that appeared there, snuff-box in hand. In that land of white clothes, that precise, ancient Castilian in black was something to remember. The black cane that had made the tap, tap, tap dangled *by a silken cord,* from the hand whose delicate, blue-veined, wrinkled wrist ran back into a foam of lawn ruffles. *The other hand paused in the act of conveying a pinch of snuff to* the nostrils of the

4 [In Kipling's 'In the Neolithic Age' the speaker's Totem tells him: 'There are nine and sixty ways of constructing tribal lays, / And every single one of them is right!']

5 [Ford himself! He quotes the opening and conclusion of *Romance*.]

> hooked nose that had, on the skin stretched tight over the bridge, the polish of old ivory; *the elbow pressing the* black cocked hat against the side; the legs, one bent, the other bowing a little back – this was the attitude of Seraphina's father.
>
> *Having imperiously thrust the door of the inner room open, he remained immovable, with no intention of entering, and called* in a harsh, aged voice: '*Señor Ramon, Señor Ramon!' And then twice, 'Seraphina, Seraphina!' turning his head back …*

The second passage contains no description at all except the description of moods, but it is none the less instructive since it shows Conrad's desire for actualities, for hard and characteristic phrases set against his collaborator's more vague personality, so that it stands out in a strong relief:–

> *It takes long enough to realize that someone is dead at a distance. I had done that.* But how long, how long, it needs to know that the life of your heart has come back from the dead. *For years afterwards I could not bear to have her out of my sight.*
>
> *Of our first meeting all I remember is a speechlessness that was like the awed hesitation of our overtried souls before the greatness of a change from the verge of despair to the consummation of a supreme joy. The whole world*, the whole of life, *had changed all round me*: it enveloped me so lightly as not to be felt, so suddenly as not to be believed in, so completely that that whole meeting was an embrace, so softly that at last it lapsed into a sense of rest *that was like the fall of a beneficent and welcome death.*
>
> For suffering is the lot of man, *but not inevitable failure or worthless despair which is without end – suffering the mark of manhood, which bears within its pain a hope of felicity like a jewel set in iron….*
>
> *Her first words were 'You broke our compact. You went away whilst I was sleeping.'* Only the deepness of her reproach revealed the depth of her love *and the suffering she too had endured* to reach a union that was to be without end – *and to forgive.*
>
> And looking back we see Romance – that subtle thing that is mirage, that is life. It is the goodness of the years we have lived through, of the old time when we did this or that, when we dwelt here or there. Looking back it seems wonderful enough a thing that I who am this and she who is that, commencing so far away a life that, after such sufferings borne together and apart, ended so tranquilly there in a world so stable – that she and I should have passed through so much, good chance and evil chance, sad hours and joyful, all lived down and swept away into the little heap of dust that is a life. *That, too, is Romance.*

Now two main facts have occurred to me in studying these passages very carefully. One of them is that every word of description is by the other writer, and every word of action is by Conrad. This is a very curious fact, for it would be absurd to ascribe to the other writer greater powers of description, and certainly that apportionment of the task was never consciously made between the two.

I have been casting about in my mind for an explanation of this fact, and just at this very moment I happened to look idly at the motto on the title page of the volume called *Youth*, and then I noticed that that motto runs:– '… *But the Dwarf answered: No, something human is dearer to me than the wealth of all the world.*' And that is the great happiness, is the great good fortune of this author's temperament. We can most of us describe, some of us can get atmospheres – but it is only the very great writer who can so interpenetrate his characters with the seas and skies, or the houses, fabrics, and ornaments that surround them. For that is what Conrad seems to do. It is not what he actually does – actually he sends through all the seas and skies the very beings of the men that look upon them. For a descriptive writer – or rather for a writer noted for his descriptions – he describes very little. Consider this passage from *Youth* – that most magical of all this author's pieces of work. The narrator, after having pulled nearly all night in the escape from a wreck, has been guided by a red light, in the depth of a great darkness, into an Eastern harbour. He has fallen asleep in the boat against an unknown quay:–

> But when I opened my eyes again the silence was as complete as though it had never been broken. I was lying in a flood of light, and the sky had never seemed so far, so high before. I opened my eyes and lay without moving.
>
> And then I saw the men of the East – they were looking at me. The whole length of the jetty was full of people. I saw brown, bronze, yellow faces, the black eyes, the glitter, the colour of an Eastern crowd. And all these things stared without a murmur, without a sigh, without a movement. They stared down at the boats, at the sleeping men who at night had come to them from the sea. Nothing moved. The fronds of palms stood still against the sky. Not a branch stirred along the shore, and the brown roofs of hidden houses peeped through the green foliage, through the big leaves that hung, shining, and still like leaves forged of heavy metal. This was the East of the ancient navigators, so old, so mysterious, resplendent and sombre, living unchanged, full of danger and promise. And these were the men. I sat up suddenly. A wave of movement passed through the crowd from end to end, passed along the heads, swayed the bodies, ran along the jetty like a ripple on the water, like a breath of wind on a field – and all was still again. I see it now – the wide sweep of the bay, the glittering sands, the wealth of green, infinite and varied, the sea blue like the sea of a dream, the crowd of attentive faces, the blaze of vivid colour – the water reflecting it all, the curve of the shore, the jetty, the high-sterned outlandish craft

> floating still, and the three boats with the tired men from the West sleeping, unconscious of the land and the people and the violence of the sunshine. They slept thrown across the thwarts, curled on bottom boards, in the careless attitudes of death. The head of the old skipper, leaning back in the stern of the long boat, had fallen on his breast and he looked as though he would never wake. Farther out, old Mahon's face was upturned to the sky, with the long white beard spread out on his breast as though he had been shot where he sat at the tiller, and a man all in a heap in the bows of the boat slept with both arms embracing the stem-head and with his cheek laid on the gunwale. The East looked at them without a sound.

Now that passage renders the East as no writer has rendered it, and yet how little of real description there is in it. It is the men – the men whose destinies had brought them to that spot who really give the passage its tone – because something human is dearer to this writer than all the pictures of all the East.

And this great and desirable faculty is his not merely because of a technical self-consciousness. We most of us – those of us who have any technical knowledge at all – know that we must not introduce any descriptive writing just for the love of a description. Anybody knows enough to know that. But Conrad's eye is so formed that it does not notice anything save what carries the story forward. To return to my illustration of the smoking-room murder. A Conrad character would not notice that the clock had stopped at 3.17, or that the cues were not in order, or that the marking of the last game had not been obliterated, unless Conrad desired to point something out – it might be that the murderer was a disorderly person, or that he had been interrupted at the end of a game of billiards by a piece of news that had made him desire to shoot his friend.

I am not by any means saying that there are no passages in the works of Conrad that are not simple pages of description. You will find, for instance, in 'The End of the Tether', whole long pages of description of land-fretted seas. But the purposes of these are the purposes of the story. They make so plain to the reader the nature of the seas in which the *Sofala* carried the burden of the old Captain's tragedy that when the sinking of the ship comes there is no need to burden the narrative with topographical explanation. All the while one has been on the ship, one has seemed to be so conscious of the ledges of rock below one that when the knife-thrust has come it has seemed for long to be inevitable, and the whole conduct of the story need concern itself only with the feelings of the human beings.

And that is the great faculty of this author – that he can make an end seem inevitable, in every instance the only possible end. He does this by every means – by the explanations of heredity, of temperament, of the nature of sea and sky, by the sound of a song, by the straws in the street.

His sense of Destiny differs in its means of expression from that of the Greeks, its intensity is always as great as theirs. Perhaps it is a part of a common Oriental temperament. The Greek Destiny was embodied, commented on, chorussed. It was an all-overwhelming cloud. The Destiny of Conrad's books is hymned by no Chorus of Captive Women, and by no Bacchantes. That is not the temper of his time or ours. When all sorts of things, all sorts of little coincidences, nowadays force us to a course of action we do not any longer say that Atropos compelled us – we say that it seemed as if every blessed thing conspired to make us do it. And what Conrad does for us is to express for us the Three Sisters in the terms of every blessed thing.

Now this is a very great achievement, a very great enlightenment for our age. I do not mean to say that Conrad is the only writer that does this for us, but I am certain that we have no other – nowhere in the Western World – so exclusively occupied with this consideration, which is, surely, one of the two most important considerations of the world and life. I have heard it said that his books are too long; that his elaboration is over great. But that is the case only for minds very hurried or temperamentally out of tune with this author. For myself I can only say that not one of his works has ever seemed tedious. I like one subject more than another, but the keen pleasure of observing the incidents, the certainty that every incident – that every word, however superfluous they may appear, will in the end show necessary and revelatory – this pleasure I am never without.

And when we consider the great obstacles of language with which this man has struggled, and the unswerving conscientiousness with which this writer has pursued his guiding lights – whether we like or dislike his books – we must be consoled. For if our age can have raised up such a conscience in any walk of life, and if our country can have attracted him to live amongst us, our age and our country must have in it something that is good – in its traditions and its teachings. Indeed, when I think that in a light-hearted way I have poked fun at the artistic conscience of this country I feel a little ashamed. For if Conrad has not earned any huge material success, he has secured a recognition, even from the more Academic, that few men of his greatness have ever secured in their age and their own day. And looking back it seems a wonderful enough thing that this writer, commencing so far away a life that after sufferings, perils, and vicissitudes borne under so many skies and upon so many seas, has its consummation here in a world so stable – that after the seas where he passed through so much, good chance and evil chance, upon this foreign shore he should receive the acknowledgment of his services from the State, and the applause alike of the Orthodox and of the Critical. That, too, is Romance.

English Review, 10 (December 1911), 68–83.

D.G.R.

The trouble about forming an estimate as to the literary or aesthetic value of Rossetti the painter-poet was just Rossetti himself. There are, of course, many writers whose personalities have very much affected or very much obscured the merits or the defects of their work. Yesterday, as it were, we had Henley, the day before yesterday, FitzGerald, a hundred years ago or so, Dr Johnson. (As I have been very much hauled over the coals lately, for using dates figuratively, I should like to add that these dates are also used figuratively. I am, for instance, aware that Henley has been dead more than twenty-four hours, and FitzGerald more than forty-eight.) But Rossetti's personality did not swamp his work, as did those of Johnson or the other two. Nobody really knew – in spite of the ham and egg story – whether he ate his meals with his waistcoat buttoned or unbuttoned. No one really had as clear an idea of him as they had even of Thackeray or of Dickens. (In the interests of strict accuracy I should like to add that when I say 'no one had an idea of his personality' I am speaking only figuratively. I do not mean to say that Miss Sidall, the servant at Red Lion Square, Mr W. M. Rossetti, Mr Watts-Dunton, or Mr Hall Caine, who served the poet-painter so faithfully – I do not mean to say that none of these gentlemen or ladies had a personal acquaintance with Rossetti.) But what I mean is that, during Rossetti's life, the large body of his readers, the large body of those who never read him, the personages who formed public opinion, and the more numerous persons who tried to form public opinion – none of these persons had anything but the very haziest idea of what Rossetti the man really was. There was really an extraordinary buzz about his personality during the seventies and eighties – a romantic clamour. But since no one knew anything at all about the figure itself, the buzz and the clamour were extraordinarily vague. It was as if all these people were talking romantically about the equator. The imaginary line was certainly there, and there, romantically, Rossetti undoubtedly was, cloistered with Mr Watts-Dunton, or with Mr Hall Caine, as the case might be. But, in the popular estimation – in everybody's estimation – Rossetti was just a solar myth, a golden vision, a sort of Holy Grail that the young poets of the seventies pursued, but seldom saw. And I think this romantic vacuum was extraordinarily good for the seventies. It meant that they had the feeling – that everybody had the feeling – that somewhere in the world there was a glorious, a romantic figure, cloistered up and praying for the poetry, the romance, and the finer things of this world. I think it was a good thing for the seventies, just as I think it is a good thing for me every now and then to remember that in the cloisters of Catholic Christianity there are, even today, a great many religious spending all their hours in just praying for the poor souls of all of us. (In the interest of accuracy I should like to add when I here write 'all of us', I am stating an exact and not a figurative fact.)

The edifying log-rolling by which in the seventies Rossetti's poems were, very properly, forced into the hands of the public – the organized and efficient log-rolling was again worked with extreme decency. Rossetti's poems were boomed – just as my works have been boomed, and just as the works of every writer of any position or merit must be boomed if he is to continue to live by his pen. But Rossetti's poems were forced upon the public without his publishers, his friendly critics, or his uncritical friends calling in the aid of personalities. They decently let Rossetti alone. They did not ask anybody to buy the volume which contained 'Jenny' or the volume which contained 'The White Ship' because Rossetti wore eccentric trousers, collected postage stamps or disliked caviare. At that date he was hardly even celebrated in public places or weekly periodicals because, very sensibly, he desired to spread the fame of his beloved wife and so he took the manuscript of his poems out of her coffin, where in his first grief at her loss he had placed them. No, none of the energetic gentlemen who boomed this poet-artist tried to do it by means of sarcophagic details. They did their work decently, talking only of the glorious sonority of the polysyllabic lines, of the romance, of the tenderness, of the splendour, of the morbidness, of the high moral purpose, of the mystic inner meaning that were contained in 'The Stream's Secret', in 'Sister Helen', in 'The King's Tragedy', or in all those glamorous poems with the golden haze around them.

And so for every one the personality of Rossetti became the personality that is expressed in his poems, and in the very few pictures of his that had really been seen. According to what was our idea of the personally poetic (again in the interests of accuracy I should like to add that here I am employing a purely figurative modesty when I write 'our', for of course I knew what Rossetti was like) – according to what was our ideal of a poetic personality, so we vaguely imagined Rossetti in the seventies – all we young writers, young painters, middle-aged merchants, royal princesses, peers, and bankers, all we unimportant persons who so enthusiastically blazed abroad the Rossetti legend. We imagined him as well-fleshed, bearded, or with ascetically scraped lean features; we imagined him hollow-eyed, or with the perpetual tolerant smile of Shakespeare. But we had not the least idea of what he looked like. (Again in the interests of accuracy I should like to add that this does not represent my state of mind during the seventies, and that during that period I was not either a peer of a royal princess, either a merchant prince or a banker. I was not even a young writer. No, at the end of the seventies I was a child of seven. But I have been trying to identify myself with the spirit of that age.) Of course there was the reverse of the medal. The other day I was travelling from Nauheim to Frankfort. There got into my carriage an elderly pepper-and-salt bearded, well-brushed gentleman with a strong North-country burr. He revealed himself in conversation as a survival of the merchant princes of the seventies. He had kept himself alive by taking the waters of Nauheim yearly, and by constantly consulting a Frankfort physician about his gout. In short, he was a keen, sensible Lancashire man. He began to talk about George Rae, the Leatharts, the Grahams, the Leylands, about many picture buyers and about many picture bargains. He related how, cheque-book in hand, he had gone into the studios of Royal Academicians and had bought off their easels unfinished pictures which he had afterwards sold at greatly advanced prices. He was a keen business man, and talking to him was delightful to me. I seemed to hear in his voice the accents of all those dead and gone merchant princes and picture buyers. Yes, it was a voice from the past. And suddenly he said: 'Now there was Rossetti! What a warm man Rossetti might have been if he had not wasted his talents in those extravagant dissipations!'

And this again was the dear old voice of the seventies. My North-country friend was uttering the pleasing remarks that he had heard in the studios of Academicians when he went to buy pictures. And he spoke of Rossetti with a sort of sincere regret exactly as he would have done of a friend of his who had not made all that he might have done out of an iron foundry with excellent prospects inherited from his father. He gave me other horrid details of Rossetti's career and habits (they were all of them quite untrue, and most of them quite impossible). Yet this gentleman had never seen Rossetti, had never read a word of his writings. He had never so much as read one of the innumerable biographies – not even Mr Hall Caine's. No, he was just echoing the whispers of academic studios of the seventies.

And after Rossetti's death the biographies began. They poured forth, official and unofficial, sending out smuts or deluges of whitewash. Frenchmen wrote them, Germans wrote them, Japanese wrote them; I wrote them, Mr Hall Caine wrote them, Mr Watts-Dunton did not write them, Mr William Rossetti did. For thirty years or so they poured from the press, nearly all of them exceedingly dull, nearly all of them misleadingly accurate in things that did not matter. For thirty years or so Rossetti's figure was perpetually before the public, getting more and more pompous, more and more priestly, more and more like a German professor of the beautiful, growing duller and duller and duller, and at last he was dead. Last year he was as dead as a doornail. And that was a thousand pities, a triumph of obscuring pompousness over a man who was very great, and a poet who was very rare.

To get at the value of Rossetti the poet, as to get at the value of any original spirit, there is only one test. You have to ask yourself what you would be, what your mental development would have been, how your intimate self would have grown, if that man had never existed. And think of what we should all have been if Rossetti had never existed!

For, putting ethics and the technical criticism of art and letters for the moment aside, we have to consider that the real value of the work of Rossetti and his school was the preaching that the Arts are joyful and comfortable things – are things as joyful, as comfortable, and as natural as is the light of the sun. They are indeed the sunshine of the soul.

Think then, again, of what England would have been without the influence of Rossetti during these last thirty years. We should have been Prussianized, we should have been Americanized. No doubt it would have been a good thing had we paid more attention to the evolution of a cast-iron military class as they have done in Prussia, which began to grow so mighty about the time when Rossetti published his first volume of poems. No doubt we should have had a few still more and still richer men had we developed enormous industrial systems like that of the Standard Oil Company, which began its depredatory career about the time when Rossetti published his second volume of poems. But I do not know that we should have had a better England or a happier.

I do not mean, of course, to say that Rossetti, alone and unaided, repelled armed invasions from the Mark of Brandenburgh, or that he said to Mr Rockefeller 'thus far and no farther'. But Rossetti was a great man. He was great in the exact sense of the word – for greatness in a writer, as in a statesman, as in a world conqueror, implies the power to voice great multitudes. A technically perfect artist may create characters that will live for ever and yet he may not be a great man. For a great man does not merely win battles or create characters – no, he creates frames of minds, he creates enthusiasms in great bodies of people. 'Create' is perhaps not exactly the just word. What he does, rather, is to prove to large bodies of people that they have enthusiasms slumbering within them. He strikes within us little silver bells, or the great chords of large war harps. And the measure of his greatness lies in the wideness of his appeal. So that my own private image of Rossetti the writer and the painter is of something a little vague, very romantic and exceedingly great. He seems to sweep his fingers over the harp-strings of innumerable hearts, calling out the music that is in them.

Nowadays, Rossetti is generally called the poet of the young. And this is a curious fact, creditable enough to Rossetti, but not very creditable to us who are no longer young. And it contributes still more to the general glamour of vagueness that surrounds his personality and his greatness as a painter and as a poet. We cannot say how wide his appeal is because his appeal is to the young, and the young have little opportunity of voicing themselves. They don't get into the papers, we don't listen to them at our clubs; they are generally packed away in their universities, and when they are at home we manage to shut them up over the dinner-table. So in those mysterious young hearts things are going on, and it is certain that Rossetti holds a large share of their enthusiasms. It is certain, because we can divine it from our own hearts where 'Rossetti' – the mere sound of the name 'Rossetti' – causes to arise a whole strain of vague and yet regretted emotions. It suggests something fine, generous. It suggests that part of our youth which, although we have outgrown it, we regret. There are the many follies of our youth which were not fine and which, we thank God, we are permitted to forget. But if we no longer think very often of Rossetti, it is just because we no longer read poetry. We have outgrown that and we are not really glad of it, for it was one of the finenesses of our youths.

And of course in a sense it is the biographers who have killed Rossetti for grown men and women, just as chatter about Harriet, atheism, and advanced opinions killed Shelley as a poet. For you cannot read the 'Ode to the West Wind' without having it at the back of your mind that Shelley and his mistress rode about Italy on a donkey, and that many excellent people have used this fact in order to prove that marriage as an institution ought to be abolished. And in that way your enjoyment of the 'Ode to the West Wind' has been spoiled. Yet the 'Ode to the West Wind' is a noble poem and has nothing to do with Italy, donkeys, or the fact that Shelley found his first wife to be an imbecile schoolgirl. No doubt he found his second wife trying enough, but the whitewashers have washed that out, so Mary Shelley for many excellent people remains an arid argument for free love.

Much the same thing has happened to Rossetti. For most of us he is the gentleman who dug his poems out of his wife's coffin, a solitary fact which does not, if a respectable paper will allow me the expression, matter a damn. Nothing that Rossetti did matters a damn. He was a great poet of not flawless technical gifts. He was a great literary painter, with a defective technical education, but with a great skill in shirking difficulties. And he was a great man. To attempt to whitewash the private character of Rossetti, Shelley, Lord Nelson of the Nile, Goethe, or the Emperor Tiberius is profitless folly. You can say that you believe that they had the highest moral purposes, but some other man will always come along and prove in black and white that each of them ran away from his own wife, or with someone else's. The fact is that it is utterly unprofitable to expect to find greatness and a personal high moral purpose in the same body. It cannot be done. There is not room for them, alas! I used to know a great writer who always lost his ticket when he travelled. Always! I had many hundred hours of pleasure in reading the works of this writer. But I never could understand how he could be such a fool as to lose his railway tickets. It seemed a silly sort of a habit to me and it upset him very much. I went on reading his books and getting the utmost pleasure from them, and then, one day, the answer to this riddle came to me. The great writer in losing his railway tickets was paying for my pleasure. He lost them because his mind was taken up by his work.

In his life Rossetti lost quite a number of railway tickets of one kind and another – perhaps, if Providence is not more just than are we in our anecdotal blindness, than we with all the whitewash in our eyes – perhaps he even lost his ticket to Heaven. But it was because he was thinking of other things – of the things that have given us pleasure, that have saved us from Prussianization and the adoption of American methods. In a sense he is our scapegoat – the scapegoat of you and me, who in our intellectual vacuities have time and the duty to attend to all the tickets and all the labels of the world. In one of my several dull biographies of this painter-poet I have said that he had the private tastes of a pork butcher. This was true. Whistler on his death-bed said: 'You mustn't say anything against Rossetti, Rossetti was a king', and this also was true, and any proper man will understand how these two irreconcileable truths came to reside in the same body, But the fact is there are millions and millions of pork butchers. We are all pork butchers,[1] if we are not all socialists. But every now and then one of us, forgetting that the sole end and aim of humanity is not to be found out and so to die churchwarden or, at least, sidesman of our church or chapel – every now and then one of us keeps his eyes on the pale light of the stars, the golden light of the grail or of romance, or the blood-red light that hangs over battlefields.

Then he walks on with his eyes upon those lights of the horizons. His feet will not avoid any puddles if they are in the way. But we, the white-washers and the gentlemen of the other persuasion, shall observe only the feet and the puddles. That is because that is our nature. But the exceptional pork butcher[1] will walk on and will become such a saint as was Augustine; such a saviour of his country as was Nelson, or such a poet as was Shakespeare – being one or two in a million million, in an infinite multitude of pork butchers.[1] But saint, or saviour of his country, or poet, this pork butcher was a king, and you must not say anything against him or you will be a dirty, ungrateful little pork butcher.[1] That is the penalty that you will pay, not the king. Such a great, easy, fine king was, to the measure of his lights, Rossetti. It is well to get it said and to leave it at that. He once gave a sovereign to a beggar, he once borrowed some books and did not return them. We cannot afford to do either of these things, because with us they matter. They are – such things – our achievement. But then Rossetti wrote 'Jenny' and painted *The Annunciation* –

1 This will not bear statistical examination. I mean *hommes moyen sensuels*.

(In the interests of accuracy I should like to add that I do not *know* that Rossetti ever gave a sovereign to a beggar. What I mean is, that it is the sort of thing that he would have done. I should like also to add that in the later years of his life – 1869 to 1882 – Rossetti did not lose, or, at any rate, it is unlikely that he lost, his railway tickets. They were probably taken for him and carefully guarded during the journey by Mr Watts-Dunton, Mr Hake, or Mr Hall Caine. But what I meant is, that if he had travelled alone he probably would have lost his railway tickets. Besides, in this context I am using the words 'railway tickets' as a figure of speech meaning one or other of the Commandments.)

Bookman (London), 40 (June 1911), 113–20.

The Critical Attitude: Applied to the Affairs of the World in General: essays from *The Bystander*

Some of Ford's editorials for his *English Review* had appeared under the heading 'The Critical Attitude', and were included in his 1911 book of the same title. After he lost control of the *Review*, he wrote this distinct series of more journalistic pieces for *The Bystander*.

A Tory Plea for Home Rule (1)

FATAL IRELAND

Africa is the grave of reputations, and from there comes always something that is new; Ireland is the ruin of good men and great causes, and from her comes always an old story. There is about Ireland something that causes a madness akin to the African madness. You take a soldier and a gentleman of the type of Sidney, the sort of man who at Zutphen gives his water-bottle to a dying man, the very perfect gentle knight, the mirror of chivalry. You send him to Ireland and he becomes a robber and a low sneak thief, watching the murder of women before his eyes with a Christian complacency and a snobbish contentment. You take a soldier like Cromwell and make him turn his attention to Ireland, and he becomes an atrocious butcher. Why, the only decent Governor that we ever sent to Ireland was Lord Chesterfield, who is known only as a cold fop, the author of worldly letters to a bastard son. It is not that we need worry sentimentally over the murderers. I think we could contemplate Ireland with less humiliation if Cromwell had rooted out every Irishman. It would not matter much; they would be dead and gone and quiet in their graves, which would be better for their descendants. But the furiously interesting – the saddening – thing is that it was the fop who made the only good Governor.

WHY WE HAVE FAILED

That is really the point that ought to teach us humility – it ought to teach us that we should mind our own business. And really the domestic government of Ireland – that little remote island of the Western Seas – is none of our business. The essence of its problem is a geological fault. By some accident the flake of rocks that Ireland is, tailing off into the deeps of the Atlantic, contains not a trace of the minerals that are necessary for the building up of a successful modern State. It contains some marble – but we are an age of brick and ferro-concrete. That is really what it comes to. We cannot make Ireland pay. No one can make Ireland pay; then, for God's sake, as we have left still some Irish alive, let us leave them to starve in their own way. Let them have their abuses in their own way. We cannot prevent abuses, because we can only govern where there is money. We can govern where there is that by the simple expedient of fines, or of teaching the world how that money may be made to increase. But where there is no money fines do not count, and all that historically we have ever been able to try to take from the Irish is their lives, their lands, their cattle, and their Faith. And those last are the things that men fight to the death for. When it is merely a matter of money men grumble, hold in Trafalgar Square mass meeting after mass meeting, peddle away a constitution or so, and squeal vigorously in the last ditch, as all we Tories have been so discreditably doing in the last six months. But fight! We have not got a kick in us. It is only our pockets that have been in danger. If it had been our cattle, our homes, our lives, or, above all, our Faith, Mr Asquith would have had another story to tell.

THE STUPID PARTY

But we are a frightfully silly lot, we Tories. We have always been called the Stupid Party, and, by Jove! we are it. Why, we get even our party name from Ireland; why, we love the Irish so that we never can get past trying to treat them like naughty children – but when in the world have we ever been able to think about that poor and martyred land? Never. Never since Chesterfield, whom we sent there because he was a fop. Roughly speaking, we have treated them systematically, for the last century, to fire and the sword, and that, in all the disgusting muddle, has been the better way. The other party has, roughly speaking, given them constitutions and hanged them for objecting. For a Liberal cannot understand anyone objecting to a constitution – for him it is the Sin against the Holy Ghost, as long as the Constitution is one that can be jerrymandered to suit the party in the House. For the Liberals are the Clever Party. They are that. Their job is to keep in power, and splendidly the records of the last century show that they have done it.

OUR BUSINESS

But we Tories really love the Irish – we love them as we love naughty children and lost causes – with a deep, stupid, sentimental love. Only we cannot forget that it is our business to govern. It is: we are the ruling classes. It is our business to govern England, Scotland, Wales, the Isle of Man, the United States, Canada, Australia, and some other places. But not Ireland. There are limitations to every art, and you cannot govern Ireland. You could not even keep an Irish servant in order. You have no rewards to give that would move him; there are no punishments you can give that he can feel as a humiliation. The best that you can do is to win his loyalty, and then he will die for you. This is a very profound truth. For we do not for the moment govern the United States; all we do is to squeal in the last ditch and grumble at our leaders, whilst the Liberals use the Irish to jerry-mander the House of Lords, and will then use Home Rule to give them a permanent majority in the House of Commons. But we – we govern nothing. Nevertheless, it is probable that in the year 2711 we shall be in power again, if the Permanent Liberal Government have not by that date leased these islands to Prussia under the suzerainty of a permanent Liberal Front Bench.

OUR SENTIMENTALITY

Yes, it is our business to govern – but not Ireland. When the late Mr Gladstone – who was a Tory traitor – introduced the first Home Rule Bill, he had simply realized that great fact. He had thrown up the sponge, as we ought to have done years before. But he was a Tory traitor, and we had to 'go for him'. That was perfectly proper, but we ought not to have gone for his Bill. (We are, you see, the stupid party because we are the sentimental party. We were not going to have any truck with the devil.) Only, in this case, as they say in Ireland, a blind hen had found a pea. For what possible objection was there to Home Rule? Rome Rule? But the poor devils fought, for us, well enough – the poor Papists – at the Battle of the Boyne. German dominion? But it was to keep out some sort of Germans that they fought then – for our sakes. For in the end we are Tories – not Conservatives, that most hideous of all words. We are Tories, and it was for us these men's fathers were harried, these men's mothers were murdered all through the days of the Stuarts, all through the days of the Georges. There was a day when we were not so tender for the Nonconformist succession and the Curse of Cromwell.

VOTE CADGERS

Historically considered, Toryism has made two great opportunist mistakes in the course of the last twelve decades – three, if we include the throwing out of Mr George's Budget by the Peers.[1] By our senseless opposition to Napoleon we gave life to Prussia, the flail of the world. By our senseless opposition to Home Rule we flooded the party with Whigs that spawned upon us Democratic ideas. Democratic ideas! Whig place-hunters! What use have we for them? We are, you understand, speaking merely historically. Mr Goschen was an excellent, quiet gentleman, but he ruined Consols, and makes the credit of the country shake today.[2] Lord Hartington was a fine Whig and a perfectly honest gentleman. Neither of them could be suspected of merely seeking office. But Lord Hartington made us ridiculous by going to sleep in the House. Mr Chamberlain was a magnificent debater, but he taught the party to cadge for votes, and forced the hand of his leader so that the Lords threw out that Budget. Yes, all those three politicians taught us the trick of cadging for votes. For what Tory now but says that the business of statesmanship is to promote the greatest good of the greatest number?

OUR CRY

What Tory before the Whigs came over would have dared to talk such nonsense? For the business of Tory statesmanship is to secure the greatest good of the best elements in the community. That is just as good a party cry for a working-class audience, and it has the advantage of being honest. What is the good of saying that Tariff Reform will solve all social problems? It certainly will not, though it might help by steadying prices and hastening our Imperial federation. But we are paralysed by fear of the working man. And that paralysis came from Ireland – through our Whig 'allies'. We cannot get on if we try to spread the net in the sight of that particular bird, the working man. The working man is perfectly right, and he is not a silly fool. He may believe in the sincerity of the Left when the Left preaches the greatest good of all incompetent and whining working men, but he will not believe in the sincerity of a Right using those words. That is a theory like another, but it cannot be our cry. What we desire, what we stand for, is the greatest good of the competent working man and the blotting out of the incompetent. What the Whig desires is a margin of incompetent labour with which to keep the price of labour down. That is a simple, self-evident proposition that the working man can understand. He has intelligence enough to read the hearts of men, if only because he stands in the midst of the realities of life. It is no good our saying that we stand for Equality. We do not. We stand for a ruling class,

1 [Lloyd George, Chancellor of the Exchequer 1908–15, and later Prime Minister. The rejection of his budget of 1909–10 by the House of Lords led to the constitutional crisis and Parliament Act of 1911.]

2 [Sir William Edward Goschen was British ambassador in Berlin, 1908–14. Consols (abbreviated from 'consolidated annuities') were securities without a maturity date.]

recruited from the working-class just as often as the working-class produces a man good enough to become a ruler. It that is not a good enough cry to go to the country we do not want – we ought not to want – our side in office. We ought to disdain it.

A NEW POINT OF VIEW

As it is, we have the miserable spectacle of Mr Balfour, who is a great man and a great leader, being forced out of the leadership by the pusillanimous and office-hunting wing of the party, because he felt unable to put up miserable cries about anything that comes along in order to catch the working-class vote. And that is the direct consequence of Ireland. For Heaven's sake let us get Ireland cleared out of the way. We cannot rule Ireland, for we cannot understand what Ireland wants, for, of a real truth, what Ireland wants – and what England can never understand that every Irishman wants – is not wealth or an equal opportunity of wealth for every man, but an equal opportunity for every man for a romantic chance of distinction upon an Irish political theatre. But in the meantime the country is drifting to ruin because we will not let the Irish alone. I have had a singular experience. I was talking about Home Rule to the best Tory that I know. I wasn't looking at him, but suddenly I heard in his voice such deep emotion that I did look up. He had just said, 'It would be too awful!' and I observed that he was as near to tears as a good Tory country-man could be. I said, 'In the name of heaven, what would be too awful?' He replied, 'What Ulster would do.' I said, 'What would they do?' He said, 'They would harry the whole land from north to south. It would be too awful for the poor, lovable Irish.' Now, there is a point of view! Is it not purely admirable? For, you see, we *cannot* let those distressful creatures alone. We cannot even let them get their own heads bitten off if they wish it. We are dismayed at the spectre of Mr T.P. O'Connor's head carried on a charger before Sir Edward Carson up College Green! I suppose we could not get on without the cheap literature that Mr O'Connor supplies to us.

Bystander, 32 (22 November 1911), 397–8.

A Tory Plea For Home Rule (2)

THE POWER OF COMPACTNESS

What we have to insure in the first place for Ulster is that Ulster should have a fair proportionate representation in the Irish Parliament, and it will then remain for the Orangemen to form themselves into a compact, solid minority that will work as one man. And anyone acquainted in the least with the opportunities that be ready for a compact, sectarian body in a legislative assembly will know how easy it is for that compact, sectarian body entirely to dominate that legislative assembly. In the German Empire, Catholics are to Protestants as two to five. Yet it was the German Catholics alone in the world who brought Bismarck to his knees, and the German Catholics have ruled Germany ever since, do so to this day, and very probably will continue to do so to the end of time.

THE CASE FOR ULSTER

If you will consider the figures two to five, and will change the colour of these religions, you will see how very easy the task of the Orangemen is. Political unity is theirs already, because of their common sectarian interest. Their opponents will split up into factions the moment outside oppression of Ireland ceases. It is mere folly to imagine that every Irishman, if he were left alone, would be the blind tool of priests. France is a Catholic country, but where are the priests? Italy is a Catholic country, but where is the prisoner of the Vatican? At present the priests do more or less guide the counsels of the Irish Nationalist Party, but that is because the Irishman knows that when it is a matter of an oppressed nation the Church of Rome, which, in times of prosperity, may or may not be anti-national, becomes the most profoundly inspiring of national factors. It is Rome that has kept Polish national feeling alive through centuries of oppression; it is Rome that has kept alive Irish national feeling through centuries of oppression. I am not now stating my personal preferences, but merely putting the common sense of the case for Ulster. And the common sense of the case for Ulster forces every sane man to see that the moment outside pressure is removed from Ireland the Nationalist forces will break up in a most extraordinary way.

FOUR IRISHMEN AND MR BALFOUR

I do not in the least profess to understand Irish internal questions. But when I was conducting the affairs of a certain periodical, four Irish gentlemen came to see me on four successive days to ask me to write something about some Irish abuse. Each of these gentlemen revealed himself as being extremely gifted, eloquent, sincere, and even inspired. Three of them were Members of Parliament, all were Nationalists, the fourth being the principal leader-writer of one of the Nationalist organs.

But when it came to the stories they told, each one was inspiringly but absolutely different from each other story. I couldn't in the least doubt that each was telling the absolute truth, but here were four absolutely different truths relating to the same incident. The one thing that united all these gentlemen – for each detested the other, and said that if any views but his own prevailed it would spell ruin for Ireland – was a quite sincere, a quite deep liking for the Rt Hon. A.J. Balfour.

THE SLEEPLESS WIFE

When I wrote that Lord Chesterfield was the only successful Viceroy we ever sent to Ireland, I did not mean to say that he was the only successful Governor – for the only successful Governor we ever gave them was Mr Balfour, and, official political screaming apart, he was the only popular one because he was the only one that ever put up a square fight, just as he is the only living politician of prominence who has ever put up a square fight against anything. (And my feelings will not let me omit to quote here a passage from a letter I have just received from a Yorkshire Tory friend – the same Tory friend who was so amiably concerned at the thought of the dreadful things that the Ulsterman would do to the poor lovable Irish.) 'Here,' he writes, 'with cheerful indifference we roll down the slopes. Myself I see bureaucracy at the bottom. And of all nations, except the Russian, we have the least aptitude for the bureaucratic. I met yesterday a miner's wife who had lain awake all night because Balfour had gone. It amazed me.' I do not know why this should amaze my friend, for, when he has been able to act of his own free will, there has been no occasion upon which Mr Balfour has not done the right thing and said the right word. And there is nothing astonishing in the fact that a Yorkshire miner's wife should have felt these things and have had her rest disturbed. We have all felt them, and all of our rests have been disturbed. For myself, as long as I can remember, I have been for Mr Balfour, right or wrong – and, of course, for Miss Pankhurst; but that that falls in another department. Mr Balfour has officially opposed Home Rule. He was, it must be remembered, only the Constitutional Leader of his party, and not its autocrat. If only he had been! But he had to be the protagonist of the majority of his party, and the majority of Mr Balfour's party was Lord Northcliffe. I don't in the least blame Lord Northcliffe, though I don't in the least want what Lord Northcliffe wants. But he, at any rate, was the only man of the Conservative democracy who had the courage to go on grinding his axe until he was grinding all alone; until he was the Conservative Party, and Mr Balfour had, as his loyal duty to voice Carmelite House, which is where Lord Northcliffe has acted. At the eleventh hour, as I have said – or, really, it was at 11.59 – some of us Tories got into the last ditch and squealed, but until then we were the most discreditable mob of cowards shivering before the democratic sheet and turnip. Mr Balfour's business was to voice us, and we were not there to be voiced. There was only Lord Northcliffe. What else could Mr Balfour have done?

INEVITABLE HOME RULE

But even in Ireland Mr Balfour did the right thing – did the only thing which could have been done to make Home Rule possible. He settled the question of the Irish landlords. Without that a Parliament on College Green would have been impossible today. I don't particularly care about Irish landlords – or, at any rate, they are the landlords I least like. But, of course, we could not have deserted them any more than we can now desert Ulster. Fortunately, Mr Balfour equitably disposed of the landlords' claims – and all that we have to do is to look after Ulster. Of course, if Ulster fights with the weapons of the flesh, we shall have to send British soldiers against them, as we should have to send British soldiers against Mohammedans in India if they marched upon Hindus. We can't have sectarian nonsense of that sort in an empire or even a bureaucracy today. And we shall have to exile Sir Edward Carson to Ceylon, where beneath a palm tree he can emulate Arabi Pasha. But let me repeat again, Home Rule is inevitable; and that is a good thing, because we, as Tories, cannot go on having the rags of Kilmainham blowing for ever in our faces. We have been hindered by the Irish question in everything that we have had to do for the last twenty-five years. We have to see that Ulster gets its proper share of representation, which the Liberals will diddle it out of if they possibly can, and then Ulster must see to it that it maintains a compact body of disciplined men that will be overwhelmingly strong among the twenty-four parties with violent hatreds and incomprehensible ideals with which the Irish Parliament will seek to administer the affairs of the parish pump. We must see to it that their control is limited to the affairs of the parish pump. And above all, we must see to it that in the Imperial Parliament there must be fewer Irish members than those who represent London. For the population of Ireland is somewhat smaller than that of London.

END OF THE WHIGS

With these cries, and with this conscience, we may very safely go to the country, which is not such a confounded fool as the party Leaders think. It ought to be easy to make it plain to every decent man in these realms by means of amendments to the Whig Home Rule Bill – it ought to be perfectly easy to make it plain to the country that the whole end and aim of Whig statesmanship today is so to jerrymander the constituencies that the Whigs may remain in power for ever. When once the country realizes that, there will be an end of the present Whig leaders.

Bystander, 32 (29 November 1911), 438, 440.

Pan and The Pantomime

G.B. PAN

When I first thought of the title for this article it struck me as admirable, for, by 'Pan', I meant Mr Bernard Shaw. But now I see that there is a certain ambiguity; for looking on Boxing Night at the boards of Drury Lane I was overwhelmed by the remembrance of Peter. Yet, if you come to think of Mr Bernard Shaw, he would make an admirable Pan. He is everywhere; he is sweetly humorous with the remarkably bitter after-taste; it is impossible to get away from him; and he is a great god. All these things was He who invented the Pan-pipes.

VICTORIOUS SHAW

Mr Shaw has conquered the world – the real world, not merely the world of Intellectuals – in a most amazing, in a most bewildering manner. He has really even conquered the pantomime. For the lines upon Boxing Night that made the most impression upon the immense house at Drury Lane were not those referring to the licking of stamps, and were not those referring to the fact that, if you have any money at all, it is nowadays much cheaper to be dead than to be alive, and were not even those referring to Mr Bonar Law. No, they occurred when Miss Fanny Brough,[1] who was making her first appearance in that class of entertainment, advanced to the footlights to speak her two lines of the epilogue. They were to the effect that this was Fanny's first pantomime, and she hoped the audience would not greet it with 'pshaw!'[2] The house did not greet it with 'pshaw!' It rocked; it was brought down; there was nothing that it did not do that it could have done in the circumstances.

THE HUMOUR OF UNHAPPINESS

Of course, a good deal of this was due to Miss Fanny Brough's personal charm. It was an extraordinary charm. I have never seen anybody look so gloriously unhappy upon the stage. In the wings they had shoved her into a pierrot's costume, and she obviously did not like it. Later, they shoved her into a paper-bag in order to cook her in the Ogre's oven, and she still more obviously did not like it. And during the whole unwieldy entertainment she looked upon all the other performers on those boards with the sort of disgusted dislike that you will see upon the face of a suburban lady who has got by accident into a third-class smoking-compartment that contains already the eleven members of a half-intoxicated football team. It was real Shavian humour introduced into the realms of Harry Payne.[3]

1 [Fanny Brough, 1854–1914; leading actress, known particularly for comedy.]
2 [Allusion to Shaw's *Fanny's First Play* (1911).]
3 [Harry Payne, clown and pantomimist.]

And although Miss Brough did not herald herself with the words, 'Here we are again!' there was no doubt that she was saying for herself and Mr Shaw, 'Here we are for the first time.' And it will certainly not be the last.

SHAW'S FIRST PANTOMINE

No, it will certainly not be the last. For Mr Shaw is everywhere. Not only is he at the Little Theatre, where you would expect him to be, but he is also at the Criterion, where his success mildly surprises one, and he is at the Palace, where he is just simply amazing. (He is not, that is to say, at the Palace at the moment of writing, but I understand that he is to re-appear there by the time these words reach the eye of the public. Also I am informed that he has been commissioned to write the Drury Lane pantomime for 1915. By that time Messrs Glover, G.R. Sims, Dix, Arthur Collins, and everybody else connected with the present *régime* at 'The Lane' will have received their peerages, will be millionaires, and will no longer write for this or any other stage.) But at the Palace yesterday Mr Shaw was, and tomorrow he will be again, just simply amazing. And why he is so really amazing is that there he is really so enlightening. As I have said elsewhere, I am one of the old guard of admirers of Mr Shaw. When I was a boy in the eighties I applauded him for being an Anarchist. Afterwards, in the nineties, I groaned at him for 'ratting' to Socialism. Afterwards, but still in the nineties, I applauded rapturously the very first performance of *Arms and the Man*, and since then I have applauded with a gradually decreasing fervour every one of Mr Shaw's plays. Now I have found him out – with the aid of the audience of the Palace Theatre.

SHAW – SUBURBAN!

For years, and years, and years – for all these years, in fact – Mr Shaw has been telling us that he is an acute Irishman. But he is not; he is just a muddled Englishman. For years, and years, and years – for all these years, in fact – Mr Shaw has been telling us that he is a cosmopolitan writer of modern drama. But he isn't. He is a suburban writer of 'well-made plays'. Let me dispose of the second accusation first – the accusation of suburbanism. If you go to the Palace Theatre to witness the performance of *How He Lied to Her Husband*, you will be astonished – if, like myself, you are an ardent Shavian of twenty years' standing – to discover that the quite enthusiastic audience does not laugh in the least at what for twenty years you have considered to be excruciatingly funny. It does not begin to laugh when, for instance, the poet announces that he is a first-class boxer. It does not see anything funny in that. Because it just simply does not know anything about poets. It does not even know that they are invariably immoral. But we of the suburbs, who for twenty years have read Mr Shaw with amusement, tempered by awe, do know all about poets. We know that they are frail creatures, like John Keats, who died of a *Quarterly*

Review. So we laugh, so we used to laugh consumedly, when the young poet of *How He Lied to Her Husband* proposed to smash the husband to a pulp after he had abducted the wife. And all the jokes of Mr Shaw's at which we used to laugh were calculated to appeal to a suburban audience – to a small clique whose men wore flannel shirts, whose women wore dresses of curtain serge and amber beads; whose favourite reading consisted of the 3,198 Fabian tracts; who were all of them members of the Fabian Society, and who had the most sternly and Puritanically immoral views about the sanctity of marriage.

A BLOW FOR THE EARNEST

But the good audience at the Palace Theatre, and the good audience at the Criterion, know nothing about these things. The audience at the Criterion is slightly more suburban than that at the Palace, but even there Mr Shaw has come out into the open. Mr Loraine's reading of *Man and Superman* is not Mr Granville Barker's. The Fabian jokes of the play are not underlined, but the cranky amiabilities of Mr Stephen Tanner appear not Fabian, but human oddities, fit to appeal to people who have never heard about Fabian tracts. Similarly, to return to the performance at the Palace Theatre, what we old Shavians used to regard with awe and reverence the audience there just roars at. For the audience does just roar with delighted laughter at the eccentric husband who wants to be smashed into pulp by a young poet insufficiently eager to abduct his wife. This struck the Palace audience as being merely the turn of genius in a cranky and amusing story. To us of the old guard who wore flannel shirts or curtain serge and amber beads, it was the voice of the master prophet preaching an inspired ethics – to the effect that the marriage tie is not sacred, and that every commercial husband ought to desire to facilitate his wife's running away with a poet.

THE PROFESSIONAL PLAYWRIGHT

That was what it really amounted to. And you see Mr Shaw, with the ingenious plots of all his plays from the time when he wrote *Man and Superman* until the time when so dismally he failed with his 'conversation plays', was just giving us 'well-made' plays in disguise. It was just Gilbert and Sullivan without the Sullivan, and with immensely better construction. *Arms and the Man* was a well-made play; *Man and Superman* was a well-made play; *John Bull's Other Island* was a well-made play. *Major Barbara* was not quite such a well-made play. *Getting Married* was rather a bore. For the fact is that Mr Shaw is too English to write 'conversation plays'. If you want a good and really thrilling play of that description, you have to go to some sort of foreigner – *The Lower Depths* was thrilling and sustaining because poor, dear Maxim Gorky really felt, and his emotions carried you along. So it was with the Irish Players, too. So it is with some

German writers. But Mr Shaw is absolutely heartless. He doesn't feel anything at all. That is why his humour is hard and unpleasant; that is why his characters are all hard and unpleasant characters. I am not in the least reproaching him for this. It is a jolly good thing that in some manifestation of English art there should be something that does not taste like the cream from inside an inferior chocolate. But in his 'conversations' Mr Shaw does not feel and he does preach, and a preacher who preaches without feeling is inevitably a bore.

LITERATURE IN THE THEATRE

Indeed, when it comes to putting a problem upon the stage, Mr Arnold Bennett, who is a vastly less experienced playwright, simply does 'stunts' all round Mr Shaw. On the whole, I think we may be glad that the literary touch is bubbling up through the fissures of theatrical slate. For Mr Shaw is a literary man; Mr Barrie is a literary man; M. Maeterlinck is a literary man; Mr Gordon Craig is more a literary man than anything else. And Boxing Night's pantomime at the 'Lane' showed the influences of all these gentlemen. The stage was frequently in complete darkness, and there were all sorts of lime-light effects. That was Mr Gordon Craig. The introduction of Miss Fanny Brough, who, in a lady-like way, was quite out of the picture, was just a Shavian touch. The adorable little Hop-o'-My-Thumb, played in a way to bring tears to your eyes by Miss – or was it Master? – Renée Mayer – that was just a miniature edition of Miss Pauline Chase playing Peter Pan. And there were boring interludes with ingenious scenic effects that were for all the world as unbearably dismal as M. Maeterlinck's *Blue Bird* itself. But the old pantomime humour was almost altogether gone. There was no bibulous comedian in woman's clothes, but there was a dry, quaint king who had lost his memory, played by an actor who was a genius in his way. There was also quite a funny horse that bit a strolling player. But that was the last relic of the old days.

THE NEW PANTOMIME

And what an amazing house! How it roared. It suggested that it was the arbiter of the destiny of great nations. But, at any rate, Mr George R. Sims and his colleagues have discovered that what the public wants is *The Blue Bird* plus *Peter Pan* plus the stage effects of Mr Gordon Craig – plus, above all, the suburban English humour of Mr Shaw. Nevertheless, I hope when Mr Shaw comes to write the pantomime in 1915 he will leave us the comedian of genius playing a king who has lost his memory and a funny horse that will bite out, let us say, the red whiskers of the stage dramatist. But probably he will not. Well, well, the old order changeth, yielding place to …

Bystander, 33 (10 January 1912), 82, 84.

Literary Portraits and Other Essays from *The Outlook*, 1913–15

I. Mr Compton Mackenzie and *Sinister Street*

I.

Some years ago I contributed to an extinct – and by me at least sincerely regretted – organ, the *Tribune*, a series of articles under the above heading. I take them up again partly because I had not, at the time of that paper's death, finished saying all that I wanted to say; partly because the personnel, or at any rate the aspect of the personnel, of the literary world in this country has undergone a very considerable change. At that date the outlook was full of hope; there were writers like Mr de Morgan who were just beginning careers; others like Messrs Wells, Bennett, and Galsworthy who were lions young enough, but already emitting, if I may use the term, formidable roars; there were the established artists in their vigorous primes, like Mr Conrad and Mr Henry James; there were the still living writers who appeared to have almost classical positions, like Mr Meredith, Mr Swinburne, and Mr Hardy, who, since Providence is sometimes kind, is still with us. Today we shift the canvas of the panorama a definite step onwards…

The classical writers of yesterday are dead – Swinburne and Meredith. Mr James, having published his definitive edition, has, as it were, taken classical honours; Mr Conrad is the undisputed Prince of Prose; Messrs Wells, Bennett, and Galsworthy have now given us a sufficient bulk of work to sit assured, and classed in what I believe are called the seats of the mighty. And the outlook – *The Outlook* too, for the matter of that – is full of hope; there is, that is to say, a sufficiency of younger men coming on to make the job of continuing such a series as this worthwhile: there is Mr D.H. Lawrence, on whom I at least pin the most enormous hopes; there is Mr Stephen Reynolds, who continues to analyse the life of what he chooses to call the Poor Man; there is Mr Pound, who, with his humorous appearance is seriously enough undertaking the considerable job of starting a new movement in poetry. (This is not an inclusive survey, but merely a list of the two or three names that jump into my mind. Lord Randolph Churchill forgot Goschen upon a memorable occasion; I may well have forgotten the Henry James of tomorrow. Well – there is Mr

Onions!) At any rate, they are there all right, les jeunes!

Men, however, and however young, don't matter much; even a genius or so does not matter much! The real point for the contemplative critic is whether the collective action of those young men with the vine-leaves in their hair, or of those two or three geniuses, is sufficient to form consciously or no, a movement. For it is only by movements that literature – or anything else – can be carried forward. If the effort of today does not to some extent carry on the effort of yesterday; if the effort of tomorrow does not show some signs of carrying forward the effort of today, thus solidifying the edifice, or, if you like, broadening out the stream – then the contemplation of the Body Corporate of Literature becomes a comparatively unprofitable task – the consideration not of a fine town or stream but that of congregation of unrelated buildings, of unconnected pools. I do not mean to say that even this latter might not be an interesting task, but it is a task not so interesting as the discovery of a systematized effort in a group of beings, though the effort, or even the system, may be unconscious enough. What we desire is to be able to say of our day as was said of a certain Roman: 'Opera sub Tiberio semi-imperfecta...' and so on; to be able to say that whereas certain men have set up edifices of sumptuous marble, certain others are still engaged in building in the nobler material further edifices upon vacant lots. This, I think, we can do today.

In the series of articles that I contributed to the *Tribune* it was possible enough to feel at the time – and it has become a certainty now – that the quality of Hope attached mostly to the three writers Mr Wells, Mr Bennett, and Mr Galsworthy. At that date both Mr Wells and Mr Bennett did two separate types of work – the story-telling type by which they purported to support life, make their names known, and obtain popularity – and the more earnest or, at any rate the more significant type of novel which, in essence, is a work of history. And to this latter class of work in these three writers most of the hope of that dead day attached itself. (Mr James was doing it all the time; Mr Conrad was a separate genius.) What one hoped was that Mr Wells and Mr Bennett would make enough money by writing 'stories', and that Mr Galsworthy would take himself seriously enough to set out upon the exclusive writing of the historic novel. For in the end the really historical novels are the chronicle of Brakelond, the works of Defoe, Richardson, Smollett, Mark Rutherford, and George Gissing – the chroniclers of their own day. The Gadzooks style of thing, whether it be *Julius Caesar*, *Salammbô*, the *Castle of Otranto*, the *Tower of London*, or my own contrivances, is merely a display of ingenuity with no further significance than just the amount of ingenuity displayed...

Mr Wells, Mr Bennett, and Mr Galsworthy, the fates being propitious, did really continue their historical labours almost to the exclusion of the 'story-telling' vein, and thus the reproach to the English novel of being a merely negligible collection of desultory anecdotes began to pass. For if the novel, as literature, is to have any serious claim to the position of a saviour of society – and it is no good bothering one's head about anything if that anything has not got at least a sporting – a ten to one – chance of becoming a potential saviour of society – the novel must be a picture of manners, a chronicle of movements, or of parts of movements.

II.

From this point of view (I am leaving out for the moment the question of Art) you could not well have a better book than *Sinister Street*, and I am very glad of it, because Mr Compton Mackenzie is a young man whose work I have been, as the phrase is, 'following' for some years, and whose personality I find attractive. Mr Mackenzie is of distinguished theatrical origin, which is in itself a significant matter. For whatever may be said for or against theatrical people as a class, they have before them the perpetual necessity of being observers of manners. If they observe well they make good actors; if they don't they can, at best, but rant. (I think, at least, that I am right in saying this.)

Trained then in what must have been a school of observation and, one presumes, in reasonably easy circumstances, our author attended a presumably slipshod public school of the usual type, and then one of the usual old universities where, as was probably right and proper he paid more attention to the social side of things and to amateur theatricals than to the curriculum. Given in addition a gentlemanly-scholarly contemplation of the Classics –

> *Valle sub umbrosa locus est, aspergine multa*
> *Umidus ex alto desilientis aquae*[1]

and so on; given a by no means German attention to the picturesque parts of history, and temporary passions for one game or another, and there you have, I should say, puer felix – or a very unfortunate one, as the cat jumps. Happily felis catus came down on the right side of the wall.

Beginning his publishing with poems, our author presented us successively with a patch-and-powder comedy of great ingenuity, and a theatrical story notable for minute observation of detail. *Carnival*, however, whatever its merits, and they were considerable, was still a 'story', and suffered from being too much written, from being a little too extravagantly picturesque. The danger was that our young friend might find tales more ingenious, and language more florate, and end in the school of the late R.L. Stevenson – the gentleman who put back the clock

1 [Ovid, *Fasti*, 4.427–8; 'In a shady vale there is a place moist with the abundant spray from a high waterfall']

of English fiction fifty years. (That remark is not mine, though I heartily concur in it; it was actually, in all its truth, made by that great poor genius, Stephen Crane!)

But it was on the right side of the wall that the good cat descended, and with *Sinister Street* our author joins the goodly band of historians. For *Sinister Street* is really history – the history of a whole class, in a whole region, during a whole period of life. Mr Mackenzie's central figure is an apparently ordinary boy, in an apparently ordinary English home in West Kensington, going to the ordinary slipshod preparatory school, to the ordinary slipshod London public school, in preparation for the ordinary good time at one of the older universities. It will thus be observed that Mr Mackenzie knows of what he writes. I have indeed never read a more carefully documented study of real life in boyhood and in early adolescence – or, at any rate, I have never read one that was so documented and yet so interesting; or one in which it is so subtly and so cleverly brought out that the apparently ordinary English boy in the apparently ordinary English home is really the odd creature in an odd establishment that all English people really are. (It was Mr Galsworthy in that most delightful of all his plays, *Joy*, whose governess made the tremendous discovery that the situation of every soul in these old islands is a 'special case', and that, really, is Mr Galsworthy's chief benefaction to humanity.) *Sinister Street* itself, then, is a special street; West Kensington is an extraordinarily odd, even a romantic quarter; the boy of the book is a special case – and that is English life of that class. All the while we have been talking of the drab lives of the suburbs…

I don't mean to say that *Sinister Street* has not got its artistic faults; though, since these are more apparent whilst one reads the novel, they may well be slighter than struck me at first. Whilst, that is to say, I was reading the book, I was struck by the hardness of the handling. The details about schoolday caps, stamp collections, sweaters, high collars, struck me as being in a sense too provincial – too exclusively appertaining to schoolboy life, and given with too little sense of fusing and of atmosphere. How exactly I should want to alter the handling I could not say; I should want myself to get a little more of haze between the definitenesses; a little less of the continual definition of material objects. And yet I may well be wrong. After all, for eighty years or so the great French writers have preached the lesson that the only way in which to render a psychological state is to render the material objects that evoke it, and that is the truest of all truths. And indeed the memory of *Sinister Street* – I read it about three weeks ago – is a peculiarly atmospheric one. I seem to see the twilights amongst the not at all high plane-trees, amongst the labyrinthine streets of not very high brick villas, the lights shining out in the paper-shops; the 'buses, just lit up, too – I seem to see, extraordinarily, the landscape of my own boyhood. So that possibly *Sinister Street* is a work of real genius – one of those books that really exist otherwise than as the decorations of a publishing season – exist along with *L'Education sentimentale, Fathers and Children, Heart of Darkness*, and *The Purple Land*. One is too cautious – or, with all the desire to be generous in the world, too ungenerous – to say anything like that, dogmatically, of a quite young writer. But I shouldn't wonder?

At any rate there is a fine movement stirring in English literature – I mean amongst novels – and novels are the only things worth writing.

Outlook, 32 (13 September 1913), 353–4.

VI. Mr John Galsworthy and *The Dark Flower*

I.

It is the curse of cynicism, just as it is the curse of handling social grievances in terms of art, that, as if they were acids working on alkalis, the satirical characters of any novel utterly destroy the virtuous protagonists of the author in his constructive moods. The virtuous protagonists, on the other hand, invariably destroy the effect of the book altogether. Becky Sharp, I mean, kills Amelia Osborne so effectively that Thackerayan Virtue was knocked out of the world for good and all by *Vanity Fair*. No woman, after reading that work, could ever have wanted to be like Amelia, no man like Major Dobbin. Amelia and Dobbin, on the other hand, take their revenge on their creator by making *Vanity Fair*, whenever they appear on the moving canvas, utterly, oh, desolatingly dull! And they do it even when they are not on the canvas, for when the author is describing his adventuress's adventures, suddenly a prick of conscience comes into the midst of his gusto. He remembers that he has forgotten the Amelia-cum-Dobbin point of view, and straightway starts in to tell you that his own heart is really in the right place…

As it was with Thackeray of *Vanity Fair*, so was it with Dickens of *Bleak House*, with Alphonse Daudet of *L'Immortel*. For, in that one particular, the French are no whit ahead of their English colleagues, and nothing is more desolatingly dreary than the Virtuous Artist and his wife in the French writer's masterpiece…

And as it was with his predecessors so it is apt to be with Mr Galsworthy. Mr Galsworthy is the best man in the world – absolutely the best, with a heart of pure gold! He is also the best satirist in England – the only satirist. Now, to be a finished satirist and to have a heart of gold is a very ticklish affair; just as to have the gift of ironical observation and to desire to be a constructive observer is to be in some peril. On the one hand, you are keenly alive to the ridiculous contrasts of a comic world; on the other you desire to construct caryatids, with moulded breasts and hair like corn, groaning under the weight of all the balconies of unreformed Society.

Mr Galsworthy, with his fine, pretty smile – I don't mean his physical smile, though I don't see why I shouldn't, for the matter of that – goes through this ant-heap of ours, through our dining-rooms with the heavy oak furniture, the steel engravings of the Good Shepherd and the Stag at Bay, the tantalus on the sideboard, the cigar-cabinet made to hold two thousand cigars beside the black marble and steel of the fireplace. He lifts the violet velvet window-hangings that let a little dust powder on to the head because the poor parlourmaid is *so* tired. In the street without he perceives the Watercress-seller, and the fine smile vanishes; the grim jaws clench together (I don't mean the physical jaws of our author); the note-book comes out; echoes from the *Woman Who Did*, from William Morris, from Jean-Jacques Rousseau, from the Chancellor of the Exchequer, from Henry George, from Ibsen, and St Vincent de Paul whisper through the suddenly shuddering air. And along with the fine smile goes Observation.

Now that is a pity. It is a pity for Literature; it is a pity also for the Watercress-seller and for the Woman Who Has Left Her Husband. For Mr Galsworthy could do so much for these poor people if he relied on his own satiric temperament (which, heaven knows, might be a solvent powerful enough!). He could, if he only would, stand so well upon his own bottom and forget about Jean-Jacques. Even St Vincent he has enough of in himself...

It is especially a pity for the woman who has left her husband, because it is apt to turn her into a bore, so that you forget that hers really is a Hard Case. I was thinking, of course of *The Fugitive* (Duckworth and Co.), which is being played at the Prince of Wales'. Mr Galsworthy is such a magnificent dramatist. *The Silver Box* was such a fine play; *Joy* is such a fine play; *The Fugitive* is almost always such a fine play. I don't know any other dramatist who, for me, really counts.

I say this advisedly, though in my moments of irritation with our irritating author I am apt to call him a dreary nuisance. For the feeling of almost mad rage, that comes to one when Mr Galsworthy shouts soliloquies bang in the middle of something really fine and dramatic – just when you want to forget that his crew of doctrinaire humanitarians exist in this distracting town – that feeling of exasperation is apt to persist in the form of sullen resentment ages and ages after one has left the playhouse. It is the most exasperating thing that I know. There was the *Pigeon*. Nothing could have been finer. It went on and on; it was making every one of its points. Anyone not an ox could have seen what was at the bottom of the piece of life that was being presented. And then – Bang! Some chap on the stage sat down on the corner of a table and began to shout and spout an interminable river of the praise of vagabondage. One did not want it; the play did not need it. It hardened hearts. Yes, it actually hardened hearts…

I was talking during one of the entr'actes to a gentleman who is, let us say, the biggest whisky-distiller the world has ever seen. Said he, rather musingly 'Charity! Yes, I've tried Charity and it did not work. I once sent two guineas to a laundress in the Temple and she tried to blackmail me afterwards. But I think I will try Charity again. I suppose if I founded an orphanage… They couldn't get up a blackmailing case out of an orphanage – could they now?…' But as we went out of the theatre he said, 'Oh, Charity! Damn Charity! I've had enough.' And I'll be hanged – I'll really be hanged – if I did not feel like him. Alas! for the poor Watercress-seller. That soliloquy did for him.

I suppose that Mr Galsworthy will say that, being what he is and having done what he has done, he can afford himself the *menu plaisir* of a soliloquy. But he cannot, because outside his window there stand the figures of the indigent and of the woman who has left her husband. It is his duty either to let their insistent figures alone or to do his real best for them.

The Fugitive is a very excellent illustration. Whenever Mr Galsworthy's characters are making their hard material points the mind of the audience is apt to be set running – the mind of the reader is apt to be set going – upon what might well be a 'hard case' of sufficiently frequent occurrence to be worth considering. When that is to say, the heroine suggested – for she only just suggested – that her husband's embraces were distasteful to her, the audience could feel for her position varying degrees of real sympathy. She was really in a tight and odious place. It is, in fact, impossible to imagine a more horrible position for a woman. But when the well-developed, not neurasthenic, and quite attractive lady writhed about the stage and groaned because her husband found Big Ben more interesting than a sunset cloud, almost all sympathy went away from her. When her friend, the literary gentleman, urged her to grow her wings, cut the galling knots, and affront the boundless empyrean – then, then! the whole sympathy went round to the afflicted family. It really was, as one of Mr Galsworthy's characters would say, a bit thick.

Ibsen is so very dead – though even he was once alive; 1882 is so very dead, though it was, truly, once the current year, like this year. And we poor literary gentlemen …. Ah, we poor literary gentlemen – these are no longer our fat years. We cannot afford – not any one of us can afford – to squander our substance of sentimentality in that way. We could in 1882. The guileless public of that decade accepted us and our long hair, our unpaid bills, our spoutings about free love and all the rest of it. But that is all gone. We jolly well have to behave ourselves nowadays, as one of Mr Galsworthy's characters would say. So that not one – not one solitary one!

– Literary Gentleman of today would dare to talk as Mr Galsworthy's Malise talked to the unfortunate lady whose suicide on the threshold of a brothel (for Mr Galsworthy – in heaven's name why? – had not the strength of mind to let her get as far as the brothel itself!) he so dismally caused.

No, there is not one Literary Gentleman who would talk like that, though I am advised that one solitary swallow from the tepid eighties still flits across our wintry landscapes and would like to write that sort of stuff. But it can't be done...

It is amazing to me that Mr Galsworthy, with his fine sense of irony, will not delve so far into the nature of humanity – of the humanity for which he writes – as to see these patent facts. We *want* nowadays – really the whole world wants nowadays – to sympathize with ladies who are uncongenially married. Even the Churches would welcome some putting of a case that would give them a chance to relax their rules relating to marriage. But talk about clouds and the growth of wings will not do it – only the hard and convincing putting of the material facts of hard cases will do it. And there is nothing that Mr Galsworthy can do better, and there is no one can do it better than Mr Galsworthy. Look at *The Silver Box*.

Given a lady who wants to leave her husband for valid reasons – physical abhorrence, drink, cruelty to a dog or a kitten, or if you like, merely because she wants to have some fun and will take the risks; given, if you must have a Literary Man, one who will say, 'My dear child – to leave your husband is a devil of a job; but if you positively *must* do so I will give you all the legs up that I can'; and given all the rest of *The Fugitive* just as it is, but without the cup of cold poison at the end, and there you have something. You have considerably something...

For, mind you, *The Fugitive* is already something; but it is a thing like a picture of which the foreground is painted by a chocolate-box manufacturer, the rest being forceful, vigorous, arousing. You have to cover the foreground with your hand before you get any real enjoyment out of it...

There was once some infernal chap in the Dark Ages who was given a satire to read. He said, 'This is all very well, but it isn't *constructive*. Where is the author's remedy for the evils that he girds against?' You hear his shocked and imbecile tones... And ever since that distant day every fool who has had a satire to consider has always asked that imbecile question; and every poor fool who has ever written or contemplated writing a satire has always asked himself, 'This is all very well, but where is *my* constructive remedy?' And straightway he has indulged himself in floridities that are more fatal than drink. But no woodman, cutting down brush, finds it necessary to have a plan for planting the woodlands with geraniums or formulates it in impassioned soliloquies...

No, satire is in itself constructive. For, as certainly as when you cut down underwood in a copse the wood-flowers spring up in your introduced sunlight, so surely does satire clear out the dark forest that is the hearts of men,[1] so that the decencies and kindnesses that there are in that soil do find the happy sun. But you must let the bluebells grow in their own way…

Well, perhaps one day Mr Galsworthy will give us again a work of pure and delicate satire, and will enshrine the kindly and generous thoughts that its production causes to arise in him, in a separately published volume of poems or dreams or visions. That would be all that the most exacting of critics would demand, for that would give us two very satisfactory works, differing in kind.

★★★

Outlook, 32 (18 October 1913), 527–8.

VII. Mr Percival Gibbon and *The Second-Class Passenger*

I.

The writers of whom I have latterly treated, Mr Wells, Mr Bennett, Mr Galsworthy – and to some extent Mr Mackenzie and Mr W.B. Maxwell[1] – have been rather concerned with modern Occidental life as we live it than with romance or art. In a sense they are all of them sociologists, rather grave, rather depressed, not markedly full-blooded, concerned rather to read the solution of some riddle suggested to them by the baffling grey pattern that our life is than with telling good tales in a rattling way.

Yet, really the whole concern of art is the telling of a good tale in a rattling sort of way. That was, in essence, the task of Maupassant, of Flaubert, of the Goncourts, of Turgenev. They were not interested in solving for the reader the riddle of the universe; they wanted to 'grip'. The technical essentials of the French school of fiction – the *progression d'effets*, the architectonics, and even *le mot juste* itself – were not so many mysteries of a priesthood. They were just gropings after methods of interesting *l'homme moyen sensuel*. If English critics and English writers would

1 [Ford frequently echoed this remark from Turgenev's 'Lisa'. See *Ancient Lights* (London, 1911), p. xi; and the title page to *The New Humpty-Dumpty* (London, 1913).]

1 [William Babbington Maxwell (1866–1938), one of the illegitimate children of M.E. Braddon and her publisher John Maxwell, was a prolific novelist, specializing in social satire and stories of sexual betrayal.]

just make the effort to realize this simple fact they might carry the banner of fiction one step further, which is what decency demands of them. France, exhausted by the great productive struggle of last century, is enjoying a period of rest – is turning its attention to the re-birth of poetry as seriously and as practically as it took up the task of making prose a medium of just expression for reasonable and proper men. Germany never did and never will – until its barbaric language is regenerated – produce anything in prose that non-Germans could want to read. Russians are all too individualistic and obstinate to make any collective, any 'group' advances in an art the first of whose necessities is the final sacrifice of self. The Russian has to lecture.

It would remain then for England, where, whatever else may be said about the country, literature is alive, adolescent, and striving in a muddled way. But, just for that very reason, it is remarkable to observe how the virus of French influence has 'taken' in this land. It has produced sociologists. Anything that today 'counts' in an established sort of fashion, from Mr Bernard Shaw's productions to, let us say, Mr Maurice Hewlett's, is sober, earnest, purposeful realism, if it does not happen to be fantastic Utopianism. Now realism was only one side of the French movement, and certainly nothing was further from those writers than earnestness or depression. They might be harrowing, but it stopped at that. Even 'Coeur Simple' is cheerful in its treatment beside *Clayhanger*; it is vivid with episodes, with material objects, with curiosity.

No, the work that is being turned out for us by our novelists who now 'count' suggests nothing so much to me as a modern Anglican church with a brass-railed pulpit, and an active vicar directing with energy 'social endeavour' amongst the respectable poor. That of course is an excellent thing, but it is an odd one. It is rather like religion with theology left out and with faith turned materialist. For again, whatever the French school had or hadn't, they had faith – the faith that, if they turned out good art, sociology and the rest would follow. That is what Flaubert meant when he said that if his countrymen had read *L'Education sentimentale* France would have been spared the horrors of the débâcle. It is a very simple and human claim. The blacksmith is not decried for having as his motto the device: 'By hammer and hand all art doth stand.' The baker again will at most be smiled at if he claim that bread is the most important thing in the world, and that, so he but bake well, he may save his soul alive. No one expects the baker to deliver lectures on the land question before he turns to his ovens, or blacksmiths to march about demonstrating in favour of super-Dreadnoughts, though, at the back of the baker in the end is the land, and the apotheosis of smithery is the huge battleship. Those cobblers, in fact, are praised and get to heaven by sticking to their lasts. It is only the literary gentleman who is expected to be – who desires to be – a sort of a blooming hermaphrodite!

These ideas are suggested to me by falling by chance upon a book by Mr Percival Gibbon.

I do not know what Mr Gibbon may desire to 'do' with his books – promote Imperialism, found bull-rings? – Heaven knows what. At any rate nothing of the kind sticks out from the context of his work. *Frau Grobelaar's Leading Cases* was a set of good stories about Boers and things of that sort. *Margaret Harding* was a good story about some decent English people in South Africa who were much worried by a nigger. *The Second-Class Passenger* is a book of good short stories. But, although I have been carefully reading the last two books for the last ten days, I cannot gather from them any philosophy, code of morals that the writer may desire to promote, or any sociologically constructive desire. That is a great relief.

It is a great relief for, if you can read in any writer's – any English writer's – books for ten days at all; and if you can then discover none of those abstract attributes, you may then be certain – from the fact of the readability – that that writer is either something of an artist by nativity or that he has some artistic aspirations. And that I really mean.

The author of *Mr Sponge's Sporting Tour*, for instance is for me one of the most readable of novelists.[2] Now any English novelist or critic will tell you that that chap wasn't any sort of artist after the model of the French writers; therefore the French writers must be fools and art is all my eye and Betty Martin... But I think that is the wrong way of looking at it. The right way would be to study *Mr Sponge*; to study then *Boule de Suif*, or *La Maison Tellier*, or *Yvette*, and to do what you can with the lesson. The probability is that you would produce something really readable.

Mr Gibbon then must be either something of an artist by birth or he must have artistic aspirations. And, since I believe our author has some dislike to being styled the former (though I can't for the life of me say why it should be objectionable to be told that one has a certain gift!), I will limit myself here to saying that traces of Mr Gibbon's artistic aspirations are visible on every page of Mr Gibbon's books. To test quite genuinely that statement, whilst I was writing those words with my right, my left hand was opening, without looking at it, one of Mr Gibbon's books. I came upon these two sentences:

> It was a journey of a day and night, while that little train rolled at leisure through a world of parched sand, beyond the sand-hills to the eye-wearying monotony of the desert. Sometimes it would halt beside a tank and a tent, while a sore-eyed man ran along the train to beg for newspapers...

Now that last sentence is really good selection, observation, projection. Anyone of course could have written the first sentence; 'parched' as

2 [R.S. Surtees]

applied to the sand of a desert is not particularly illuminating; 'at leisure' strikes me as wrong when applied to a slow train, because the train had its job of getting somewhere and the very meaning of leisure is to have no preoccupation. Similarly, even in the second sentence Mr Gibbon ought not to have written 'the train' because he had already called that conveyance 'it'; 'carriages' or some word that would have visualized the train would have been better. But that having been said, there remain the tank, the tent, and the sore-eyed man who begged for newspapers. That is real observation; that is real art because it conveys to the reader not only information and interest (for it is interesting to be told that a man in the middle of the desert desires newspapers); it also gives a picture, an atmosphere, and, for what it is worth a civilization. It does it moreover in very few words.

Pray pardon my minute examination of such matters. That is my preoccupation in this world. I will try again:

> Two other figures brought up the rear, and likewise entered at the doorway and passed from sight. The first, as he became visible in the gloom beyond the light, was dimly grotesque; he seemed too tall and not humanly proportioned, a deformed and willowy giant. Once he was opposite the door his height explained itself: he was walking with both arms extended to their full length above his head and his face bowed between them. Possibly because the attitude strained him, he went with a gait as marked as his posture, a measured and ceremonial step as if he were walking a slow minuet. The light met him as he turned in the doorway, and Ford, staring in bewilderment, had a momentary impression that the face between the raised arms was black...

Now that is a very good piece of writing. It is true that 'likewise' is a disagreeable word when you mean 'also', that 'sight', 'light', and 'height' occurring so close together are disagreeable assonances and, by impeding the ear, impede also the run of the paragraph – and that is always to be avoided because the first thing that you have to do is to get your reader on. But the rest of the paragraph is quiet and formal English, with no Stevensonian epithets sticking out; and the matter of the paragraph, apart from the good picture, is valuable. The picture, that is to say, represents the nigger of the book (*Margaret Harding*) walking before an extended revolver, with his hands up – and it is all the better 'technique' because it is a little mysterious. It fixes itself on the imagination once the answer to the riddle is propounded.

Mr Gibbon is in fact possessed of a very sober and very sufficient technical equipment. He brings about his dramatic incidents very naturally and quietly. And that is all the better in that his subjects are usually subjects of action – subjects set in South Africa, in Algiers, in places where argument as a rule is represented to us as being of the 'kick him in the belly' order. But there is not so very much violence in Mr Gibbon's work. Occasionally he lets himself go, as when Christian Dupreez hits Boy Bailey in the saloon-bar; but Kamis on the other hand sets to work on that unfortunate individual with a proper economy of effort which makes him all the more effective. The Second-Class Passenger lays about him with a bronze image; Miss Gregory uses a hatpin with effect, in the dark; Mr Lucas bangs the Russian lieutenant on the head with a flute.

In addition Mr Gibbon has none of the meretricious omniscience of Mr Kipling – that omniscience that at first delights and afterwards causes so many misgivings; and he has none of the browbeating superiority of the usual Colonial novelist. I suppose him to be an Imperialist, but I do not know; I suppose him to have a sense of sympathy with negroes mishandled in South Africa, with Jews the victims of pogroms in Russia – but it does not stick out worryingly.

★★★

Outlook, 32 (25 October 1913), 571–2.

XII. Herr Arthur Schnitzler and *Bertha Garlan*

I.

★★★

Now, German is a good enough language for verse – a better, really, than English. The female rhymes are frequent and commodious, the vowels are less ugly. (There is not the short u sound of love and butter; the vowels are also more purely pronounced. If the word 'impossible' existed in German it would not be spoken 'impossibull'.) At any rate, it is a good enough medium and, since poets are not expected to be men of reason, they are allowed to use simple sentences. Heine could write 'Du bist wie eine Blume', and, as all the world knows, it is quite passable poetry. But if I wished gravely to report the fact to you, I should have to say something like 'Der Dichter versichert das Maedchen dass sie wie eine in Venedig gekaufte in Luxus-Zuge expedierte und mit "Raedler" abgelieferte Magnolia Blume aussieht'; I should have to add the inserted particulars whether I wanted to or no, in order to give sound, length, dignity to the statement. (The statement means, 'The poet assures the Maiden that she, like a, in Venice bought, by train-de-luxe despatched, and by express messenger delivered, magnolia blossom looks.') This is, of course, a rather burlesqued phrase; but here is another from the pages of a quite beautiful book by a quite beautiful writer: 'Und so sehr sie es mit ihrem Verstande wusste dass der Hugo, der da drin im Nebenzimmer mit jenem neuen schmerzlich gespannten Zug um die Lippen, auf dem Diwan schlief, dasselbe Menschenkind war, das vor wenig Jahren noch im Gartengespielt hatte –' ('And however much she might be intellectually convinced that the Hugo who was asleep, within the room, upon the sofa, with that new, strained fold about his lips, was the same child of Adam who, a year or so ago, had still played in the garden –') And you will observe that this is only the beginning. The full sentence contains forty-one words – ninety syllables – and three inversions, ending with 'hatte sterben sehen'.

Now, Arthur Schnitzler, from whom I have quoted, is one of the clearest stylists that ever used the German language for the expression of his thoughts, and the book from which I have quoted (*Frau Beate und ihr Sohn*) is one of the most touching and the most limpid of his excursions in psychological analysis. It is plain, then, that this writer has much to contend with.

Yet his day and his hour have arrived. He is known to two continents as the 'Austrian Maupassant'. Leaving Maupassant out for the moment (and *The Outlook* prints this week one of the most typical of Herr Schnitzler's contes, so that the reader may make the comparison for himself) let us consider the Viennese writer for himself alone.

To Germany Herr Schnitzler stands for a great deal – for a retracing of steps more than anything else. The usually sober enough critic of the *Berliner Zeitung am Mittag* becomes almost dithyrambic in his praise of *Der Weg ins Freie* (which is, indeed, a sort of Pilgrim's Progress of a poet's soul). It has just been capably translated into English by Mr Horace Samuel under the title *The Road to the Open* (Howard Latimer). The critic of the *Neue Freie Presse* calls *Frau Bertha Garlan* a masterpiece of psychological cabinet-work, and so indeed it is. And Mr Schnitzler has his school of followers that may well, as these things go, prove a lasting influence on literature.

He represents, none the less, a re-casting of steps. I have written often enough in these columns of the international main stream of the novel as an art-product, as opposed to the novels that grow like cabbages. The first effect of this tide in Germany was to force on a large growth of what was called 'realistisch' plants. These realistic books were written by authors ranging in importance from Sudermann to Bilse, who wrote the *Kleine Garnison*. They were influenced more by Zola than by the other Frenchmen, and they were very usually what in England is called 'nasty', black, gloomy, and very heavy. Of course, there were books like Freiherr von Ompteda's *Eysen* that were serious, sober, and monumental, or, like Thomas Mann's *Buddenbrooks*, that were really German interior studies, as it were, by Holbein.

II. *Bertha Garlan*. By Arthur Schnitzler

The product of the – for Germany – inevitable reaction is just exactly *Bertha Garlan*. For Germany, unlike England, is supremely self-conscious. The German Press and the German public alike began to say, 'We have had enough of this foreign influence, which is very nasty and un-German.' They began to ask for a revival of the German qualities of imagination, which is generally sentimentality. That might well have been a disaster; but it wasn't. For some years the main output of German fiction was distinguished by a sort of imbecility of super-men and *femmes incomprises*. Every second novelist was giving you the history of strong passionate engineers, wrestling with dykes against the sea, and forming affinities with super-women not their wives – that sort of thing. Then Mr Schnitzler appeared, and began to take hold of the popular imagination.

Mr Schnitzler is perhaps fifty. (I do not happen to have any German books of reference by me, but I think he was born in Vienna in the sixties.) He began life, at any rate, as a doctor, so that he looks at these careers of ours with some of that scientific and inner knowledge that doctors might possess if they were not, mostly, like other ordinary mortals, trying to hide from the facts of life. And life in Vienna is a very gay, a very sad, a very sober, a very wild affair; a little unreal, a little queer in its sense of values, a little theatrical, and extraordinarily wise. It is French in the sense that all real civilization must in the end tend towards French ideals and French culture. But Vienna differs from Paris in that it has never had a French Revolution. Its civilization is therefore very old, quite blasé, and very minutely evolved.

It is the reflection of this civilization that Schnitzler has given to the world – a civilization as full of paradoxes, of injustices, or immoralities as any play by Mr Bernard Shaw. There is, indeed, a strong undercolouring of Shaw life and Shaw situations in all Mr Schnitzler's work – the difference being that, whereas every announcement by Mr Shaw of a paradoxical injustice in English life, law, or love has the effect of a bomb, or at least of a cracker, the same thing is bedded in Mr Schnitzler's works as being part of the fabric of life – as being one of the inevitabilities. Mr Schnitzler is, in effect, so infinitely wiser, so infinitely more grown up, that Mr Shaw has, beside him, the aspect of a happy child playing in the Zoological Gardens.

It is the difference of the civilizations. In this country a man is knocked down by an insuperable disaster, and he is amazed. In Vienna – well, this is how Mr Schnitzler puts it: 'The utmost foresight and predetermined resolutions do not enable a man to bear disaster more easily, but only to meet it with a braver face.' Or again:

> Is it not a thing to shudder at, how one has the heart to speak jestingly, in one's days of prosperity, of the most fearful disasters, as if such

> things threatened other people alone and would never touch oneself! And then it comes and one does not quite realize it and one lives it down. And time passes by and one lives. (A woman is thinking of the death of a husband that she had much loved.) One sleeps in the same bed that once one shared with one's love, one drinks out of the self-same glass that once he touched with his lips; beneath the shadows of the same pines one picks strawberries where once one gathered them with one that shall never pick them again – and, in the end, one has not ever quite realized the significance of life or of death.

In the German that is a very beautiful passage with a touching, a melancholy cadence that I have not been able to render – but it gives you, upon the whole, the tone of Schnitzler's mind. And it strikes me as a very beautiful mind.

Of course, Mr Schnitzler's 'message' is not about municipal milk supplies, which is the grave, bold message of Mr Shaw; nor does he treat love and sex from moral or public points of view as do most English novelists. Viennese civilization is an old affair, and in trying to obtain readers for his books in this country I do not wish to do so by any false pretences. I should advise the English reader to begin with *Bertha Garlan* and to read afterwards *The Way into Freedom*, because the first book is less purely Viennese and the latter is very highly civilized. But neither book is one for the much talked-about but probably non-existent young person.

Bertha Garlan is the story of a woman who was satisfactorily but unromantically married to a husband who has been dead several years. She lives unromantically in a small town. One day she goes into Vienna and finds a lover. The lover treats her like a chattel, without much romance or any real love. And she goes back to the small town and the unromantic existence.

That is the whole of the story, and I do not imagine that many English readers will be found for it. It is, however, a very beautifully written, tender, and touching 'cabinet picture', as the German critic calls it. It is full of colour, of landscapes, of rivers, of woods, and of air, as are all this author's books. In all Schnitzler's writings, moreover, there is the scintillating, topsy-turvy humour, turning at times into grimness, that most people had a chance of tasting when Mr Barker produced the *Anatol* sketches some years ago; and again, last month – though that was mostly grim – in the *Green Cockatoo* at the Vaudeville. Of the two translations that have appeared this week, *Bertha Garlan* is perhaps the better done, but *Der Weg ins Freie* is a much more ambitious job. It is a difficult and sometimes a dangerous matter to translate a long book from the German; Germanisms seem to saturate your style. Or perhaps the translator of the latter work is a German. In any case both enterprises are wholly praiseworthy.

Outlook, 32 (29 November 1913), 753–4.

XXIII. Fydor Dostoevsky and *The Idiot*

I.

I must confess to having formed no settled opinion about Dostoevsky. For one thing, he seems to have been a very miserable man; for another, he had to write desperately hard to obtain a precarious living. And, finally, it is not my job to pontify, here or anywhere else. That is a thing that must be left to reviewers. If one utters confidently certain dogmas about the difficult, about the impossible, art of writing it is not because one feels any confidence about one's dicta. It is for quite another reason.

I will lay you down, very dogmatically, laws about the avoidance of assonances. I will tell you with extreme ferocity that what is to be aimed at in a style is something so unobtrusive and so quiet – and so beautiful if possible – that the reader shall not know that he is reading, and be conscious only that he is living in the life of the book. I don't want the reader ever to say whilst he is reading 'How clever this writer is!' I want him just to be happy, and to be oblivious of himself. (Of course when I write 'happy' I include in the adjective the happiness that comes in the contemplation of tragedy.) I will, I say, shout these things at you with an almost uncontrolled fury. But if you got me in a quiet moment you might very well hear me saying, 'What do we really know about it all? Perhaps an assonance is a quite desirable thing.' I don't know. And if I make these allegations confidently and hardly, with clear insulting words, it is only that attention may be drawn to them, and that more professionally critical intellects may set to work upon these matters. I don't in the least mind being disliked – *j'en ai soupé*. I don't in the least mind hurting anybody's feelings, since what I want to get up is a sort of Kilkenny row about literature. If the doctrines that I uphold prevail, well and good; if another set of doctrines, then at least somebody will be borne to heaven on their wings – quite a number of people I should think, for none of my doctrines seem to be particularly popular in these islands. But I do want anger; I do want fury; I do want either to burn or to be burnt at Smithfield.

Now the other day I chanced to utter some rather careless words about Dostoevsky. I wish I hadn't. For the poor chap was a miserable man, and I hate hitting even at the ghosts of the unhappy. For heaven's sake let him have all the glory that the world can offer him, so that his shade may be mightily rejoiced. And the poor chap had to drag his weary pen over miles and miles of paper to find himself an insufficient sustenance. May then, all the peaches and all the caviar of the world be piled up upon his altar, and all the Vouvray of France be poured over them as a libation. But when it comes to a matter of form I must a little stick to my guns, even if I have to go as far as to say that *The Brothers Karamazov* is not, in the matter of form, so consummate as *Fort comme la Mort*. What is the good of saying that it is? Dostoevsky was not aiming at Maupassant's target. He said himself that if he had had more time he would have rewritten; he would have compressed. Moreover, *The Brothers Karamazov* is not even a finished book. It is a mere preparation for writing the life of a saint. In that sense I was simply careless when I wrote that the monastery scene (and by that I was thinking only of the scene of the dead monk whose body gave out an evil odour) was an excrescence in *The Brothers Karamazov* as it stands. It is no doubt only an excrescence to that extent. As part of the preparation of Dostoevsky's hero for a saintly life, to be described in subsequent volumes, it is easy enough to see that what is for the moment an excrescence would have been no doubt a necessity for the finished work and so perfectly in accordance with the form.

The Brothers Karamazov as it stands is in fact merely the pedestal to an immense statue. What I stupidly said is that the pedestal bulges out too much upon one side. What Mr Swinnerton replies is that it doesn't bulge, and to back himself up he accuses my manner of reading of being 'digging through a book'. He has really missed his opportunity, for what he should have said was: 'Yes, the pedestal appears to bulge; but how beautifully that will be accounted for when the great statue stands upon it leaning over to the other side!' I don't of course know how Mr Swinnerton would have me read a book. I did not, I suppose, go to the same school. Usually I take a look at the first page and at the last and at two haphazard pages in the middle, and I say: 'This is rubbish!' But I very distinctly remember how I read *The Brothers Karamazov*. I was staying at a hotel for a fortnight and every morning whilst I was dressing, and every evening whilst I was dressing for dinner, and every night, whilst I was going to bed, I read in this book. I read nothing else whatever for the entire fortnight – no newspaper, no nothing. When I had finished the book I gave up two whole days and read it completely through again, intending to examine the workmanship. I didn't examine the workmanship; I was still too much interested in the story. And that really is all that I have to say about *The Brothers Karamazov*. It ought to have been all that I had to say about Dostoevsky; I couldn't have paid a greater tribute and I don't want to criticise him in the sense of finding fault with him. Let that be the province of other pens. It is not my '*Fach*', and I withdraw with apologies from the discussion.

But the essence of my self-appointed task is to record my own time, my own world, as I see it. It is an ambition like another, and I trust it will be pardoned to me. In that sense, and in that sense alone, I can say something about this great writer. I almost wish he had never written; I regard his works with envy, with fear, with admiration. I seem to see him on the horizon as a dark cloud, and the thought of his heavy books is as of so many weights upon my soul; as of so many labours for my poor brain. It is a weariness to me to think that I have got to read *The Idiot*.

II. *The Idiot*. By Fydor Dostoevsky
Translated by Constance Garnett

And I suppose that what is at the bottom of my feeling of weariness, of my aversion from Dostoevsky is just the feeling of Bertin, the painter, of *Fort comme la Mort*. It is the feeling that one is getting on in life, and that one's successors must be upon the horizon. And in the dark cloud of Dostoevsky and the school that he will make, – in that cloud of locusts one perceives one's successors. It is the Romantic Movement coming back…

The Romantic Movement coming back! For whatever Dostoevsky may be, he certainly isn't a Realist. His characters are extraordinarily vivid; but they are too vivid for the Realist School. They are too much always, in one note; they develop little; they are static. His strong scenes are strong to the point of frenzy, but they are too full-dress: everybody has to be in them at once. And they are entirely unprepared – or at any rate the author very frequently doesn't trouble himself to prepare them. There does not seem to me to be any particular reason why Nastasya should come to the house of Ganya, why she should find so many of the characters there; and there does not seem to me to be any particular reason why Rogozhin should at precisely that moment rush in with another crowd. It is mere coincidence. The French Realistic School simply couldn't handle such a situation at all, and that is, I suppose, why the French Realistic School – in which I should include Turgenev – does not deal very often with crowds. It could not handle such a situation simply because to satisfy its conscience it would have to provide every member of that crowd with a history, with an ancestry, and with an inevitable reason for turning up in that particular spot at that particular moment.

Dostoevsky simply doesn't care. He wants to prepare for you one episode of the Christ legend, and he wants to have a lot of spectators. So he just pulls them in, and the Christ-Myshkin is struck on one side of the cheek and, in the proper romantic tradition, he goes one better than Our Lord. He turns away to the wall and weeps for the shame that his persecutor will feel. And the persecutor duly feels the shame. They have to be so full-dress, these Romanticists! And it seems to me that they like to take things so ready-made. Frankly speaking, I am tired of variations of the Christ legend. Or, no, I am not tired of them; I simply never liked them at all. There used to be a German painter of sorts who used to give us pictures of Our Lord in modern peasants' houses; coming in with a wallet on His back; sitting with them at their homely meals – whatever you like. And Dostoevsky's Myshkin is too much like Our Lord in a setting of decadent Petersburg society. The book affects me much as the large pictures of Gustave Doré used to do. And, frankly, I don't like it. But no doubt Doré, too, again will have his day. What spirit he had, what invention, what industry! And Byron will come back, and Pushkin and

Lermontov. And the Flower and Fruit pieces will come back; and the whole thing will run its cycle until Preraphaelism once more will have its say with other Rossettis and newer Swinburnes.

Of course I may be entirely wrong in my diagnosis of Dostoevsky. He may not be a reversion; he may be a step forward towards a region of other-worldliness – of the other-worldliness that so desperately today we need. I hope it may be so, and that it is a mere blindness in myself if I fail to perceive it. But I seem to want something fresher, something brighter, something sharper than the Myshkin Christ. For Myshkin is the same thing all over again. But if you ask me what I want… ah, there! that again is not my job. And indeed I don't know. If I did I should try to do it myself. The only thing that I can imagine as an ideal is a book so quiet in tone, so clearly and so unobtrusively worded, that it should give the effect of a long monologue spoken by a lover at a little distance from his mistress's ear – a book about the invisible relationships between man and man; about the values of life; about the nature of God – the sort of book that nowadays one could read in as one used to do when one was a child, pressed against a tall window-pane for hours and hours, utterly oblivious of oneself, in the twilight.

I wish I knew, in the meantime, how to pay a tribute to Mrs Garnett for her translations from the Russian. This immense work, so sedulously persevered in, so high in its achievement, is one that could only be rewarded by a gratitude not to be expressed in words. It is dreadful to think of what books in English would be if we had not her translations. And indeed I think that women as a sex should be grateful to her; since she has proved herself capable of such a labour as few men could have carried through, and of a sense of phrase vouchsafed to few of us, whether we be men or women.

Outlook, 33 (14 February 1914), 206–7.

XXV. Monsignor Benson and *Initiation*

I.

I had an Anglican friend for whose intellect I had a great admiration and for whose character I had a very real respect – and that is rare, for one really respects so few people; perhaps three or four in a lifetime! So that when, one day, this friend said to me in a matter-of-fact tone, 'My mother was a saint!' I accepted the statement in a matter-of-fact way. I suppose that she worked little miracles, or did the pretty, kindly, or humorous things that, automatically, one expects of a saint of God.

But, by little and little, I began to see that my friend's mother, as he saw her – for she was long dead – was none of these things and did none of them. I questioned my friend closely, and more closely; and always as I questioned him, he became more baffling in his attitude. And for the first time, I became conscious that between this friend and myself there was a great gulf fixed. I could not get across it in any way. I remember once being present for a day or so at a congress of historians where two professors struck up a warm friendship, and their conversation impressed me as being exactly like that of my friend and myself about his mother's sainthood. For the two professors – both very distinguished men – were, the one an officially Lutheran historian, the other an adviser in canon law to the Austrian Government. But when they talked about history, although they were both transparently honest men, it was as if, though they talked about the Rastatter Congress, the Peace of Münster, the same treaties, laws or negotiations of princes – it was as if they were talking in different languages of the affairs of another planet. They did not in the least quarrel; they never, as it were, got near enough to each other for that. They were friendly beings of different species, as it might be a friendly angel and a friendly man – something of that sort.

So with my friend and myself. I got at last a sort of image of his mother's saintship. I seemed to see, at the end of an immense, serenely dark Jacobean room, an immensely tall square mirror, on a square table, between two very tall wax candles – thin wax candles in silver sticks. The mirror reflects nothing but the black serene emptiness of the room, and behind it is an immensely tall window, with square panes giving on to a perfectly black night…

I don't mean to imply anything at all by the adjectives 'black' or 'empty' – it is just physical description. But the point is, I am aware, that my mind is setting for me the background for a High Church lady of the days of Laud – and that my mind simply will not conjure up any figure at all. It simply cannot begin upon the task.

Indeed, I am a little afraid; I recognize a goodness that, to me, is almost a wickedness and almost certainly a cruelty. It is so apparently austere, restrained, non-communicative. It is so nearly exactly what I don't want religion to be; though it is also so near Papistry. I know that my friend's poets were Herbert and Crashaw and Vaughan; that his poem – the one that gave him intimate satisfaction – was:

> Sweet day, so cool, so calm, so bright,
> The bridal of the earth and sky,
> The dews shall weep thy fall to-night,
> For thou, with all thy sweets, must die.[1]

1 [A misquotation of George Herbert's 'Vertue'.]

And I think I rather hate those poets and that poem, as indeed I think I hate all sad things.

A friend, like myself, a German Papist, resident for many years in England, has expressed what I am trying to get at much better than I can.

> For me [he writes] religion is, when I really search my heart, a matter of little friendly quaintnesses and communications. To hand or to take holy water, at the finger-tips, to a good friend, on entering a church, is an intimate satisfaction. And the candles before a bad painting of Our Lady are so 'freundlich'; and the little bits of stamped tin in which we traffic, and the bits of cloth that we hang round our necks – all the business of it, all the traffics and fascinations, are so intimately childish and homelike. Yes, it is like going home. And the saints are so friendly and human and so ready to be concerned for one's welfare when one meets them in the street… It is, you see, my most worthy friend, such an extraordinarily real world. The other day I was having my things packed for going away. But all the time I was thinking of going to the Lady Chapel in the Cathedral and doing something or other. I probably answered all right the questions that were being asked me about how many collars I wanted; I must have, because my collars were all right. But, upon my soul, I was not in my dressing-room at that moment; I was in the rather dark chapel, with the candles burning and some people kneeling about, and I was standing and looking on…

My friend is not a particularly religious man; I dare say he is not orthodox at all; the German Catholics are, I believe, suspected of being latitudinarian in one way or another. But what he says expresses pretty exactly what religion means for me, when I happen to think of it; or more particularly, when I am happening to hope that my children – and all children now growing up upon this earth – may be good Catholics.

And it is extraordinarily different from the Laudian High Church atmosphere – entirely respectable though that atmosphere may be. For, good heavens! if a day is worthy to be the bridal of the earth and sky, it can't die; and our duty, as I see it, is not so much an austere preparation for a future life as so to live and play with our toys and pictures and reliquaries that, at almost any moment – like my friend over his dressing-case – we may trot away for a little into the more real side of the earth…

I hope I am not saying anything to offend anybody; I am not in the least trying to do so.

II. *Initiation.* By R.H. Benson

And of course that Laudian spirit is not merely Anglican – there is about it something of the national. It is no doubt English to regard rather the austerities than the friendlinesses of religion – no doubt the spirit of the

High Church martyrs and the spirits of Campion and the English martyrs were as nearly as possible beautiful, austere, and flamelike – the spirit of the English College at Rome, that sad, sad place, whose every stone, even on days of rejoicing, seems to whisper to the footfall of exile, of martyrdom, of the oppressions of ages.

Monsignor Benson however has very little of this consciousness of the historic oppressions of the centuries. His is – I am of course writing of him only as a novelist – a much more cheery spirit. One can't help knowing him to be a priest, so that one doesn't know how much one's astonishment may be due to the stupid impression that one never gets away from – the stupid impression that our priests live only in the clouds. But I never do get away from astonishment at the amazing powers of observation that are the Monsignor's. There is just nothing that he does not notice, and there are few things that he cannot very aptly hit off.

On those lines *The Average Man* was amazing. One said at page after page, 'How the dickens does he get to know these things?' With the wave of his pen he could give you the intricacies of a suburban kitchen; the emotions of a lady choosing a new hat; amazingly he could render for you the emotions of the process of conversion and those of a first lesson in rabbit-shooting. And in tone, in construction, *The Average Man* was as good as can be desired.

And, if I am disappointed with *Initiation*, it is still not from any lack of powers of observation or of rendering – it is simply that, in the construction of the book, the author seems to have been a little tired. He has no doubt so many further duties than the writing of novels; whereas, for me, alas! the writing and consideration of novels is the sacred side of my duties.

The opening of the book is excellent; the rendering of the Roman international society, with the marquises having tea with two cardinals, and the Americans and the chatter, and the light thin air of the city of the statue of Victor Emanuel – for the Seven Hills are dwarfed. It is so exactly what one has known; it is so exactly what one knows one will know again. The characterization, the lessons, of the architecture, of the landscape, are in their manner perfect; and the mother and daughter are hit off with real imagination; and the courtship is pretty and touching and real...

But I am tired of the English county-family atmosphere of the later chapters, even though the touch of Papistry is refreshing. I know that the thesis of the book concerns itself with a Prince in Israel, amongst the fleshpots of Egypt, finding Initiation only in death, and that, in order to show you a prince and the fleshpots, long-descended baronets with collies and parks and pavilions and death-chambers and old butlers are handy and convenient. He will have to leave all this and fare into the darkness of God.

But I should have liked something more subtle – something more passionately lovable, for the poor fellow to have to leave. The Monsignor knows so much of the human heart that he could easily enough have given that one more turn to the screw. I remember well enough a short story of his about the spiritual torments of a young priest – an unforgettable thing. And that is what I am wanting him to have screwed himself up to again. I don't know what I should have preferred – perhaps a prince of the blood royal, passionately interested in his struggles about constitutions and the suppression of dances; or a beggar passionately enamoured of his corner under the hedge and his poached rabbit-pie; or, perhaps better still, a priest passionately loving the tranquillity of his cell... That would have been it...

But perhaps I am wrong and missing the point of the whole book. Perhaps it is I who am tired. I hope it is; for I have such a great wish that Monsignor Benson should write only novels as good as *The Average Man*.

Outlook, 33 (28 February 1914), 278–9.

XXVI. Miss Amber Reeves and *A Lady and her Husband*

I.

I am driven by the thought of Mrs Blanco White into the consideration of certain aspects of various social questions. And they are, for me, just questions. I don't want to dogmatize. What I want to ask is just this: To what extent have new movements – all and sundry new movements, whether for the sterilizing of milk, or for the relaxing of Sabbath restrictions; whether for the gradual relaxation of marriage ties, or for the economic emancipation of women – to what extent have these new movements really affected the fabric of this realm of England?

I simply don't know. One's glass, with the best will in the world, is so small, and one is so compelled to drink solely in that glass, that one might come the most frightful howlers if one trusted to one's own observation. And whom is one to trust? There is Mrs Blanco White's world – I mean the world portrayed in her books – and if anyone in the world ought to know the extent to which Fabianism has penetrated the solid middle and suburban classes of this country it should be that lady who writes as Miss Amber Reeves. And in that world, there cannot be any doubt about it, Fabianism has come to stay – at any rate with the young women. They have all, all of them, read the latest Fabian tract and the latest pamphlet on the municipalizing of this or that sweated industry. They know all sorts of statistics, and the riddle of the universe has no terrors for their determined intellects. The men (and I believe it is the same in holy Russia) are more indifferent; tarred with the same stick they may be but a good deal of the tar has worn off before the stick has reached them. Still, there is the same coolness; the same contempt for you, me, and the Chancellor of the Exchequer. And of course there are the well-appointed houses in which these young people live, and the indulgent, muddled, browbeaten parents…

I don't know this class at all; there are whole classes that one does not know, and that one never will know. I sometimes go wandering at night to take the dog for a walk, or so on, along a great tract of country with squares, crescents, places and the rest of it. There will be hardly a soul in the streets (that is why it is a good region to select for the exercising of one's dog); there will be no traffic; and in a deathless silence immense white houses of painted stucco tower up into the darkness. There do not seem ever to be any receptions there – at any rate I never see awnings over the footway, or carpets laid down over the pavements. And I wonder frequently, What do all these people do? Where does all the money come from? Why do they all seem to go to bed at half-past ten? Who are they? For, in that immense region, say a mile deep to the north of Hyde Park, and for two miles to the West of Marble Arch, I do not know a single soul – not a single soul in that Imperial city of classical, white, square palaces. For hang it all! in the scale of the world's history up till today they are palaces.

Is this – do all these people form – the backbone of England? I suppose it is; I suppose they do. And I allow myself to suppose that these are the landscapes of Miss Amber Reeves' novels. It is from these doors that the fathers issue of mornings with the carefully rolled umbrellas; and there are no receptions, and no carpets in strips across the pavements, because the young people, at nights, are all up in the back bedrooms reading the Fabian tracts and the pamphlets about the municipalization of sweated industries. Then possibly there is nothing wrong – from one point of view at least – with the country. These young people, at the appointed time, will in their turn issue, of mornings, from those porticoes – the males with their umbrellas solicitously rolled by the females, who, key-basket in hand, will just see them through the doorway before going down to interview cook. And it will be a solid, if languid, Unionist constituency. As it was in 1840, as it was in 1880, so it will be in 1920, in 1960, and *in saeculum saeculorum*…

I suppose nothing ever really changes. The other day I was at a great Unionist banquet – to three hundred ploughmen, hinds, and farmers, far, far down in one of the southern counties. Do you know the difference between Kent and Sussex and the Shires? There still mothers warn their daughters: 'You see that chap? He comes from Sussex. He's a'right. He sucked in silliness with his mother's milk, and he's been silly ever since. But never you trust a man from the Sheeres.' They still do it.

II. *A Lady and her Husband.* By Amber Reeves

Well, there there was certainly an unchanging stratum. It was ludicrously unchanged; the argument that really moved that gnarled audience – the argument against Home Rule – was this: 'How would you chaps like, without a with your leave or by your leave, to be pitchforked into Hampshire? How would you like to be turned into men from the Sheeres?' So we growled, and shouted and drank beer seriously out of each other's mugs – the old blood-brotherhood, quality and ploughmen all drinking and growling together in a serious taciturnity...

And yet, in this confusing world, one is so seriously misled by going out to find what one wants to find, or by one's fat complacency. For, if Miss Amber Reeves is to be trusted, a change is working in those very stucco palaces that seem to form the backbone of England – a change that is coming about through the entry of women into social consciousness.

I take it for granted that Miss Reeves knows what she is writing about, for, as I have said, this world is no world of mine; I am much more at home drinking out of the same mug with a ploughboy. *A Lady and Her Husband* shows us however the household of a great employer of labour. The daughters are, roughly speaking, Fabians; but they get married. The son is nothing at all; the father is a constructive genius in the realms of tea-shops. He gives the public excellent poached eggs, unrivalled cups of tea, pure butter, and wholesome bread. He is honest, buoyant, persevering, unbeatable, and he has done the public great service by providing it with pure food.

His wife, I am allowed to presume, is just a normal woman, leading a sheltered life under the protection of her husband's comfortable fortune. Suddenly, however, with the marrying of her daughters, her life seems to come to an end. She finds an occupation in the study of her husband's female employees in the teashops. She discovers that these poor creatures are wretchedly underpaid; that they have to stand for too long hours; that they have to eat their meals in damp cupboards. And these facts appeal to her at first as things that can be easily remedied by her surely benevolent husband. She has always taken her husband to be benevolent.

No sooner however does she approach Mr Heyham than she discovers in him a characteristic that she had never before observed – as it were, the lust of the chase. The great business has to be kept going, because it is a great business; because it is a thing to love, to sacrifice to; because it is at once a mistress and the quarry of the chase. On the other hand, in Mrs Heyham the human side of the poor waitresses – with their miserable salaries that lead them into theft, prostitution – with their long hours of standing, that lead them to have varicose veins, neurasthenia, tuberculosis – all these miseries work in Mrs Heyham to such an extent that she becomes vividly alive to the contrasted interests of the sexes in this civilization of ours. She discovers that, long ago, her husband had been unfaithful to her, and that, in the general buoyancy of his character, he considered the unfaithfulness to have been – as indeed it was – in the nature of a bagatelle. She meets a baby's nurse, who says that women in this world have a poor time of it, especially when you consider that men will be just as well off as their wives in the next. She meets a secretary, who says: 'I wonder that any woman ever loved a man. They're ugly; they're greedy; they're coarse-minded... They've taken the whole world and made it theirs.' And this Miss Percival ends up by saying: 'I'm married, really, you know, only I don't live with my husband.' So Mrs Heyham runs down the gamut of feminine miseries...

If however Mrs Blanco White had left it at that, the book would not have been much of a contribution to our knowledge. But with a clever twist she carries the matter one turn of the screw farther. Having been the provider of half Mr Heyham's capital at his start in life, Mrs Heyham is still a half-proprietor of his immense business. So she puts her foot down and insists that the work-girls shall be better paid. Mr Heyham attempts to counter her by making plans to turn the business into a public company. In that case he will be able eloquently to assert that his duties to his shareholders will not allow him to raise wages; the other shareholders will outvote his wife, and there will be an end of her schemes.

His wife thereupon leaves home, for she is afraid that, in spite of her anger and her determination, her husband, manlike, will force her hand and make her consent to the sale of her interest to the public company. In her seclusion her resolve hardens, and she delivers an ultimatum to her husband – whom she still loves, and who still loves her. In the meantime Mr Heyham, reflecting on his whole position, finds himself able to execute a really fine volte-face. He will, by Jove! become a model employer of labour. He is a very rich man; he can afford it. On the strength of that he will enter Parliament; he has the gift of facile eloquence. He will accept the knighthood that has been offered him. He has had thirty years of hard business career; now he will adopt a career that will suit him just as well. So, in a sense, whilst giving in to his wife he 'does her in the eye'.

> And I really feel [he says to his son] that we business men don't pay sufficient attention to politics. One owes, after all, a certain duty to the nation. When we have put our relations to our employees on to a thoroughly sound footing, it seems to me that my presence in Parliament might have a real, though of course only a small, value –

I do not know whether Miss Reeves is more ingenious or more merely ironic. At any rate she is very clever. She has solved that particular riddle of the universe. For it is essential, if there is to be peace in our time, that men should have their vainglorious careers (and we can, none of us, do much harm in Parliament!), whilst women set about the task of clearing up this house of the world. Or is it that poor Mrs Heyham is really done in the eye, after all?

Who knows? In the meantime this is a very clever and a very observant book. And whilst it is a distinct retrogression in technical skill from *The Reward of Virtue*, it is none the less a distinct advance in assurance of promise. *The Reward of Virtue* was so technically perfect and so cold that one wondered how Mrs Blanco White was going to improve on it. *A Lady and Her Husband* is faulty; it is over-burdened with matter. Mrs Blanco White knows almost too much of her subject to have exercised enough of selection. But *The Reward of Virtue* was the book of an old person; *A Lady and Her Husband* is a product of youth. It is an advance on which Mrs Blanco White is to be much congratulated, since it means that she is on the road to finding herself. And that is what we all want.

Outlook, 33 (7 March 1914), 310–11.

XXVIII. Mr Morley Roberts and *Time and Thomas Waring*

I.

I have often wondered what might have been the artist's education of George Gissing. (It is Mr Morley Roberts' own fault if one identifies him with the author of *Demos* and if he does not like it.) I do not know if there are any means of knowing, or if it be mere idleness that lets me be ignorant of a fact so important in the literary history of these islands. For Gissing is an important figure in that history; I don't like him, but there is no getting away from that fact.

And of George Gissing, in essentials, one knows nothing. One knows that he had a bad time; Mr Morley Roberts has suggested that he was *infelix opportunitate domus*; but many carters have bad times and many shopwalkers tram-conductors, and private gentlemen make unfortunate marriages. I have an idea also that Gissing loved the classics, loved Theocritus, Bion, Moschus, Apuleius; but so also, very possibly, do Mr Bonar Law, the Archbishop of Canterbury, the Lord Chief Justice, and Privy Seal. But with what sort of lovers of words Gissing conversed and what sort of words he loved – of that we know as little as of what songs the Sirens sang. I at least know nothing, and even Mr Seccombe has never given us a picture of Gissing knocking down a Mr A. because he loved the word 'corybantic' whilst Mr A. laughed at the precious sounds.

Yet it is only such information that is of the slightest value to us; from that we might learn something of the real man and, with the knowledge, might amend our ways! And I have often wondered what could account for the peculiarly unattractive quality of Gissing's work, for its peculiar hodden ugliness, for its want of inspiration. It was quite odd, to me, always; because, on the one or two occasions when I met Gissing I found him attractive, with a rather beautiful nature, sanguine and by no means unattractive, a rather flame-like individual. (That is rather a stupid simile, but it is the impression that is in my mind.) Nevertheless of the few books of Gissing's that I have been able to read the only word that I can find to say is that they were ugly – essentially ugly, in soul, in construction, in wording. Or else it was the Ryecroft book which was bad sentimentalism in pretty pretty phraseology.

New Grub Street, for instance, was a work absolutely airless, unrelieved, harrowing, and creaking. It was lying awake for an interminable night listening to the monotone drip from a cistern; it went on and on, undistinguished, sordid; as if one were for ever eating a stale bun in a dirty, gas-lit, cheap tea-shop in the Camden High Street. The really great tragedies, whether they be *Lear*, or *Lisa*, or *Le Rouge et le Noir*, are never harrowing, and certainly they are never undistinguished; they never miss being intellectual stimulants. That I suppose is why poor Gissing has gone so completely out – is why, whilst he earned so full a measure of respect in his day, he made so singularly little appeal to one's imagination. It was impossible to have one's pulse quickened by the thought of him. Yet undoubtedly he was in every way respectable – sober, industrious, honest, enormously in earnest. I don't know…

At any rate I have always considered Mr Morley Roberts to have inherited the mantle of poor Gissing; I may be quite wrong, but the impression has always been very strong on me. I do not, anyhow, know Mr Roberts at all well; but I have always had a certain respect for him, combined with a certain aversion, so that when the editor of this paper asked me to write about his latest book I recoiled and protested with the exaggerated impulses that one has. Then however came the idea, 'After all, one can always slate a blessed book!' So I started in to read *Time and Thomas Waring* with every intention of kicking it from Dan to Beersheba. In the result I have wept a handkerchief into a state of complete soppiness over it. And now I am wondering why…

Years ago – perhaps in 1892 – I remember hearing my uncle, Mr William Rossetti, alluding in terms of wonderment to a clerk in his office – the Inland Revenue – who intended to give up that safe job and take to a life of adventure – stevedoring, broncho-busting, jumping the blind baggage, or whatever were the queer ideals of the queer old nineties in the way of physical adventure. And the clerk – to the wonderment of my uncle – went away and attended on cattle on Atlantic boats, and travelled in the United States without paying any fares, and to hoboes he administered the hard K.O. and did the usual things. So, at least, it was reported to me. And when his time was come he returned to London and attended an 'afternoon' of my aunt Lucy Rossetti's; and, as far as I could hear, he did not say a single word, properly filling the bill of the man of action, the bridge-builder, the Kiplingish overman of the poor dear dead decade…

So that was all I ever heard of Mr Morley Roberts until the appearance of the *Private Life of Henry Maitland*, which was a bitter bad book. Oh, a bitter bad book! I don't in the least mind that it gave away a number of the confidences of poor dead Gissing; that it may have inconvenienced several other people too I do not much mind. You must not have to do with authors unless you are prepared to have that sort of thing happen to you; that is all there is to it. But there was not about the *Private Life* a spark of elevation, of insight, of power of projection, of imagination. There was not even any invention. It was like a person sitting down to tell the truth about Mr Jones and telling all the wrong things – telling you only about what he took for his liver and where he bought his socks.

II. *Time and Thomas Waring*. By Morley Roberts

At the same time, even in the *Private Life of Henry Maitland*, whilst one was recognizing that it was all hopelessly wrong, it was impossible not to recognize also that here was, if a very plodding, then also a very earnest realist. It was the book, it seemed, of a depressed, rather hopeless individual, who had looked upon life and found it very ugly material, and uninspired, and had rendered it in an ugly, materialistic, and uninspired frame of mind. Still, in an English and what I will call a Mark Rutherford kind of way it was a rendering.

And I think it struck me then – or perhaps I am only being wise after the event – that if the writer of that book could get hold of a subject really suited to his method – which was quite a genuine method! – he might turn out something really valuable. And I am inclined to think that, with *Time and Thomas Waring*, Mr Morley Roberts really has got hold of his subject. And I am inclined to think that he has turned out a book much more significant than any of Gissing's or any of Mark Rutherford's or than any of the English school of realists. I say that I am inclined to think so, because the English school of realism is for me a thing singularly ugly, or at any rate singularly pedestrian, and I have really been very much moved by Mr Roberts' book. Quite literally I cried so much over it at times that I made myself feel ill, and do feel ill still.

It is unusual to make such a confession, but I make it for what it is worth and because, since I am trying to tell the truth about Mr Roberts, in whom I have no particular interest, he may as well have the benefit of the fact. For of course when I am writing about the quite typically English novel I am apt to get off my feet. I do not know the country – not in the least. There is, for instance, no kind of accomplishment about Mr Roberts. He cannot construct a story nearly as well as any of the novelists of commerce that one never mentions. His composition strikes me as singularly bad. What, for instance, could be worse, from the point of the beautiful and gracious thing that good writing is, than such an ending for a paragraph as the following:

> ... And for a moment there was a great flood of pity in her for her own mother, who had no high incommunicable thoughts nor any gift of contemplation, nor any dear, surrendering pity of the soul. She had no gifts; there was no fine grace in her aspect, nor any capacity for a noble calm.

I think I would cut my throat if I found I had written two sentences echoing each other like that. Just fancy repeating 'she had no...' and 'nor any...' as if it were a trouvaille! It gives the effect of some one playing the intermezzo from *Cavalleria Rusticana* fifty times over without stopping. And 'high, incommunicable thoughts'! My God! And 'dear, surrendering pity of the soul'! My God! My God!

So that one reads the book as if it were beneath a masking cloud, or as if one were wearing glasses that made everything appear astigmatic; though the conversations when they are not too long are rather effective for an English novelist. But even the conversations are ill-managed and without contrast. Thomas Waring talks, as it were, about the immortality of the soul or real morality with his mistress; then he goes down to his club and finds two journalists, a surgeon, an anaesthetist, and a nondescript and immediately they all begin to talk about the immortality of the soul and real morality in just the same phraseology as the mistresses and the hospital nurses on the next page continue the same conversations in the same phraseology. That is not handling conversation as a master, or even as a capable journeyman would handle it. We know that you must have relief, and that if conversation A be about the immortality of the soul and the higher morality, conversation B must be about the Home Rule Bill, though its more subtle bearings will carry the subject of conversation A a stage farther.

But Mr Morley Roberts just goes on and on – and on. And somehow he gets his effect – to the extent of making me weep. I am aware that in so saying I am doing what is to all intents and purposes to *renier mes dieux*. But I can't help that.

And it is by sheer power of his subject that Mr Roberts attains to this achievement. The subject is that of a man who is operated on for a mortal disease, the effects of the operation being merely temporary and he knowing that he must be operated on again and die within a year or eighteen months. There was, attached to this man, a woman he had loved very much, a wife who is always polishing the furniture (Mary, you remember, had chosen the better portion), a mistress who chose the portion of Mary; a daughter who was hopelessly and finally in love with a married man; a son, not a bad fellow, who had an entanglement with a housemaid, and who is not as brilliant as his father could have wished. The man is fifty, fairly prosperous in his profession; fairly eminent – well, you see, it is the sort of coil that any man of fifty may find himself in!

And then suddenly there comes the operation, and he knows that he has only about eighteen months to live. So he sets to work to set everything in order – for his wife; for his daughter; for his mistress; for his son; for what will remain after him of his career. That is the story – that is the 'affair' of the book.

You can see that it is rather an epic matter – an epic of our everyday life. Former ages lived in an atmosphere of knowing that death might come at any minute; in the arrow that flieth by night; in the swift pestilence; at the orders of a tyrant or an inquisitor. But we – and that is why Mr Roberts is valuable – hang on the words of a confessor who is a surgeon, and our poor souls are in the hands of nuns who are white-robed hospital nurses. I do not suppose that there is any man of fifty who is not surrounded by friends or mistresses, who may not at any moment be on the operating-table, amidst the white-robed councils of ten; or that there is any man who may not be called on to take his place. The surgeon is our confessor, is our inquisitor, is our high priest, is our pope – if not for us, then for those whom we love more dearly – oh, so much more dearly – than life. May it not, at any moment, strike our daughter who is so straight and fair, our mistress who, whilst our wife polishes the furniture, is the only thing that holds us to life, or our best friend without whom life would be rather a dull affair?

This fine, this epic subject, this real subject of modern life, Mr Morley Roberts has got hold of. And, if he has not treated it with the skill, the gloom, or the fierce indignation of a Dostoevsky, he has at least done so with a sort of honest peasant straightforwardness. If he does not appear to me to have any particular literary skill he has – at least as far as I can discern – no literary tricks. He uses cliché phrases and Anglo-Saxon, and words of Latin derivation and sentimental constructions, much as some Lancashire weaver, some hard, tender, serious and earnest workman might do – a man who had read Ruskin and Huxley and *Utopia* and the *Life of Frederick the Great*, and perhaps *New Grub Street*.

I hope this does not sound patronizing. It is merely the writing of a person of another school – of a foreigner, if you will! At any rate I hope I have brought out my meaning to the extent of making it manifest that I think Mr Roberts has treated almost the most important side of the life we lead, and that he seems to me to be the first person to have rendered it seriously, if at all. Here are the opening words of the book:

> The operating-theatre was lighted from the north end by a large window which was also partly skylight. Under the window stood radiators... The walls were of white and gleaming tiles; bright metal work

> glittered. On the left there were standing basins of white ware against the wall. The floor was of close grey concrete. Near the standing basins there was a brass structure. By this were boilers of nickel, with cold and hot water sterilised in them. To the right was a glass cupboard with shining instruments in it. Above it, in the wall, an electric fan was running...

That of course is not very striking writing; but it strikes its note right away. And it is the note of the private landscape of almost everybody that one knows and loves. The Elizabethan said: 'It is but giving over of a game that must be lost.' Mr Roberts puts it: 'Above it, in the wall, an electric fan was running.' But the note is the same.

Outlook, 33 (21 March 1914), 390–1.

XXXI. Lord Dunsany and *Five Plays*

I.

The Irish are a queer people, not because they are in any way in themselves unusual, but because, being extraordinarily normal, they contrive to produce on the rest of the world such an effect of abnormality. Thus they are cold, utterly without passion, materialist, matter of fact; as a rule, like most other peoples, they are quite without a sense of humour. They are cruel, chaste, ascetic, joyless, Puritan, Nonconformist. They are Anglo-Saxon; they are extraordinarily English. And yet look at them – look at the effect they produce on the bemused world. Is there any living soul, except Mr Bernard Shaw, himself a Nonconformist to the bone-marrow, who does not believe that the Irish are passionate pilgrims journeying through a material world with their eyes on the great stars of heaven, with the verses of the old poets on their lips, and gallant thoughts in the hearts of them? Actually they are thinking whether, if they could fill the old pig up with buckshot, they could not get eleven shillings more for him at Mullingar Fair come Thursday. Only it's a difficult job to get an old pig to fill itself with buckshot... And, if they could do a little persecuting on their fellow-Nonconformists in Ulster wouldn't they love to do it – and small blame to them! And would not they roar out great oaths, very astonishing and wild, and so persuade the whole world that it was the Ulstermen that began it by writing 'Bloody End to the Pope' under the table in a house at the corner of Square Street? And shouldn't we – all the rest of the world – go on loving them, as we do? and sentimentalizing over them as we do? and weeping the great tears over them that we do?

All this, you know, is a disquisition on literary technique – for what is literature but the producing of illusions? And for the producing of an illusion there is nothing like an Irishman. A little chap with a face like a monkey's and a queer hat (though indeed it is really only a hat just like any other Christian's) will be sitting on a stile somewhere, and he will look at you with the twinkle in his eyes. And he will say: 'Honesty – God save all here! – is the best policy! A stitch – more power to it! – in time save nine. Early to bed – the saints look down on us! – and early to rise makes a man healthy – heaven save the poor souls going all the way to Loords crost the sea! – wealthy – and it's a little of that wealth that would slip well through the holes in me waistcoat pockuts! – and wise!' And he will tell you that a nod is as good as a wink to a blind horse, and that many hands make light work, and that least said is soonest mended, and that continence, sobriety, industry, and clean living are virtues. And according as that little chap with the queer hat and a face like a monkey's desires you to laugh at his humour or weep for the sorrows of his country, so your sides will shake or the tears will pour down over your cheeks. Yet you never either laughed or wept when you first made the acquaintance with the whole inside of his head on top of your copybooks at school... But you will go on pouring out the love that is in you over him just the same! And that, you know, is the real triumph of an art – to make the hand deceive the eye though the eye knows all the while what the hand is doing. And that, again, is perhaps why the Irish have produced so few books and done so little else in the world. They have not needed to; they can make their effect – and what for do we crave for wealth and fame and achievement save that we may make our effect! – with hardly so much as the stirring of a hand – by the quoting of a few copybook maxims, as you might say! And that art is the greatest which most economizes in its means.

I think that Lord Dunsany is one of the best poets that Ireland has yet produced – he and Mr Yeats are enough to justify that distressing humbug of a country of its existence.(Fortunately I have not got to write about Mr Yeats just yet!) But I rather doubt whether Lord Dunsany has much idea of the greatness of his particular conjuring trick – or else he is as great a humbug as the rest of his countrymen. And that I do doubt. I fancy that he has the national gift of prestidigitation without really thinking that he is doing any more than eating potatoes with a fork. For as I understand it, in the considerable Irish group that now exists – in the group that more or less contains himself and Mr Yeats and the Abbey Theatre people and Mr Moore and the gentlemen that Mr Maunsell publishes – in that group Lord Dunsany imagines himself to represent the revolt against realism.

II. *Five Plays*. By Lord Dunsany

He does nothing of the sort of course, since he is one of the chief realists of them all. He is so much of a realist that he produces an effect of mysticism; just as his countryman who is thinking of filling the old pig with buckshot produces an effect of thinking of the cold ways of the stars. This is not paradox; it is part of the whole scheme of art and of the way art works… For this, more or less, is the way Lord Dunsany sets about it. Says he: 'I am sick of this world, and the Land Purchase Act, and the defectively sanitated cabins in Connemara. I will build up a world that shall be the unreal world of before the fall of Babylon. I am sick of the sogarths and their way; I will build seven thrones for seven gods of green jade.' And so he goes and does it – with all the arts of the inspired realist! One is tired of the knocking on the door of *Macbeth* as an instance, but it is still the best instance in the world of how horror is heightened – of how horror is produced – by the projection of, not the writing about, purely material things. And Lord Dunsany is doing the knocking-on-the-door stunt all the way through four at least of his five plays. (The fifth is quite negligible.)

OOGNO. What heavy boots they have; they sound like feet of stone.

THANN. I do not like to hear their heavy tread; those that would dance to *us* must be light of foot…

THANN . They should dance as they come. But the footfall is like the footfall of heavy crabs…

Now that is beautiful writing and clever imagery; but it is sheer realism all the same. And the lesson of the *Gods of the Mountain* is not a lesson for the days before the fall of real Babylon; it is a lesson for the grocer round the corner and for me at my desk – and for Lord Dunsany too. So is the lesson of the *Golden Doom*; so is the lesson of the *Unknown Warrior* and of the *Glittering Gate*. And all the effects of these last three plays too are got by the methods of the sheerest realism.

Thus the turning points, the real cruces of the *Unknown Warrior* are the bones that the slaves gnaw, the bones that are still in the flesh of the king's dog, the way the prophet's hair is cut, and the little dints in the very old sword that King Arginones digs up out of the earth. Similarly the effect of the *Glittering Gate* is produced by the burglar saying that when he gets into heaven his mother will have ready for him a glass of beer and a dish of tripe and onions and a pipe of tobacco. It is these things that make Lord Dunsany's plays differ from allegory, that most tiresome and most materialist of all things. An allegorist would have left out the bones in the *Unknown Warrior*, and would have made the dints in the sword not little ones, as dints in swords that have seen service really are. He would have let them be the great dints of stage swords such as might he borne by a Britannia in a *Punch* cartoon after she had vanquished the Gallic foe. No. Lord Dunsany is not that tiresome thing, an allegorist – though I have a vague idea that he might wish to be considered or to consider himself one. But like all true poets, like all dealers in the unseen, the imponderable, he is a realist, and a realist, and again a realist, just as all mystics in their queer way are extraordinarily full of knowledge of the world – just in fact as the most saintly of confessors will pop out at you in his confessional a queer bit of knowledge of the foolish way you will behave when you go courting. And we need realists very badly, because this world is so much too much with us. It is too much with us, and it is an extraordinarily unreal mirage. Yes, just a mirage. Three large sharp stones are in my drive; they ought to be pulled up or rolled in. There is a broken and discarded bucket in the long grass of my orchard. The rain is coming, like handfuls of small gravel cast against my window; the baker is coming in at the front gate; I shall have to paint a chest of drawers this afternoon... But all that is really mirage; there is nothing real about the stones or the discarded bucket, or the rain, or the baker coming in at the gate. Myself, my own self, is miles away – thirty miles away, thinking of things how different – how utterly different! And the future is to – the necessity is for – the artist who, by rendering the stones and the bucket and the baker and the *Daily Telegraph* that is lying on the sofa, will give the world the image of that kingdom of heaven that is behind it all. I rather fancy that the Cubists and the Futurists and the rest of the movement that is trying to get away from representational art are trying to put the kingdom of heaven too directly on to canvas, and that possibly Lord Dunsany would get farther away from the purely economic school if he set his plays in Grosvenor Square of this year.

It is perfectly true that we have had too much of the purely economic school, the imbecile Fabian society, the Rationalist Press Association and all that cretinism. We want to get back to the divine right of kings, metaphorically speaking. But I rather doubt if that is most efficiently done by dreaming about the world before the fall of Babylon; it is possible that it would be nearer the mark to present the laying of drainpipes in Connemara or the trees in Soho Square. But the fact remains that, in this odd world, two and two never make four, except in the realms of the imagination; and for the purposes of humanity – or at any rate of the poets who are the only part of humanity that are not just the stuff with which to fill graveyards – the nineteenth century, the age of gas-and-water socialism, was on a hopelessly wrong track. This I know is a sort of an Easter sermon; but I am writing in Holy Week and I cannot help myself. And if the nineteenth century was on a hopelessly wrong track and running down a siding on the one hand, I am not certain that it was not, at any rate in the case of that small band of brothers who evolved the methods of true realism, evolving the true method of rendering the realities that are behind this world of stones, buckets, and furniture that has to be painted. The formula is this: A poet contemplating a sunset has certain emotions stirred within him. Shall he then write down, 'My emotions are so-and-so', or shall he so exactly describe the sunset that the reader shall in his turn have emotions stirred within him? Realists prescribe the latter, English writers as a rule prefer the former method. But the queer Irish, with Lord Dunsany at their heads... Ah, they know what they are up to. Because the lesson of the *Gods of the Mountain* is this: There was a grocer at Putney with sandy whiskers and a lewd mind. But he pretended to be a Puritan with great skill. So the inhabitants of Putney made him a church-warden, and he was then in so prominent a position that he never, never, never once got a chance of going off to Brighton with one of his shopgirls. That is a very good lesson for *unser' Zeit*. But Lord Dunsany makes you believe that it is a story of before the fall of Babylon and that his green jade gods have taken the place of the Ancient of Days and the Fabian leaders. It is the clever man that he is!

Outlook, 33 (11 April 1914), 494–5.

XXXIV. Miss May Sinclair and *The Judgment of Eve*

I.

A gentleman who made a considerable addition to his income – an addition quite enviable – by writing short stories for American magazines, once told me that he dare not adopt that device as a permanent occupation, because all short-story writers die mad. He was rather a mad sort of person...

And I fancy that there is really the root of the matter. What my friend meant was that the 'machining' of a good short story is an employment so exacting that, after having been at it for some years, the brain of the writer gave up, not only that struggle, but all other struggles. There I think he was wrong. I fancy that none but a man with the seeds of lunacy in him can write a really good *conte*. (Very likely none but a man with the seeds of lunacy in him can write at all.) The lunacy of course may take the form merely of an exaggerated cruelty, but cruel at least a short-story writer – the writer of a true *conte* – must be. If you think of it for a moment you will see how inevitably true the dictum is.

Maupassant was the best of all short-story writers, and he had a cruel mind, and he died mad. Mr Kipling was a short-story writer of great magnificence – but that was in his youth, and youth is nearly always cruel. Mr Jacobs is, technically speaking, one of the best short-story writers there ever was, and his best short stories are always preoccupied with something cruel. They may not be all Monkey's Paws, but they always represent somebody being cruel to some one else – somebody hitting some one else in the eye, or scoring off somebody else very mortifyingly. And the best of all short-story writers in English – Stephen Crane – had something queer about him, and died young.

Let me hasten to say – for the short story is such a queer thing that one has always to be explanatory about even the very language that one uses – that by the 'short story' I mean the *conte* – the very short story that would occupy from a page to a page and a half of this journal. But what I have said applies to the longish short story quite as truly but with certainly diminished force. Mr Henry James, who has a phrase for almost anything, has given us the phrase that exactly expresses the industry of short-story writing. It is, 'The turn of the screw'. For a long short story may contain digressions. Nay, it may consist of nothing but digressions, with just the pat of the incident, the stroke from the claw sheathed in velvet, at the beginning, in the middle, at the end – where you will in the narration. But the real short-story writer must be at it with the screw-driver all the time; he must turn, and turn, and turn until the bitter end – until the last revolution of the screw does the trick – until the camel's back is broken.

For that is what it amounts to. The short story of genius – 'La Reine Hortense', 'The Three White Mice', 'The Man Who Would be King' – demands from its reader – nay, it exacts – an amount of strained, of breathless attention that is nothing short of a cruelty; and the final *coup de pistolet* – the last word – is the killing of a living thing, the breaking of a back, since it finishes that vital rapport between writer and reader.

The short-story writer is in fact a giver of news. So, for the matter of that, is the novelist, since all art is merely a means of communication between one soul and another. But whereas the novelist is the comparatively tender-hearted person who cannot communicate news without breaking it as gradually as the tenderness of his temperament will permit, the writer of *contes* is just a brute, like the gentleman of the American story who put the news of Mr Jones's decease to Mrs Jones by saying, 'Are you the Widow Jones?' In a rightly constructed novel every word is a preparation for the final effect; but there are many words, and, since it is the function of art to conceal the artifice, many of the words will possibly be misleading. This is, for instance, true of *Madame Bovary*, where the incident of the cripple or the harangues of Homais might well be taken for mere digressions were it not that they serve simply as heighteners of curiosity until the final effect of destiny is reached. But the short story has to produce its effect by means more crude – and how infinitely more subtle if they are to be effective. Of course, if the thing is to be merely an anecdote, the task is easy enough…

II. *The Judgment of Eve*. By May Sinclair

For the anecdote is just a recital of an act of sorts – an act, an expression of opinion, or a contrast, that may be quaint, or may be cruel, or may be startling. But a *conte* is one or other of these things with, in addition, a certain creation of an atmosphere, of an excitement, of a thrilling or a quivering in the reader. The writer says, as it were, 'Ah, now I am going to touch you up', and he does it. He is being cruel to you in fact.

In this gift of cruelty Miss Sinclair has been hitherto somewhat lacking – she has been too much lacking until the publication of her last novel, which very nearly, or perhaps quite, did the trick. She always possessed a power of observation, a tranquil and direct style, but until quite lately she has never seemed to me to catch hold of her subject with the intensity and vigour that are necessary – to catch hold of a theme, as it were, by the neck, and to shake the last exclamation of terror out of it. Her novels, from the *Divine Fire* onwards, until the *Combined Maze*, have generally seemed to me to be characterized by a certain listlessness, as if the writer had no real hatreds and no very strong desires. For heaven's sake do not let me be misunderstood!

I do not mean to say that a writer of novels should hate governments or institutions, or organized cruelties. Such a man is a Social Reformer. But a certain hatred for certain types, a certain cynical dislike for the imbecile, gross and stupid nature of things, for the meannesses of the human heart, for want of imagination, and for the measure of hypocrisy that is necessary to keep us poor human things all going on – that sort of hatred is an almost necessary motive power for the artist.

A sunny optimism, a cheerful outlook – such things are very salutary, but they are an end in themselves and lead nobody anywhere – at any rate in the realms of story-writing. But a settled habit of misliking for one's kind, for one's circumstances, or even for certain individuals, of certain races – that is of more avail than all the optimisms of the world, if only because it will make you more observant. Of course if you possess only a sort of kindly scepticism as to the vaunting progressions of civilizations, of politicians, of individuals, or of races, you will write excellent comedy, which is quite as good as tragedy. But a cheerful outlook is an unproductive thing, possessed by men who eat good lunches and slumber after them. It is certainly unproductive of the observant habit of mind, as who should look out upon a sunny moist field and be unaware that the anopheles mosquito might well breed in those watery pastures? No, we need the *saeva indignatio*...

Miss Sinclair has shown of course traces of this possession often enough. And I take it that her announcement in the Introduction to this volume – the announcement that she is passing 'to a more intense and more concentrated form' – really means that she is feeling the necessity for a more intense indignation with want of imaginative sympathy in her fellows and the imbecility of the nature of things. In *The Judgment of Eve* the two best stories – those that are best 'machined' and best inspired – have plenty of this quality. They have indeed as much as could be desired. They are the story called 'The Judgment of Eve' itself and 'The

Wrackham Memoirs'. The story, the given thesis, of the 'The Judgment of Eve' is indeed cruel enough for the late Catulle Mendès to have handled. It is even crueller, since the implied suggestion that the husband of the story might have saved not only the wife's life, but her personal appearance, the moral and intellectual character of the home and his own character, by infidelities to his wife, instead of a fidelity that murdered her with too much child-bearing – that suggestion, given the goodness of the character-drawing, is cruel, is exciting enough. I do not mean that it is harrowing; no good art is ever harrowing. It is exciting; it is worrying if you will. But it is stimulating. You are, in a certain sense, strengthened by the reading, since you carry away suggestions; you are not merely exhausted by the appeal to your emotions.

'The Wrackham Memoirs' is, without doubt, the better-machined story; it is more alive, more coloured, more really tragic. But I am inclined to think that it would have been better, since it would have been less provincial, if it had been translated out of literary circles. For it is provincial in the sense that, to understand it to the full, you must know something of the figures of the province of letters. And that is wrong; that is quite wrong. You should ask of your reader no knowledge whatever except that of the exact sense of words…

It would have made better art of the story. For if Mr Wrackham had been a politician and Mr Ford Lankester a statesman, or if the one had been a successful quack and the other a really good doctor, Miss Sinclair would have had to complete her story by giving some idea of the nature of their respective work. She would have known that her readers in the bulk know nothing of statesmanship and nothing whatever of doctoring. But, writing as she does a literary story, she has too much taken for granted that Ford Lankester will be recognized for the type of the late George Meredith, and that Mr Wrackham is – well, there is no doubt about him! And if she had had to define the nature of their work it would have given her a yet firmer grip of the story.

Nevertheless 'The Wrackham Memoirs' is a jolly good piece of writing and, since most of *my* readers may be taken to know something of the personalities of this province of letters, they will be safe enough to extract a good deal – a great deal – of rather cruel enjoyment from the story. And, at any rate, if this lady can keep it up – if she can keep up practising this greater intensity and this more concentrated form – I do not think that she need have much fear about her own literary future. She has served a hard apprenticeship in some mysterious and tranquil shades or other; she should now reap a good harvest from any seed she likes to sow.

Outlook, 33 (2 May 1914), 599–600.

XXXV. Les Jeunes and *Des Imagistes*

I.

Well, here they are, my young friends, with their lovelocks flowing from the seas beyond…

I suppose that, if anything characterizes this day of ours, it is a discontent – a discontent not so much with existing conditions as with existing modes of thought. There is, for instance, not much the matter with this realm of England, but Parliamentary institutions are discredited in the very birthplace of the Mother of Parliaments, and democracy is on its deathbed. This may appear an extreme statement of the case, and, since I am not a political writer, I will not stay to labour the point, which may be treated by pens abler and more serious. It is nevertheless the view of an unprejudiced observer of this odd world. And the point that I really wish to make is that the trend of all these discontents is almost uniformly reactionary. The extreme Left in France – the Syndicalists – are reactionary, are Royalist, friendly to the Church, violently anti-Parliamentary, and so on. And what the extreme Left of France says today the rest of this world finds itself repeating about thirty-nine years after. And in France the arts have a trick – which they certainly have not here – of keeping company with advanced thought, whereas in this country the general body of thought is about a thousand years behind that of the artist. Thus today the general frame of mind in this country is about that of *Piers Plowman*. In about five hundred years or so we may well have a renewed system that would have pleased Chaucer; and in a quarter of a thousand years again we shall stand with Shakespeare…

And the trend of artistic thought in France – it may well be Slav in its origin – is towards reaction from materialism. Samuel Smiles and our other national heroes would hardly get a hearing in Montmartre; pseudo-Darwinians and other deniers of mystery would hardly now found cults. The eighties, poor dear things, are finally dead. Mind, I am not saying that Marinetti and the Cubists are devout Catholics. They are not. But they represent a frame of mind that, scientifically speaking is religious – that is, at least, other-worldly. If you can once perceive that a cabbage is a wall-flower, which, scientifically speaking it is, you will then be able to see that a painter who sets down, in making a portrait, the image of his emotions in seeing his sitter and not a representation of the sitter – this painter is, scientifically, trying to paint his sitter's soul. He is trying to paint the soul of the world…

Of course you will laugh at this today; but in ten years' time you will be repeating those very words. Personally I am entirely on the side of Les Jeunes. With two exceptions they are the only persons doing anything worth considering in the world. I know that this is a very undignified attitude for me to adopt; I ought to be sitting on the benches of the British

Academy hearing Mr G— tell Mr H— how my ancestors are turning in their graves. But I cannot help it. However much I may try to resemble Socrates, I cannot keep away from the hetairai. The other ladies, like Mr G— and Mr H—, are such crying bores. Yes, one wants to be reckless nowadays…

One wants it desperately; it is a hunger; it is a thirst. One is too safe, in one's views, in one's house, in one's pantaloons. I should respect myself more if I could burgle a Wesleyan chapel and wear a purple-and-green satin dressing gown at Rumpelmayer's, and, just for once, say what I really think of a few people. But I have not the courage. That is why I admire my young friends – they do that sort of thing. They look odd; they talk violently and perfectly incomprehensibly; they label themselves with names for which they would die. (They label me too, for the matter of that!) And not one of them could write an article that the *Times Literary Supplement* would print… Think how refreshing that is! Almost anyone else can do it.

Why the particular group whom today we are considering should label themselves – and myself – Imagistes, I do not know. I do not, for the purposes of this article, know what Imagisme is. Let us examine the volume that they have put forth.

II. *Des Imagistes*: an anthology

Well, one end of this volume is Hellenic, the other extremity Sinetic, if that be the proper term for things which show a Chinese influence. The middle regions contain the very beautiful poems of Mr Flint, which are upon the whole most what I want, since they are about this city. Indeed the most memorable of this very beautiful little collection is Mr Flint's poem about a swan – and that is also the truest piece of Imagisme, at any rate in this volume. This poem however by Mr Ezra Pound is more valuable as an example of what Imagisme really is (Mr Flint's I will save for the end).

Liu Ch'e
The rustling of the silk is discontinued,
Dust drifts over the courtyard,
There is no sound of footfalls and the leaves
Scurry into heaps and lie still,
And she the rejoicer of the heart is beneath them:
A wet leaf that clings to the threshold.

That seems to me a very perfect poem of a school that I have always desired to see. (I should like to make it plain before going any farther that I am not now attempting to appraise the relative values of the poets here represented. As far as the poems are concerned I prefer – possibly for quite personal reasons – 'Priapus, Keeper of Orchards', to anything else in the book.) And these verses seem to me also extremely beautiful. They are by H.D.

... The boughs of the trees
Are twisted
By many bafflings;
Twisted are
The small-leafed boughs.
But the shadow of them
Is not the shadow of the masthead
Nor of torn sails

Hermes, Hermes,
The great sea foamed.
Gnashed its teeth about me;
But you have waited
Where sea-grass tangles with
Shore-grass.

And here again is a poem by Mr Richard Aldington that would come almost exactly into the canons of my school, if I had founded a school:

Aux Vieux Jardins
I have sat here happy in the gardens,
Watching the still pool and the reeds
And the dark clouds
Which the winds of the upper air
Tore like the green leafy boughs
Of the divers-hued trees of late summer;
But though I greatly delight
In these and the water-lilies,
That which sets me nighest to weeping
Is the rose and white colours of the smooth flag-stones,
And the pale yellow grasses
Among them...

These then are the poems that I most like in this anthology. Stop, though. This also is very beautiful:

And I wished for night and you.
I wanted to see you in the swimming pool,
White and shining in the silver-flecked water.
While the moon rode over the garden
High in the arch of night
And the scent of the lilacs was heavy with stillness
Night and the water, and you in your whiteness, bathing!
(Amy Lowell)

It is odd to me to observe how a longish poem of my own that these young men have appropriated for their collection appears amongst this abstract and refined verse like a Gothic gargoyle introduced amongst the Elgin Marbles. I do not mean to say that I would not rather have written Mr Aldington's verses on the Bayswater Fountains. I would. I also have sat in Kensington Gardens, and there was nothing to prevent my doing it except the absence of the Muse at such moments. But the point is that in this collection the only poem that is rhymed is my own.

My own attempts at verse are longish things, and I suppose that what I am aiming at is to produce the hobbling jolting metres of the Gothic ages. And the reason why I adopt rhyme is that it quickens up the form. I wrote the other day a quite long poem that no paper in this country will print – not even this Journal, which stands, as you see, a good deal. Well, I wrote it carefully in unrhymed irregular metres. And it seemed of a length, intolerable, unbearable, inexpressible. I then went through it carefully, inserting rhymes to every line. The result was a singular shortening in effect. (I do not mean to say that the poem is not still intolerably long, but still the effect of the rhymes is to shorten it by at least one-half. I suppose that to be because the ear, leaping forward to find the rhymes, does its work more quickly. I cannot at any rate imagine any other reason.)

The poems however of these young men are almost invariably short. The effect then of their unrhymedness is to give to swallow-flights an appreciable weight, a certain dignity, a certain length. I do not know quite about the metres. Or rather I know quite well what is my private opinion about them; but it probably differs from any explanation that would be given by the Imagistes themselves. They, would probably tell you – if you could understand what they say, which is more than I mostly can – that rhyme and metre are shackles. And so indeed they are. Reasoning the matter out with myself, I seem to find that the justification for *vers libre* is this: It allows a freer play for self-expression than even narrative prose; at the same time it calls for an even greater precision in that self-expression.

It is the perpetual torment, it is the ignis fatuus of the artist, in whatever medium, to seek for new forms. I do not know how much of my time has not been spent in discussing the possibility of finding a new form for the novel. One discusses it hopelessly, as if it were floating in the air above the mist in which we live; one discusses it irritatedly, as if it were a word that is for ever on the tip of the tongue and yet will never come forth. But in *vers libre* as it is practised today I really think that a new form has been found, if not for the novel, then for the narrative of emotion. Mr Pound's poem that I have quoted is in reality a tiny novel, and as such it is doubly interesting to me who am only a dabbler in verse. But at any rate the immediate interest of *vers libre* is that whatever its form, it is in its unit an expression of the author's brain-wave. The unit of formal poetry is the verse of so many lines, or the line itself. The unit of cadenced prose is the paragraph. But the unit of *vers libre* is really the conversational sentence of the author. As such it is the most intimate of means of expression...

The subject is however so large a one that I hope to be permitted to return to it next week. In case however fate or the editor of this Journal intervenes – which I hope they will not, since the subject is that of the whole future of imaginative thought – let me say that this tiny anthology of the Imagistes contains an infinite amount of pure beauty – of abstract beauty. That is my simple opinion. It is the beauty of music – that is to say, of music without much meaning, but of very great power to stir the emotions. And that is the sole real province of all the arts. Here is Mr Flint's poem:

> *The Swan*
> Under the lily-shadow
> and the gold
> and the blue and mauve
> that the whin and the lilac
> pour down on the water
> the fishes quiver.
>
> Over the green cold leaves
> and the rippled silver
> and the tarnished copper
> of its neck and beak,
> toward the deep black water
> beneath the arches
> the swan floats slowly.
>
> Into the dark of the arch the swan floats
> and into the black depth of my sorrow
> it bears a white rose of flame.

Outlook, 33 (9 May 1914), 636, 653.

XXXVI. Les Jeunes and *Des Imagistes* (Second Notice)

I.

It is interesting – it is like a dim recollection of the early nineties – to consider that in the new movements of which I am writing there are two distinct strains that, it would appear, must become hostile with the bitter hostility characterizing the struggles between Socialists and Anarchists in the year 1893. In 1893, as I recalled elsewhere, I was a full-fledged

Anarchist, and I can remember going to William Morris's meeting at Kelmscott House with the deliberate intention of interrupting those tranquil and lamp-lit affairs. I don't know that I ever did anything more than shout a question or two, but certainly, there was what is called an 'ugly feeling' in the air.

The great mass of humanity at that date regarded Anarchism and Socialism as indistinguishable and as indistinguishably connected with ragged appearances, red ties, and bombs. Well, the years have rolled along, Anarchism has become Syndicalism; Syndicalism in despair has become reactionary, has become even aristocratic, as it was bound to become; and here we all are. And, in the Futurism of today – which is the aesthetic, the intellectual expression of Syndicalism – there can be discerned two main streams. And poor Mr Marinetti is understood to be having already trouble with his followers.

For, on the one hand, whilst all the literary, all the verbal manifestations of Futurism are representational, and representational, and again representational, all the plastic-aesthetic products of the new movement are becoming more and more geometric, mystic, non-material, or what you will. The Futurist painters were doing very much what novelists of the type of Flaubert or short-story writers of the type of Maupassant aimed at. They gave you not so much the reconstitution of a crystallized scene in which all the figures were arrested – not so much that, as fragments of impressions gathered during a period of time, during a period of emotion, or during a period of travel. Thus, in one corner of the picture you would have a large Roman 'I', showing that the painter either travelled first-class or would so much like to have travelled first-class that the desire left a permanent impress on his mind. Similarly, in another portion of the canvas there would be a rendering of an old gentleman with a face like a goat, and in other places locomotive funnels – the funnels of steamboats, the Arc de Triomphe, a *voiture de remise*, and so on. Such a Futurist painting was very much what Flaubert or Maupassant would have tried to render in words forty or fifty years ago. The effect produced indeed is very much that of Turgenev's account of an execution. And the effect produced by one of Mr Marinetti's poems is almost exactly similar. It is literally impressionism and nothing more. And the fact that the *mots* are *en liberté* affects nothing more than the fact that the word *flamme* will be standing on its head instead of lying down. The Cubists are however entirely different in spirit and, whatever they are, they aren't impressionists. They are, if you will, emotionalists. Looking at the leaves on a tree, at a man's head, or at a petticoat makes them want to draw certain patterns, and they go and draw them. That, at any rate, sums the matter up as clearly and in a few words.

Now it is obvious that a very pretty fight might arrange itself between the Cubists, who are anti-materialists, and the Futurists, who are really realists. And I dare say that, humanity being what it is, that fight may yet arrive. And yet I do not feel at all certain that there is any necessity for this Armageddon, since the real crux of both methods is a matter of arousing emotion. I will try to illustrate what I mean. Some time ago I was passing through a period of extreme mental distress – a period that lasted for a long time – of a distress for which there was no remedy. But one day, going downstairs and looking out of the window, I saw a shape of an extremely vivid – but an incredibly vivid! – green. It was one of those greens that transcend any thinkable colour – that transcend any green flame, any possible painted surface, and it was extremely clear and sharp in outline. It was in fact the underside of a parrot climbing up a vertical wire trellis. And at that sight an extraordinary calmness descended upon my depression; it was like the end of the Church service when the clergyman says 'The peace of God which passes all understanding'.

II. *Des Imagistes*: an anthology

Now the point is that, if I had been a Futurist, I should have rendered a bit of the staircase, my shoes which I had just put on, certain details of the circumstance or of the person who was depressing me. I might have put in the representation of a postage-stamp because I was expecting a letter, or the representation of a telephone-receiver because I hoped against hope that some one would ring me up; and somewhere about I should have put in a very sharply defined shape of a very vivid green. I should then expect the spectator to have the emotions that I had then felt. If, on the other hand, I had been a Cubist I should have rendered no material object. I might have given you a streak of clear grey, possibly subconsciously suggested by the sky, a streak of scarlet for the colour I should like postage-stamps to have, a black octagon because the telephone is mechanical in suggestion, and so on. But equally with the Futurist, I should be trying to convey my emotions to the spectator, since the whole province of both these schools of art is the conveying of emotions.

My Imagiste friends fall, it seems to me, into the category of realists. They render, that is to say, concrete objects, and expect the reader to have aroused in him certain emotions. And indeed, if you will consider Mr Flint's poem about the swan you will see that it is an exact setting forth of my own anecdote about the parrot, and almost the same effect will be produced by Mr Epstein's sculpture of birds, or by any other of the Imagiste poems that I quoted last week.

The fact is that any very clear and defined rendering of any material object has power to convey to the beholder or to the reader a sort of quivering of very definite emotions. In its very clearness and in its very hardness it seems to point the moral of the impermanence of matter, of human life, or if you will, of the flight of birds. You can get indeed more emotion out of the exact rendering of the light reflected in the bonnet of an automobile than out of the lamentation of fifty thousand preachers. The point is, I suppose, that just as very vivid and perfectly disproportionate emotions are aroused in you by meeting certain persons, so equally vivid emotions will be aroused if you come in contact with their manifestations, with their records, with their art. And the justification of any method of art, the measure of its success, will be just the measure of its suitability for rendering the personality of the artist.

I am thinking of course of the *vers libre* of my Imagiste friends as a vehicle for the expression of personality. Last week, if you will remember, I said that the unit of verse of the poems in this particular volume appeared to be the conversational sentences of the poet. You must, I think, be aware that whenever you frame a conversational sentence with any care you try to get into it a certain cadence. If you are merely asserting to your fishmonger your reasons for considering the prices he charges for red mullet to be exorbitant, if you are asserting it carefully, you must be aware that, whilst you are listening to his reply to your last sentence, you will be preparing in your mind, you are balancing, you are stressing the sentence with which you will reply to him. You may open your conversation with a long sentence to which he may reply as best suits his temperament. You will then utter a sentence which he may interrupt; you will probably take up your sentence and finish it, partly because you wish to convey certain facts to that fishmonger, but almost certainly very much more because your ear does not wish to be cheated of its cadence, of its stresses, of its balance. And those sentences will be extraordinarily characteristic of you. They will be more characteristic than your hands, than your eyes, than the set of your shoulders, or than the way you lift your feet when you walk. And, if any really observant friend wished to render you to an admiring or to a perturbed world he would render you more exactly by catching the cadence of your sort of typical sentence than by almost any other means. (I do not mean to say that this is the only form characterization takes, but I certainly think it is the most subtle and the most intimate.)

And the more formal your conversation may be the more characteristic will your cadences become – the more characteristic, that is to say, of your mood at the time. If you are at a stiff and frigid tea-party you will arrange them so as to conceal emotion, but they will be none the less you. Or if you have ever had occasion to plead for a long time for something that you very much wanted, with a rather silent person, you will, if you take the trouble to remember – not the context of what you said, but the sound, the rhythm of your utterances – you will remember an effect like that of a sea with certain wave-lengths going on and on and on. They may be long rollers, or they may be a short and choppy sea with every seventh sentence a large wave.

And that seems to me to be the importance of the *vers libre* of this volume. It seems to me to be important not so much because of the context of the poetry as because it is a definite progress towards the intimate rendering of the writers' personalities. The *vers libre* that we have had up to this date has been, as far as its cadence is concerned, more or less derivative. Whitman, for instance, is nearly always blank verse, arbitrarily distributed, and as much might be said of Henley. They wrote, that is to say, rather to satisfy an existent metre, a metre evolved by ages of convention, than to satisfy the personal needs of their ears. And that is true of all other verse forms, whether the line be octosyllabic, or deca- or endecasyllabic, or spondaic, or what you will. I am not of course decrying all other forms of metre and I am not throwing rhyme to the dogs. All that I am trying to say is that verse which is cut to a pattern must sacrifice a certain amount – not necessarily very much, but still a certain amount – of the personality of the writer. And inasmuch as the personality of the writer is still the chief thing in a work of art, any form that will lead to the more perfect expression of personality is a form of the utmost value. I suppose that what I have been aiming at all my life is a literary form that will produce the effect of a quiet voice going on talking and talking, without much ejaculation, without the employment of any verbal strangeness – just quietly saying things. Of course I do not lay that down as a canon for the whole world. The universe is very large and in it there is room for an infinite number of gods. There is room even for Mr Marinetti's declamations of his battle-pieces. But one is very tired; writing is a hopeless sort of job, words are very hard to find, and one frequently wishes that one were dead, and so on. It is at such times that one welcomes the quiet voice that will just go on talking to one about nothing in particular, just to keep one from thinking. It is at such times that one welcomes such a poem as

Sitalkas

Thou art come at length, more beautiful than any cool god
In a chamber under Lycia's far coast,
Than any high god who touches us not, here in the seeded grass.
Aye, than Argestes
Scattering the broken leaves.

(H.D.)

Outlook, 33 (16 May 1914), 682–3.

XXXVIII. Mr W.H. Mallock and *Social Reform*

I.

If the Tory Party had any sense it would buy 6,000, or 60,000, or 600,000, or 6,000,000 copies of Mr Mallock's book and distribute them throughout the constituencies. But the Tory Party has always been the stupid party and now it is purely imbecile, so I suppose it will do nothing of the sort. From the days of the *New Republic* Mr Mallock has been the most distinguished, the most active, and the most typical of what it is customary to call reactionary thinkers in this country. I should be tempted to call him the only actively reactionary propagandist that we have; but if I did so some one would write and say that Mr Jones, of Putney, has been writing reactionary pamphlets for the last seventy-two years; and that would be a nuisance. Still, it is my private opinion that Mr Mallock is the most important of our reactionary writers (by 'reactionary' I mean really sceptical; for there is in England a school of thought, though it would seem preposterous to say so and though nothing ever really appears to make the Englishman think. Still, here and there in colleges, in vicarages, in surgeries, and in odd houses there are two or three men with cool, unhurried sceptical, cynical minds of the type that is peculiarly English, and that I must confess to finding quite attractive).

What I really do desperately want is to see a good Tory history in use in the schools in this country, to take once and for all the place of stuff of the Whig type like that of the late Mr John Richard Green. It is really time that the idea of precedent broadening down to precedent[1] should be got out of the heads of this afflicted people.

For, looking at the state of the nation from the standpoint of the independent observer, it is perfectly obvious to me that we are approaching the stage when we shall have for Government a permanent Left – such a state of things as they have today in France. I am convinced that, once the Irish question is out of the way, our side will never have a chance. Never, never, never. And why in the world should they have a chance? They don't deserve it. For years and years, for decades and decades, they have been letting their children be filled up with the Whig cant of the greatest good of the greatest number and things that I have not the patience to write about. I do not suppose that there is a single child in this country who is not being taught to say that Oliver Cromwell was a democrat or that the Great Rebellion was a constitutional movement to resist a new and unjust tax and to free a groaning people. As a matter of fact, ship-money was the oldest tax of England – a tax that was levied before the

1 [Tennyson, 'You ask me, why, though ill at ease': 'A land of settled government, / A land of just and old renown, / Where Freedom slowly broadens down / From precedent to precedent'.]

days of the Heptarchy – and the Cromwellians were a lot of people who objected to paying their taxes just as you and I object to paying them, only more efficiently. They were indeed so efficient about it that, at the death of Oliver Cromwell, the national exchequer was bankrupt.

I do not make these statements as being of any importance, but simply as instances of what should be taught in schools if children are to have any just view of history and if the Tory Party is to survive. The Tory Party has a very proper contempt for men of letters. We are, poor dears, a weak people; but our home nevertheless is in the eternal hills. Last Sunday a lady said to me that she had never met a man of letters who was not a Liberal. I instanced several distinguished employers of the English language, and she retorted that they were none of them Englishmen, though they were certainly strong Tories. I left the matter at that.

But there you have it really in a nutshell. The Tories have always quite properly, but none the less stupidly, despised men of letters. It is like despising your cook; it is just as stupid as kicking your cook in the face. For it is the man of letters who has evolved the monstrous nonsense that is taught in the schools of today. It is the man of letters who is filling up the minds of your children with daily messes just as the cook fills their tender stomachs. And no man, having secured for himself a good cook, would go and kick him or her in the face. I don't mean to say that the man of letters has any valid moral excuse for being treated better than your butler, your governess, or your curate. But if you don't treat him better he will go and be a Liberal and get asked to the 'at-homes' of the leaders of the party and get a knighthood or so thrown to him. So he will go on writing about precedent broadening down to precedent, and he will go on being a democrat *in seculum seculorum*.

Hang it all! Why cannot the Tory Party treat men of letters as my co-religionists treat their priests? Quâ man, it is possible for a priest to be the nastiest little bounder imaginable, but, inasmuch as he has to do the dirty work of scraping our ignoble souls into heaven, he has about him something of the divine and is accorded great pomp and precedence in the proper places. The Tory Party, like our ignoble souls, has always had to have somebody to do its dirty work. And, if it could put on a sufficient semblance of deference to make Toryism worth while before the foreign Jew like Disraeli, it could surely pretend to bend its proud neck before followers of my own calling – for the sake of the little children. If you come to think of it, there are no fewer than three men of letters – Lord Morley, Mr Birrell, and Mr Masterman – in the present Cabinet.

II. *Social Reform: its relations to realities and delusions.*
By W.H. Mallock

I have already avowed the greatest admiration for Mr Mallock's book. Mr Mallock has set himself the task of destroying one of the great historic fallacies – a fallacy which, having been in the first place the assumption of Karl Marx, has become as great a menace to society of today as has been for a long time the ideas of Rousseau. Rousseau is of course much the more formidable sentimentalist, and as such he is much the more difficult to combat. Rousseau fastened upon the neck of this world that collar which is the idea of the rights of man. Of course it is purely nonsensical to talk of any man having rights when all that a man really has are duties and privileges. But these are very indefinite matters. Rousseau may make his statement and you your counter-statement; yet the matter will remain pretty much where it was, and the degree of its acceptance by the world will be nearly the relative degree of the loudness of your shouting or the persuasiveness of your manner. But Marx was not an artist like Rousseau. He dealt with facts and figures, not in sentiments. He and his followers, that is to say, evolved, not the theory, but the direct statement that, under the system of capitalism the rich are daily growing richer and richer and the poor daily more and more poor. This statement is simply a lie.

This statement is simply a lie due to the non-scientific minds of Marx and of his followers. These gentlemen are sentimentalists like you and me and the Chancellor of the Exchequer. They are sentimentalists who, having once seen some ragged children playing in the gutter whilst an opulent lady in silks and satins – this is rather the phraseology of social reformers than my own – at any rate, having seen the opulent lady in silks and satin roll by in an elegant barouche, drawn by two pampered horses and having upon the box-seat two pampered menials – these social reformers then have their sentiments stirred. They say, here are the rich battening upon the poor. Some time afterwards they go into Hyde Park upon a Sunday morning, and they perceive a perfect galaxy of opulent women drawn by pampered steeds, or at any rate conducted by pampered menials. Having perceived only one lady before and perceiving now a great many, they start and say, 'surely the rich are growing richer'. At the back of their minds remains the thought of the poorer quarters of an immense London which they seldom visit – because social reformers as a rule do themselves rather well – they quite conscientiously believe that the poor remain as poor as they were. They might then say with truth, as far as they have perceived it, that the rich are growing richer and that the poor remain as they were. Even that would be an untruth, since in actual fact, although a few rich people are growing richer, the whole body of the population, including the poor, are growing immeasurably more wealthy. To put the matter picturesquely, and of course exaggeratedly, there are practically no poor in the England of today.

There are no poor in the sense that there were poor in the year 1801. In the year 1801 the number of earned and unearned incomes was 4,100,000. And the number of incomes below £60 a year was 3,752,100. That is to say, that upwards of three-quarters of the wage-earners of this country were living at what today would be considered very near starvation level. Today the number of incomes below twenty-two shillings a week has decreased to 2,000,000, although the population of wage-earners has increased from four to eleven millions. The number of incomes between thirty shillings and sixty-two shillings was in 1801 90,000. Today it is 6,000,000. These are all official figures quoted by Mr Mallock from census and income-tax returns. It must therefore be obvious to anyone with any eye at all for figures that, far from the poor having grown poorer, or even having remained as poor as they were, not only the relative but the actual number of the very poor has enormously decreased in these islands during the last hundred and fourteen years; and that the relatively comfortable amongst the wage-earning classes have enormously increased in number. Without however inquiring into these facts, and carried away by emotions conveyed to them through their eyes, the Marxian reformers add to their axiom that the rich are growing richer every day, not merely the corollary that the poor are growing poorer – no, for the sake of emotional appeal, for the sake of the balance of phrase, of rhetoric, of epigram, they must add the corollary that the poor are growing poorer.

It is to these arguments, to these particular sentimentalities of the Marxian reformers, that Mr Mallock devotes his keen attention in this remarkable volume. Remarkable the book is, because hitherto the only data that there have been were the vague speculations of party politicians, whereas Mr Mallock has, first of all statisticians, availed himself of 'specific official information, the existence of which appears to have been overlooked relating to the amount and distribution of incomes at the beginning of the nineteenth century'. And if you come to think of it, if you come to think merely of the drawings of Rowlandson and Cruikshank, or of the depictions of the life of the poor in the pages of novelists from the days of Fielding to those of Dickens; if you come to think of that picture of rags, filth, squalor, darkness, disease, and what is called crime, you will have a picture of horror and brutality compared with which the life of a working-man of today is little short of heaven. This however is mere sentimentalism of my own.

Mr Mallock presents you with the definite and hard statistics reviewed from every thinkable standpoint. He puts the statistics statistically; he puts them in terms of buildings, in terms of eating, in terms of drinking, in terms of furniture – there is no limit to his inexhaustible vitality. I must confess to having found it rather tough reading for the exhausted and inattentive brain that one carries about with one nowadays. But that is not Mr Mallock's fault; his statements are clear enough when he desires to be clear, and picturesque enough when picturesqueness is his aim. And, as I said at the beginning of this article, the Tory Party, if it had any sense, would trumpet, would telegraph, would telephone, would communicate by every thinkable and unthinkable means Mr Mallock's discoveries throughout these islands. But of course the Unionists will not.

Outlook, 33 (30 May 1914), 751–2.

XXXIX. Mr W. B. Yeats and his New Poems

I.

Mr Yeats's figure has always singularly intrigued me. Humanity is not a nice animal, and I must confess to having for seven-eighths of my life, with the best will in the world, regarded Mr Yeats as almost a grotesque. I never took much stock in poets. Shelley to me was always a nuisance, Keats a negligible consumptive, Tennyson a smooth prig, and William Morris a bore. I had some respect for Browning, I suppose because he was fond of talking of the duchesses of his acquaintance, and it appears to me to be respectable to want to know duchesses. I should like to know lots and lots of them, and, if I did, I should certainly talk about them all day long.

What this all amounts to is that I want poets to be natural creatures; and they very seldom are natural creatures. And I suppose why I regarded Mr Yeats with so little respect for many years was simply that he seemed to me exceedingly affected. I don't mean to say that he seemed to me to be personally affected, since I never, until quite lately, came into personal contact with Mr Yeats. But, from the nineties onward, Mr Yeats really did seem to dispense across this city of London a sort of aura that I found exceedingly irritating. That may have been mere jealousy, of course; but I hardly think it was jealousy, since Mr Yeats was always so immeasurably more distinguished than myself that I might just as well have been jealous of Sappho.

But certainly the thought that Mr Yeats was somewhere about, probably leaning on a mantelpiece with his face to the ceiling, irritated me exceedingly. I didn't like his confounded point of view. I hated and do still hate, people who poke about among legends and insist on the charms of remote islands. And all that I had read of Mr Yeats's work was *The Countess Kathleen*, which seemed to have to do with legend, and a poem which began, 'I will arise and go now'. This always seemed to me to be particularly irritating. How, I used to ask myself, could that gentleman get to Innisfree, supposing he were then lying down, without rising? And why then should he state that he was going to arise? You will observe that this was a prose-impressionist irritation. The prose-impressionist, if he has to deal with a gentleman going out of a door in an ordinary way, does not say that the gentleman walked to the door, starting with his right foot, put his hand upon the handle, turned the handle, drew the door towards him, and stepped across the mat. No, the prose-impressionist treats the matter somewhat as follows: 'Mr Humphrey said he must be going. When the door closed upon him Inez threw herself into a chair and wept convulsively.' So, Innisfree being the centre of Mr Yeats's poem, and I being, presumably even at that early age, a prose-impressionist, should have preferred Mr Yeats's poem to have run:

> At Innisfree there is a public-house;
> They board you well for ten and six a week.
> The mutton is not good, but you can eat
> Their honey. I am going there to take
> A week or so of holiday tomorrow.

There might have been in addition some details about the landscape and whether the fishing was good. That was what I wanted in a poem of those days; that is what I still want in a poem. And the Mr Yeats of the nineties seemed to be always – when he wasn't leaning against a mantelpiece – reclining by the side of some lake or other, and then arising and going to some other lake. He seemed, in short, to be self-conscious about his attitude.

I don't think that as the years roll on I have grown more tolerant. Indeed, I am perfectly sure that I have grown much more ragingly one-sided. But I have certainly acquired a great respect for Mr Yeats. Outside my young friends he seems to me to be the one poet that matters in a world where only poets matter. Did you ever happen to know by repute a notorious villain and then gradually get to know that villain? And have you then gradually discovered that that villain was a serious and a striving personality, and gradually, further, that he was a hero, a prophet, the apostle of a cause? It is not an uncommon experience amongst generous people.

Something of the sort must have taken place in myself as far as Mr Yeats was concerned. It was probably Mr Yeats as theatre director that first impressed me. Nothing could be more unlike a theatre director than Mr Yeats in his apparent distraction; but somehow things seemed to get themselves done by the players of the Abbey Theatre in a way infinitely better than that of any gentleman whose pince-nez did not fall off every two minutes. And the Abbey Theatre was a very fine and a very memorable achievement. So, having acquired considerable personal respect for Mr Yeats, it began to occur to me that his Celticism might be genuine, or might be a pose, but that in any case it did not matter very much beside the importance of the personality. It was as if the saviour of a country should choose to wear a shocking bad hat. And then someone kindly induced Mr Yeats to send me some poems for publication in *The English*

Review, and I began to have larger hopes of this poet. One of them began:

Being out of heart with government
I took a broken root to fling
Where the proud wayward squirrel went,
Taking delight that he could spring...

This seemed to me to be more encouraging, since a poet who is dissatisfied with government will probably have something in him. Or it might be better to put it that an Irishman who was not out of heart with the government of his country would be so little of a man that he could not possibly be a poet.

II. *New Poems*. By Mr W.B. Yeats

And in his new poems Mr Yeats shows more and more signs of coming out of Celticism. I do not mean to say that he is any less an Irishman, but he seems to occupy himself less with going up into the mists and reading about the old ancient kings of all when he gets there. Mind, I am not so violently Futurist as to object to a man having any truck at all with old legends. But dwelling upon them is just a sort of building of castles in the air, and building castles in the air is an occupation over which every man should spend a portion of his time if he is to keep his mind sweet. But I think it should not be too much indulged in, any more than drinking, to which pursuit it is closely allied. It is a too easy type of stimulant.

A considerable portion of Mr Yeats's new book is made up of legendary matter, and beautiful enough it is. But a considerable proportion too is given up to actualities, to pictures, even to pasquinades. And that is a very good thing. You have poems with titles like 'To a Wealthy Man who promised to send a second subscription if it were proved that people wanted pictures', or 'September 1913', or 'To a Friend whose work has come to nothing'. And it is a very good thing that Mr Yeats has come out into the world. It is a good thing for the public generally. To have your poets perpetually chanting that your own day is vulgar or mean, and that beauty can be found only in other centuries or in other climates, is a thing very enervating. If you are perpetually to be told that heroism, beauty, fineness, or chivalry are only to be found in the records of the year 1415 or the Malay Free States, you will gradually cease your efforts to be beautiful, fine, heroic, or chivalrous. And that man who, having the power, ceases to depict for you the possibility of chivalry is accursed beyond all other men, since in the end chivalry in yourself and in those around you and loyalty to your ideals are the only things that make life worth living.

And Mr Yeats's emergence into this curious and beautiful world of ours is of benefit to the world of letters because it is very interesting. I have, for instance the vague conviction that Mr Yeats is nowadays as subconsciously abandoning beauty as in the nineties he sought it. He seems to strive after harsh effects, harsh words, harsh consonants. I haven't much right to dogmatise about these matters, but I rather fancy that in these last two particulars he is mistaken. A harsh effect is always a good thing, because it is arresting to the attention – a harsh effect in matter I mean. But harsh verbiage I rather fancy is always a mistake, simply because it stops the run of the eye and gives a sort of dramatic effect where dramatic effect is a nuisance. And dramatic effect is a nuisance not only when it forces the note, but because it lessens the effect of such passages as are designedly dramatic. The effect of a gentleman's weeping or swearing will at any given moment be very much less if he is in the habit of being in tears or frequently utters expletives; thus Mr Yeats's harsh and crabbed use of English, although I can quite well imagine it to be design, takes away to some extent from one's pleasure in reading his verse. 'Beggar to beggar cried, being frenzy struck' is an ugly line not only because the matter is ugly – which is perfectly legitimate – but because the gs and ks and the comma and the unusual construction arrest the ear almost as badly as if a train had run off the line. And I cannot see that any purpose is served by letting this train run off its rails five times in the course of five verses – since this line is five times repeated.

But Mr Yeats may reply – as it is open to every artist to reply – that he could not get his particular effect if he did not use this particular means. And, no doubt in saying so he would be perfectly justified in his own view. But I think I should be right in rejoining that in that case Mr Yeats must be still aiming at what, for lack of a better word, I would call the rhetorical. He is no longer aiming so much at the adventitious beauty, the rhetoric, of legends and of the indefinitely remote, but he is trying to get a sort of swagger into his gait, a sort of harshness into his voice.

God forbid that I should be taken to deny the right of existence of any d'Artagnan[1] amongst the poets, but, for myself, I do seem to need something quieter and something more subtle: I suppose that the person of whom I am always thinking is in the end Heinrich Heine in his more satirical moods.

But in the end I suppose that it does not matter. There was Mr Yeats, with his harsh words or with his words that are not harsh, evolving a new method and adumbrating a new point of view, and I must confess to unfeigned satisfaction at the new point of view. I have said somewhere else that Mr Yeats's earlier work suggested to me a landscape, or perhaps rather a territory all of mist, through whose swathes there gleamed here and there a jewel, a green cap or a white owl's feather. But the landscapes of Mr Yeats's new poems suggest to me rather high skies, with toppling clouds and the shore of the sea and harsh rocks and people leading the life

22 [Hero of Alexander Dumas' *The Three Musketeers*.]

that we lead. I cannot think of any other way to express it; and if I have meticulously, and possibly with the air of a pedant, examined the mere verbiage of these poems it is only because that is my poor old job. I wish it weren't my poor old job and that I had the faculty of expressing more ungrudgingly my admiration for this great personality and fine poet.

Outlook, 33 (6 June 1914), 783–4.

XLII. Mr Robert Frost and *North of Boston*

I.

★★★

I have heard depressed Americans – and nearly all Americans are very depressed when you praise their country to them, though they will knock you down with a fire-shovel if you hint at a word of blame – I have heard depressed Americans assert that the end of New England has come, because all the sons of the old-standers – the men whose families went over with the *Mayflower* – marry the French ladies' maids of the summer boarders, and so the old stock is dying out. But I think that that must be an exaggeration. The agricultural New Englanders are horribly poor because their country is unfertile, their climate inclement, and they have to suffer – just as English farmers have to suffer – from the competition of the West. But there still remains a large population supporting itself by agriculture – hard, rigid, determined men, instinct with the New England conscience, with cold virtues of early Nonconformity rendered colder by the harshnesses amongst which they dwell. They are extraordinarily provincial, formal, old-fashioned, and unbending; some of them strike one as a little mad, because of course their values are not one's own values. But there they are, and it is to me at least incredible that summer boarders enough can be found to populate the country from Connecticut to the State of Maine with French ladies' maids.

II. *North of Boston*. By Robert Frost

It is because of the revelatory light that it casts upon the nature of this queer population that Mr Frost's book may well be of value to the general reader. Because it is as interesting as a book of travel. The story of the dangerous man with the hundred collars for which he has no use because they are size sixteen, whereas his neck now requires sixteen-and-a-half; the picture of the two neighbours walking down opposite sides of a loose stone wall, replacing boulders that cattle, time, or the weather have thrown down; the real pictures of haymaking and of the man who tried to smother his employer beneath trusses of hay because that employer had nagged him to a state of frenzy; the pictures of the berry-pickers; of the mountains, of the springs – all these things are better done by Mr Frost than by any writer that I know. There are these natural objects and scenes – and always there is present the feeling of madness, of mysterious judgements, of weather-hardened odd people – people very uncouth and unlovely, but very real.

I have the privilege of knowing Mr Frost quite well, but if I did not know him I should imagine him to be a queer harsh sort of fellow, in a hacked-out black frock-coat, with a round soft black hat, a goatee going grey, driving a dilapidated buggy over sandy roads filled with boulders the size of an armchair. A sort of deacon from the State of Maine he would be – one of those silent dour Americans who appear sane enough until suddenly, as if you touched in them something that clicked, they become frighteningly vocal, impassioned, *hurlant* – there is no other word for it – about the Second Advent or something of the sort. Maybe it will only be about a patent-medicine.

I have omitted to state that Mr Frost's stories and pictures are in verse, so that I may have been attracting attention to his book by false pretences. But Mr Frost's verse is so queer, so harsh, so unmusical, that the most prosaic of readers need not on that account be frightened away. This is the sort of verse that it is:

> I don't just see him living many years,
> Left here with nothing but the furniture.
> I hate to think of the old place when we're gone,
> With the brook going by below the yard,
> And no-one here but hens blowing about.
> If he could sell the place, but then he can't:
> No-one will ever live on it again.
> It's too run down. This is the last of it.
> What I think he will do is let things smash.
> He'll sort of swear the time away. He's awful.
> I never saw a man let family troubles
> Make so much difference in his man's affairs.
> He's just dropped everything. He's like a child.
> I blame his being brought up by his mother.
> He's got hay down that's been rained on three times.
> He hoed a little yesterday for me…

He had been left by the woman he lived with, who had gone off and married some one else, and that is the girl's mother speaking. She had lived with them, as I make it out; but she also was going off… That is the queer sort of story, and those are the queer people the stories are about, and that is the queer sort of verse.

Mr Frost no doubt has theories as to prosody. He seems to make people, or the narrator, talk with the abrupt sort of rhythms that do undoubtedly distinguish his compatriots north of Boston, and then to insist on jamming all the utterances into decasyllabic lines. You can hardly call it blank verse. Occasionally lines with nine syllables or seven hit you in the face and make you feel as if you had fallen out of a window, or, at any rate, set you counting on your fingers. Here are the first lines of the book:

> *Mending Wall*
> Something there is that doesn't love a wall,
> That sends the frozen ground-swell under it,
> And spills the upper boulders in the sun
> And makes gaps even two can pass abreast.
> The work of hunters is another thing;
> I have come after them and made repair
> Where they have left not one stone on stone...

That last line is a truly bewildering achievement.

But I daresay Mr Frost does not care whether his lines are regular or not. And yet, on the other hand why does he bother to put his work into lines at all? I am not insinuating that Mr Frost is not a poet. He is a very fine one. But there is such a thing as *vers libre*, which is an excellent instrument for rendering the actual rhythm of speech. I am not in the least suggesting that Mr Frost should write *vers libre*; I am only saying that it seems queer that he does not. There was Whitman... But Mr Frost's achievement is much finer, much more near the ground and much more national, in the true sense, than anything that Whitman gave to the world. I guess he is afraid of the liberty of *vers libre*; to shackle himself probably throws him into the right frame of mind. It is another form of the New England conscience.

Anyhow it is no affair of mine. As long as Mr Frost goes on getting his effects I don't mind how he gets them. He may use rhymed Alexandrines for all I care. As long as he will go all on, croak-croaking about his queer people, I shall be satisfied. Because he does give you a very excellent, a very poetic, a very real sense of his meadows and woods and rocks and berries, and of night and of showers and of wildnesses and dangers – of an America that really matters far more than the land of endless trickery, make-believe, and lying and empty loquacity. That is the face that – Heaven knows why! – America seems to like to present to these parts of the world; but those are its least desirable features. Anyhow Mr Frost has called in on us to redress the balance of that particular New World. And I hope he will get a hearty welcome.

For he is not a remains of English culture grown provincial and negligible as were the writers that abounded near Concord, Mass. He is as different from Holmes and Whittier as he is from Whitman or Bret Harte or Mary E. Wilkins. He is not in fact a sentimentalist. Not to be a sentimentalist is to be already half-way towards being a poet – and Mr Frost goes the other half of the way as well, though to describe what that other half is beats me. Here is the little poem – rhymed for a change – in which as it were he proffers his invitation to read *North of Boston*:

The Pasture
I'm going out to clean the pasture spring.
I'll only stop to rake the leaves away
And wait to watch the water clear, I may;
I shan't be gone long – You come too.

I'm going out to fetch the little calf
That's standing by the mother. It's so young
It totters when she licks it with her tongue.
I shan't be gone long – You come too.

Why is that beautiful and friendly and touching and all sorts of things? I don't know. I suppose, just because Mr Frost is a poet.

Outlook, 33 (27 June 1914), 879–80.

France, 1915 (continued)

I.

The distinction between the French mind and the non-French mind – nay, the absolute distinction of the French mind – is almost entirely a matter of language. For it has never been sufficiently recognized in this country how language holds sway over character, over action, and over all the attributes of humanity. When a French peasant-woman observes somebody hanging about her house, the men being absent in the fields, she says: 'C'est que'que maoufatant!' – 'It is some malefactor.' A Kent or Sussex peasant-woman in the same circumstances would remark: 'Reckon he bëant after no good!' And, as you progress further northward through the English shires towards the Border so you will approach the still greater caution of 'I'm not saying that he's there for any good.' And very similar reservations will characterize the common speech of almost all European countries, even when the matter of comment is something absolutely immaterial. In the brightest of sunshine in High Germany the peasant will say: 'I am not saying that the weather is not good'; and the Russian peasant, in answer to your query, will put it that perhaps it is five versts to Moscow, but that the matter is in God's hands. The Latin mind – or what it is convenient to call the Latin mind – seeks, in fact, for definite statements and, before making a statement, must of necessity form a mental appraisement as exact as possible. This leads to an extreme concreteness of mentality.

These things are of course matters of aesthetics, and matters of aesthetics, usually despised in this country, are at the present moment very much at a discount. Why they should be at a discount, the prevailing system having broken down and having proved so absolutely unworkable, Heaven alone knows! This country, and this world having drifted into the greatest of catastrophes for want of plain-speaking, one might think that sanity would lead the populations of this country and of the world to see the desirability of cultivating the exact use of speech. We are at war today very largely because of the imbecilely figurative language that prevails in German Ministries and Chancelleries, and of the imbecilely phrased reservations that characterize the diplomatic language of the rest of the world. We are, in short, at war today because German allegories of Mailed Fists, shining armour, and the rest of it seemed ludicrous to the rest of the world, and because the cautious indefiniteness of phraseology of the rest of the world seemed to the German office-holders to be a sign of timidity. The Germans loudly proclaimed to the rest of the world that if anyone sought to cast the shadow of dishonour upon their unspotted eagle-banner they would unsheathe the sword that their fathers had bequeathed to them, and would gird on the shining armour fashioned for them by Thor, the God of War, and, with the words of Luther upon their lips, under the auspices of the God of the Germans, would 'let loose' (*losschlagen*) upon an effete Europe and so conquer a place in the sun. The rest of the world, with Great Britain at its head, replied that in the event of certain unfortunate eventualities certain other unfortunate eventualities might eventuate. At that point, which had been reached by July 27, 1914, the rest of the world believed that Germany was engaged on farcical rodomontades, and Germany believed that the rest of the world meant nothing at all, and did not know what it did mean. Had Germany, on the other hand said: 'We are a very efficient nation; our military organizing has been carried to a pitch of human perfection; it is absolutely necessary for us and Austria to have at least one open strip of territory through the Balkans to our allies the Turks, and so through to the Persian Gulf. If this strip of territory is not guaranteed to us and our allies we shall march through Belgium to Paris'; and if the rest of the world had then replied: 'We are not so efficiently organized as you, but we are determined to support France, and if you violate the neutrality of Belgium we shall put into the field all the forces that we can raise to oppose you' – here would at least have been a clear issue.

I am not presuming to criticize the diplomatic steps that were taken by this country or by any of the Allies. They, like the rest of the world, have to take the world as they find it, with its periphrases, its reservations of language, and its cliché phrases. But I am very much concerned to point out that if similar blunders of diplomacy are to be avoided in the future it is important that clarity of phrase and exactness of thought should be cultivated. And here at once the question of aesthetics comes in.

II.

For to be precise is the most difficult thing in the world, and it is only the French, following in the traditions of classical Rome, who have at all appreciated the value of this precision. Nicenesses of phrase are not merely part of the private pleasure of the artist; they are the necessity of the common man in every function of his life. Relatively, even the present war is of small importance; what is of importance is that the ordinary affairs of life should be conducted as quietly, as efficiently, with as little discussion and as little waste of time as possible. The farmer who can instruct his hind in the fewest and most exact words how deep to plough a field, how low to cut a hedge, at what time to take up a young team from the field, is doing a greater service to humanity than another farmer who fumbles over his instructions, and whose instructions are, in consequence, less fully carried out and yield smaller return. A man who, in courting a woman, or a woman who, being courted by a man, can exactly define his or her emotions or what their subsequent relationships will be, is doing some service to the State, since less time will be lost from their subsequent labours over the adjustments of their personal relationships. A mother is doing most service to the State when the language with which she enjoins moral reflections upon her children is exact, convincing, and thus most likely to bear fruit. It is in all these departments that France has so far outstripped the rest of the Occidental world that we may well say that it is only France that matters. If, in short, Europe, save for France, were depopulated, France could provide Europe with a much saner, much more efficient race of men – of men capable of making something decent, dignified and enjoyable out of life.

There is no minuteness to which this does not apply. If, being a man, you go into an English hat-shop you try on a hat and don't like it; you try on another and don't like that. At last you put one on and the hatter remarks that that is how they are being worn now. If you go into a French hat-shop, the hatter, being a practical man, will try you with several hats, and will finally arrive at one of which he will say, 'Cela vous dégage mieux la physiognomie' – 'That disengages your physiognomy better' or, as we should say, 'brings out your features more'.

To this gem there are several facets. In the first place the French hatter is better educated in the traditions of his trade; it costs him as little effort to discern and decide that a hat 'disengages your physiognomy' as it costs his English confrère to say that it is a fine morning when it probably isn't. And, again, the Frenchman talks like a book. In England this is a term of reproach. But that is probably one of the worst symptoms of English life, for, however near it may come to exactness of expression, or however far it may fall away from that first of human necessities, your book is at least an attempt to express something more exactly than it is usually expressed in everyday parlance. And, if national obloquy attaches itself to the phraseology of literature, then national obloquy attaches itself to exactitude of expression between man and man. Yet it is only by exactitude of expression between man and man that honesty and decency in human contacts can be attained to. In England, in short – still more in Germany, and even more, I believe, in Russia – the cleavage between the spoken language and the written is very wide and grows daily wider. This is a great calamity for the world. On the one hand the spoken language tends to become more and more figurative and less and less exact since it is more and more divorced from written language, which should be at least an attempt at exact expression. On the other hand, literature becomes more stilted, becomes more a matter of preciousness, and delights more in words as decoration rather than as the means of exact expression – literature then becomes of less and less influence on the life of the people, and leaders of thought lose at once their influence and the desire to express their thought. It is because in France these tendencies are less developed than in every other country of the Occidental world that we may most welcome an alliance in which the hegemony of the civilized world falls to this great, sober, and beneficent country. Other things matter very little. The greatest victories of mankind are over and done with by the next autumn, when the stubble is over the graveyards; but we shall only make a decent thing of peace when we can see human issues clearly, and we shall only see human issues clearly when we have learnt to effect their just expression.

Outlook, 35 (8 May 1915), 599–600.

Sologub and Artzibashef[1]

I.

To Western minds the main characteristic of Russian writers is just the atmosphere that they, all alike, render for us – a physical atmosphere of

1 *The Old House*. By Feodor Sologub. Translated from the Russian by John Cournos. *Sanine*. By Michale Artzibashef. Translated by Percy Pinkerton.

wooden, cell-like rooms, of leather, of smoke and of immense fields, where – I do not know why – I have the impression that I shall always find summer. I suppose that is because the immense majority of Russian stories that I have read are stories of the country, and the winter shuts up country-life in Russia. But, whether it is the matchless 'Bielzhin Prairie', the matchless 'Rattle of the Wheels', or the matchless description of the peasants' singing contest in the *House of Gentlefolk* or in *Torrents of Spring*, it is always the summer of a green land of willow-fringed streams that comes up in my mind when I think of them. And as with Turgenev, so with the new great of Russia:

> The river winds its way among the green, full of capricious turnings. White tufts of mist, dispersing gradually, hang over it like fragments of a torn veil…
>
> Everything, as before, was green, blue and gold, many-toned and vividly tinted; truly all the objects of Nature showed the real colours of their souls in honour of this feast of light…
>
> It was an old, large, one-storeyed house, with a mezzanine. It stood in a village eleven versts from a railway station and about fifty versts from the district town. The garden which surrounded the house seemed lost in drowsiness, while beyond it stretched vistas and vistas of inexpressibly dull, infinitely depressing fields.

That is the landscape and that the old house of Sologub. And here is the landscape of *Sanine* – and an open window:

> After crossing the meadow, they again got on the main road, which was thronged with peasants in their carts and giggling girls. Then they came to trees and reeds and glittering water, while, above them, at no great distance on the hillside, stood the monastery, topped by a cross that shone like some golden star.
>
> Painted rowing boats lined the shore, where peasants in bright coloured shirts and vests lounged…
>
> Gently, caressingly, the dusk, fragrant with the scent of blossoms, descended. Sanine sat at a table near the window, striving to read in the waning light a favourite tale of his. It described the lonely tragic death of an old bishop who, clad in his sacerdotal vestments and holding a jewelled cross, expired amid the odour of vestments.

It will be observed that the landscape of Artzibashef is more exotically rendered and more coloured than that of Sologub, just as his comparatively vulgar soul is more hotly expressed than that of the much greater artist that Sologub is.

Sanine one may dismiss with a very few words. It is one of those works, written no doubt honestly enough, whose popular appeal lies in the fact that it supplies justification for men to misbehave with other men's wives or women with other woman's husbands. The philosophy of the chief character Sanine – who is a perfectly unreal Superman related to the Monster of Frankenstein – reduces itself to the saying, though it takes a hundred thousand words to say it in: 'Do what you damn well like.' That is not a very new philosophy.

It is not a very new philosophy; it may be right or it may be wrong; that is no affair of mine in these columns. But a life lived on those lines is apt to be a very uninteresting life; and literature written on those lines, since it accentuates life, is bound to be drearily, drearily uninteresting. A literature of morality, in short, can only be interesting when it deals with the interplay of scruples. One may, that is to say, find an interest in considering the story of a gentleman who is not certain whether he will pick a pocket, cut a throat, punch a head, or go off with a till or another man's wife. But most of the interest goes out of a story when it is a foregone conclusion that the hero always will do what he damn well pleases. It is like going to races where it is always Eclipse first and the rest nowhere. And the story becomes excruciatingly monotonous when the hero not only breaks all the commandments with machine-like regularity, but talks about the breaches – and talks and talks – and talks.

From that point of view *Sanine* is one of the worst books ever written. Nevertheless it is obvious that a work that has had the enormous sale, all the world over, that has been enjoyed by this work of M. Artzibashef cannot be wholly uninteresting. And the fact is that M. Artzibashef, if he is not an artist, and if he very certainly is not a master, is a considerable genius as a teller of artless and coloured stories. He is in short one more product of the Russian return to the Romantic movement. The incidents of *Sanine* are not quite real; the seductions and suicides are too frequent and suggest that the writer has gone through life looking for seductions and suicides. Of course if you do that for forty years or so you may find quite a number, so that, like the landscapes of this work, the mental atmosphere is too highly coloured to be artistry. The real weakness of this writer is unerringly pointed out by Mr Cannan in the introduction to the English edition. 'M. Artzibashef,' says Mr Cannan, 'is fascinated by the brutality of human life.' He is in fact a specialist, like any other stamp-collector. And that is wrong. For life may be cruel, but it is always varied and subtle even in its cruelties; or life may be gay, but it is always varied and complicated in its most elemental gaieties. And the amount of time occupied by brutalities in the mental life of the most brutal of life's brutes is relatively very tiny. Let us say that it is a matter of two minutes a day. To put it very roughly: A man may be all his life an honest, sober, and industrious bank clerk, a good father, a loving husband, a cheerful friend. At the end of his life he may commit a murder in a moment of passion. Well, throughout all time, so long as his name is remembered, that man will be known as So-and-So the murderer. The artist is the person who perceives that that is not a true appellation, and Michale Artzibashef is not one of these. Therefore he does not deserve much consideration either as a novelist or a thinker, though *Sanine* is well enough worth reading for the matter that it contains, just as one may read an account of the doings at the Court of the King of Dahomey.

II.

Feodor Sologub is an altogether different pair of shoes, and in introducing him to us Mr John Cournos is doing us a real service. For Sologub is Russian in a sense that Artzibashef is not, and that even Turgenev is not, since Turgenev was something more than merely Russian. And we have got to live with Russia for the rest of our lives. It is well then, merely from that point of view, that we have *The Old House*.

The Old House is a story of the quiet dwelling in the mournful fields where the river winds amongst the willows. It is lived in by four women, a grandmother, a mother, a daughter, and an old nurse, who all await the return of the man-child of the house – and the man-child has been hanged. He has been hanged for a political offence, and they know he has been hanged, and they continue to wait for his return. They wake up, drink their chocolate in their beds, open the rooms, see that his rooms are exactly in order for his return, cross the garden and the river to meet him as he comes, sit all together in the evenings and await his return. They live, you see, their orderly, quiet, grave, and mournful lives in the old house, one-storeyed and with a mezzanine, entirely on that pivot. From time to time one says to the other: 'This is all nonsense. Borya has been hanged.' But the other continues to read the newspaper, even while she is speaking – to read the newspaper for tidings of Borya's whereabouts.

This story is a remarkable masterpiece in the art of telling. It so gets itself in, recapitulates, spots in a point here and there, is so misty and so extraordinarily real that – impatient as one may be in the reading of it – at the end and for days after one has been in Russia. For, indeed, all Russia – or, at any rate, the secret of Russian lives – is here. One has asked oneself again and again how it is that Russians bear the hardships that are theirs – the hardships of poverty in one case, of oppression, of foul weather, of unceasing toil for little material profit or enjoyment. And there it is – the power to endure that comes from the obstinate determination to ignore material circumstance, to live amongst visions and unrealities – to live in short, obstinately in the kingdom of God that each of us has within him. This is the main 'note' – it is the note of the *Letters of a Sportsman*, of the stories of Chekhov, of the immense epics of Dostoevsky, as it is of the comparatively ostentatious careers of Tolstoy or of Maxim Gorky. And this at least should rid us of the fear of Russia as a militarist or an aggressive Power of the future. The Russians simply have not enough practicality to wage any calculated war of aggression, though for defence their visionary nature makes them incomparable.

I am inclined to find a little fault with Mr Cournos for his selection of the other tales of Sologub that he here gives us. There is, that is to say, too much of the arbitrary-supernatural and not enough of the beautifully real. I call visions of beasts, monsters, dispossessed souls and the like, the arbitrary-supernatural because they have no communal basis or interest. I see myself visions, every day of my life – this morning I had a vision of a huge crab burrowing into a sandbank; yesterday of a buxom, dark lady in blue satin with a large blue hat, with a dog beside her, carrying a huge bunch of wild flowers and walking down my drive. I put them down to ocular fatigue and leave the matter at that, for I do not regard them as matters of legitimate art, though I suppose it is not illegitimate, now and then, to depict a character haunted by visions and to weave some sort of story into a series of apparitions.

The point that I wish to make is that the interest of such tours de force lies so entirely in the handling that one specimen would have been enough in the present volume. Here, out of eleven stories four deal with bogies, horribly enough, two with lunacy, and only five with real life. That is a pity, for the stories of real life are masterpieces. Read, for instance, 'The Search', which is about how a little boy feels when he is wrongfully accused at school of having pilfered from his comrades' overcoat pockets. It is a wonderful revelation of the human heart – of that heart of another which is a dark forest, as the Russians say.

It will be a great disgrace to the British public if it neglects this volume, on the accustomed plea that life is too sad already for one to read sad books. We have consumed edition after edition of *Sanine*, which is a riot of animalism and chockful of suicides – let us, for goodness' sake, do something for a book which will show us our Allies are good, gentle visionaries. That would be a real compliment.

I must add that Mr Cournos has done his work very exquisitely, with that touch of poetry in his prose that is the gift only of a translator who is himself a delicate poet and a patient thinker, and spiritually akin to the writer whose works he interprets. I hope Mr Secker will commission Mr Cournos to translate the complete works of Feodor Sologub. It would be a fine achievement – a fine monument with which to celebrate that peace for which we all long.

Outlook, 35 (26 June 1915), 830–1.

A Jubilee (review of *Some Imagist Poets*)

I.

It is as nearly as possible twenty-five years since I wrote my first review.

★★★

Well, twenty-five years is a long time to have been bothering one's poor head about literature; it is, as it were, a jubilee period.

★★★

Please God, my next twenty-five years will be spent in other fields; if I get my poor chance life will probably wear a different aspect for me, and from that I shall draw other lessons. If not today, then tomorrow, I hope to be up and away to regions where I shall be precluded from uttering injunctions to find *le mot juste*, and *le mot juste*.[1] And *le mot juste* again! That shall be as it chances but let me give at least as much alms to oblivion as this: that if any poor soul is heartily sick of my writing – and I suppose that there are such poor souls in plenty – he cannot be half as heartily sick as I of my writing. Where, then do we stand?

I do not suppose that I have led a movement, though I dare say I have. There isn't, you know, any knowing in these matters. Supposing that I should say that my young friends the Imagists were children of my teaching, I expect that, with one accord, they would get up and say that they had never heard of me. The world is like that. But still, unceasingly, in season and out, for a quarter of a century I have preached the doctrine that my young friends now inscribe on the banner of their movement. So I may have led their movement – blowing, as it were, into a discordant gourd, in the dust of the wilderness, miles ahead, and no doubt unworthy to unloosen the shoe latchets now that I am overtaken.

What, then, is this doctrine? Simply that the rendering of the material facts of life, without comment and in exact language, is poetry and that poetry is the only important thing in life. This is an absolute truism that any city merchant or any crossing-sweeper or any newspaper manager would subscribe to if he took the trouble to know what it meant; the misfortune is that inferior writers and loose thinkers have so befogged the meaning of the word 'poetry' that I shall, to most readers, have the appearance of having written nonsense. Let me put the matter, then, in several differing aspects.

Let us say you are a hero on the fields of Flanders. You have rescued wounded, you have taken trenches, you have kept the machine-gun all on going. But you will do all this unrewarded and unseen by any save God unless some poet – who may be your commanding officer, who may be a private reporting to your commanding officer – unless, then, some poet in exact and convincing phrases conveys to the bestower of decora-

1 [Ford got his commission as an officer in the Welch Regiment by the end of the month.]

tions or to the heart of a people the presentation of your deeds. Those phrases will be poetry because they have the power to rouse emotion; they will have the power to rouse emotion because they are exact, simple, and sincere. Widdrington of Chevy Chase lives today, and today, if we meet people called Widdrington, we say: 'That is an honourable name', not because he fought on when his legs were cut off below the knee, but because some balladist had the wit to write: 'He fought upon his stumps.' It is just the semi-grotesqueness of the phrase expressing a feat that the mind afterwards recognizes as one of extreme obstinacy, vitality, and heroism that makes Widdrington live in our memories whilst millions of other heroes have been forgotten since his day. Or, again, the early dispatches of Sir John French were poetry of a very high order – were 'reading' of a very high order – just because they were, in phraseology, exact, preoccupied, simple, and unaffected. They were just renderings.

II. *Some Imagist Poets*: an anthology

I differ therefore from my Imagist friends in one very important particular. They dismiss 'prose' with a sniff. That is wrong, since they only exist by descent from the great prose writers – and I will go so far as to hazard the dogma that the prose form is the only satisfactory vehicle for expressing the poetry of life. Says the writer of the preface to *Some Imagist Poets*:

> We attach the term ('free-verse') to all that increasing amount of writing whose cadence is more marked, more definite, and closer knit than prose, but which is not so violently nor so obviously accented as the so-called 'regular verse'.

This is a survival of an ancient superstition descending from barbarous days when primeval savages first found that rhythmical grunts could be used for the accentuating of group emotions. I express this fact as incisively as I can because this pronouncement of the preface writer is a perpetuation of the greatest nuisance in the world. The fact is that cadenced prose is poetry, and there is no other poetry. Rhythmic prose, regular verse forms, and 'free-verse' itself as soon as its cadence is 'more marked, more definite, and closer knit than that of' properly constructed prose – all these things are departments of rhetoric which is a device for stirring group passion. In this sense Chateaubriand's sentence:

> It is sad to think that though eyes may be too old to see with they will yet not be too old for shedding tears,

though it may have its defects of expression, is yet much truer poetry than:

> People – uproar – the pavement jostling and flickering –

Women with incredible eyelids:
Dandies in spats:
Hard-faced throng discussing me – I know them all;

which is a rhetorical expression of an uneasy egotism and has little of the repose that stamps the caste of Vere de Vere. And in this sense:

That night I loved you
in the candlelight.
Your golden hair
strewed the sweet whiteness of the pillows
and the counterpane.
O the darkness of the corners,
the warm air, and the stars
framed in the casement of the ships' lights!
The waves lapped into the harbour;
The boats creaked;
a man's voice sang out on the quay;
and you loved me.

Or:

Reed,
slashed and torn,
but doubly rich –
such great heads as yours
drift upon temple steps…

are poetry – and very great poetry – whilst

Where are the people and why does the fretted steeple sweep about in the sky? Boom! The sound swings against the rain. Boom again!

with its rhymes and detestable assonances and inexactitudes, though they be printed as prose, are sheer artificiality.

Of the six poets printed in this anthology only two – H.D. and Mr F.S. Flint – have the really exquisite sense of words, the really exquisite tranquillity, beauty of diction, and insight that justify a writer in assuming the rather proud title of Imagist – of issuing, that is to say, that challenge, that they will rouse emotions solely by rendering concrete objects, sounds, and aspects. Mr D.H. Lawrence is a fine poet, but he employs similes – or rather the employment of similes is too essential a part of his methods to let his work, for the time being, have much claim to the epithets restrained or exact. (What I mean is that although it may be ingenious writing to say that a wave looks like green jade, Stephen Crane's statement as to waves seen from a small boat, 'the waves were barbarous and abrupt' is the real right thing.) Mr John Gould Fletcher, Mr Aldington, and Miss Lowell are all too preoccupied with themselves and their emotions to be really called Imagists. It is no doubt right to be dissatisfied with the world, or with the circumstances of your life in childhood, or to make your mark in the world by writing as if you were Paganini or Tartini of the 'Trillo'. But that is really not business – though of course it is business as usual. Still, Miss Lowell is extraordinarily clever. What could be more clever than:

> My thoughts
> Chink against my ribs
> And roll about like silver hail-stones.
> I should like to spill them out
> And pour them, all shining,
> Over you.
> But my heart is shut upon them
> And holds them straitly.
>
> Come, You! and open my heart;
> That my thoughts torment me no longer,
> But glitter in your hair.

I suppose the real trouble with Miss Lowell is that she has no heart.

Mr Lawrence, on the other hand, has the touch of greatness. No doubt one day he will be great enough – and it is a very good thing for him that he has joined the Imagists. Their movement is about the only literary thing that much matters today. With H.D. and Mr Flint – (it is a scandal and a shame that Mr Flint is not recognized as one of the greatest men and one of the most beautiful spirits of the country – it is a scandal and a shame that Mr Flint is not the head and body of a national commission for making England understand France – it is a scandal and a shame that Mr Flint should be a power in Paris and unchronicled here; though we may put it to the credit of this out-of-joint world that it has produced H.D., who seems to have found what he desires) – with H.D. then and Mr Flint as the hard pebble core, and with the others that I have mentioned, more or less amorphous, but marked enough around them, this little group of poets is rolling its hump along the world. It is a good thing. My eyes – though they are not yet too old to shed tears – will, metaphorically speaking, close upon this twenty-five years of stump-oratorship in favour of direct thinking and low speaking, contentedly enough – in the conviction that England, whatever may happen, will continue to hold a worthyish place still in the serener regions of good letters.

P.S. – At the risk of occupying more space than is allotted to me by the Editor, I will transcribe the manifesto of this little group. I hope readers will pay some attention to it, for it is very well put – indeed I have written most of the generalizations at least ten monotonous times in these columns during the last two years – and it will afford the reader a pretty good standard or touchstone for judging what other work is poetry:

1. To use the language of common speech, but to employ always the exact word, not the nearly exact, nor the merely decorative word.

2. To create new rhythms – as the expression of new moods – and not to copy old rhythms which merely echo old moods. We do not insist upon 'Free-verse' as the only method of writing poetry... We believe that the individuality of a poet may often be better expressed in free-verse than in conventional forms. In poetry a new cadence means a new idea.

3. To allow absolute freedom in the choice of a subject. It is not good art to write badly about aeroplanes... Nor is it necessarily bad art to write well about the past...

4. To present an image (hence the name Imagist). We are not a school of painters, but we believe that poetry should render particulars exactly and not deal in generalities, however magnificent and pompous. It is for this reason that we oppose the cosmic poet who seems to us to shirk the real difficulties of his art.

5. To produce poetry that is hard and clear, never blurred nor indefinite.

6. Finally, most of us believe that concentration is of the very essence of poetry.

Outlook, 36 (10 July 1915), 46–8.

On a Notice of *Blast*

II. *Blast, War Number*. Edited by Wyndham Lewis.[1]

The first number of *Blast*, issued so many thousand years ago, was mostly larks. The second number is a much more serious affair. Of its contributors only Mr Pound – who is, of course, a neutral – keeps much of his original jauntiness; and Mr Lewis has discovered a new poet who shows signs of being very much after my own heart in Mr T.S. Eliot – an American. Upon the rest – upon Mr Lewis, upon Gaudier, upon even Miss Dismorr and Miss Sanders, as upon Mr Nevinson, Mr Roberts, and

1 [In the first part of this article, Ford takes issue with a derogatory review of the Vorticist magazine; a review he thought insulting to his friend Henri Gaudier-Brzeska, who had been killed in the previous month.]

Mr Wadsworth – the pressure of these times leaves its solemn traces. And, indeed, they would be bad enough artists if it did not, since, in the end, all good art is, in however distorting a mirror, a reflection of its own time. And, indeed, that the Vorticist movement should have survived a year such as that we have just passed through argues a grimness and tenacity of purpose such as must needs reflect itself in the works of these contributors. So that it is not a very gay *Blast* that thus greets the storms of summer.

And, when everything is said and done, *Blast* offers itself, modestly enough, as pioneer work, as exploration. 'We are not Hindu magicians,' says Mr Wyndham Lewis, 'to make our mango-tree grow in half an hour.' And that is a very sensible statement. And, whilst I am quoting, I may as well give you Mr Lewis's statement of the practical position of the Vorticists. They have been called violent – though why a drawing of five superimposed planes should be more violent than, say, a representation of Britannia with a trident, passes me to imagine. So, says Mr Lewis:

> Many people tell me that to call you a 'Prussian' at the present juncture is done with intent to harm, to cast a cloud over the movement, if possible, and moreover that it is actionable. But I do not mind being called a Prussian in the least. I am glad I am not one however, and it may be worth while to show how, aesthetically, I am not one either… The Junker, obviously, if he painted, would do florid and disreputable canvases of nymphs and dryads, or very sentimental 'portraits of the Junker's mother'. But as to the more general statement, it crystallises topically a usual error as to our aims. Because these paintings are rather strange at first sight they are regarded as ferocious and unfriendly. They are neither, although, they have no pretence to an excessive gentleness or especial love for the general public. We are not cannibals. Our rigid head-dress and disciplined movements which cause misgivings in the unobservant as to our intentions are aesthetic phenonmena; our goddess is Beauty, like any Royal Academician's, though we have different ideas as to how she should be depicted or carved, and we eat beefsteaks, or what we can get (except human beings) like most people… This rigidity, in the normal process of Nature, will flower like other things…

I do not know that eclecticism ever found a more modest trumpeter, which makes the vindictiveness of my friend the critic of the evening paper still more inexplicable. It is so very unusual to spit on the grave of a young man who is quite gently trying to find a new road. And obviously a new road is needful for the young. I confess to finding a certain strangeness in the cubes, the revolving astral bodies, the periphrases, the notes of exclamation of Vorticism. But the contemplation does not move me to defile last resting-places. I say to myself: The aspect of the world must be vastly different to those born within the last quarter of a century. My existence began, consciously at least, in the country. Rounded limbs of horses progressed there before rounded hay-wains; cherries hung upon boughs; speech was slow; brooks gurgled very gently. That was the normal basis of human life. But, for those born since the nineties the earth is a matter of hurtling, coloured squareness, of the jar of telephone bells, of every kind of rattle and bang, of every kind of detonation, of every kind of light in shafts, in coronets, in whirls and blaze and flash. The ocular and phonetic break between today and the historic ages is incredible. To all intents and purposes the Kent of my childhood and adolescence differed very little from the Greece where Sappho sang. There were railway trains, but one used them little; there was gunpowder, but one saw its effects seldom enough. Nowadays, ten times a day we are whirled at incredible speeds through glooms, amidst clamours. And the business of the young artist of today is to render those glooms, those clamours, those iron boxes, those explosions, those voices from the metal horns of talking-machines and hooters.

Upon this task the Vorticists have set out, quite tentatively. And I repeat that I find a certain strangeness in their effects. I imagine that I should prefer to be where Christobel low-lieth and to listen to the song the sirens sang.[2] But I am in London of the 1910s, and I am content to endure the rattles and the bangs – and I hope to see them rendered. And I certainly do not hope to see them rendered with the palette-effects of the late Lord Leighton or the verbal felicities of the late Lord Tennyson. I am curious – I am even avid – to see the method that shall make grass grow over my own methods and I am content to be superseded. I think that that should be the attitude of the composed and reasonable human being. We – my friend the critic of the evening paper, myself, the executors of the late Lord Leighton – have got to go out sooner or later, and the really exciting thought is: What is going to give the world the good time we had with *Flaming June*, the *Derby Day*, *Bubbles* or the *Idylls of the King*?[3] I think what I should like best in the world would be to know what form human expression will take in ten centuries from now, and I think that what I should like least in the world to have recorded of me is that I should have hindered that oncoming or have ridiculed the mortuary inscription over the tomb of the untimely dead.

As for the methods of the supporters of *Blast* I will quote for you a few words that poor Gaudier wrote in the trenches. I do not think you can want anything gentler or wiser as an expression of artistic ideals.

2 [Apparently a confusion of Coleridge's 'Christobel' with Tennyson's 'Claribel, A Melody', which opens: 'Where Claribel low-lieth'. Sir Thomas Browne, *Urn Burial*, chapter 5. See p. 137 above.]

3 [Paintings by Lord Leighton, William Frith, Sir J.E. Millais, respectively, and Tennyson's poems (completed in 1885).]

I have been fighting for two months and can now gauge the intensity of Life. Human masses teem, and move, are destroyed and crop up again. Horses are worn out in three weeks, die by the roadside. Dogs wander, are destroyed, and others come along. With all the destruction that works around us nothing is changed, even superficially. Life is the same strength, the moving agent that permits the small individual to assert himself… The bursting shells, the volleys, the wire entanglements, projectors, motors, the chaos of battle do not alter in the least the outlines of the hill we are besieging. A company of partridges scuttle along before our very trench…

Just as this hill where the Germans are solidly entrenched gives me a nasty feeling because its gentle slopes are broken up by earthworks which throw long shadows at sunset, just so I shall get feeling, of whatsoever definition, from a statue according to its slopes, varied to infinity.

I have made an experiment. Two days ago I pinched from an enemy a Mauser rifle. Its heavy, unwieldy shape swamped me with a powerful image of brutality. I was in doubt for a longtime whether it pleased or displeased me. I found that I did not like it. I broke the butt off; with my knife I carved on it a design, through which I tried to express a gentler order of feeling, which I preferred. But I will emphasize that my design got its effect, just as the gun had, from a very simple composition of lines and effects.

I find that a very touching and wise passage of prose. And I will ask the reader to observe that it contains the thoughts of an artist who had a mystical and beautiful mind and who had been long under fire. Is it not interesting and valuable to observe what such a mind selects? If *Blast* had presented us with nothing else it would have been justified of its existence.

Outlook, 36 (31 July 1915), 143–4.

'Thus to Revisit', *Piccadilly Review*, 1919

Ford wrote three series of articles under this title. Those in the *Dial* and *English Review* were collected in *Thus to Revisit: Some Reminiscences* (London, 1921). The following, from a short-lived periodical, were not.

I. The Novel

Time and Eternity. By Gilbert Cannan
Night and Day. By Virginia Woolf

In the beginning, as far as one knows, were the *Satyricon* and the *Golden Ass*; then came the *contes*, *fabliaux*, *nouvelles*; then Cervantes, Defoe; then Fielding and Smollett; then Richardson – and so the mainstream of imaginative prose passed again across the Channel to flow from the pens of Diderot, Chateaubriand, and Stendhal, and not to return to these islands until Flaubert and Turgenev had elevated the spinning of loose and formless Romances that you 'read in', into the art of constructing novels that you must read.

I trust the reader will allow me to get so far without violently cavilling; for this series of papers is intended rather as a friendly enquiry into how literature has survived Armageddon than as any browbeating disquisition. And it would be a good thing if we could come, now, to some agreement as to the definition applied to varying forms of writing. For before the 4th August 1914, we certainly had not even the rudiments of an agreed critical language. If one had, for instance, to write about the production of novels considered as an Art, one had to use almost exclusively French words – to write of *progressions d'effet*, *mots justes*, and so on. I used, I remember, to write high-spiritedly of Novels and Nuvvles, and, thus to cause offence.

NOVELS AND ROMANCES

I propose, now, for the purpose of these Causeries to use the words 'Romances' and 'Novels'. Let us say that amorphous, discursive tales containing digressions, moralizations and lectures are Romances, and that

Novels have unity of form, culminations and shapes. In the Romance it matters little of what the tale-teller discourses, so long as he can retain the interest of the reader; in the Novel every word – *every word* – must be one that carries the story forward to its appointed end. The Romances then would be the *Satyricon*; *Don Quixote*; *Tom Jones; Vanity Fair*; or the *Brothers Karamazov*, of Dostoevsky; the Novels – well, there are very few Novels. There are the *Neveu de Rameau*, of Diderot; *Le Rouge et le Noir*, by Stendhal, *Madame Bovary*, and *Education sentimentale*, of Flaubert; practically all the imaginative writings of Turgenev, and of the late Mr James.

The disadvantage of this nomenclature is that, if we adopt it, we must include amongst Romances a great many works eminently unromantic in texture. For you could not say, however loosely constructed they may appear to be, that *Humphrey Clinker*, the *Satyricon*, or, on the face of it, the works of Dostoevsky, are inspired by what is usually called the Romantic Spirit. On the other hand the two almost perfect novels by Mr W.H. Hudson – *Green Mansions* and the *Purple Land*, are the very embodiment of the Spirit of Romance. As, however, I do not propose to say very much about formless narratives, I am content to leave the matter there. But I should like to add that I do not wish to be taken as thinking – or as trying to induce the reader to believe – that all formless narrative is to be regarded with contempt. I am ready to aver that the *Way of All Flesh*, by Samuel Butler, is one of the four great books in the English language, and that *Humphrey Clinker* is, when one is in the mood, as 'good reading' as *Fort Comme la Mort* – when one isn't! I hope, indeed, to be allowed to return to Butler next week.

And again; it must not be forgotten that certain writers are sometimes Romancists and sometimes Novelists; that certain books of Novelists have the aspect of Romances – and that many books which appear to be loose in texture are actually almost devilishly intent on carrying their 'story' forwards. In *Madame Bovary* or in *Education sentimentale* you have pages and pages that appear to be nothing but digressions. You have Homais and you have the cripple – but every word devoted to either of them makes the suicide of Emma more a matter of destiny; and, if you take the greatest – present company always excepted! – writer of today you will find that Mr Conrad goes to almost extraordinary lengths of apparent digression in order to 'justify' the existence of a Police Sergeant who shall arrest a cornered criminal. Or again, you have the Mr George Moore – that great writer of *Esther Waters* and the *Drama in Muslin*, – or the Maupassant of *Une Vie* and *Bel Ami*. These books do not appear to be tight constructed – but he would be a bold man who said, dogmatically that they are without 'form'. I hope, therefore, that it will appear that nothing strikingly dogmatic is intended in these arguments, for no proper man can today be dogmatic, since all proper men for the last five years have been shaken, earthquaked, and disturbed, to the lowest depths of their beings. It is the queerest thing in the world to return to the grey regions of Covent Garden and to find that still there are 'firms' in Henrietta Street, in Bedford Street, or in King Street, and that an 'Autumn Publishing Season' is apparently in contemplation. Queer! One walks the grey streets wondering where they all are…

MODERN INSTANCES

So that this is an enquiry into that question which has tormented me all my life – as to where we really stand. And here are Mr Cannan, who before the war was one of *les jeunes*, and Mrs Woolf, of whom I know nothing. *Time and Eternity* and *Night and Day* are interesting examples of the two tendencies of which I have written. Speaking as it were in shorthand, you might say that Mr Cannan's book is a Novel, Mrs Woolf's a Romance. Mr Cannan carries excision almost to extremes: in reading Mrs Woolf one seems to hear of families [in an] unmistakable voice of one's childhood. It is surely the voice of George Eliot – but it is the voice of a George Eliot who, remaining almost super-educated, has lost the divine rage to be didactic. Mrs Woolf records passionlessly the mental attitudes, the house furnishings, and the current literature of the intellectual governing class just before the war. You find it difficult to know whether she approves of them or whether – as is probably the case – she isn't mocking at them tenderly. Her characters are the descendants of great, but rather academic poets, the editors of huge monthly reviews:

> The Hilberys, as the saying is 'knew everyone', and that arrogant claim was certainly upheld by the number of houses which, in a certain area lit their lamps at night, opened their doors after 3 p.m., and admitted the Hilberys to their dining rooms, say, once a month. An indefinable freedom and authority of manner, shared by most of the people who lived in these houses, seemed to indicate that whether it were a question of art, music, or government, they were well within the gates and could smile indulgently at the vast mass of humanity which is forced to wait and struggle and pay for entrance with common coin at the door.

How different from us, Miss Beale and Miss Buss! Or rather, how different from the characters and the atmosphere of Mr Cannan's book. For, whereas *Night and Day* is a severe love-story, a *chassez-croisez* of engaged couples in a Parnassian and prewar atmosphere, Mr Cannan's book is written with lurid heat and deals with murder in an atmosphere of alcoholic and rag-time Bohemia when Armaggedon was at its height.

> He was horrified when he called on Valérie, after her plunge for independence, and found her at tea with Freda and Freda's motley acquaintance in the studio. To begin with, it was not a very nice studio. It was very big, dark, very dirty and neglected. The artist who had occupied

> it was at the war, and his indifferent canvases disfigured the walls... the only redeeming feature was an immense fire that blazed in a great fire-place. By this sat Valérie shivering, while Freda and her friends were sitting round a table bolting cakes and bread and jam as though they had not seen food for a very long time....

And here is the murderer in the role of Samson:

> He was enormously strong. He picked up men and women three at a time and threw them towards the door, and they went, laughing and giggling; some of the women, screaming as a body went flying over them or landed on top of them. Before very long no one was left but the drunken painter, who had slipped down on the floor and was asleep, with a Stilton cheese for a pillow.... He thought: 'I've got to go out there and fight and kill for this: while this is going on. It is always going on – on and on and on. It never stops. It always will be.... And Valérie, oh my God, Valérie!'

Eventually he suffocates Valérie with a pillow – being like Othello, a Militarist.

It is queer to find that, in these modern developments, Mrs Woolf, who is the spiritual descendant of the George Eliots, the Ruskins, the Spencers, the Pollocks, and all the other moral adornments of Victorianism, writes skilfully a moral-less but very entertaining book which is all ado about nothing; and that Mr Cannan, the literary descendant of the Maupassants, the Goncourts, and all the non-moral overseas writers, has become an almost virulent and certainly an incoherent moralist. Incoherent is not, perhaps, the exactly right word. For, just as Mrs Woolf is a mistress of inclusion, so Mr Cannan is to such an extent a master of excision that you cannot quite tell what are the ideals which he violently proclaims.

I shall probably return to both these books when it comes to discussing other technical points. My space is, I imagine, at an end. But I should just like to add that if I did not think that the books of these two writers were not interesting and suggestive I should not write about them.

I do not know what space the Editor of the *Piccadilly Review* will allow for correspondence on literary matters, but if readers of this periodical, who are seriously interested in technical literary points, care to write to me personally, I will try to answer their communications from time to time, since I take some such arrangement to be of the essence of causeries.

Piccadilly Review, 23 October 1919, 6.

II. The Realistic Novel

An Honest Thief. By Fyodor Mikhailovich Dostoevsky. Translated by Constance Garnett
Bengy. By George Stevenson

Novel-writing is the youngest, as it is the Cinderella, of all the arts. For this reason it is the only art that is supremely worth pursuing. The fields that lie open to it are illimitable, and the possibilities of new forms inexhaustible. For the actual forms that have been exploited hitherto are so few that you could almost number them on the fingers of your hands. The earliest and most rudimentary conceptions of fiction writers were based upon the simplest forms of tale-telling. You took a story, which was generally the story of a man favoured by women and the gods, audaciously endowed and superhumanly fortunate, and you pursued him through various adventures until you thought the reader had had enough of him. Very few writers attempted to convince the reader; it was enough that he should be kept breathless. Occasionally you had an author like Lope da Vega or like Smollett who, whilst investing their central character with heroic qualities, immersed him in atmospheres of actuality that today would be called realistic. Occasionally, too, you had authors like Defoe who produced fiction in the guise almost of forged documents, thus attaining to some sort of form or to some sort of realism. Richardson, however, was the first creative writer to found a school, and that school may be said still to exist. For the late Mr Henry James was as much a descendant of Richardson as the present Throne is the descendant of the Throne of Henry VIII. Richardson begat Diderot and the encyclopaedists; who begat Chateaubriand; who begat Stendhal, and later Maupassant, Flaubert, Turgenev, the Goncourts, Daudet, and the great French school which dominated the world during the closing years of the Second Empire and of the last century. This school had two descendants – the late Mr James and Mr Joseph Conrad – who are the only two writers whose works since that day have demanded any serious attention from the technical and purely literary point of view.

I am aware that this is a highly provocative statement and I mean it to be so.

REALISM NOT SUFFICIENT

Let me then particularize a little more. I do not mean to say that during the latter half of last century and the whole of the present one, as far as it has gone, no good books have been written under the guise of fiction except by the Paris school or by Mr James and Mr Conrad. It would be idle – and indeed it would be very wrong – to deny the sombre poetry, the extreme charm, or the tragic gloom, of Mr Thomas Hardy. It would be impossible to deny that *The Way of All Flesh* is one of the four great books in the English language, but a great book – a book that is great because of the information it conveys or of the characters that it sketches, or of its author's temperament – is not the same thing as a consummate novel, nor is the power to convey a sense of reality, or what in the nineties of the last century was called realism, a sufficient passport to perfection in art.

For, in the nineties of last century, the immediate effect of the great French school, which was then only just dying, was to produce in the West Central district of London, a passion for what used to be called 'slices of life'. In those days you had Mr Somerset Maugham and Mr Edwin Pugh, to tell you stories of how heroic coster girls were 'bashed' by drunken husbands or lovers; Stephen Crane gave you *Maggie, a Child of the Streets*; even Mr Kipling tried it in a story called, I think, 'Badalia Herodsfoot', which appeared, as far as I can remember, in the *Detroit Free Press*, and was subsequently suppressed (at any rate, there was some sort of row about it).[1] Mr Wells was contributing the adventure of Mr Hoopdriver to the columns of *To-day*; Mr Zangwill was writing of the Ghetto; Mr Bennett *The Man from the North*, Mr Gissing and Mr Mark Rutherford were writing tales of lower middle class life. And I fancy Mrs Mary E. Mann had also begun to publish by then. (I am talking of the years around 1895 or so).[2] There was thus a very promising 'slice of life' school in existence. As a school it has disappeared, though I believe many of the writers who graced it are still amongst us.

'LIFE'

It concerned itself, however, practically not at all with novel-writing as an art – whether as an art that demanded beauty or exactness of language, or as one necessitating a sense of form. Its preoccupation was with what it called 'Life' – and Life meant alcoholism, fog, kerosene lamps, barrel organs and depression. It did, however, one thing – it swept the divinely and feminely supported central figure into the limbo of the commercial novel, and it paid some attention to what is called in French the 'justification' of its characters. That was a step in advance.

DOSTOEVSKY AS A MODEL

Of this strain in the development of the novel not very much trace remains apparent to one who like myself, is revisiting the glimpses of the

1 [Andrew Lycett, *Rudyard Kipling* (London, 1999), pp. 226–7, recounts a row with Harper and Brothers who planned to publish a volume of stories without Kipling's permission. Eventually the publishers included the story 'The Record of Badalia Herodsfoot' instead of another, on the grounds that they already had the serial rights for it.]

2 [Mr Hoopdriver is the protagonist of Wells's *The Wheels of Chance* (1896). Mary Mann (1848–1929) wrote over forty volumes of fiction, many set in Norfolk.]

moon.[3] I do not know if Mr D.H. Lawrence is still writing novels – I hope he is. And Dostoevsky, in a sense, is still with us, since Mrs Garnett, to whom this country is so enormously indebted, is continuing to give us volumes of her translations *The Honest Thief* will not much increase this indebtedness, since all the stories contained in the volume are excruciatingly bad, with the exception of 'The Honest Thief' itself, and that is no great shakes. But it is cheering to see that *The Friend of the Family* is announced by Mrs Garnett's publishers as being in preparation. That Dostoevsky who is, in fact, a pure romantic, and only when it suits him to be, a sort of pseudo-realist – that Dostoevsky should have appealed so enormously to the English reader, and still more to the English writer, is only in the nature of things. The English writer is always trying to break back into Romanticism. For any band of artistic effort, of clearness of vision, of sustained thought about human affairs, are troublesome to him as to all men – and they do not seem worth while since our Literary Press, our Preachers, and our Social Hierarchy alike tell him that novel-writing is a contemptible occupation. So, if you have to make a living by it you do it along the lines of least resistance. For this Dostoevsky is the best possible model since a large section of the public nowadays demands realism with its intellect but, in its heart, loves heroes, and Dostoevsky is a realist of the 1895 school inasmuch as he places his heroes in atmospheres of alcoholism, fog, kerosene lamps, gaols, lunatic asylums and mortuaries. But his heroes – I use the word advisedly – always have vast empires in which they are the central figures – those empires being the kingdoms of their own minutely examined psychologies.

★★★

Piccadilly Review, 30 October 1919, 6.

III. The Serious Books

Seven Men. By Max Beerbohm
Birds in Town and Village. By W.H. Hudson

My friend the late Arthur Marwood[1] – who possessed, upon the whole,

3 [What may this mean, / That thou, dead corpse, again in complete steel, / Revisitst thus the glimpses of the moon…' – *Hamlet* I. iv. 32–4]

1 [Ford drew upon Marwood in constructing many of his fictional characters; in particular, Christopher Tietjens in *Parade's End*.]

the widest and the most serene intelligence of any human being that I have yet met – used to say that for any proper man there could only be four books in the English language that could be worth reading. Each proper and serious man, that is to say, could find his own four books, but he could not find more than four. Two of these four he was dogmatic about; he said, I mean, that every man must have, as two out of the four, Clarendon's *History of the Great Rebellion*, and Mayne's *Ancient Law*. As for the other two, you might select from, say; Beckford's *Letters from Portugal*, Johnson's *Lives of the Poets*, Mr Doughty's *Arabia Deserta*, or any one of Mr Hudson's books – preferably *Nature in Downland* or *Idle Days in Patagonia*. But, for any man there could only be four books.

It was a sweeping statement to which my friend thus committed himself, but if the reader will take my word for it that Arthur Marwood was a man of extraordinarily wide reading, of a memory so tenacious that he appeared to be encyclopaedic in his knowledge, and of singular wisdom – if we may give to wisdom the definition that it is the power to apply to any given incident the generalizing habit, and the ability to take various points of view that comes from a very wide knowledge and understanding of other given cases – the reader may well think it worth while to pay some serious attention to this dictum. For myself I love sweeping dicta; they awaken trains of thought: they suggest; and, the more obviously sweeping they are, the less they need to be taken *au pied de la lettre* and the more they may be refined down until the exact and balanced judgment is arrived at. If you wish to think, you must sketch in a rough design of the region that your thoughts may cover so that you may proceed towards rendering it more exact and more precise.

THE DESPISED NOVEL

It will be observed that all the books selected by my friend were of the variety that is called in the bookselling trade, and by reviewers, the serious book. The novel, that is to say, did not exist for this friend of mine. I don't mean that he despised novel-writing as an art; he simply did not know that it was there; for, in essence, he was the last of the Tories, and, if Toryism is certainly wisdom, its logical practice calls, on occasion, for a certain wilful colour blindness. He did not, then, condemn novel-writing; he was not of the type, most frequently found amongst deans, who says that the reading of novels promotes offences leading to the Divorce Court; nor yet was he of the type of academic conductors of reviews, magazines, and the more ponderous periodicals, which devote infinite oceans of space to works about the love affairs of Keats and Shelley; the addiction of Elizabeth Barrett to the society of charlatans; the campaigns of Marlborough: the varieties of parasites of the genus pig; the incidence of taxation on the middle classes in Uruguay: the cultivation of beetroots; the production of commercial alcohol; the morganatic wives of the sons of George III; and the prevalence of the *mal Anglais* at the Court of Peter the Great; whilst imaginative literature is dismissed in two pages, the one headed 'Recent Poetry.' and the other 'Notes About Novels'.

'YELLOW-BACKS'

I was examining the other day the files of one such literary organ, and, upon my word, this was the exact proportion allotted respectively to serious books and to literature. My friend Marwood was more sincere. He simply did not consider that novel-writing was a serious pursuit, any more than stamp collecting, or the playing of diabolo, which in those days had become suddenly prevalent. I suppose that his only contact with novels had happened when, one day as a boy in the seventies, he had pulled open an old cupboard in his North Country ancestral manor house. There fell out upon him hundreds and hundreds of yellow-backed novels by Ouida and novelists of her generation. These his father had read contemptuously and chucked – *le mot juste* – into the otherwise useless cupboard, much as a cigar-smoker might trifle with a cigarette at odd moments to throw the end into a dustbin. That is a reasonable and Tory point of view.

Its logical end, however, is to leave you with only four books in the world, and that is not a very cheering prospect on long winter evenings. For, unfortunately, the writing of serious books has never been taken very seriously in these islands – not the actual writing. The practice of producing matter which will ultimately appear on the two sides of the printed page, the sheets making up the pages being then bound into ponderous volumes, is, of course, sufficiently prevalent. The more ponderous the volume, the more satisfied will the producer be, and the more chance will he have of extended attention in the literary reviews. But you do not write such books with any literary motive. Generals, alas, and Chancellors, produce enormous tomes in order to justify disastrous strategy or political courses that have gone wrong; the widows of generals and the daughters of chancellors produce books from motives of filial piety. Gentlemen with no literary gifts, with no love of literature, and with no literary insight – though this tendency is mostly Teutonic – produce lives of Keats, Shelley, Browning, Crabbe, George Darley, Donne, in the hope of attaining the fame that descends upon the erudite, of the rewards that are reserved for the persistently dull. These are the most pernicious of all writers of serious books – but there are an enormous number of others.

As written today, then, the Serious Book is generally Teutonic in its origin – that is to say, it is produced by gentlemen more distinguished for their industry than for their gifts, insight, or love of their subjects. That a serious book should possess form, imaginative insight, or interest for anyone not a specialist, would, generally speaking, be considered a very unsound proposition. To say that its writing should be distinguished by the quality of style, would be universally condemned.

And yet if a book, no matter what its subject, does not possess qualities of form, imaginative insight, and that catholicity of outlook which is the poet's gift and that sense of style which conduces to clarity of thought in the reader, that book will have no chance of survival into the future, and, on the day of its birth, will be below contempt.

FACTS THAT SWAMP IDEAS

For the province of literature is to educate, so that the reader may be stirred to the perception of analogies or to the discovery of the sources of pleasure within himself. It is for that that you go to the Arts, and for no other purpose. It is this issue that the Teutonic mode of pursuing learning began so fatally to obscure in the latter years of Queen Victoria's reign, so that the production of works of ponderously stated and industriously collected fact has swamped the very idea that the province of the printed book is to civilize and to show how sympathy and joy may be arrived at.

To read a sentence of Mr Hudson's is to receive little or no instruction –

> One of the first birds I went out to seek – perhaps the most medicinal of all birds to see – was the Kingfisher; but he was not anywhere on the river margin, although suitable places were plentiful enough, and myriads of small fishes were visible in the shallow water, seen at rest like dim-pointed stripes beneath the surface, darting away and scattering outwards like a flight of arrows at any person's approach. Walking along the river bank one day, when the place was still new to me, I discovered a stream, and following it up arrived at a spot where a clump of trees overhung the water, casting on it a deep shade. On the other side of the stream buttercups grew so thickly that the glazed petals of the flowers were touching; the meadow was one broad expanse of brilliant yellow. I had not been standing half a minute in the shade before the bird I had been seeking darted out from the margin almost beneath my feet, and then, instead of flying up or down stream, sped like an arrow across the field of buttercups. It was a very bright day, and the bird going from me with the sunshine full on it, appeared entirely of a shining splendid green. Never had I seen the Kingfisher in such favourable circumstances; flying so low above the flowery level that the swiftly vibrating wings must have touched the yellow petals, he was like a waif from some far tropical land.

Or to read a page or two of Mr Beerbohm who, as far as I know, is the last survivor of the English school of essayists, is to acquire little or no new factual instruction. Yet to read Mr Hudson is to become a man very much better, since various aspects of the world will become newer, brighter and more vivid, and, to come in contact with this limpid writing which is as simple as the utterance of a child, is to acquire, by degrees, a distaste for pomposities of diction and inexactitude of thought. It is not that the habits of the kingfisher matter any more than the habits of Marlborough or Mme. de Maintenon. On the 27.12.18 and the 4.1.19, being on leave, I twice saw a kingfisher seated on a twig near the miniature lake at the eastern end of the Serpentine in Hyde Park. But unless I state the fact vividly it might just as well go unrecorded.

QUALITIES OF THE ESSAYIST

It is the same with the essay – that form which unites the Novel to the 'Serious' Book. Hazlitt's description of the Great Fight happens – I write this on the authority of our principal boxing expert of today – then to be, out of all the immense welter of words that was poured out about the noble art before its eclipse, the only piece of writing conveying practical information as to the early Prize Ring that has any value for the student of boxing today. But for the general reader it survives because of its vivid and simple writing and because it shows you how to look at the world. To read Mr Beerbohm is to receive practically no instruction. The following passage will show you neither how not to write, nor how to write a play:

> He made me understand, however, that it was rather the name than the man that had first attracted him. He said that the name was in itself a great incentive to blank verse. He uttered it to me slowly, in a voice so much deeper than his usual voice, that I nearly laughed. For the actual bearer of the name he had no hero-worship, and said it was by a mere accident that he had chosen him as central figure. He had thought of writing a tragedy about Sardanapalus; but the volume of the *Encyclopaedia Britannica* in which he was going to look up the main facts about Sardanapalus happened to open at Savonarola. Hence a sudden and complete peripety in the student's mind. He told me he had read the Encyclopaedia's article carefully, and had dipped into one or two of the books there mentioned as authorities. He seemed almost to wish he hadn't. 'Facts get in one's way so,' he complained. 'History is one thing, drama is another. Aristotle said drama was more philosophic than history because it showed us what men *would* do, not just what they *did*. I think that's so true, don't you? I want to show what Savonarola *would* have done if –' He paused.
>
> 'If what?'
>
> 'Well, that's just the point. I haven't settled that yet. When I've thought of a plot, I shall go straight ahead.'

But if you read Mr Beerbohm at his best you receive a certain stimulation and, if you follow him, you will be led up to a point of view, which will enable you subsequently to be less subject to being overawed by solemn humbug. Of course, *Birds in Town and Village* is not Mr Hudson's best book any more than *Seven Men* is Mr Beerbohm's most valuable contribution to comparative sociology. But it is cheering to return to a world that might be full of sad surprises and to find that they are still there.

Piccadilly Review, 6 November 1919, 6.

V. Biography and Criticism

Samuel Butler: A Memoir. By Henry Festing Jones
The Caliph's Design. By P. Wyndham Lewis

There are few inventions that have not proved a curse to humanity; the gentleman who invented the Biography as applied to the artist or the thinker cursed humanity more than any soul before or since his hateful day. For there is no great man that is not belittled and rendered common by his biographer, since no man may be a hero to his valet. A star danced – and underneath it Shakespeare was born. So he found none to write his biography, and, serene, enigmatic and elusive his face smiles up at us through his pages. Had the bottle washers or parasites who usually attend on the Great, washed the bottles and designed the costumes of the Swan of Avon, we should have read him as little as we read Johnson. So we should have been cursed….

'CHATTER ABOUT HARRIET'

I never could read Shelley or Keats. I never have been able to, try as I will. And this was because when I was a young child I lived amongst people whose real use for these poets was to discover that when Shelley eloped with Mary Someone or other – Godwin or Wollstonecraft, I fancy – Mary rode upon a donkey, and Harriet drowned herself [in the Round Pond I always used to think]. And Keats was the tuberculous son of a livery stable keeper, who wrote love letters to a lady called Fanny Brawne. You see, *in illo die*, there were terrible people called Professors Dowden and Buxton Forman,[1] my uncle William Rossetti; my aunt Lucy Madox Rossetti. They never told you that Shelley or Keats could make you happy for ever if you read them. They never left one alone to read the poems. But they told me to distraction that Shelley was an atheist or that Keats was killed by the *Quarterly*.

1 [The great Shakespearean scholar Edward Dowden also wrote a *Life of Shelley*. Henry Buxton Forman, editor of Shelley and Keats, worked for the Post Office.]

I find even the editor of the *Athenaeum* (how jolly for once to be on the side of the Angels!) repeating this plaint:

> (*Athenaeum*. Review of *Samuel Butler*, Oct. 24. 1919.) And if it be said that a biography should make no difference to our estimate of the man who lives and has his being in his published works, we reply that if it shifts the emphasis ... *The Way of All Flesh*, which as an experimental novel is a very considerable achievement, becomes something different when we have to regard it as a laborious and infinitely careful record of experienced fact(!) Further still, even the edge of the perfect inconsequence of the 'Notes' is somewhat dulled when we see the trick of it being exercised(!!) ... Butler *loses almost the last vestige of a title to be considered a creative artist* when the incredible fact is revealed that the letters of Theobald and Christina in the *Way of All Flesh* are merely reproduced from those which his father and mother sent him(!!!!!)

I have tried by means of notes of exclamation and italics to reveal my profound and agitated disagreement with the amazing statements of the editor of *The Athenaeum*. (But, indeed, nothing is so disquieting as thus to revisit the glimpses of the moon and to discover that moon and *Athenaeum* alike have so extraordinarily little changed.)

BUTLER AND HIS BIOGRAPHER

'After all,' says the editor in the same review, 'Butler was not a great man.' Butler was the greatest Englishman the nineteenth century produced, and the *Way of All Flesh* is one of the four great imaginative works in the English language. And the review of Mr Jones's book by the editor of the *Athenaeum* is in fact just a lament – a lament because Mr Jones has destroyed for him his mental image of Butler, so that he will never again read the *Way of All Flesh* with his old pleasure. That is why I have ventured to say that I agree with the spirit if not the letter of this review!

As for Mr Jones, one wishes one knew quite how, justly, to sum him up. His admiration for Butler is admirable. It has been admirable for years. But for years he was a dependent – as it were a musical valet – to his hero. If you are anybody's batman a curious thing happens to you, in that you lose all sense of proportion one way or another. If you are a bad servant you will libel your master beyond recognition; if you are a good batman you will think your master was a hero – but your chief talk will be about his feet of clay. I remember asking about his master of an exceedingly devoted – a heroically and touchingly devoted – servant. My friend – a fine fellow and one of a beautiful nature, as I knew him – had been killed three weeks before. His servant would say: 'Mr —, a fine officer! A keen gentleman! Keen!' and then he would relate an anecdote showing that my friend had been mean in money matters, mean in his relations with women, deceitful to his senior officers, not very considerate of his men, and, in most things, what used to be called 'slim'. I dare say my friend had a touch of 'slimness' in his composition – yet I will aver that he had a beautiful, self-sacrificing, courageous and far-seeing nature – with a devotion to his and my battalion, to his senior officers and to the men such as is given, alas! to few of us. His batman, absolutely devoted, had admired mostly his occasional feats of slimness and, being at the moment his master's biographer, mentioned nothing else.

A MONSTROUS FIGURE

It is like that with Mr Jones. He wishes Butler to shine in controversy, to appear shrewd, right, agnostic, *ergoteur*,[2] prudent, sceptical, disillusioned, just as the batman wished to represent his master as always getting the best of it whether by fair means or foul. Mr Jones shows us a Butler who was sound, mean, mercenary, hypochondriac, selfish, lying and, in the end, monstrous – a Butler who was all these things in order that he might 'score' every one 'off' – from Charles Darwin to the custodians of Italian churches. His Butler bleats and whimpers about 'truth' as only a confidence-trickster can do about honesty – and, in the end, it amounts merely to giving 'old Darwin the best warming that I can manage to give him – and I think I shall manage a pretty hot one'. For 'Darwin' you might substitute the world – and the Victorian world's view of this personal Butler is pretty well summed up in Darwin's own words: '… A clever and unscrupulous man like Mr Butler would be sure to twist whatever I may say against me, and the longer the controversy lasts the more degrading it is to me.' That is the epitome of the great case Butler versus Mundum-Victoriae.

The world of today is infinitely his debtor, just as Butler is infinitely greater than the shivering and fearful wretch that Mr Jones presents us with. For fear – ceaseless, degraded, and all-pervading fear – is the note of this character; it dreaded friendship, love, wine, the three per cents, Persian cats, emotions, matrimony, life itself. But what do these things matter unless they spoil for us the great projection of life that he left behind him? They matter nothing. And Mr Jones was devoted to Butler. So we may leave it.

A GREAT POET

The fact is that Butler was a great poet – and just as only great writers can translate the writings of great writers in other tongues – so only great poets can write the lives of great poets. And they have other things to do. It is the work of art alone that matters in the case of Butler as in the case of all other poets. Unfortunately parasites obscure all these things to the world.

2 [Quibbler or caviller]

I am, however, not attaching that disagreeable word to Mr Jones. Long friendship gives a man certain human rights in the direction of descanting on the characteristics of a dead friend. A man in such a case writes from a certain fullness of the heart – and Mr Jones had every right to publish his biography. That it has taken the form it has is a tragedy – since he has belittled for us a man who, had he been left to stand by his work alone, was at once the epitome and the corrective of his race. Your true parasite is the professor who gives us lives of men he has never seen and whose works he has never loved. He calls the result criticism, and hates alike all real criticism which concerns itself with Art, and all real Art of which he himself is incapable.

MR LEWIS'S SELF-CONTRADICTION

In a queer, muffled, incoherent way this is what Mr Wyndham Lewis does in his latest pamphlet – and he does it the more effectually in that he contradicts himself on each successive page. In that he descends alike from Samuel Butler and from Samuel Johnson before him. Just as was the case with Butler – and no doubt with Johnson – Mr Lewis seems to feel the necessity for a theory, so that, having formulated it, he may sleep soundly. On the morrow he will develop his theory until it is altogether different. Then he will formulate that and, so again, sleep soundly; and, at the bottom of all his theorizing there is good, sound, solid, common horse sense. So it was with Butler, so also with Johnson – and as with these two, so in the case of Mr Lewis the good sound sense is united, as a rule, with the desire to 'score off someone', for reasons personal, obvious or obscure. This personal motive may or may not be usually wrong; aesthetically it is impeccable. A work of art, a piece of criticism, is an attempt to spread, to strengthen or to render prominent, your own type – an attempt to render the world a more fitting place for the survival of men sympathetic to you. If then, 'X.' attempts to damage you, either by injuring your public reputation, by carrying off your young woman, or distraining on you for rent, 'X.' becomes an enemy of humanity. So you try to destroy him, quite legitimately; you typify him as a being belonging to another School of Thought, and, either by name or veiledly, you destroy him. Your solicitor – or your Professor of Etiquette – might try to dissuade you; but they function in another dimension, a dimension not yours.

THE ONLY ART CRITIC

So, smashing at those who have inconvenienced, discouraged, publicly condemned him, Mr Lewis voyages down the Ages. He is, as far as I know, the only writer about the Plastic Arts of today who matters twopence – just as, in his day, Whistler, for all his defects, was worth a wilderness of Ruskins and Tom Taylors. At any rate he is the only writer about the Plastic Arts whom anyone could want to read and to digest. He has no doubt thought; he has for certain, felt a great deal, and he smashes the Pompous and the Worthy.

That is as much as I feel called upon to say about his fulminations on the Plastic Arts. Personally, I agree with him when he says that X=X; and I applaud him when he says that X=really ω. But I do not profess to dogmatize about the Plastic Arts – I am more concerned with the dominable and cantankerous way in which Mr Lewis puts things.

For myself I wish – and I always have wished – that Mr Lewis would leave paintings alone, and devote his enormous and spasmodic energies to writing. I don't at all know where he stands as a painter – but how admirably is this put:

FRENCH REALISM

> As a 'Romantic' … the Frenchman is a failure compared to the better equipped Romantic of more romantic nations. Delacroix and Géricault are not as satisfactorily romantic as Turner; Victor Hugo's novels are not as good romances as Hoffman's or Dostoevsky's. Dostoevsky is [nearer] the real and permanent romance of life. Turner is a delightful dreamer, nearer to the quality of romance than an equivalent Frenchman.… The next thing you notice, having come to these conclusions, is that a variety of Frenchmen – Stendhal, Flaubert, Villon, Cézanne, Pascal – a big list … do not fit into the French national cadre. They are less local than the successes of other modern European countries. Dostoevsky, the most intoxicated of his worshippers must concede, has the blemish of being sometimes altogether too 'Russian' to be bearable, too epileptic and heavy-souled. Turner had too much of the national prettiness of the 'dreamy' Englishman.
>
> French Realism means, if it has a meaning, what these best Frenchmen had; they were almost realer than anything in the modern world. They have made France the true leader country.

I have been trying to say – and indeed, saying, at great length – all that since before Mr Lewis was born – and without any particular effect – or any effect at all. But put so shortly, in a form so portable to the mind, Mr Lewis's statement is bound to have its effect – even on our own Academics. Our own Academics – who are more poisonous than those of any other nation, since they act on readers more sluggish and more 'dreamy' – must, that is to say, either adopt enough of Mr Lewis's statement to keep them alive, or they will find their ground cut away under their feet in the minds of the sluggish and dreamy public. (I notice, indeed, that several of our Art critics have already altered their views as to the relative values of Cézanne, Gaugin, Picasso or Matisse, in order to get in line with some of Mr Lewis's classifications.) For the life of the Academic is always an anxious one. If he slay the body to which he is parasitic he must die. So, every now and then, he must admit some new life, and thus, even in this country, the Arts carry on. And Mr Lewis is one of those rare creatures who, sending out as it were lightning flashes, reveals to this parasitic class the awful precipice that is just at their feet. I notice indeed that even *The Times* puts the *Caliph's Design* amongst books recommendable to its readers. So that once again – twice in one week! – I find myself on the side of the – what?

Piccadilly Review, 20 November 1919, 6.

Letter to the Editor of *The Athenaeum*

Sir, –

In your last issue the whole subject of Vers Libre is dismissed in a third part of an unsigned review.[1] But such a matter cannot be so dismissed – so light-heartedly, summarily and flippantly. Neither can the poems of the most consummately exquisite and gentle master of the form that in England we have be so dismissed, and you hope to escape protest.

Not even *The Athenaeum*, with the prestige of all its great obscurantist dead trailing behind it, can so dictatorially put back the clock. It is as if, once more from your columns, we heard the voices of our dear old friend Norman MacColl or our dear old preceptor Theodore Watts-Dunton snuffling, as they and their contributors used to snuffle, when they were confronted by anything that had not the support of their close corporation; that was beautiful, sincere and unguarded. You are probably less acquainted than am I – who for twenty-five years lived as it were in the *bas fonds* of those formidable shadows – with the Great Traditions of your journal! So you will not remember the Great Number in which you, dismissing Walt Whitman with two semi-obscene words (Swinburne), stated that the sonnets of a Mrs Augusta Webster were 'superior to anything that had been written' since the days of the 'Swan of Avon', and surpassed indeed the similar metrical efforts of that Bard (W.M. Rossetti). And in the same Great Number you stated that the orchestration of the then Queen's Master of the Music, Sir Somebody Somebody – he had supplied two lost parts for instruments in Hummel's Quintette – wiped out for ever all the orchestral works of the composer of *Tristan* (Joseph Knight). When I was still *le jeune homme modeste* and very, very innocuous, an odious old gentleman, having damned in your columns my infant works, addressed to me the galling exhortation *Patrem et avum habes; eos exorna!* ...[2] May I now return those your words to your address?

Returning, then, to the present century, let me put it in this way: Your Reviewer must be a man with some of the knowledges and experiences of a man. He *knows* that when human beings are undergoing fears, joys, passions or emotions they do not really retire to studies and compose in

1 [Reviewing F.S. Flint's *Otherworld: Cadences*, Edith Sitwell's *The Wooden Pegasus*, and Iris Tree's *Poems*, the critic argued that Ford's friend Flint lacked poetic intensity.]

2 [You have a father and grandfather: extol them!]

words jigsaw puzzles: they relieve their minds by rhythmical utterances. These, if rendered by an artist, make up the utterances of passion that are endurable or overwhelming. He must have read some of the Authorized Version and be acquainted with the Book of Job; the Lament for Absalom; the Psalms Of David; or the idyllic utterances of Ruth to her mother-in-law. Perhaps your Reviewer may never have come across really simple persons, peasants and the like at moments of great losses, great joys, great upheavals. In that case he will be surprised to hear that such elementals do not express themselves in rhyme. They do not. They come very near to the Vers Libre of the Translators. I have heard them say:

1. By God! We're alive: I never thought we should be./ 2. After tonight./ 3. Give it a name, Old Bird. It's a damn fine thing to taste hooch./ 4. After a straf like last night./ 5. Evans copped it; so did Dai Morgan./ 6. Swallow it down, have another of the same./ 7. Cor! I am all of a tremble. Or they say: sometimes with tears, sometimes not:

> That was my eldest son,
> Muss 'Uffer!
> He lay with his head twid my breastesses
> Six hundred mornings and more
> Before it was properly light;
> Counting the flies on the ceiling,
> And me never to see him no more.

That may not be poetry; but it is *vers libre* and it is the expression of emotion. Nevertheless it does not rhyme 'Greenwich' with 'spinach', or get entangled in 'ation' rhymes as the young do. (Heaven knows I do not wish to run down the young ladies your Reviewer so likes: Good luck to them, now and hereafter! His quotations are probably unfair to them, and they are no doubt emotional enough in other places. It is hard on them that he should have used their verses as sticks with which to beat his dog.)

And then... one does not like to see dog eat dog. One understood that *Normanno mortuo*[3] – *The Athenaeum* was to become the organ of the Morning Star; the New Day; the Young... Entreat, sir your Reviewer to look up your files for the great number of Whitman v. Augusta Webster and Sir William Blank v. Richard Wagner, and then let him reread his review of Mr Flint and the two young ladies....

Or at any rate let me say in your columns, you have trailed on the ground your august mantle-of-Elijah-tail, that for certain temperaments – *hominibus bonae voluntatis* – the poems in Mr Flint's *Otherworlds* are exquisite, and extract from the life that we today live all the poetry and all the emotion of a non-blatant kind that can be got out of the poor old

3 [Norman (MacColl) being dead]

thing by those not suited for skipping about in meadows and exclaiming:

> Ring a ring of roses!
> Pocket full of posies!

Though that too is a lovely occupation.

And Mr Flint's prose introduction is so quietly and beautifully written; so gentle in its cadences that are like those of Mr [W.H.] Hudson; it expresses so modestly and so completely what the whole great world outside these fortunate islands is expressing, feeling, or discovering as to the art of poetry, which is the pursuit of intimate expression between poor lonely man and poor lonely man.... Well, your Reviewer might surely have let it alone if you were unable to place at his disposal space in which seriously to consider, or worthily to condemn, that manifesto.

I have the honour to be, Sir, Your obedient servant,

The Athenaeum, 16 July 1920, 93–4.

An Answer to 'Three Questions'

1. Poetry always was, and always will be, a necessity for the human being. Verse-reading and verse-selling are no doubt temporarily in a decline, and will so remain until verse-poets make their verses interesting to grown men.

2. The function of poetry in the Republic is still, always has been, and always will be to instil imagination – that is, sympathetic insight! – into the Human Brute that man is. It civilizes. Rhythms or broken rhythms are a necessity for humanity. If it cannot get verse that interests it it will hum 'Tumty-tumty-tumty-tum' whilst lacing up its boots, or will revel in formally rhythmic or jazz music. Its reading will be novels and the newspapers.

3. Creative prose *is* poetry; the novel is narrative poetry and displaces nothing. The success of Messrs Kipling and Masefield proves that when verse-poets will write of subjects or in frames that interest adult humanity they can secure large followings in modern Anglo-Saxondom. Hardly anyone – naturally enough – wants to read imitations of Milton or the Jacobean poets written in frames of mind inspired by the Shelleyan or Keatsian attitude to life. Purity and refinement are no doubt good things, but you cannot expect to sell vegetables if you grow them on sterilized soil in vacuum chambers. But if verse-poets only want to be awarded 'marks' for poetical compositions by refined yet illiterate professional critics of professorial rank and attainments: well, that is quite a good, gentlemanly, spare-time occupation. But it has nothing to do with poetry, neither will it 'sell'. Or 'live'.

But why drag in the newspaper reports as the villains of the piece? Servants always did gossip at backdoors; masters and mistresses, poets, novelists, business men – and particularly solicitors! – always did gossip in parlours or offices; washerwomen over soiled clothes, officers on parade, ploughmen under the hedge. Gossip is as much a necessity as oxygen for humanity: it always has and always will take up the major portion of human leisures and interests. For the lonely people of large cities the daily press nowadays supplies vicarious inter-human oxygenation moderately well, supplemented as it is by the fiction of commerce. But if anyone supposes that, say, Elizabethan gentlemen spent five minutes over reading

Lear whilst they had eight hours a day for the discussion of dainty gossip hinted at in the Sonnets, that person is probably mistaken. No, the daily press has nothing to do with the lack of 'poetry-sales' in the modern world!

If the conductor of this periodical could secure a good, rattling account in rhymed verse of a late murder, with names of ladies of title hinted at with asterisks and startling insight into the psychology of the murdered unfortunate, and if the Poetry Bookshop has the distributing organization and could do it for one penny, those rhymed verses would sell two million, six hundred copies. If, in addition, it was poetry, it would be an immortal masterpiece of the type of Kyd's *Spanish Tragedy* – or the *Cenci*!

Chapbook, 27 (July 1922), 14–15.

A Haughty and Proud Generation

It is easy to say who are our British novelists of the first flight: they are Mr Conrad, Mr Hardy, Mr George Moore, Mr W.H. Hudson – and possibly Mr Bennett. That I regard as indisputable if we may take the novel as giving us something more than the tale – as being a tale with a projection of life, a philosophy, but not an obvious moral, or propagandist purpose. First-flight novelists, then, will be those who have perfected their methods and are resigned.

The second flight will be, in our literature, Pushkin's 'haughty and proud generation: vigorous and free in their passions and adventures'; they are such writers as Norman Douglas, P. Wyndham Lewis, D.H. Lawrence, Frank Swinnerton, Katherine Mansfield, Clemence Dane, Dorothy Richardson, and James Joyce. Your first flight will be wise; your second, dogmatic. One likes to thank them, for what it is worth, with one's note of applause. But they will not thank you much in return because they are going on to the new adventures, the new explorations of method.

Let us for a moment differentiate between the novel and the tale – or let us at least try to get at a working definition. The novel of today is probably the only intellectual, poetic, or spiritual exercise that humanity is engaged in performing. It is probably, too, the only work of exact and dispassionate science.

We may consider the tale first. Mr Kipling, speaking at his reception at the Sorbonne, talked recently of 'the literature of escape'. I don't know whether this phrase is an accepted classification of academic criticism, or whether we owe it to the genius of Mr Kipling. Mr Arthur Symons said long ago that all art is an escape – but that is another matter. Anyhow, that is a very valuable phrase. For the literature of escape embraces whole century-long ranges of effort from *The Golden Ass* of Apuleius to the last sadic rubbish of Miss Dash; all the works from the story of Morgiana and the Forty Thieves to *Treasure Island* or *Lorna Doone*, reading which the tired city typewriter or the millionaire's office boy may escape from their environments and so recruit their vital forces.

The tale – even the novel of commerce – should not be despised. Mr Gladstone sought refuge from the Irish Question in *John Inglesant*; Edward the Seventh read the nautical romances of Captain Marryat to solace himself whilst he was negotiating the Entente Cordiale, and thus we see the tale interlaced as it were with the greatest of international happenings.

The King's taste was sounder than that of the Prime Minister – but King or Premier, *midinette*[1] or millionaire, you must come at last to this: you must find escape from yourself in the artless tale – in the fiction of commerce. The late Mr Meredith used to await with impatience the daily instalments of *feuilleton* in one of our ha'penny papers.

But when it comes to criticism of the tale one is, in England, thrown back almost entirely upon the 'short story'. The English long tale is practically always merely anodyne, without art, construction, presentation, or progressive effect. You read it and 'escape', but you have no comment to make. It calls for none. And the short 'short story' is a very old form. Told by story-tellers in bazaars, by medieval queens to their courts, or by anecdote-cappers round the fires of smoking-rooms, the tale was constrained by time to be short and by the exacting nature of audiences to be well told. For people who listen must be gripped more firmly than people who read.

And one may say that all the pure art of the English-writing peoples has until quite lately gone into the short story. You could cite Mr Kipling, Mr Wells, and even Mr W.W. Jacobs without absolute shame against Continental writers of this one form. For the whole art of these three writers of genius has gone into their short stories – the whole, that is to say, of their senses of proportion, of narration, and of construction. The *Country of the Blind* volume of Mr Wells, any volume of the Indian tales of Mr Kipling, and any volume of Mr Jacobs are products of sheer genius in narration. Naturally any volume of Maupassant in his greatest vein – say, the original *Yvette* collection – excels the English books because in addition to skill of narration Maupassant had a great, gloomy, philosophic outlook which transfused all his really representative writing. And when an artist has the temperament that will let his work be transfused by a profound or a lofty perception of the broader aspects of human vicissitudes, his work will have greater value to the republic than that of the most skilled constructors of anecdotes. Chekhov, though not so practised in elisions as Maupassant, was to all intents and purposes as skilled a narrator and so, for the matter of that you might say, is Schnitzler.

Let us then put it that, although the writing of good short stories is not an essentially English occupation, when English men of genius do turn their attention to that form, they not infrequently attain to high achievement in pure art. But as far as this country is concerned, the practice of that form seems to be in abeyance. I cannot, at any rate, think of any English writer who could be classed as in the second flight of writers of the short story. Mr Kipling and Mr Wells of the indisputable first flight have turned their attention to other things; I have seen nothing by Mr Jacobs for a long time.

I ought perhaps to make a reservation in favour of Miss Katherine

1 [Young Parisian dressmaker or milliner]

Mansfield. I have had for this lady for so long so considerable an admiration that, though dates are not my strong point, I think it possible that she stands chronologically with Mr Lawrence, Mr Joyce, and Mr Lewis. Certainly in prewar days – and that is probably the criterion for 'second-flightness' – Miss Mansfield had arrived at a strong, severe, at an almost virulent skill in sheer elision: relevancy. I can still remember with precision some of her contributions to a journal called *Rhythm* that must have lived out its quite valuable life in 1913 or 1914; and certainly in her volume entitled *Bliss* Miss Mansfield has carried the methods of tight, hard, cold – I wish there were some translation for the Latin word *saeva* – selection further than it has ever been carried in English work. I wish she did more. Bulk is not a quality for which one need feel any respect; but a number of instances is helpful when it is one's task to generalize. And anyhow there is not too much in the literature of escape that one can read, not only to get away from the remembrance of one's creditors, but also with the keen pleasure of appreciating the skill of chisel work. Miss Mansfield has spent a good deal of time, lately, in exercising a mordant pen on contemporary fiction. I wish she had not: we have so much more need of good stuff than of analysis of indifferent matter.

So we arrive at the novel and at the second generation of its practitioners. Compared with the short story which as an art form was certainly perfected in the day of the Parables – and who knows in how many generations of earlier Books of the Dead and on how many myriads of incised bricks? – the novel is still a babe in arms. Henry James was our first novelist; Mr Conrad our next – and then we come to the second flight. Henry James was our first Anglo-Saxon writer to perceive that this life of ours is an affair of terminations and of embarrassments. Mr Conrad was our next. He realized that the records of human lives cannot be set down as they are set down by the amiable, learned, and incompetent contributors to Dictionaries of National Biographies, as a straightforward 'article' with dates but not too many references.

Of course, the great master of both these great men was Flaubert, and, if you read the account of the adulterous courtship of Emma Bovary by Rodolphe, you read the germ of *Ulysses*, of *Tarr*, of all the works of Miss Dorothy Richardson, of most of the stories of Mr Lawrence. Rodolphe, the rather bounderish country gentleman is trying, at a cattle show, to seduce Emma Bovary, the wife of the country doctor. They are seated side by side on the seats of the tribune. Rodolphe says: 'My love for you shall be eternal. We shall live as do the little birds in the sacred odour of Paradise.' The Prefect cries out: 'Trois boeufs; trois cochons; douze poules, et un coq! – Maitre Cornu!' – 'Three oxen; three sows; twelve hens, and a rooster! – First Prize: Mr Hornimann!' Rodolphe continues: 'Gracious being! At the mere sight of your form my heart…' The Prefect shouts: 'Four onions; twelve potatoes; twelve turnips! – First Prize: Mr

Sprout!' It is something like that: the constant alternation of the romantic-heroic with the products of dung and sweat. And that is our life.

Mr James must have known too many shrinkings, embarrassments, and fine shades to render them without remorse; Mr Conrad, much coarser and much less shuddering in fibre than the Master from New England, has limited himself – as far as form goes – to registering how human lives, in a thousand devious, unconnected anecdotes, present themselves to the memory of the teller of a story. Mr Conrad, in fact, is reconciled to, is tranquil in face of, his world of ships' captains and revolutionaries. Mr James, much more akin in spirit to the Flaubert whom he could not bear – to the Flaubert who was really a good Christian horrified at the way in which Christian men mangled in their practice the precepts of Our Lord – Mr James, then, never got over the crudities of merely living.

It has remained for our novelists of the second flight to unite, as best they could, the practices of Mr James and of Mr Conrad and to carry the process that one step further that art forever demands. The formula, the discovery, has trembled as it were on the lips of generations of novelists the world over. You find it in the banquet of Trimalchio; in the Sancho Panza of Cervantes; in Shakespeare's clowns; in Thackeray's comments on his characters – the sense of the gross, the ironic, or the merely smug world that surrounds and nullifies the hero. It has remained, let us repeat, for our novelists of the second flight to carry the conviction of the grinning, complex world into the consciousness, into the springs of action of their characters – to render it, not objectively, but from the inside.

Gissing had got so far as to emphasize that the gross, ironic, smug – and sordid! – world paralyses the lives not only of heroes but of the least significant human beings. *New Grub Street* falls short of being a masterpiece of the first order only because, like Zola's *L'Oeuvre*, it is perpetually harrowing – so ceaselessly harrowing that the mind cannot react against its protracted and heavy dragging. Still, *L'Oeuvre* and *New Grub Street* are serious studies of the hero as artist in process of strangulation by the drag of sordid material detail; just as *The Town Traveller* and *Demos* show the quite ordinary man's character being preyed upon by the mere sordidnesses of dirty table-cloths, greasy bacon, and frayed trouser-ends.

Gissing is little read today, which is a pity, for he was a sound, industrious, and honest craftsman; and he has left practically no following. That is not so much to be regretted because his methods, as far as I can see, lead only into a cul-de-sac. And that brings me to Mr Swinnerton.

To read Mr Swinnerton at his best is to hear all the time the cadences of Gissing; and even in such carefully psychologized work as the character called Jenny of *Nocturne* there is the perpetual undertone of the dirty tablecloth and the greasy bacon. The mental states of the girl are continually at the mercy of re-hashed mutton and wet hat-trimmings – or of *bisque de homard* and peaches. Psychologically these are not *trouvailles* –

only Mr Swinnerton's neck of mutton and the bread pudding of the domestic hearth, as well as the Beaune in the glass of the seducer, are excellent renderings of still life.

But Mr Swinnerton – and *Nocturne* is incomparably his best book – is not just doing the sordid surroundings plus the young woman's reaction into luxurious seduction on board a lordly yacht, that being the 'plot' of this work stated unsympathetically. (And the plot of every work worth consideration should be capable of standing up against unsympathetic statement.) He has sufficient perception of the complexity of life to attempt to crowd into the story of five or six hours the whole mental history, the whole progression, of his young woman's 'fall'. And not only does he attempt this but he succeeds in the attempt. That is a very considerable achievement. It may or may not be merely a technical feat; but the effect is to convey some at least of the flicker and waver of the human soul in the life that we live.

Descending then from Gissing – though I am quite prepared to have Mr Swinnerton or someone else write to the papers and declare that he has never felt the influence of the author of *Henry Ryecroft* – Mr Swinnerton makes his assault upon the Modern Position. Descending from Henry James, Miss Clemence Dane makes hers – not quite so uncompromisingly. *Legend*, which is Miss Dane's most interesting book, though *Regiment of Women* contains more harrowing stuff, is another attempt to work into a single evening the story of a whole life, the whole work of an artist, the complete love affairs, and the death of an unknown, problematic woman of letters. Without Mr Swinnerton's courage or technical 'chic', Miss Dane not only provides herself with a narrator, which of course is a necessity for her form, but provides the narrator with a humble, Jane Eyre-like psychology, vibrating sympathies, love affair, and marriage. Thus she carries the 'story' on, though only in a 'prologue', for months after the evening is over. Mr Swinnerton just leaves the evening there as far as *Nocturne* is concerned: we do not get told whether the skipper of the lordly yacht marries the girl, or whether the young woman has a baby, or any of the other details that, rounding up endings, leave the voracious reader with a comfortable feeling of repletion.

Nevertheless, Miss Dane's attempt is an attempt – less to get at the complex impressionism of life than at the complexities of human judgements. A glamorous literary female figure is talked about from every point of view within the Jamesian-At-Home sphere of life, by almost every imaginable human type to be found in a South Kensington 'highbrow at home'. A nasty writing man thinks 'She' does not love her husband; a nice painting man preserves discreet but illuminative silences; a 'cattish' writing woman thinks 'Her' second book a sentimental failure; a nice writing woman thinks it a monument of irony. So a curiously fussy image of the Figure is built up, the Figure herself dying in the distance whilst the 'at home' proceeds. Miss Dane in short employs Mr Conrad's method in unfolding her story and goes to the Henry James of 'The Aspern Papers' and 'The Real Thing' for her curiously provincial atmosphere.

The point, however, about both Mr Swinnerton and Miss Dane is that they do have conceptions of life as a very complex affair of cross motives. Neither treats characters as simple beings whose story is a matter of straightforward achievement under one dominant passion – achievement of fame, fortune, automobiles, heroines, offspring. Nor does either of them seek to render the world a better place. Those are very good things.

We come, then, to the more obviously motive forces of the English novel of today. We may begin with Mr Douglas – the Mr Douglas of *South Wind* and *They Went*; though really you might just as well call *Alone* a novel with modern Italy as central character – modern Italy set down from as many angles, cut into as many-faceted a thing as the central figure of *Legend*, and provided with even more wines and dishes than the central figure of *Nocturne*.

In a sense Mr Douglas is a writer of an older generation – of a generation infinitely old, critically. To come upon passages of appraisement in *Alone* is to be bewildered by the feeling that one's young, young youth has returned. You have Ouida and Mathilde Blind – Mathilde Blind of all people! – exalted at the expense of James; for all the world as if the late Mr Watts-Dunton were still setting the standard of the late *Athenaeum*. There is hardly anyone old enough to remember *that* literary point of view.

So that Mr Douglas, as far as his gifts are concerned, must have sprung fully armed from some militant head. He does not descend from Gissing or Mr Conrad; certainly James has not influenced him; it is impossible to imagine his having the patience to read *Education sentimentale*; he has none of the swift attack of Maupassant. He is most like Anatole France – and yet he is very unlike Anatole France. He is like, that is to say, because at any moment he will illuminate a modern predicament with an anecdote from the depths of a most profound antiquity – only you feel that Mr Douglas is quite capable of inventing his anecdote and conveying to it, with tremendous gusto and smacking of the lips, an almost too gorgeous patina. Not for nothing has he told us the story of the faun of Locri.

South Wind is the story, tremulous in surface and in treatment, of an affair – of, that is to say, an atmosphere. The bishop is nonsense; the duchess is nonsense; the millionaire, the boy, the count – they spring for moments into life that is more real than life and cast light, not on any humanity, but on a place that quivers in Mediterranean sunshine. Or let us put it that Mr Douglas's central figure is the season of 19— in Taormina or Capri or some such place, and that Mr Douglas's human dolls illuminate with their actions and illustrate with their disquisitions that period of fashionable time. I think this is the best way to put it: for this author's savage, mordant dislike for humanity would hardly let him make his central figure a bishop or any other created human being. The central figure of *They Went* is the Devil, who, I imagine, was not created; but even with his own devil Mr Douglas has not very much patience, not enough to dwell very much or very often upon him. But here again his real hero is the fabulous city of the catastrophic end.

Loving the souls of places, not of men, Mr Douglas can afford to write a great deal more than the human-centred novelist of today; so he can afford to be relatively personal too. For it matters very little if the personality of your writer sticks out in the foreground of places where the sunlight always quivers. It does matter a great deal if that personality intrudes on the always shadowy renderings of human interplay. That is the weak spot of *Tarr* – which Mr Lewis wrote, not with as much aplomb, but quite as obtrusively as Mr Douglas. That is no doubt because both these important writers began as essayists – a school that is exceedingly deleterious to the novelist-beginner. For your essayist learns to rely on his personality rather than on anything else of all the things there are under the sun. What, for instance, might not the Mr Beerbohm of *Seven Men* be if he did not perpetually and for a living have to be Max – more blasé, more unpractical, more cynical, and less interested than any other man of London Town?

Mr Douglas probably imposes his personality out of sheer damn-your-eyes don't-careness; but Mr Lewis does it of set purpose – and sometimes he forgets to do it, out of sheer fatigue, one suspects. Then he writes the straightforward story of the tale-teller, as he does throughout the adventures of Kreisler in *Tarr*, the Tarr episodes themselves being, except for the discussions, shadowy and unconvincing.

But in the discussions Mr Lewis shows himself an extraordinarily great artist, not, heaven knows, in what his characters say, but in the rendering of their temperamental and physical reactions one upon the other. Mr Lawrence is a great realist – except when he is recording conversations. Mr Lewis is our greatest anti-realist; but when he is rendering conversations he is so great a realist that he makes you shiver. His characters writhe – over the marble table-tops of restaurants where the waiters rush about, harried, in the serving of 'bocks', or over the gas cooking-stoves where they are making 'lunches' out of the débris, the scraps from paper parcels purchased from an adjacent *crémerie*. They indulge in meaningless scraps of talk; but their personalities are set 'one over against another', currents crossing, embarrassments, agonizing shynesses, remembrances – and nothing can be more bitter! – of points they might have made in their last speech but seven. That is very wonderful.

The characters of Mr Lawrence, infinitely more real, infinitely more provided with ancestries, their feet infinitely more on the ground, sit about in punts, in fields of asphodels, and talk pathologic nonsense, every word of which Mr Lawrence records as if he had been sitting on the other side of the hedge with a stenographer's tablet. But as for interplay of personality with personality, in the works of Mr Lawrence there is none. Absolutely none. Lawrence's men and women discuss Love and discuss Liberty as if they were looking up those words in the *Encyclopaedia Britannica* and reading out what there they found, with a profound solemnity, an unwinking preposterousness.

On the other hand, the author of *Tarr* could never have written 'Odour of Chrysanthemums', the descriptions of how a coal-miner's widow washed the body of her husband, killed by a fall in a pit. The odour of chrysanthemums drifts in all the while, it being autumn.

That is Mr Lawrence being almost greater than it is proper to be. For the Mr Lawrence of *The White Peacock*, of *Sons and Lovers*, is a writer of genius. But he indulges his moods too much – at the expense of his subject. And self-indulgence is the last thing that a writer at all concerned with realism can allow himself. Temperament is, of course, necessary for the genius; but the genius who lets his books be nothing but temperament falls either into boredom or the ridiculous. And so, in *Women in Love*, a recent novel, Mr Lawrence gives us in all seriousness, during a discussion of Love-in-Liberty and Liberty-in-Love the most ridiculous sentence that was ever set down by the human pen. I regret that it is too indecent to be quoted in this context.

The fact is that sex discussion occupies – such is the idiocy of the repressive laws of Great Britain and the still more stupid laws of the United States – far too great a part in the public mind of the lands that border the Atlantic. It becomes an obsession; it ends as a nuisance. Sex is, I suppose, one phenomenon in a chain of the phenomena of growth and of reproduction. It has its importance along with eating and other physical processes. One should – the novelist, above all, should – regard it with composure. But so few do.

Indeed, I fancy that Mr Joyce is the only artist we have today who with an utter composure regards processes of reproduction, of nourishment, and of physical renewal. But then Mr Joyce, the supreme artist, regards with an equal composure – all things. That is why the law of the United States has persecuted his publishers. For law cannot – any more than the average of excitable humanity – contemplate, composure with equanimity. It is in itself abhorrent. If we were all always composed, we should have no war, no crime, no daily journalism, no outcry, nothing contemptible, very little that was base. We should have nothing but the arts. What then would become of poor humanity – of *l'homme moyen sensuel*, of the preacher, the writer on morals and the always excited scientist? They must die! Some day they all will. But that time is not yet.

And Mr Joyce is a writer of very beautiful, composed English. To read *A Portrait of the Artist as a Young Man* as against, say, *Interim* of Miss Dorothy Richardson is to recognize the difference between singularly fussy inclusiveness and absolutely aloof selection. There is really more enlightenment as to childhood and youth in the first three pages of Mr Joyce's book – there is more light thrown on the nature of man – than in all Miss Richardson's volumes.

And that is not to belittle Miss Richardson; for to be infinitely little set over against Mr Joyce, is to be yet considerable enough. But Mr Joyce measures his effects by things immense and lasting, Miss Richardson by the passing standards of the lower middle-class boarding-house. It is as you might say Flaubert against Gissing.

Mr Joyce's work is a voyaging on a much higher spiritual plane: the embarrassments and glories of Miss Richardson's young women are bound up in material details. You are embarrassed because of the fichu about your neck; you glory because, finding a restaurant open long after normal closing time, the Italian proprietor serves you himself, with an air of distinguished consideration, with a shiny roll and a cup of chocolate – at a table laid with the plates and cutlery for a party of four! Now, I am not decrying the rendering of that sort of glory or melancholy. A large part of the elation of our poor lives as now we live them may well come from the fact that with our insufficient means we have received at some restaurant more consideration than we had expected. Proprietors and waiters have some of the contempt of public officials for poor humanity, and some of the clairvoyance in appraising purses that belongs to the really successful tradesmen. To hoodwink such fearsome creatures is to achieve a feat such as seldom falls to our portion. But it is only a momentary pride. And the depression that comes with shabbiness of clothes, deep though it be, is not the essential depression of the healthy man.

That is why the school of Gissing is a lesser thing than the school of Joyce. You may put it medically. Doctors tell you that all your life you have in your throat seven million germs of the cold in the head: but it is only when your vitality is at a low ebb that those germs invade your system. For the Gissing of *New Grub Street* sordid tablecloths; monotonously passing lives, and material indigences were the fulcra, the essential motive powers, in the lives of heroes. But that is not true to life – or it so happens only when the system is in a state of low vitality. It is possible that the sudden perception of a dirty tablecloth, all other things being unbearable, might make a hero-poet rush out and sell his soul to an evening paper. But that would be an accidental culmination; a pathological state. The contemplation of mutton hash contributed largely to the seduction of Mr Swinnerton's Jenny – and that, given all the sordidnesses of her day, was true enough. But a whole procession of days of mutton hash, a whole Sahara of tablecloths stained with rings from the bottoms of stout glasses, would not turn Mr Swinnerton's brave London Jenny into a prostitute by temperament or a real poet into a born journalist. In fact mere irritation at the sordidness of his surroundings will do no more than make a sound man or woman commit now and then a *lâcheté*;[2] it will never change the essentials of a character.

It is the perception of that fact that gives such great value to Mr Joyce – and to the whole movement of the second flight. The mind of every man is made up of several – three or four – currents all working side by side, all making their impress or getting their expression from separate and individual areas of the brain. It is not enough to say that every man is homo duplex; every man is homo x-plex. And this complexity pursues every man into the minutest transactions of his daily life. You go to a bookstall to ask the price of a certain publication. Yes! But part of your mind says to you very quickly: 'This clerk has the nose of my uncle George!' Another part feels that you have plenty of time for your train; another that the fish you had for breakfast is disagreeing with you. Generally you are under a deep depression caused by the morning's international news, but you have a particular elation at some movement in the stock market. A lady passing leaves a scent of wallflowers; that calls up associations to which you hardly attend. Almost unknown to yourself, beneath your breath you are humming a tune that has yet other associations. It is this tenuous complexity of life that has its first artistic representation in the works of our second flight – and it is this that makes one feel hopeful in the general depression of the English literary world. It is true that it finds almost its sole appreciation in America; but America does at least keep it going. And as long as it keeps going – *les idées sont en marche*.

The *Portrait of the Artist as a Young Man* is a book of such beauty of writing, such clarity of perception, such a serene love of and interest in life, and such charity that, being the ungenerous creature man is, one was inclined to say: 'This surely must be a peak! It is unlikely that this man will climb higher!' But even now that Mr Joyce has published *Ulysses*, it is too early to decide upon that. One can't arrive at one's valuation of a volume so loaded as *Ulysses* after a week of reading and two or three weeks of thought about it. Next year, or in twenty years, one may. For it is as if a new continent with new traditions had appeared, and demanded to be run through in a month. *Ulysses* contains the undiscovered mind of man; it is human consciousness analysed as it has never before been analysed. Certain books change the world. This, success or failure, *Ulysses* does: for no novelist with serious aims can henceforth set out upon a task of writing before he has at least formed his own private estimate as to the rightness or wrongness of the methods of the author of *Ulysses*. If it does not make an epoch – and it well may! – it will at least mark the ending of a period.

Yale Review, 11 (July 1922), 703–17.

2 [Baseness or meanness]

Ulysses and the Handling of Indecencies

I have been pressed to write for the English public something about the immense book of Mr Joyce. I do not wish to do so; I do not wish to do so at all for four or five – or twenty – years, since a work of such importance cannot properly be approached without several readings and without a great deal of thought. To write, therefore, of all aspects of *Ulysses*, rushing into print and jotting down ideas before a hostile audience is a course of action to which I do not choose to commit myself. The same imperious correspondents as force me to write at all forward me a set of press-cuttings, the tributes of my distinguished brothers of the pen to this huge statue in the mists.

One may make a few notes, nevertheless, in token of good will and as a witness of admiration that is almost reverence for the incredible labours of this incredible genius. For indeed, holding *Ulysses* in one's hand, the last thing one can do about it is to believe in it.

Let us, if you will, postulate that it is a failure – just to placate anybody that wants placating in that special way. For it does not in the least matter whether *Ulysses* is a success or a failure. *We* shall never know and the verdict will be out of our hands: it is no question of flying from London to Manchester under the hour. That we could judge. It fails then.

Other things remain. It is, for instance, obvious that the public – the lay, non-writing public of today – will not read *Ulysses* even in the meagre measure with which it reads anything at all, the best or the worst that is put before it. Perhaps no lay, non-writing public will ever read it even in the measure with which it reads Rabelais, Montaigne, or the *Imaginary Conversations* of Walter Savage Landor. (I am not comparing Mr Joyce with these writers.) That perhaps would be failure.

Or perhaps it would not. For myself, I care nothing about readers for writers. It is sufficient that the book should be there on the shelf, or the manuscript, down the years, slowly gathering the infiltrated dust of the bottom of a chest; indeed, it is enough that the words making it up should have ever been gathered together beneath a pen. Force once created is indestructible; we may let it go at that.

And yet, even though the great uninstructed public should never read *Ulysses*, we need not call it a failure. There are other worlds. It is, for instance, perfectly safe to say that no writer after today will be able to neglect *Ulysses*. Writers may dislike the book, or may be for it as enthusiastic as you will; ignore it they cannot, any more than passengers after the forties of last century could ignore the railway as a means of transit.

I have called attention in another place to the writers' technical revolution that in *Ulysses* Mr Joyce initiates. The literary interest of this work, then, arises from the fact that, for the first time in literature on an extended scale, a writer has attempted to treat man as the complex creature that man – every man! – is. The novelist, poet, and playwright hitherto, and upon the whole, have contented themselves with rendering their characters on single planes. A man making a career is rendered simply in terms of that career, a woman in love as simply a woman in love, and so on. But it does not take a novelist to see that renderings of such unilateral beings are not renderings of life as we live it. Of that every human being is aware! You conduct a momentous business interview that will influence your whole future; all the while you are aware that your interlocutor has a bulbous, veined nose; that someone in the street has a drink-roughened voice and is proclaiming that someone has murdered someone; that your physical processes are continuing; that you have a headache; you have, even as a major motive, the worry that your wife is waiting for you at the railway terminus and that you may miss your train to your country home. Your mind makes a psychological analysis of the mind of your wife as she looks at the great clock in the station; you see that great clock; superimposed over the almanack behind the head of the bulbous-nosed man, you see the enormous hands jumping the minutes.

And that is a rendering of a very uncomplex moment in the life of the most commonplace of men; for many, such a scene will be further complicated by associations from melodies humming in the ear; by associations sweeping across them with scents or conveyed through the eye by the colours and forms of wainscotings.... Or merely by pictures of estates that you may buy or lands that you may travel in if the deal on which you are engaged goes through.

Of this complexity man has for long been aware, nevertheless in Anglo-Saxondom until quite lately no attempt has been made by writers to approach this problem. For that reason in Anglo-Saxondom the written arts are taken with no seriousness as guides to life. In Dago-lands it is different. There for the hundred years that have succeeded the birth of Flaubert huge, earnest works distinguished by at least mixed motives in psychological passages or consisting almost solely of psychological passages that shiver with tenuously mixed motives – such works have been the main feature of European literature, from *Education sentimentale* to the *Frères Karamazoff*.

To this literature Anglo-Saxondom, or at any rate England, has contributed nothing at all, or nothing of any importance,[1] and because of that Anglo-Saxondom remains outside the comity of civilized nations. So the publication of *Ulysses*, success or failure, is an event singularly important. It gives us at least our chance to rank as Europeans.

No doubt we shall take it – for I do not believe that it is the Anglo-Saxon publics that are at fault in the matter of civilization. *Ulysses* will go on being miscalled or ignored by our official critics and will go on being officially disliked by our writers with livings to get. But the latter will have to take peeps at it so as not to let the always threatening 'other fellow' get ahead; and gradually across our literature there will steal the Ulyssean complexion. That, I think, will be so obvious to any student of past literature that it hardly needs elaborating. Then our publics, learning to find their ways amongst complexities, will approach at least nearer to the fountain-head. This sounds improbable. But it should be remembered that there was once a time when the works of Alfred Tennyson were hailed as incomprehensible and when Charles Dickens clamoured for the imprisonment of Holman Hunt, painter of *The Light of the World*, as a portrayer of the obscene![2] Such strange revolutions have taken place; but they are conveniently ignored, as a rule.

I know that a thousand readers of *The English Review* – or is it twenty thousand? – are waiting to tell me that Mr Joyce is not Tennyson. But indeed I am aware of the fact and glad of it, since one more figure such as that must push English literature a thousand – or is it twenty thousand? – years back. And this is not to attack Tennyson!

It is to say that in matters of literature at least we have an ineffable complacency to which another such a Figure as that of the Bard of Haslemere could only immeasurably add: on the principle that 'it is certain that my conviction gains immensely as soon as another soul can be found to' … put it into rhyme.[3] Let that be how it may, it is certain that in Mr Joyce we have at last, after one hundred and fifty-one years – I leave the date 1771 for the unriddlement of the literary learned – a writer who forms not only a bridge between the Anglo-Saxon writers and grown men,[4] but a bridge between Anglo-Saxondom and the Continent of Europe.

1 I may as well say that I am not unaware of the *Tarr* of Mr Wyndham Lewis; of the works of Miss Dorothy Richardson; *Nocturne* of Mr Swinnerton, or even of *Legend* by Miss Clemence Dane, each of which three last attacks one or other corner of Mr Joyce's problem, whilst *Tarr* makes a shot, unrealistically, at the whole of it. I am, however, writing notes on *Ulysses*, not a history of a whole movement.

2 [Actually Rossetti's *Christ at the Home of his Parents*; not as obscene but as blasphemous.]

3 [The quotation, a favourite of Ford's, is a variation of Novalis' epigram used as Conrad's epigraph for *Lord Jim*: 'It is certain my Conviction gains infinitely, the moment another soul will believe in it.']

4 'I should be said to insist absurdly on the power of my own confraternity' (that of the novelists) 'if I were to declare that the bulk of the young people in the upper and middle classes receive their moral teaching chiefly from the novels that they read. Mothers

Ulysses, then, is an 'adult', a European, work. That is why we fittingly call it incredible. For who, a year or so ago, would have believed it possible that any work having either characteristic would have been printed in the English language?

The question of the expression of what are called indecencies in the arts is one that sadly needs approaching with composure. I will claim to approach it with more composure than can most people. On the whole I dislike pornographic or even merely 'frank' writing in English – not on moral, but on purely artistic grounds, since so rare are franknesses in this language that frank words swear out of a page and frankly depicted incidents of a sexual nature destroy the proportions of a book. The reader is apt to read the book for nothing else.

On the question of whether the Young Person[5] should be 'told' truths about sexual matters I keep a quite open mind. If she should, well and good – as long as subtle souled psychologists[6] can be found at first to know and then to reveal that truth! If she shouldn't, there are locked bookcases and Acts of Parliament such as prevent the supply of cigarettes and racing circulars to the adolescent. But it is probably impossible to keep sexual knowledge from the Young Person who is determined to obtain it. Personally, I never had a bookcase locked against me in my childhood; my father expressed to one of my school masters the mild wish that I should not be encouraged to read 'Byron', and naturally, as soon as I heard that I read three or four lines of *Manfred*. But I cannot remember a single indecent passage in any literature that I read before I was twenty, unless four lines of Milton that used to make one of my classes at school shiver with delight can be called indecent. My schoolfellows – at a great public school! – used to approach me, sometimes in bodies, I being reputed bookish, with requests that I would point out to them the 'smutty' passages in the Bible and *Tom Jones*. But I did not know these, and I remember being severely manhandled on at least one occasion by ten or a dozen older boys, because I refused. I formed even then the opinion that the appetite in humanity for sexually exciting written details was an instinct of great strength, and nothing that I have since experi-

would no doubt think of their own sweet teaching; fathers of the examples which they set; and schoolmasters of the excellence of their instructions. Happy is the country that has such mothers, fathers, and schoolmasters! But the novelist creeps in closer than the father, closer than the schoolmaster, closer almost than the mother. He is the chosen guide, the tutor whom the young pupil chooses for herself. She retires with him, suspecting no lesson… and there she is taught how she shall learn to love; how she shall receive the lover when he comes; how far she should advance to meet the joy; why she should be reticent and not throw herself at once into this new delight….'

I leave it to the reader to guess what – very great – novelist wrote that in the year 1880.

5 [Mr Podsnap in Dickens's *Our Mutual Friend* worries over what might bring a blush to the cheek of the 'Young Person'.]

6 [Shelley's phrase about Coleridge in 'Peter Bell the Third'.]

enced has caused me to change that opinion.

My own 'suppressions' – three in number – have been merely funny, and yet, reflectively considered, they are nearly as revelatory as any others.

Thus: A great many years ago an American publisher who afterwards became United States Ambassador to Great Britain,[7] proposed to publish one of my works in his country. It was a novel, Tudor in tone. He sent for me one day and protested: 'You know, we could not print this speech in the United States!' … To indicate something of great rarity one of my characters said: 'You will find a chaste whore as soon as that!' I suggested mildly that he should print it: 'You will find a chaste — as soon as that!' But, 'Oh!' exclaimed that publisher diplomat, 'we could never print the word "chaste"; it is so suggestive!' And my book was never published in the United States.

Again: One of my colonels, formally using his powers under King's Regs, prohibited the publication of one of my books. He was of opinion that it was obscene; besides, he thought that 'all this printing of books' ought to be stopped. He was a good fellow: he is dead now. My book he had not read. It was published by H.M. Ministry of Information over that officer's head – as British Governmental propaganda, for recitation to French Tommies!

Again: Years ago I had a contract with a very respectable Liberal journal to supply once a week a critical article. Being in those days a 'stylist', I had inserted in my contract a clause to the effect that the paper must publish what I wrote and must publish it without the alteration of a word. I had occasion then to write of two of the characters of some novel: 'The young man could have seduced her for the price of a box of chocolates.'

Late, late one night the editor of that journal rang me up on the telephone to beg me not to insist on his publishing those words; his readers, he said, were not so much strait-laced as particular. After I had gloated over his predicament a little I told him that he might alter the words to suit his readers.

He altered them to: 'The young man could have taken advantage of her at small cost'!

Now I hope I may be acquitted of personal resentment if I say that that publisher-ambassador and that editor – we may leave the colonel out of it, since he was purely irresponsible, desiring to suppress all books and authors on principle – that publisher and that editor credited their respective readers with minds extremely objectionable. For the person who prefers the phrase 'take advantage of' to the word 'seduce', like the person who cannot read the word 'chaste' without experiencing indecent sugges-

7 [In *Return to Yesterday* (London, 1931), pp. 320–1, Ford retold this story, identifying the publisher as Walter H. Page.]

tions, must have the mind of a satyr. It would be better not to write, to publish, or to edit for him at all.

It is, of course, a fact that the serious artist is invariably persecuted when he trenches on matters that are open to the public handling of any pimp as long as he grins. It seems impossible to change that amiable *trait* in Anglo Saxon officialdom. But that is not the same thing as saying that a change would not be a good thing. Before the war, when I was less of a hermit but much more ingenuous, I used to be shocked by the fact that a great many ladies whom I respected and liked possessed copies of, and gloated as it appeared over, a volume of dream-interpretations by a writer called Freud – a volume that seemed to me to be infinitely more objectionable, in the fullest sense of the term, than *Ulysses* at its coarsest now seems to me. For I can hardly picture to myself the woman who will be 'taught to be immodest' by the novel; I could hardly in those days imagine anyone who could escape that fate when reading that – real or pseudo! – work of science. Yet I find today that the very persons who then *schwaermed* over Freud now advocate the harshest of martyrdoms for Mr Joyce.

That is obviously because Mr Joyce is composed, whilst Mr Freud has all the want of balance of a scientist on the track of a new theory.

Composure, in fact, is the last thing that our ruling classes will stand in anything but games; that is to say that it is permitted to you to be earnest in frivolities, whereas to be in earnest about serious matters is a sort of sin against the Holy Ghost and the Common Law. That will have to be changed – or we as a race shall have to go under. And we shall have to go under because of the quality of our minds; and the quality of our minds is what it is – because we cannot *stand* the composure of Mr Joyce!

I cannot help these things; but I expect to be severely censured for making the constatation. As Matthew Arnold pointed out, we were in his day the laughing-stock of the world; today we are the laughing-stock and the great danger to civilization. That is largely due to the nature of our present rulers – but only partly! Other nations have bad Governments and are yet not so universally distrusted. We are distrusted, lock, stock, and barrel, and every man jack of us because we are regarded not merely as a nation of shopkeepers, but as personally and every one of us hypocrites to boot.

Here is a passage which, I suppose, Mr Joyce risks – possibly quite justifiably, who knows? – a long sentence for writing. It comes from the very height of his *Walpurgisnacht*:

> PRIVATE COMPTON (*waves the crowd back*). Fair play here. Make a b……g butcher's shop of the……
>
> (*Massed bands blare 'Garryowen' and 'God Save the King.'*)
>
> CISSY CAFFREY. They're going to fight. For me!…

STEPHEN. The Harlot's cry from street to street
Shall weave old Ireland's winding-sheet

PRIVATE CARR (*loosening his belt, shouts*). I'll wring the neck of any .... b......d says a word against my... ... King.

BLOOM (*shakes* CISSY CAFFREY's *shoulders*). Speak, you! Are you struck dumb? You are the link between nations and generations. Speak, woman, sacred life-giver!

CISSY CAFFREY (*alarmed, seizes* PRIVATE CARR's *sleeve*). Amn't I with you? Amn't I your girl? Cissy's your girl. (*She cries*) Police!....

VOICES. Police!

DISTANT VOICES. Dublin's burning! Dublin's burning! On fire! On fire!

(Brimstone fires spring up. Dense clouds roll past. Heavy Gatling guns boom. Troops deploy. Gallops of hoofs. Artillery. Hoarse commands. Bells clang. Backers shout. Drunkards bawl. W......s screech. Foghorns hoot.... In strident discord peasants and townsmen of Orange and Green factions sing 'Kick the Pope' and 'Daily, Daily, Sing to Mary'.)

PRIVATE CARR (*with ferocious articulation*). I'll do him in, so help me.... Christ! I'll wring the b......d ......'s ......d......g windpipe!

OLD GUMMY GRANNY (*thrusts a dagger towards* STEPHEN's *hand*). Remove him, acushla. At 8.35 a.m. you will be in heaven and Ireland will be free. (*She prays.*) O good God! Take him!

BLOOM. Can't you get him away?....

STEPHEN. *Exit Judas! Et laqueo se suspendit!*

BLOOM (*runs to* STEPHEN). Come along with me now before worse happens. Here's your stick....

CISSY CAFFREY (*pulling* PRIVATE CARR). Come on. You're boosed. He insulted me, but I forgive him (*Shouting in his ear*). I forgive him for insulting me...

PRIVATE CARR (*breaks loose*). I'll insult him!

(He rushes towards STEPHEN, *fists outstretched, and strikes him in the face.* STEPHEN *totters, collapses, falls stunned. He lies prone, his face to the sky, his hat rolling to the wall.* BLOOM *follows and picks it up.)*

That appears to have been an ordinary Dublin Night's Entertainment; the English reader may find it disagreeable to peruse. But I do not see that the adoption of a suppressive policy towards such matters does anyone much good. I ought to say that in Mr Joyce's pages the epithets that my more coy pen has indicated with dots are written out in full. I don't see why they should not be: that is the English language as we have made it and as we use it – all except a very thin fringe of our More Select Classes. And that, in effect, is our civilization of today – after a hundred years of efforts at repression on the part of those with Refined Poetic Imaginations.

For that, looking at the matter with the complete impartiality, and indeed the supreme indifference, of one who breeds animals, seems to me to be the main point about the whole matter. We have for just about a hundred years had, in Anglo-Saxondom, firstly repressive tendencies in the literary pundit, and then repressive legislation; at the present moment we are a race hysterical to the point of degeneracy in the pursuit of the salacious; our theatres cannot pay their way without bedrooms on the stage; our newspapers cannot exist without divorce-court and prostitute-murder cases, and the lubricities of the Freudian *idées fixes* creep subterraneous – 'creeping-rootstocks', to use a botanical term – in the under-minds of our More Select.

The language of our whole nation, except for a tiny and disappearing class, is of an aching filthiness that would add to the agonies of the damned in hell! Those *are* the facts: no one who has lived with men during the last eight years will deny them.

Then, a hundred years of repression having brought us to that pass, it would seem to be better to drop repressions! The promotion of them is an excellent way of making a career – as the late Mr Comstock found it; an excellent way of extorting boodle; inflicting pain on the defenceless; of attaining to haloes whilst perusing scabrous matter. All these ambitions, God knows, are human. Whether they are commendable would seem to be a matter of doubt. That they are extremely bad for a people is obvious to the composed in spirit. For if you expel Nature with handcuffs and the Tombs, it will burst forth on Broadway in pandemonium. Mr Mencken in a *Book of Prefaces* presents us with evidence enough of that.

There is not very much about Mr Joyce in all this – *et pour cause!* Mr Joyce stands apart from this particular world of ambassador-publishers, lay and ecclesiastical editors, intelligentsia, and Comstockian orgies. To call a work that deals with city life in all its aspects 'serene' would probably be to use the wrong word. And yet a great deal of *Ulysses* is serene, and possibly, except to our Anglo-Saxon minds, even the 'disgusting passages' would not really prove disgusting. That is what one means when one calls *Ulysses* at last a European work written in English.

For indeed a book purporting to investigate and to render the whole of a human life cannot but contain 'disgusting' passages; we come, every one of us, into a world as the result of an action that the Church – and no doubt very properly! – declares to be mortal sin; the great proportion of the food we eat and of the food eaten by the beasts that we eat is dung; we are resolved eventually into festering masses of pollution for the delectation of worms.

And it is probably better that from time to time we should contemplate these facts, hidden though they be from the usual contemplation of urban peoples. Otherwise, when, as inevitably we must, we come up against them we are apt to become overwhelmed to an unmanly degree. As against this weakness it would probably be good to read *Ulysses*. But I am not prescribing the reading of *Ulysses* as a remedy to a sick commonwealth.

Nor indeed do I recommend *Ulysses* to any human being. In the matter of readers my indifference is of the deepest. It is sufficient that *Ulysses*, a book of profound knowledges and of profound renderings of humanity, should exist – in the most locked of bookcases. Only... my respect that goes out to the human being that will read this book without much noticing its obscenities will be absolute; and I do not know that I can much respect any human being that cannot do as much as that. But I daresay no human being desires my respect!

Let us copy out a random page from this book: this is Mr Bloom, the advertisement canvasser of a Dublin paper, coming out from Mass and, on his way to a funeral, entering a chemist's to get a lotion made up for Mrs Bloom:

> He passed, discreetly buttoning, down the aisle and out through the main door into the light. He stood a moment, unseeing, by the cold black marble bowl, while before him and behind two worshippers dipped furtive hands in the low tide of the holy water. Trams; a car of Prescott's dyeworks; a widow in her weeds. Notice because I'm in mourning myself. He covered himself. How goes the time? Quarter past. Time enough yet. Better get that lotion made up. Where is this? Ah, yes, the last time Sweny's in Lincoln Place. Chemists rarely move. Their green and gold beaconjars too heavy to stir. Hamilton Long's founded in the year of the flood. Huguenot church near there. Visit some day.
>
> He walked southwards along Westland Row. But the recipe is in the other trousers. O, and I forgot the latchkey too. Bore this funeral affair. O well poor fellow it's not his fault. When was it I got it made up last? Wait. I changed a sovereign, I remember. First of the month it must have been or second. O he can look it up in the prescription book.
>
> The chemist turned back page after page. Sandy shrivelled smell he seems to have. Shrunken skull. And old. Quest for the philosopher's stone. The alchemists. Drugs age you after mental excitement. Lethargy then. Why? Reaction. A lifetime in a night. Gradually changes your character. Living all the day among herbs, ointments, disinfectants. All his alabaster lily-pots. Mortar and pestle. Aq. Dist. Fol. Laur. Te Virid. Smell almost cure you like a dentist's door bell. Doctor whack. He ought to physic himself a bit. Electuary or emulsion. The first fellow that picked an herb to cure himself had a bit of pluck. Simples. Want to be careful. Enough stuff here to chloroform you. Test: turns blue litmus paper red. Chloroform. Overdose of laudanum. Sleeping draughts. Love philtres. Paregoric poppysup bad

for cough. Clogs the pores or the phlegm. Poisons the only cure. Remedy where you least expect it. Clever of nature.

– About a fortnight ago, sir?

– Yes, Mr Bloom said.

He waited by the counter, inhaling the keen reek of drugs, the dusty dry smell of sponges and loofahs. Lot of time taken up telling your aches and pains.

– Sweet almond oil and tincture of benzoin, Mr Bloom said, and then orangeflower water....

It certainly made her skin so delicate white like wax.

– And white wax also, he said

Brings out the darkness of her eyes. Looking at me, the sheet up to her eyes, smelling herself, Spanish, when I was fixing the links in my cuffs. Those homely remedies are often the best: strawberries for the teeth: nettles and rainwater: oatmeal they say steeped in buttermilk....

That is a page of *Ulysses*, selected at random and exactly measured. There are in this book 732 such pages; they were written in Trieste, Zurich, and Paris during the years 1914 to 1921. The reader will say they are not exhilarating: they are not meant to be. And yet ... how exhilarating they are!

English Review, 35 (December 1922), 538–48.

Mr Conrad's Writing

> The helmsman's eyeballs seemed to project out of a hungry face as if the compass-card behind the binnacle glass had been meat.... The rudder might have gone for all he knew, the fires out, the engines broken down, the ship ready to roll over like a corpse. He was anxious not to get muddled and lose control of her head, because the compass-card swung far both ways, wriggling on the pivot, and sometimes seemed to whirl right round. He suffered from mental stress. He was horribly afraid also of the wheelhouse going. Mountains of water kept on tumbling against it. When the ship took one of her desperate dives the corners of his lips twitched.

Let us consider the writing of Mr Conrad. Other pens more weighty, more authoritative, or for a hundred reasons more acceptable, shall no doubt attend to his moralities, his geography, his knowledge of the sea and even to his 'style', since the appearance of this admirable collected edition will make the works of Mr Conrad more extendedly accessible than ever they were before.[1] Let us, then, for a moment limit ourselves to the consideration of his writing.

If you call it 'style' you will be at once in a frame of mind more monumental and much less intimate. Style implies a man in parade uniform; writing, the same man in working dress. The paragraph set at the head of these columns has always seemed to the writer the high-water mark of Mr Conrad's, and in consequence of English prose. It resembles, and perhaps with cause, the extraordinary passage ending 'et comme il était très fort, hardi, courageux et avisé il obtint bientôt le commandement d'un bataillon', in 'Saint Julien l'Hospitalier'. In Flaubert's passage of a few short lines the whole career of a soldier of fortune is summed up, pictured, professionalized and done for ever. It *is* the soldier of fortune. Mr Conrad's passage about the helmsman *is* the helmsman; his whole life *qua* helmsman is there, his whole career and all his preoccupation, and that, looking at the work of Mr Conrad more aloofly, is the secret of his magic. His books are an unending procession of exact presentations, in the first place of men and then of their vicissitudes and the fascination of his books is the fascination of that most fascinating of all things, gossip. It is as if you

1 Uniform Edition of the *Complete Works of Joseph Conrad*, in 19 Vols (London: Dent).

stood at a window giving on to a not too crowded but lively street with, beside you, an instructed companion who said continually, 'You see that man. He ...' or 'There is Mrs Witcherly. She has just ...' Only instead of your own unobservant organs you look upon the passers-by with the eyes of Mr Conrad that miss nothing. Nothing.

It then becomes a matter of selection, and in selecting what he shall render in order to give the exact balance and the exact truth of a life Mr Conrad is as unerring as he is in his observation. His leavings-out are as matchless as are his inclusions, and that is all a question of the 'writing'. In the passage quoted from *Typhoon* you have the flashed picture of a helmsman's eyes; you have his preoccupation with the strains on the rudder, the fires, the engine and the hull; you have his preoccupation with the strain upon himself; you have his fear; you have the actual circumstances of the moment, and then once more in 'when the ship took one of her desperate dives the corners of his lips twitched' you have the man himself considered from the outside, and that last sentence is 'writing' as distinguished from style. For style, we may presume, would concern itself with cadence, with the atmosphere, with, as it were, the dressing-up of the paragraph. When you write – or still more when such a writer as Mr Conrad writes – you have to concern yourself with the getting in of 'things'. That must come first, and that is the essential. The stylist, on the other hand, concerns himself firstly with dressings-up, the tonalities of words, the cadences of paragraphs. So that it is best to consider Mr Conrad as a writer of prose, rather than as a stylist in the horrible sense in which the late Mr Pater or the late Mr Wilde were stylists. For Mr Conrad the *mot juste* is the word that exactly expresses a material object; for the stylist the *mot juste* expresses the mood, the manner and more particularly the prose of the concocter. It is thus the writing much more than the style that is the man, the style being only too often his trappings.

Considered exteriorly the 'style' of Mr Conrad will be observed in this collected edition to vary very considerably from the relatively thin, Daudetish, phonectic syzygies of *Almayer's Folly* to the richer Elizabethan organ-rollings of *Heart of Darkness*; from them to the drier precisions of *Typhoon*; from those to the looser textures of *Nostromo*, and so to the relative fluencies of *Chance*, of *Victory* or 'The Inn of the Three Witches'. There is in all these succeeding works obvious progression, or at least a gradual alteration in attack. For the present writer the high-water mark of Mr Conrad's style is reached in the passage quoted from *Typhoon*, and this because at this point his 'writing' and his 'style' more intimately approach the one to the other, so that *Typhoon* is at one and the same time a tremendous poem of pure humanity and a tremendous *tour de force* of pure writing. But appreciation of style is very much a matter of individual tastes. The reader may very well prefer the concluding paragraph of 'A Smile of Fortune' or he might prefer:

> It enveloped me, it enfolded me so lightly as not to be felt, so suddenly as not to be believed in, so completely that that whole meeting was an embrace, so softly that at last it lapsed into a sense of rest that was like the fall of a beneficent and welcome death.

There is, in short, room in the stylistic world for the brave inclusive decorations of the Renaissance as for the dry selectiveness of Cranach, and if the reader prefer the grand staircase of the opera-house in Paris on a gala night to the cold mud of the trenches, he need not, therefore, be contemned. And the same latitude must be allowed to the writer of prose, who changes his cadences so that they may be in tone with the changing stresses of his narrative. Mr Conrad came to England, an Elizabethan, with a prose that almost continuously burst into polyphonic organ effects. But these sounds have gradually nearly died out of his pages. You have to look with some care through the pages of *The Rescue*, the latest of Mr Conrad's novels to be included in Messrs Dent's edition, before you come upon such passages as:

> The sun had sunk already, leaving that evening no trace of its glory on a sky clear as crystal and on the waters without a ripple. All colour seemed to have gone out of the world. The oncoming shadow rose as subtle as a perfume from the black coast lying athwart the eastern semicircle; and such was the silence within the horizon that one might have fancied oneself come to the end of time.

Whereas the present writer once occupied himself for an hour or two turning *Heart of Darkness* into blank verse and found that a very creditable production of Christopher Marlowe's could be made by adding a very few syllables here and there. This is not to say that Mr Conrad writes blank verse: the addition of the syllable here and there making all the difference, but it does say that the effect of that most wonderful of *nouvelles* is attained by mighty lines and cadences enormously cared for. In *The Rescue* these are largely absent, yet probably the atmosphere of the Shallows is as all-pervading in the later book as is that of the Congo in the much earlier. It is probable, in short, that the later and more assured Mr Conrad was satisfied that with the rarer 'atmospheric' passages of *The Rescue* he had established in the reader's mind as lasting an effect of place as in *Heart of Darkness* he had done with a far greater number of polyphonics. For the province of the 'atmospheric' passage is merely to give a sense of place to the reader; to strike a note that shall hold throughout the reading. Once this is achieved every word of atmospheric writing becomes a longueur, or at very best an excrescence.

And Mr Conrad is the greatest English poet of today because, more than any other writer, he has perceived – he has gradually evolved the knowledge – that poetry consists in the exact rendering of the concrete and material happenings in the lives of men. It is obvious that, like every other writer, he has the secret longing now and then to produce abstract writing – writing which shall be as devoid of material significance as a fugue of Bach is of 'programme' and that yet shall have the beauty of pure sound. But few writers have so well resisted this craving – few at least of those who have so supremely the gift. And, indeed, to find Mr Conrad in the purely symphonic mood for any length of time you have to go to such personal writings as was *The Mirror of the Sea*. Here for page on page you got pure word painting, but in the end, and for the most part all the way through, Mr Conrad is the humanist. The swing of his sentences is achieved less by falling in to time with studied or derived cadential measures than by the fact that they time themselves to the measure of Mr Conrad's thoughts when he is thinking of his fellow-men. So they have, his cadences, a unity that is the unity of an incomparable observer of his kind.

Literary Supplement to *Spectator*, 123 (17 November 1923), 744, 746.

Literary Causeries from the *Chicago Tribune Sunday Magazine*, 1924

II. Vill Loomyare

★★★

There used to cover the United States when I was last there a cunning advertisement that read: 'Drink Moxie! You will not like it at first!' It is a good advertisement to remember when it is a matter of considering the works of young men who are abused by the middle-aged and the established. And indeed I will concede that the works of wild young men are wild – and bad. But as I said last week there are badnesses that, to those who study these things, are worth a whole wilderness of virtues. Let the reader remember the worldly fates of those who – like myself, alas! – were the really model boys at school.

I may have seemed to wander a long way from the Vill Loomyare – but I have not got very far from Paris, the sober, quiet and incredibly industrious city. For I have been driven to these speculations by happening to look down the publishing list of the Three Mountains Press which consists of six works selected by my friend Mr Pound as marking the high-water mark of English literary psychology and execution of the present day – these works all having been published in Paris and being all by writers who have been profoundly influenced by the curious, indefinable, unmistakeable spirit of workmanliness that breathes in the Paris air – though not in the air of the Vill Loomyare. Mr Pound has selected three English and three American writers for publication under his aegis. I will leave out of account the three English writers: any English Critic – I mean Reviewer – would tell you that he had never heard of one of them.[1] I will also leave out the *Indiscretions* of Mr Pound himself. Dealing as they do with family history in an American society of two decades or so ago they may, for all I know, occasion personal discomfort to the actual present reader, and if he dislikes that at first he may, and with some reason, go on disliking it. The *Great American Novel* of Dr William Carlos Williams – unless the reader happen to be a Great American Novelist – and the *In*

 [One of them was Ford himself, whose pamphlet *Women & Men* appeared in the series.]

Our Time of Mr Ernest Hemingway do not, I imagine, start with any such handicaps. Each of these works is distinguished by a singular, an almost unsurpassed, care of handling, Dr Williams in a mood of fantasia presenting you with a sort of madly whirling film in which Greater America flies over, round and through your head whilst Mr Hemingway gives you minute but hugely suggestive pictures of a great number of things he has seen whether in the days when the late war was a war of movement, or in the gardens and presence of the King of Greece, or again in the *corridas* of Southern Europe. Mr Hemingway stays in Paris and his work is in the hardest and tightest tradition of the French, inspired with a nervous assiduity that is the American contribution to the literary forms of today. Dr Carlos Williams is a practising physician in the United States who dashes now and again through Paris on his way somewhere. So, if the American reader will pardon the gaucheness of a phrase that I cannot think how otherwise to put, his work is more European. For whereas French work on the whole retains the aspect of hard chiselling that distinguished even their most impressionist writers, Europe around Paris has developed Impressionism almost to its logical ends, so that to read Dr Williams is to be overwhelmed by the bewildering remembrances that, with their blurred edges, are all that remain to us of life today. To read Mr Hemingway is to be presented with a series of – often enough very cruel – experiences of your own that will in turn be dissolved into your own filmy remembrances. Dr Williams, in short, presents you with a pre-digested pabulum of life, Mr Hemingway with the raw material. These are the two main literary trends of today and each of these writers in these several ways is singularly skilful. I daresay both of them might distress a quite lay reader, for that is a branch of diagnosis in which I am singularly inexpert.

★★★

Chicago Tribune Sunday Magazine, 24 February 1924, 3.

III. And the French

★★★

And masterpiece or no masterpiece the French literary stream pursues its way, engrossed and uninterrupted. The masterpieces may be there or they may not; if they are they are as like as not ignored. But the general level is amazing. I have lately had the luck to have to pass some days in quinined retirement and so to do some reading! And during those three days I have read three French books of varying literary calibre, but coming my way almost by hazard and not one of them ignoble. You would have to find a month of Sundays before you could find a chance three of our books of which the same could be said. The French are said to be insular, to ignore the outside world. One of these books – *Oxford et Margaret* by Jean Fayard – which I take to be the work of a very young man concerns itself solely with Great Britain; another, *A la Dérive*, by Philippe Soupault, very largely with Australia; the third, *Lewis et Irene*, by Paul Morand, flits around the world from the Levant to the Strand as deviously as it flits around its cosmopolitan characters. From the literary point of view M. Fayard's book is the least satisfactory of the three; it is relatively formless and abounds in the author's comments which we were taught to regard as taking away from the vividness of the depiction. Nevertheless its insight into the life of the devious, divagating thing that is the British young soul of today is amazing. To read it is like listening, as from time to time one is privileged to do, to the long, long talks of the Young Things of a Britain profoundly under the influence of Dostoevsky; so under the influence of Dostoevsky that the adolescent British mind seems to drift without any tangible aim, conception of a Cosmos or guiding spirit. So, at last you see us as we are, almost as talkative today as were the Russians before the war – and almost as fusionless!

Thus M. Fayard's work has a real sociological value. From it the seer into international futurities might learn a great deal as to the future. For young Oxford, aimless and drifting as it is, will give us the men and women that tomorrow will mould our Imperial destinies. And so nicely balanced and tight a place is the world of today that the moulding of our Imperial destinies must enormously influence the destiny of every soul in the world.

M. Morand, on the other hand, views the world from the more unconcerned – and more indulgent – armchair of the diplomatist who has travelled, who knows where and seen who knows what. He concerns himself very little with ethics, with frames of crowd minds and the last thing that can have influenced his world must have been any book of Dostoevsky's. The aimlessness of his cosmopolitans is the aimlessness of the entirely disillusioned and his handling of his immense problem – which is actually: What will happen when Woman, as she now does, enters the Temple and takes her place among the moneychangers – this immense problem is handled with such disillusioned aloofness that the Problem becomes merely an individual falling out of a Prince and Princess in a Parisian Night's Entertainment. That in itself is an achievement and the work is in a genre almost unknown amongst Anglo-Saxon publications. If you compare it with, say, *Antic Hay*, of Mr Aldous Huxley, a young English writer who, is apparently coming to occupy, *mutatis mutandis*, something of the position occupied by M. Morand in France – and for the matter of that in Anglo-Saxondom – if you make that almost impossible comparison you will see how infinitely more consummate in this literature of cynicism is the French method of which M. Morand is so admirable an exponent. It is Stendhal against Sir James Matthew Barrie, that terrible influence which together, again, with Dostoevsky, has so taken the quality of blind potency out of our British life of today. So that in M. Morand you have international passion against a tapestry of the isles of Greece and the rue St Honoré; in a working almost too slight; whereas in Mr Huxley's book you have a drawing by a hypercultured, rather heavy-handed Englishman of good traditions, almost without atmosphere, rendering a sort of pawkily promiscuous life that is without passion or background. Both are fairy tales, at the end of the story – and the fairy tale is a species perfectly legitimate amongst the fauna of the Arts! – but M. Morand's work is consummate, the other merely tentative.

M. Soupault, on the other hand, is a poet – and if any Frenchman's work of today can shew influence of any English writer, M. Soupault's *A la Dérive* shews the influence of the author of *Lord Jim*. His book on account of its sheer writing – lucid, cadenced, and tranquil – is singularly beautiful. It is indeed, on that account so beautiful that, lulled by the cadence of the words the reader rather forgets the energetic, the harsh and the sometimes even very cruel nature of the story. That is an achievement in art, since usually the writer of the 'strong' book seeks only to make his incidents harrowing and so fails to be an artist. The story of *A la Dérive* is the story of a Hamlet amongst tramps, pursuing his unknown aims from Paris to Australia and its great desert, to Singapore, all the world over to end in the Ile St Louis.

So if last week has not brought us three masterpieces of the scale of *Salammbô* it has at least brought us three books that one can read without feeling oneself mentally lowered by one's company.

Chicago Tribune Sunday Magazine, 2 March 1924, 3, 11.

VIII. So She Went into The Garden …

I am frequently asked – I am indeed almost *too* frequently asked: 'Do you really take pleasure in the works of all these so-called advanced writers and artists. Or…' But at that point the interlocutor boggles, the only implication remaining open to him being: 'Do you only do it because of a pose? Or because you are paid by a publisher? Or by Bolsheviks?' However even the Anglo-Saxonly boorish do not get as far as that to one's face.

The other day, however, a critic, a Frenchman and therefore a man of some intelligence and politeness, varied the form of the enquiry and asked: 'How is it possible that you take pleasure in the work of Mr Joyce? You, a Classic?' He did not mean that I was yet of that band of half-calf bound importances the thought of whose works casts glooms over festive occasions, but merely that he acknowledged that I endeavour to express myself with limpidity. It was nicely done! And you observe that he conceded without question the fact of my pleasure in the Advanced.

And indeed I do take that pleasure. And I am not paid to do it and to do so does not pay. Indeed I imagine that my diet of a little thin oatmeal would speedily become turtle and old port if only I would consent to deny I took that pleasure. For another question that reaches me almost every day is: 'How is it that your books with their... and their... and their... do not sell by the tens of hundreds of thousands in the United States?' And not infrequently the questioner will supply the answer: 'It's because we Americans can never really tell whether you are in earnest, and no American can stand *that*.'

If in turn I question the questioner it does not take long to discover that I am suspected of a want of earnestness and of the quality of uplift – if uplift be a quality! – just because I, a Classic, do profess to take pleasure in the works, say, of Mr Joyce... Now I am for the moment very much in earnest and I am about to try to explain to the Indulgent Reader why it is that I take the pleasures that I take. This would be a task of no value or importance were it not for the fact that no man, however much he may be a Classic, is very far in the end from being an *homme moyen sensuel* – so, if I can explain myself, it may explain to a number of my fellow-beings how they, in turn, may take that pleasure for themselves. That is the function – the sole function of a critic!

The Lay Reader – and I imagine myself to be addressing almost solely the reader who has neither practised nor made any very deep study of Literature – the Lay Reader, then, must start by remembering that, in Literature as in every other department of life, the point of view of the professional differs inevitably in certain departments from that of the layman. A charming lady, leaning delicately over the wall of a pig-sty will exclaim: 'Oh what a darling little thing that pink lop-eared one is,' and well it may be. But the expert pig-rearer beside her knows that that little pig is too narrow through the heart to be up to its meals, too spindly in the quarters to run to good hams, too short in the snout to grub well for its victuals – and that the lop-ears will ruin him for the show-bench. It is much the same with books.

We professionals with a passion for our art are not looking out for, we have no use at all for, the pink-piggy Peter-Pannishnesses that, charmingly bound and colouredly illustrated, shall decorate a lovely lady's drawing-room table – any more than the professional pig-rearer attempts to produce a breed of piglings fitted, with pink bows on tail and ears, to trot after a dimity flowered skirt. We are out, really, to discover what grim uglinesses of today shall make the poetically admirable flakes of ham of next year's breakfast table.

II.

The parallel is almost exact. For the Lay Reader should remember that, inevitably and unchangeably, today finds horrible in literature what tomorrow finds adorable – or even merely insipid. There was for instance in my youth a writer called Rhoda Broughton who used to be considered the last outrageous thing in advanced opinions. Her heroines had latch-keys, rode in omnibuses or walked the city streets unchaperoned – I forget the other horrors.

Well, that is merely a matter of manners, not of writing but it is emblematic enough – for it is not merely the literary methods of advanced books that are always shuddered at by the conservative of any given day, it is also the depiction of manners. In their day Keats and Shelley were howled at by the Quarterlies not alone because they invented between them the poetic jargon that became the stock in trade of all Victorian poets, they were also pilloried as Atheists, Revolutionists, advocates of Adultery … as every imaginable type of suborner of the established; and as writing, for the sake of a pose of exclusiveness, incomprehensible and wicked mystifications. *Exactly* the same epithets were hurled a little later at Tennyson. But exactly the same. Exactly the same at Browning, Exactly the same, odd as it may seem, saluted the early works of Dickens – and to make the circle come truer, a very little later, in the *Daily Telegraph*, Dickens himself was clamouring for the imprisonment of the Pre-Raphaelites – and for exactly the same reasons. D.G. Rossetti, who is now considered a very mild writer for very young men, was accused of writing in an incomprehensible jargon, atheisms, obscenities, lustfulnesses, and all the rest of it. A little later the same charges of incomprehensibility and looseness of morals were made against *Tess of the D'Urbervilles*, *Jude the Obscure* and the poetry of Mr Hardy.

When then the Reader finds today exactly – but exactly, exactly! – the same charges being made against the most prominent of the younger writers of today, what, even if he do find those younger writers a tough proposition, must he conclude? I leave the answer to the Reader. The moral however will bear a moment's adumbration. It is, that is to say, disagreeable to adopt a position of humility towards that which one finds at first reading, incomprehensible and strange, or shocking because of its too great definiteness of outline. I am quite acquainted with the feeling. But it is worth while, the most enduring of pleasures being those that one acquires at the expense of trouble, to make several essays of the works of one or other of one's younger contemporaries. The probability is that they will be the adored poets of tomorrow; for history whether of men or of literatures is one long tale of repetitions. Then, if one can get from their work, before tomorrow, some of the pleasure that tomorrow will almost inevitably feel, one's gain will be great indeed.

It may, that is to say, be disagreeable to read and re-read – though I find it pleasurable enough!

> And there they were too listening in as hard as they could to the solans and the sycamores and the wild geese and gannets and the auspices and all the birds of the sea, all four of them, all sighing and sobbing, and listening. They were the big four, the four master waves of Erin, all listening, four. There was old Matt Gregory and then besides old Matt there was old Marcus Lyons, the four waves, and oftentimes they used to be saying grace together right enough…

It is a lovely, sleepy cadence, if there is nothing else to it and, if you permit yourself to be choked off the enjoyment of it by the fact that you do not quite understand it or by the suspicion that there are no such birds as sycamores and auspices, you will just lose that enjoyment and gain nothing in particular.

III.

I am driven into these speculations by being asked by my editor to explain to his readers, precisely the pleasure that I take in the work of Mr Joyce…

For myself then, the pleasure, the very great pleasure that I get from going through the sentences of Mr Joyce is that given me simply by the cadence of his prose, and I fancy that the greatest and highest enjoyment that can be got from any writing is simply that given by the cadence of the prose. This may seem a hard saying to the Reader, but if he will consider the pleasure – the definite pleasure apart from any other consideration – that he will get from the more glowing passages of, say, the English Bible, what I mean will begin to suggest itself.

> In the days when the keepers of the house shall tremble, and the strong men shall bow themselves, *and the grinders cease because they are so few,* and those that look out of the windows be darkened. And the doors shall be shut in the streets when the sound of the grinding is low, *and he shall rise up at the voice of the bird and all the daughters of music be brought low…*

I do not know the precise significance of the passages I have underlined but I do get extreme pleasure from reading them, and so I imagine does the reader.

Or let us take again a passage in which the 'sense' might be almost unpleasant, since we may care nothing at all about the interior of ships and, having a great deal to do, dislike burdening our minds with matters that are of no use to me:

> It was stayed like the gallery of a mine, with a row of stanchions in the middle, and cross-beams overhead, penetrating into the gloom ahead – indefinitely. And to port there loomed like the caving in of the sides, a bulky mass with a slanting outline. The whole place, with the shadows and shapes, moved all the time. The boatswain glared: the ship lurched to starboard and a great howl came from that mass that had the slant of fallen earth.

That seems to me to be supremely beautiful writing – and merely because of the cadence.

Now I must not be taken as saying that there is any kinship or resemblance between the writings of Mr Joyce, the Scriptures or the prose of Mr Conrad. All that I am saying is that immense pleasure *can* be obtained from letting the cadences of Mr Joyce pass through the mind.

There comes in then another factor. There is hardly any writer caring about his art who has not longed at one time or another to compose mere fantasias in words, just for the sound of them. And this is no exclusive desire of the writer, for almost all adults at one time or another and all the children that ever were born indulge in bursts of pure nonsense-speech, just to create rhythms for themselves and to have an outlet for high-spirits. And, if every one has had the desire to utter such verbal sounds most unspoiled human beings like to have communicated to them such rhythms with little, or with quite grotesque, meanings.

The liking for these qualities of pure sound through which penetrate glimmers of incongruous or grotesquely contrasted half-ideas is merely the liking for the quality of surprise and the dislike for the obvious that is at the basis of all art. It is shared by all human beings but it is perhaps more relished by us Anglo-Saxons than by other races. This you may learn from the fact of the immense popularity of purely 'nonsense' writers like Edward Lear of the Limericks. And how many generations since the death of Miss Edgeworth – if the writer was indeed Miss Edgeworth – have not been ravished at the sound of:

> So she went into the garden to cut a cabbage leaf to make an apple-pie. And the Great She Bear put his head in at the window. 'What, no soap?' So he died and she very imprudently married the barber. And there were the Picaninnies and the Glubyillies and the Great Panjandrum with the little button at the top and all. And they all fell to playing the game of catch as catch can and they danced till the gunpowder ran out of the heels of their boots?

'But,' the Reader will exclaim, 'surely there is no relation between the delicate foolery of Miss Edgeworth and the blasphemous pages of *Ulysses*.'

Nevertheless consider the cadence of: 'And there they were too listening in as hard as they could to the solans and the sycamores and the wild geese and gannets and the auspices and all the birds of the sea,' and you will find that your [ear?] is being pleased by a cadence that is [one?] of the universal old cadences of all, [Miss] Edgeworth having struck on the same [caden]ce decades ago.

Or for sheer incongruousness consider:

> Malachias, overcome by emotion, ceased. The mystery was unveiled. Haines was the third brother. His real name was Childs. The black panther was himself the ghost of his own father. He drank drugs to obliterate. For this relief much thanks. The lonely house by the graveyard is uninhabited. No soul will live there. The spider pitches her web in the solitude. The nocturnal rat peers from his hole. A curse is on it. It is haunted. Murderer's ground.
>
> What is the age of the soul of man? As she hath the virtue of the chameleon to change her hue at every new approach, to be gay with the merry and mournful with the downcast, so too is her age changeable as her mood. No longer is Leopold, as he sits there, ruminating, chewing the cud of reminiscence, that staid agent of publicity and holder of a modest substance in the funds. He is young Leopold, as in a retrospective arrangement, a mirror within a mirror (hey presto!) he beholds himself.

That passage, chosen really and truly at random as *Ulysses* opened itself, is surely genuine and high-spirited fantasia and I take a good deal of pleasure in reading it. It is not one of the finest passages or I should take more, but its essential quality is typical enough and it very well supports my thesis.

The reader will by now be saying: 'Well, but this fellow says nothing about what we want to hear of. There is not a single word about the obscenities, the blasphemies, the Bolshevism of which we have heard so much.' And there is not, simply because I have been asked to explain what makes me take pleasure in the work of Mr Joyce, and I take no pleasure in obscenities, blasphemies or the propaganda of the Soviets. And indeed, of this last there is not a word in the works of Mr Joyce. There are obviously passages that, in the ordinary vernacular, would pass for obscenities and blasphemies and, if they were not necessary for the texture and construction of *Ulysses* I should prefer to be without them as also I should prefer to inhabit a world that had no sewers, no refuse pits, no avarice, greed, slander, hate, detritus or indigestion. And the reader who prefers to ignore the existence of these things in the world has one very simple remedy, as far as *Ulysses* is concerned. He can refrain from reading the book. I am not asking him to do otherwise.

Chicago Tribune Sunday Magazine, 6 April 1924, 3, 11.

Stocktaking: Towards a Revaluation of English Literature

In the first of this series of essays for the *transatlantic review*, published under the pseudonym 'Daniel Chaucer', Ford wrote: 'It is obvious that these years of the revision of all values must witness a revision of literary estimates'.

II. Axioms and Internationalisms

How much knowledge of imaginative Literature, then does it need to make a proper man? Ah! How many miles to Babylon: and shall we get there by candle light! So we used to sing when we were children.

The answer is not very formidable nor will any student find such of us as are men of good will very forbidding professors. It used to be said that a proper man was one who had built a house, planted a tree, begotten a son, written a book and something else... played in a county cricket match, let us say. At any rate the implication was: a civilized human being should devote a fifth of his time and thoughts to the arts and the humaner letters. The time is really more than enough if the studies should be pursued with intelligence. Eternity shall be insufficient to civilize us if we pursue our slipshod courses. For the question is not: How much have you read; but how have you read? knowledge of books being entirely immaterial, knowledge of writing everything. One man will in fact read twenty books whilst another is reading one and, at the end, know less of his twenty than the other of his one. For if you are a decently civilized man you can tell a whole book from the turn of one phrase as often as not.

And there is no very special virtue in reading: it is an occupation bad for the eyes; it curbs the shoulders and, if you read too much you may go mad. At any rate there was once a man who did. He had been studying the *Faerie Queene* for ten years with the idea of writing a commentary with an emended text. And he had earned golden opinions from his professors. Suddenly he realized that he had never read *The Way of All Flesh* by the late Samuel Butler. So he threw up his job in the University and became a railway guard in order to have time to read novels between stations. But the railway workers threatened to strike if he continued in his employment since he was a non-unionist, so he lost that job. I do not know what has since become of him…

Anyhow it does not matter how much or how little you have read so long as you are acquainted with what we will call the axioms. You are, say a lawyer: you desire to impress your clients with the idea that you are a man of culture: It is not necessary that you should be acquainted with all the late Professor Lazarus' writing on Shakespeare's derivations from Robert of Gloucester: indeed it is very necessary that you should *not*. The Professor's style is so circumlocutory and so contagious: for a time after reading only one of his monographs you will be unable to write a comprehensible letter. But let me explain what an axiom is:

A great many years ago, being in a company fairly mixed and fairly favourable to the work of James McNeill Whistler, I grew irritated with the way my fellow guests went talking on, always non-committally, about the *Nocturnes* and the *Symphonies*. I said at last, rather rudely:

'What's the use of talking about Whistler? Whistler is an axiom!' Some other gentleman afterwards printed that statement. But the aphorism is rather a useful one for my present purpose, so I re-claim it. I do not however accuse the other gentleman of being a plagiarist. That Whistler was an axiom is a truism and, in those days that sort of saying was much in the air.[1]

In the plastic arts, in music, in all foreign literatures there are artists whom one calls axioms – not because they are supremely great by temperament but because they worked supremely along one or other technical line. You may not like Whistler: but you have to accept him as a prototype of a form of art. You may not like Jan van Eyck; Dürer; Holbein, Velasquez; Rubens, Rembrandt; Ghirlandaio; Praxiteles or even Raphael but you cannnot ignore them even should Hokusai be your own master. Similarly you may not like but cannot ignore Bach and Palestrina.

It is the same, as far as foreigners are concerned, with literature; no Frenchman can ignore, not the temperaments, but the technical skill, of Chateaubriand, Racine, Villon, Gautier, Musset, Maupassant, Flaubert and a great many other writers from Mallarmé back to Ronsard. Indeed no human being can afford to ignore them – or Heine, Goethe, Leopardi, Lope da Vega, Turgenev, Chekhov, Dante, Bertran de Born, Boccaccio, Catullus, Petronius Arbiter, Apuleius, the Greek Anthologists or the author of the Song of Solomon. To be ignorant – to be utterly ignorant – of the *methods* of any one of these writers is to be to that extent ignorant

1 The Good Lawyer ought to know that J. M. Whistler was a painter who, in the course of a long libel action against the late Mr Ruskin, made the Law and its practitioners look more grossly, clumsy, barbarous and ignorant than most men have done. Had the then Attorney General had one spark of artistic training or intelligence he would, in his long duel with Whistler, have come off a great deal better and Mr Ruskin today might have been a good deal less despised.

of the ways by which humanity may be approached, cajoled, enlightened or moulded into races. To know all the writings of Heine is not necessary; but not to know how Heine mixed, alternated or employed flippancies and sentiment is to have a blind spot in your knowledge of how a part of humanity may be appealed to. It is true that Heine is detested by a great number of Germans – by perhaps all 'good Germans' using the words in the sense that 'good Americans' is used by inhabitants of the United States. But that does not preclude his being so adored by so large a proportion of all the 'bad' ones that his appeal may be called relatively universal. So, if the lawyer have before him in the witness box a witness; the master working in his garden a gardener; the orator before him under the rostrum an audience; or the casual acquaintance beside him at dinner a guest, all of these being of a type susceptible to the Heine-influence, he, lawyer, master, orator or guest will be to that extent a man more or less proper according as his appreciation of the Heine-method is keen or not so keen. And so it will be with a man's knowledge of the methods of all the world's writers who are – axioms!

★ ★ ★

transatlantic review, 1:2 (February 1924), 56–9.

[III. but headed] II. (continued)

During the last century English official criticism has erected as it were a stone-heap, a dead load, of moral qualities: A writer must have optimism, irony – but not mordant or painful irony; a healthy outlook; a middle-class standard of morality; as much religion as, say, St Paul had; as much Atheism as was possessed by Shelley… and finally, on top of an immense load of self-neutralising moral and social qualities, above all Circumspection! So that, in the end, no English writer according to these standards, can possess authenticity. The formula is this: Thackeray is not Dickens, so Thackeray does not represent English Literature: Dickens is not Thackeray so *he* does not represent English Literature. In the end Literature itself is given up and you have the singular dictum of the doyen of English official literary criticism. Writing a history of English Literature in the Eighteenth Century this gentleman writes – but always rather uncomfortably – of Dryden as divine, of Pope as divine, of Swift as so filthy as to intimidate the self-respecting critic. But when this Historian comes to Pepys his enthusiasm is unbounded. The little, pawky diarist he salutes with an affection, an enthusiasm for his industry, his pawkiness, his thumb nail sketches. Then he asserts amazingly: 'This is scarcely literature' and continues with panegyrics that leave no doubt that the Critic consider the Diary to be something very much better. Pepys, in short, is the crown of the seventeenth–eighteenth-century writers – the one man who makes the not immensely susceptible bosom of the official critic glow; but his achievement is not literature.

The judgement is typically English: the bewildered foreigner could only say: 'But if the Diary is all that you assert of it it must be literature; or, if it is not literature it cannot be all that you assert of it.' And obviously... Let us now look at the matter from the point of view of internationalism!... this sort of timid official panegyric is not the sort of thing to make the Foreigner read Pepys; nor will the coldly polite ascriptions of 'divinity' to Pope and Dryden be much more attractive. And that sort of thing is endless. Glancing by chance last week down the columns of one of our weekly journals that devotes some space to reviewing, you might have seen a notice of the transactions of an obscure English royal society. The 'transactions' contained an Anglo-Ecclesiastical plea for Tennyson by the Dean of Westminster: quite the proper thing for a Dean to have written. The Reviewer however fell foul of the Dean not so much because of anything that the Dean had written but, by implication because the Dean had given a friendly lift to Tennyson instead of to another; 'Tennyson was verbose, otiose; in his highest flights he never removed very far from the allegorical. How different would his position today not have been had his weapon been the "keen drypoint", the scalpel of... Pope!' The gentleman who wrote that sentence has since announced the forthcoming publication of his edition of the *Rape of the Lock* with notes, annotations and a biography founded on some new discoveries as to the more questionable transactions in the life of Pope!

That is English official criticism at its best – at its very best, because it does take some heed of method rather than merely of morality. Tennyson would undoubtedly have been a different writer had his methods been those of Pope. The assertion cannot be contested. But the criticism is something more for those who can read between literary lines. It appears in a journal – the official journal of a party devoting itself to the abolition of the English Church, the English Throne and the British Empire. So the Reviewer is bound to attack a Dean, any Dean, anywhere. That is all right. Deans are harmless men of business with a great deal to do, but if anyone can make his bread by attacking them there is no reason why it should not be done. Bread must be made – or so it is said.

The trouble – the very great trouble! – that might arise is this: If Tennyson is to be made a Dean-supported person every writer of the Left must attack him: if Pope is to be supported by the Reviewers of the Left Press every writer of Tory persuasions must attack him – and there is another possible English Literary Axiom gone. Because if every Tory writer in England of today found it necessary to attack Pope, Pope would certainly be damaged; so would almost any English writer who was attacked by the entire Left Press of these realms.

And this is no very exaggerated view. When it comes to Mr Kipling it is no exaggeration to say that our entire Left Press, quietly and subtly at work, has for the last twenty years enforced the lesson that Mr Kipling has none of the serene cosmopolitanism of Matthew Arnold – or let us put it that the laureate of the banjo cannot be a poet. Our Right preachers and moralists, when it comes to Mr Wells being, as Tories and Deans should be, more blatant, limit themselves to saying that, they would rather see their daughters dead at their feet than reading one of Mr Wells's later novels; whilst for a decade or so an influential branch of the Left group was accustomed to state – that they intended to and could 'ruin' Mr Wells, his brand of advanced opinion differing from their own.

These vile parages are in short no place for men of genius. The pity is that men of genius in England are as fatally attracted to that sort of ruin as are sea-birds in the night to the great lanthorns of lighthouses. It is true that Mr Kipling is distinguished by all the banjo-Jingoism, the 'You-bloody-niggerisms'... of Shakespeare! But that does not make him any less national a voice: we Anglo-Saxons have those characteristics and the rendering is authentic. It is equally true that Mr Wells, whose short stories are as authentic as those of any writer, has a public mission varying with the years.... And such of the Left as have no personal feuds with Mr Wells beat all the drums of that side; and the more courageous Tories publicly desire the deaths of their daughters... And the one lot ignore the authentic and wonderful *Country of the Blind*; and the other lot ignore the authentic and wonderful *Invisible Man*; and the daughters reading *Ann Veronica,* get into terrible scrapes and never again have time to read anything else. And there is always a great dust and we may very well have a war with France!

In any case *The Man Who Would be King* and *The Liner She's a Lady* get forgotten and Mr Kipling forgets how to write such things. So Literature suffers. And Mr Wells forgets how to write: and Literature suffers still more. And the years pass and the sort of thing continues and less and less does our sceptical Foreigner believe that our literature is anything other than pettinesses utterly lacking in distinction – provincialisms! For, very comprehensibly, the Foreigner has little or no use for Anglo-Saxon morality; still less – *pace* the Editor of the *transatlantic review* – can he admire or awaken in himself any interest for our internal politics...

I once met a Peruvian who had come to London to study English Literature. He said:

'Oh! but your *writers*! They pant and they pant; producing and producing! And then, as the type, the Archetype you have... Charles Lamb On Buttered Toast!'

I said:

'Ah! that is because you are not an Englishman!' But I felt it.

It is time then, that we had a re-valuation of the literary assets of Anglo-Saxondom: a re-valuation in which the style of Trollope shall not be estimated by the morality – or by the latest editor – of Bunyan; a re-valuation in which no political hack and as few Deans as possible: no biographers, bibliographers, emendators of texts or persons commercially interested in the sales of books shall have any say. How that re-valuation is to be brought about does not fall under the heading of this chapter. Why it should – why it must – be brought about is the more immediate matter.

It is because enthusiasms are a necessity for the human being. For the Anglo-Saxon to believe himself wanting in one of the great faculties and resources of humanity is calamitous for the Anglo-Saxon. It forces him to believe that because he is relatively gross and relatively commercial he will best express himself by exaggerating his grossness, his more brutal qualities and his worship of money. So our business men pretend to take pride in the quite false assertion that they have no time for reading books…

And so we remain a blot on the world and our populations are regarded as more and more suspect. That is a misfortune because our writers, hampered as they are by political necessities, by hypocritical and crystallized moralities and by commercial pressures have yet, as it were between the blasts of those storms, produced a great body of beautiful and humane work: in such a sufficiency as to entitle us to occupy a place in the comity of the civilized nations. To bring that about a certain enthusiasm is needed – a certain racial assertiveness which we lack…

Supposing a British Cabinet Minister or an American high politician were asked to stand up in a Walhalla of the nations and claim for our twin civilizations our place in the sun: upon what achievements would he base our claims? He would talk about the steam engine, the spinning jenny, the steam-hammer, the electric telegraph, submarine cables, the gramophone, the 'movies', wireless… Being at this point probably coughed down he would hazard, more dubiously, a new departure. He would begin to talk of evolutions of freedoms and moralities: of houses of Representatives, of Congressmen, Commons, County Councils; of Colonial traditions, ballot boxes; constitutions; of the perfecting of the factory system; of modern industrial life which is nowhere so… as in our favoured lands… the purity of… in our great cit… initiation of legislation against the White Slave Traf… Anti-Alco… Non-Secret Dip…

His voice being drowned, puzzled and irritated, he would cease and in the eventually resulting silence a kindly Scandinavian would be heard to prompt:

'Speak about Mr Shaw!'

'Oh! ah yes!' he would grasp at the proffered branch… 'There's Shakespeare… and… Shakespeare and… Lord Byron… but perhaps he's a little too... and... Of course Shakespeare... and... Did someone say Herbert Spencer? Yes! Yes!... There are few branches of human activities in which by the temperate employment of non-sectarian religion in social problems our favoured nations......'

And so our cases go by default!

It is not in that way that the rest of the world frames its *apologia*! In the forefront of *Toutes les Gloires de la France* are set not merely the names of Napoleon, the Great Condé, le Roi Soleil, or merely Pasteur, Robespierre, Danton, or Lafayette: it is not by the name merely of Bismarck, Moltke, Marx or Ehrlich that Germany claims pity from Europe; nor does Italy ask your patience solely because of Mazzini, Garibaldi, Savonarola; nor Russia only because of Peter the Great, Schuvalof, Bakunin, Kerensky or Lenin... Nor yet is it because of the names of Gianaclis, Thetocopoulos or Venizelos that the name of Greece survives among the nations.

Indeed such great names as those, of thinkers and of men of action in fields purely material are the names that separate Europe into nations... They provide the separate glories of France, of Italy, of the Alemannic peoples, of Greece... But the others, the glorious names of all the imaginative writers and artists: from Homer to the Brothers Grimm; from Flaubert back to Apuleius; from Catullus to Turgenev; all these form the glories of Europe, their works going together to make one whole and each work being one stone in a gigantic and imperishable fabric. Outside stand we Anglo-Saxons for want of a little faith.

It is possible that a change might come: in the general re-valuation that is taking place all the commercial considerations, the moral queasinesses, the Professors of Literature, *Vorschungen*, university curricula, honours examinations, all these phenomena commercial at base which stand in the way of the taste for and the honouring of our Literature, may be estimated at their true price. To seek to abolish them is not much good, for they are parts of the essential imbecilities of pompous men – of the highly refined imaginations of the more select classes. They should be left isolated in little towns, but their existence should not be forgotten or they will come creeping in again.

Working in that way one of our peoples may well evolve and re-erect in English a literature that shall be really of the masses, really national, really beloved and really great. It is probably from the United States that that movement will come: at any rate today the United States with her awakening consciousness has an opportunity such as she never had before of entering into the great comity of civilized nations. We, for the moment are too tired, too bound down by vested interests, too poor; bled too white – and of our best blood.

transatlantic review, 1:3 (March 1924), 51–7.

IV. Intelligentsia

Let us put it as an axiom that books are written for the Reader; that books should be written for the Reader: and for the Reader and for no one else. It will follow then as a corollary that the existence of a large class of Intelligentsia will be a calamity for Literature; as indeed it will be for all other activities in the world.

Humanity is as a rule lazy in things of the intellect. Why should it not be so, since one of the chief luxuries of having an intellect is to rest it? So men are prone in these matters to take advice from largely self-constituted Boards. Humanity, indeed, is only a little less lazy in practical matters: less, but only a little less! I am at the moment more interested in the hay- than the muck-rake but few people can be ignorant of trades, crafts or Mysteries in which the Public is deliberately misled by interested practitioners, sometimes as a mere matter of the purse, but as often as not because of some Tradition invented by the practitioners' great grandfathers. Try for instance to plant a garden with the aid of a professional gardener!

Or let us suppose that a Board of Automobile Wardens should form itself upon the lines of a priesthood the qualification for membership being that all the individuals making up the board regarded motoring upon public roads as a vulgarity! Quite a large section of the public, for one reason or another, would try to live up to that ideal and would pass portentous hours driving majestic automobiles round tracks in their private grounds. That sounds ridiculous but it is some such doctrine and an analogous practice that the Intelligentsia have attempted to force upon humanity.

Literature exists for the Reader and by the Reader: that is Bolshevist doctrine or platitude according to the point of view. The quite natural tendency of the Intelligentsia is to make of literature as unconsumable a thing as may be, so that, acting as its High Priests, they may make mediocre livings and cement their authority over an unlettered world. It is an ambition like another but more harmful than most.

The ambition of the writer as writer is to cast light; to make clear. His purpose is to make man, above all, clear to his fellow men: the purpose of the Intelligentsia is to suppress all such illuminations as do not conduce to rendering more attractive their own special class. It is sheer good fortune that the comprehension of one's fellow men should lead to civilization; that, *tout comprendre* should be *tout pardonner*; for if it were the other way the writer would go on just the same casting light into the dark places of the human soul, and then what a wilderness of Armageddons the world would be! But that is a pure by-product.

The Reader may, if he wishes, retort that this is another of those cases, so frequently occurring in the realm of the Applied Sciences, in which the by-product is of greater value than the original object of manufacture and that may well be the case. But it is of no consequence. The fact remains that the only civilizing agency that is at work today as in other dark ages is the Arts and that the Arts do not work by direct means. They make you understand your fellow human being: they may indeed make you understand your fellow brute beast. In either case in the train of comprehension come sympathy and tolerance and after subjecting yourself for some time to the influence of the arts you become less of a brute beast yourself.

This is the only humanizing process that has no deleterious sides since all systems of morality tend to develop specific sides of a character at the expense of other sides. Thus the Anglo-Saxon Victorian code as preached by moralists of the Charles Kingsley-Samuel Smiles type of popular teacher enjoined industry, sobriety, superficial honesty, personal economy, moderation and circumspection – all virtues having for their objects the saving of money. Money being thus deified as never before it was, many resultant evils have since afflicted humanity, the worst of them being body politics and a political economy founded almost solely on one or other unit of coinage to the total ignoring of all other civilizing influences; a vast sweating system with sempiternal industrial conflicts; immense cornerings of commodities and an universal ruthessness. Nor is it easy to think of any system of morality that is for certain much more desirable, the deification of openhandedness, frequent intoxication, promiscuity and recklessnesses without bounds – the old German panaceas for life – producing individuals on the whole preferable to the heroes of Mr Smiles but still ill to live with when crossed and with certain obvious defects when moulded into races. Neither have the idyllic-logical moral projections of the Marquesan Islanders which were lately described and lauded by a settler in those island-paradises done very much to preserve that highly civilized and gentle race. For a polite anthropophagy they have exchanged a taste for gin; for an untroubled promiscuity, monogamy and venereal disease; for a community of goods exactly such as that prescribed by the early Christians they have exchanged a state that is usually called wage-slavery. It appears that they were visited by a ship or ships whose captains were disciples of Charles Kingsley and Samuel Smiles and whose crew ardently carried out the Old German virtues. I should imagine that the Lord Bishop of Winchester, author of *As a Dog to His Vomit*, a treatise for the use of Unrepentant Prisoners, may have had some sleepless nights when they brought him news from the Marquesas, the first ship to visit that group of islands with civilizing views having been captained by a captain and manned by a crew from his diocese. But perhaps he did not.

Anyhow it is no business of the imaginative writer, the producer of Literature, to bother his head with creative systems of morality. No doubt he will have an instinctive morality of his own but usually, outside Anglo-Saxondom, and sometimes even within those bounds, he refrains from attempting to impose, except instinctively and without benevolence prepense, his own views upon his fellow men. His business is to project as exactly and with as little bias as he may, the results of pursuing certain courses in certain climates or latitudes: he has nothing to do with forcing humanity into moulds devised by himself. He is, in short, to the measure of the light vouchsafed him,[1] reporter or Creator; he is never a prophet whether of good or evil.

That measure of artistry for the sake of art must be allowed to him by an indulgent public: he must report for the sake of reporting; create for the sake of creating. The Public will usually, the Intelligentsia never, permit this necessity of his existence to be enjoyed by the artist. (The evolving of Literature is an Art.) Usually, that is to say, the public will take what it gets, dividing itself into three large but by no means equal-sized bodies. It can consume a large body of work allegorical or allegoric-classical in inspiration: it can consume a large body of work purely realist in technique; but the normally immense body of readers reserves itself for work of the careless romantic type.

According to a computation made by a German trade-paper just before the war and intended to show the consumption of books the world over by persons reading European languages, the most widely read books in the Western Hemisphere during the twentieth century had been: firstly, the *Pilgrim's Progess*; next to that *Madame Bovary* and the short stories of Maupassant, the orignal *Yvette* volume coming first, but the whole consumption of Maupassant being equalled by the sales of *Madame Bovary* alone; finally a group of sheer romanticists ranging from *Tom Jones* to the works of Hugo and Dickens. In this group the *Pickwick Papers* stood easily first and the *Travailleurs de la Mer* second. The *Pilgrim's Progress* was easily first, of all single books in the matter of sales and editions; *Madame Bovary* came next, but a long way behind; but the combined sales of the Romanticists was vastly greater than the sales of the French Realistic writers from Flaubert to Zola. On the other hand of any individual writer, taking the sales of all his books, Maupassant was the most widely read.

I am not going to pause to make any comments on these constatations here, my only intention in calling attention to them being to prove that large sales of books very differing in character – and of books quite out of the fashion of the moment – can go on side by side. As far as one has any means of checking them the statements are correct and they ring all the more true in that, coming from a German source, no claim is made for any specific German book or author. On the face of it one might have

1 [A favourite allusion of Ford's, to Wordsworth's late sonnet 'If thou indeed derive thy light from Heaven'.]

expected to find at least Grimm's *Fairy Tales* somewhere near the *Pilgrim's Progress*, but that is not the case. Such Anglo-Saxon attempts to gauge these figures as I have seen have always placed Shakespeare and Dickens at the head of all their lists – but those estimates I take to be due rather to pious aspirations than to actual figures, and indeed their compilations have a tendency to confine themselves to Anglo-Saxondom paying only the sketchiest of attentions to the rest of the Western World. But the great proportional preponderance of the French Realists is due to the fact that in South America and in Eastern Europe there are – or perhaps it is only 'there were' by now – immense populations of avid readers, all reading French and all with a strong taste for knowledge of life and a strong distaste for what we are accustomed to call the 'serious' book.

At any rate, there you have a projection of a world taste untrammelled by the dictations of any one black-coated class – a picture of the world reading what it wants to read. Anglo-Saxondom, except for specimens of the weakest types of Literature of Escape, is not, as a rule, given what it wants to read in its more serious moments and when it is given what it wants is not usually allowed to read it. It takes refuge in the feebly pawky and the feebly negational – or the feebly immoral: in, that is to say, *Tom Jones*; the essays on buttered toast of Charles Lamb; the works of Lewis Carroll; nonsense rhymes; in the London periodical called *Punch*; in the negational nonsense plays of Mr Shaw, the more positive, sentimental nonsense of Sir James Barrie, the topsy-turvey Ballades of Mr Belloc and Mr Chesterton.

This *genre*, more specifically English than American, is Anglo-Saxondom's sole exclusive contribution to the literature and thought of the world. Considering it aloofly from almost any philosophic standpoint you can only regard it as purely immoral, as almost always negational, as the last protest of a Comfortable Class against any fine-nesses that can be achieved without the accompaniment of Comfort. But it is all these things, as a rule, in only a very gentle, gentlemanly degree and as a literature of escape for the Wealthy or for those who consider that they ought by divine right to be wealthy, it has no doubt its place in the world. It is England's substitute for Realism.

In this department of thought England and the United States very early parted company, American humourists being historically more savage, lately more mordant, and momentarily, more depressed. That is because American humour is an affair more really national. Someone – I think it is Mr Mencken in a passage that I cannot recapture, or it may have been Mr Mencken quoting someone else – has complained that nineteenth century America was a nation of peasants and its literature a peasant literature – this especially in reference to Mark Twain. But it seems to me that a nation that can produce so considerable and typical a writer may well be proud enough of its peasants even though Twain – and I daresay for the matter of that Artemus Ward – went continually in fear on the one hand of the Intelligentsia of Concord and on the other of what precursors he might have had to encounter, of the Comstock brigade. And it is typical of the two branches of Anglo-Saxondom – or at any rate it is a good illustration, to point to the difference, in the matter of writings called *contra bonas mores*, between Twain and Robert Louis Stevenson: Twain in a private letter says that he cannot write what he really thinks about certain matters because of the pain an outcry against him would cause him; in a similar letter Stevenson says that he is determined never to spoil his market by writing about women. And Twain at least, in volumes to be published after his death so that the labour brought him in no money, did write what he really thought about certain matters.

The question of the treatment of such subjects as sex in literature is one of some difficulty: at any rate it presents certain difficulties in Anglo-Saxondom. I shall have to face it before finishing this volume, but this is not the place. Let me set down here, to illustrate what I mean, a quotation, an estimate by a writer whom I have already styled the doyen of English official critics, of a certain book:

> When we come to the story itself it is to find ourselves moving among the healthiest company ever devised by a human brain. The winds of heaven blow along the pages... and so long as wit and wholesomeness, manly writing and generous thinking, with a genial appreciation of all that makes life worth enjoying, are welcome among us, this truly sunny book will never lack its admirers.

That might have been written of any book of the 'English Classic' type: it might be praise of *Tom Brown's Schooldays*, of *Lorna Doone*, of *Midshipman Easy*; of *Rob Roy* or *Treasure Island*. But it isn't. It is praise of *Tom Jones*.

I make no professions to write about morality, but that has always seemed to me an amazing passage. I came across it when I was just over fifteen and it has remained so clear in my mind that, just now, for the purposes of transcription, turning up the book, my finger went instinctively to about the thickness in the volume and my eye to the position on the page, of that amazing passage. For I read it just after I had come back from school; and at school that day a number of boys of my own age and older, and of my Form, had come to me as one unusually well-read in books, to ask me to point out to them the 'smutty passages' in... *Tom Jones*! There are certain coincidences, certain concatenations of circumstance, that will alter for you your whole life. That, for me, was one. *The winds of heaven blow along the pages...*

I remember looking at the writer of those words who in those days was a frequent visitor to the then rather influential 'highbrow' home in which I lived and wondering how he could walk into a room with head moderately erect, how he could look anyone in the face, or why a thunderbolt did not 'Strike him dead', as boys say. It is to be remembered that I was not sixteen at the time and that to have been surrounded, just before, by a grinning half-circle of boys asking to be guided towards sexual emotions, had been a real torture. I think I am glad – though I do not know why I should be! – to remember that I stoutly refused, in spite of threats of boyish tortures. It was my first martyrdom!

Under the old regime it was the custom of the Tsar, on Easter morning, to say to the private on duty outside his door, '*Christ is arisen*' and to kiss him. Perhaps that was why our Tsar of Orthodox Criticism presents with such an accolade, Private Henry Fielding, a selected soldier in the ranks of imaginative writers. The knout is the more usual instrument of discipline for the novelist. But once in a year there must be a festival of Unreason, a feast of the Boy Bishop, Saturnalia, Thanksgiving Days, Eleusinian mysteries! Then they let out Henry Fielding and he is kissed on both cheeks.

My French Literary Tutor, a Monsieur Henri Andrieux, since, I believe a critic of some position in France but to me, in those days a romantic figure as the son of one of the leaders of the Paris Commune, spat sideways when I shewed him that passage. He had waxed black moustaches that stuck out sideways like the whiskers of a very fine tom-cat; and he swore quite violently about the hypocrisy of the English critic as a race, he too being particularly struck by the *winds of heaven*. He said indeed that all English critics had functions in the state similar to those of the old gentleman in *Troilus and Cressida*.

He was unjust as all French critics are to all manifestations of English criticism; but I am bound to confess that, coming when they did, his analyses of his English *confrères* made a profound dint in my mind. So that I am bound to extend my confession still further and to avow that I can never find myself in the presence – but it happens so seldom! – of an English-orthodox critic without feeling distinctly uncomfortable. These gentlemen distinguished by such a worship of circumspection; providence; continence; sobriety: and stand there still so conscious that I have never grown up and maybe never shall grow up: and the dint made by the words of M. Andrieux is always at the back of my mind; and I grow afraid... But that too is unjust. I know, really, how safe in their hands is my adolescent mind.

Thackeray, too, worshipped Tom Jones as he did his own Becky and Barry Lyndon and Ravenswing. Indeed it is probable that Thackeray finally established, if he did not invent, the worship of Fielding's paean to the old German virtues. But, then, it is universally granted in the higher circles of the Intelligentsia that Thackeray as a writer was an eighteenth-century figure and not really imbued with the ethical hubris of Victorianism.

So that where we get to, I do not quite know: possibly back to another witches' sabbath, another kiss from the Emperor of All the Russias...

It might be best to consider the matter historically...

transatlantic review, 1:4 (April 1924), 168–75.

IX. The Serious Book (continued)

Let us for a moment consider how the mind of the Naturalist works. What follows is from the pen of Samuel Smiles, the words being taken down from the dictation of Thomas Edward but put – Heaven knows why – into indirect narration. Thomas Edward, the cobbler, 'who never earned more than eighteen shillings a week', and on that brought up, well-clothed and educated a large family, had made a large collection of 'Preserved Animals, comprising Quadrupeds, Birds, Fishes, Insects, Shells, Eggs and other curiosities'. This Collection, made in the neighbourhood of Banff, at night since he had by day to work for his master, stuffed and cased by his own hands, he exhibited during Brandon feeing fair in Banff, in a house he took for the purpose – thinking to 'improve his circumstances'. This was in 1845 when he was 31.

> In preparing for the exhibition of his Collection Edward brushed up his specimens and cleaned his cases, before removing them to the Trades Hall. But in looking over his Collection he found that he had suffered a serious loss... Some time before he had put nearly 2,000 dried and preserved plants into a box which he had placed at the top of the stair in order to be out of harm's way.... They were the result of eight years' labour employed in collecting them. But, when he went to overhaul the box, he found that the lid had been shoved to one side and that numerous cats had entered it and made it their lair. The plants were completely soaked. The box smelt so abominably that he was under the necessity of making a bonfire of it in the back-yard.

He had also 'twenty glazed boxes containing 916 insects'. When he went to catalogue them he found that the boxes 'were all empty. They contained nothing but the pins which had held the insects, with here and there a head, a leg or a wing': the work of mice.

Nevertheless the Exhibition was a success and Edward removed it to the large city of Aberdeen. Here no one visited it and Edward was on the point of bankruptcy, an intolerable prospect for this absolutely honest, peasant-minded man. This is his account of his solution of the difficulty:

> The afternoon was far advanced. His dinner, which had been brought to him an hour before still lay untasted. He was pacing up and down the apartment, pondering over his miserable condition, when his father entered. Edward was looking so agitated that the old man enquired 'what ailed him'. He said he was going out, and went towards the door, fearing lest his wife or any of his children should appear. His father stepped between him and the door, remonstrating with him and saying he was not fit to go out in such a state. But a woman entering attracted his father's attention and Edward was thus allowed to slip away unobserved.
>
> Edward rushed down Union Street on his way to the sands. At first he thought of going to the Dee at the Craiglug; but he bethought himself that it would be better to go to the seashore where it might be thought his death was accidental. From the time of his leaving the shop in Union Street until about four hours after, when he recovered his senses, his memory remained almost a complete blank. He had a vague idea of crossing the links and seeing some soldiers at the foot of the Broadhill… He remembered however the following circumstances:
>
> He had thrown off his hat, coat, and waistcoat when a flock of sanderlings lit upon the sands near him. They attracted his attention. They were running to and fro, some piping their low shrill whistle, whilst others were probing the wet sand with their bills as the waves receded. But amongst them was another bird, larger and darker and apparently of different habits to the others… They rose and flew away; he followed them… at length he was stopped by Don mouth. When he recovered his consciousness, he was watching the flock of birds flying away to the farther side of the river…
>
> He found himself divested of his hat, coat and vest and he went back to look for them… He found that he had been followed by some people who were watching him. When he returned they followed him until he reached his clothes. And when they saw him dressed and ready to depart they disappeared. Not wishing to cross the links again that night, he turned and went up Don side to the New Bridge and took the road from thence into the town.

I do not quote this as a specimen of prose: in spite of elisions there remains too much of the generalization of Mr Smiles: but it is rare to get the mind of the field naturalist really at work; the soldiers at the foot of Broadhill are valuable!

Let us consider a word or two of prose as prose… Edward sold his Collection, went back penniless to his cobbler's stool; made More Collections; learned to read and write; corresponded with Learned Men and Societies; had honours bestowed on him, crustaceans named for him.

– Is there not even the *Coucshia Edwardii*? All this without books and without the afflatus of the Carlyles and the Ruskins. When he was first asked 'What made you a Naturalist?' he was completely dumfoundered. 'What, make a Naturalist as you would make a tradesman! My answer to those who put the question was and still is *I cannot tell.* I never knew of any external circumstance that had anything to do with engendering in my mind the never-ceasing love which I entertained for the works of the Almighty; so that the real cause must be looked for elsewhere.' And he sold his collections to clothe his children; and old age came and deeper poverty – and another learned honour or so. But: 'All my honours', as he puts it 'came to me from a distance. I have kept the museum of the Banff Institution for about twenty-one years, for almost nothing; and though the Linnean Society thought me worthy of being elected an associate, the people here do not think me worthy of being an honorary member of their Society. Still I am not complaining. The people of Banff had no right to make me a gentleman.' And his wife sums him up: 'Weel, he took such an interest in beasts that I didna compleen. Shoemakers were then a very drucken set, but his beasts keepit him from them. My man's been a sober man all his life; and he never negleckit his work. Sae I let him be.'

As for the prose? Well, all my life this has seemed to me to be a very beautiful passage, for its simplicity and its cadence. 'As a last and only source', he concludes a sketch of his own life,

> I betook myself to my old and time-honoured friend, a friend of fifty years' standing, who has never yet forsaken me, nor refused help to my body when weary, nor rest to my limbs when tired – my well-worn cobbler's stool. And here I am still on the old boards, doing what little I can with the aid of my well-worn kit, to maintain myself and my family; with the certainty that instead of my getting the better of the lapstone and leather, they will very soon get the better of me. And although I am now like a beast tethered to his pasturage, with a portion of my faculties somewhat impaired, I can still appreciate and admire as much as ever the beauties and wonders of Nature, as exhibited in the incomparable works of our adorable Creator.[1]

1 S. Smiles, *Life of a Scotch Naturalist*, 1877.

After the publication of this book Thomas Edward received a small pension from the Civil List. I believe he had it at the direct intervention of Queen Victoria who sent for him to Balmoral and, bidding him on account of his age and infirmities, to be seated, remarked to him: 'Mr Edward, you are the only man except Mr Carlyle who sat whilst I remained standing.' I hope that is a true story; it was told me by either my father or my grandfather both of whom knew Thomas Edward; but I was a very young child at the time and my mind may well have embroidered the mere granting of a pension on the civil list. If it *be* – and I shall take leave so to consider it! – it embodies the finest royal compliment that I know of.

I may be wrong: one is apt to be, perhaps, when one returns to the favourites of one's extreme youth and finds in them all that one had remembered of them. But I think that extremely beautiful prose, the expression of a beautiful, exact and simple personality. And the fact that the prose of Field Naturalists has as a rule those qualities seems to me to point certain lessons.

I have no wish to dogmatize at this point on the nature of Style; it seems to be according to the rule of nature that you should attend to mass before you examine texture. Even in Pablos Alto, or maybe in Santa Fe, where the air is very clear, you see first the form of the horse, and that before you are near enough to perceive that the blue sky is reflected on its shining quarters.

The quality that I – and I hope the Reader – ask of a Style is that it should be as clear and as simple as is consonant with the subject treated. Abstract thought for example will not bear the same simplicity of statement as concrete storytelling where the necessity is to get a situation in quickly and there is no strain on the mind. When writing an Essay on History in the abstract it is bad writing to say:

> There is one mind common to all individual men. Every man is an inlet to the same and to all the same. He that is once admitted to the right of reason is made a freeman of the whole estate. What Plato has thought he may think; what a saint has felt, he may feel; what at any time has befallen any man he can understand. Who hath access to this universal mind is a party to all that is or can be done, for this is the only and sovereign agent.
>
> Of the works of this mind history is the record. Its genius is illustrated by the entire series of days. Man is explicable by nothing less than all his history...

That would be all very well in a short story by Maupassant, though he would have more mercy on his reader; but it is simply bad art when it is the first paragraph and three sentences of a volume 538 pages in length. It was I think Carlyle who said that it was like a discharge of buckshot. Carlyle was never kind to his best friends and at his wrongest as a rule in being kind to them, but he was right enough in that.

And, from our point of view, this discharge of rattling platitudes is nonsense, and pernicious nonsense at that. It would be as sweeping, and much more true to say: Man is explicable by his imaginative literature alone. The man who has read the whole of written history and all the Essays about it knows nothing of man. Let him read the Book of Job. Man is explicable by nothing less!

For of a truth, if you had examined the whole of Wiltshire with a microscope, going over the whole county your eyes two inches from the ground, you would know less of that region than the Reader – who has probably never been in and not improbably never heard of the Downs – will know after reading Mr Hudson's little story. To reverse the dictum I will say that I knew more of the United States before visiting it after I had read the little books of Mr Burroughs the naturalist than after some week's study devoted to Professor Woodrow Wilson's voluminous history of that country – and more of the sort of place Walden would be than after reading Thoreau twice or so, That may be a matter of personal idiosyncracy; but human nature being what on the whole it is will gain more insight from a little flash cast on an immense subject than from an infinite wilderness of generalizations drawn from what are called *Quellen*.

That is a fact. I can't help it. It might be in the abstract better – though I don't know why it should! – if humanity read Emerson to obtain insight into the minds of their fellows. But they certainly do not in the vast, vast, vast majority. They will read *Huckleberry Finn* some; some the works of Mr Hudson; some the *Life of a Scotch Naturalist*; some, according to taste, the more vivid, the more accurate or the more sensational reports in the daily papers, of murder, adultery, sudden deaths or heroic rescues. Few I think will deny that, if some deplore. But our business is not with lamentations; our little affair is to discover what man really likes in books. When we have discovered that we shall know what Literature is. After that the Reader, dropping this pilot, may go on to the improvement of his fellows.

Almost alone, then, amongst the writers of Serious Books the Field Naturalist from Hudson back to Aristotle may be fairly well trusted to keep to his work of earnest observation and lucid rendering. It may be replied that he is fortunate, because that is his job. Well, he is fortunate and that is his job; but more than that goes to the making him – conscience that lets him leave well alone. Supposing that Mr Hudson instead of going about in the fields and thinking his thoughts had been filled with a passion for reforming the habits of the Robin Redbreast! For the robin is a cruel devil; invariably he beats out the brains of his aged father, not unusually devouring them too.

I suppose the robin could be reformed; we might train great numbers of bird-catchers to remove all fledgling robins from their nests, retaining them in captivity till all the fathers died in the ordinary way. But it would be a difficult job.

Far more difficult is the job of that House Naturalist, the writer of 'serious' books: he desires as a rule to reform Man, a task as easy as that of teaching the wind to blow always in one direction. It might be set about; but it can only be set about reasonably and with modesty by gentlemen who have made some study of their fellow men. For the purpose of this fascicle on the Serious Book I have, for a number of years now, passed the greater part of my reading time over such works – a practice I had abandoned since the time of my late childhood. And I have been much struck by the recurrence in the most unrelated philosophers, the most antagonistic biographers, the most unharmonizing historians, of one Sentiment. That Sentiment is always expressed more or less epigrammatically according to the genius of the writer. You find it – to limit it to works in our immediate purview of the moment – in Boswell's Johnson, apropos of nothing; in Roscoe,[2] apropos of the quarrels of Platonists and Aristotelians; and – apropos of Carlyle, for I do not think that in Carlyle himself you find it succinctly expressed – you find it in Emerson's *Essays*, in James Anthony Froude who had the unenviable job of editing the Carlylean remains of all sorts, in the study of Carlyle by Dr Garnett who hated Froude for the way in which he discharged his task; and in the *Thomas Carlyle* by John Nichol, LLD, MA, Balliol, Oxon, Emeritus Professor of English Literature in the University of Glasgow who lets Froude down easily but, publishing in 1892, dislikes everyone else who before him has got in with a Life or a Study of Carlyle. The Sentiment then is this: '*The highest function of the Philosopher* (a term embracing all writers of Serious Books) *is to promote the Higher Happiness of humanity*: (Professor Nichol, LLD, MA, Balliol, Oxon naturally styles this the 'Summum bonum'); *unfortunately no man has yet settled in what the Highest Happiness of Man consists*.' And Messrs Froude, Garnett and Nichol unite in saying that of all men in the world the subject of their pens was least likely to settle this.

Faced with this seeming unanimity of a number of the high priests of the Serious, we, creeping more humbly between their mighty legs, may find some millet seeds of truth. And one truth would seem to be this, that humanity likes to be pleased. That is a truism that is not very often stated. Let us advance one step more along the perilous way and say that humanity is more surely improved by being pleased than it [is] by being Improved. Put in a purely literary way that is to say that any given man is rendered more of a 'better man' when he has read Mr Hudson's non-moralized vignette of the rook-scarer alone on the downs than after reading the definitely-moralized criticisms of Carlyle on John Keats:

> The kind of man he was gets ever more horrible to me. Force of hunger for pleasure of every kind and want of all other force. Such a structure of soul, it would once have been very evident, was a chosen 'Vessel of Hell'.

But indeed some philosopher of the commonplace has said that when he is happy man is more merciful to his fellow man than when he is unfortunate – and it hardly needs a philosopher to arrive at that conclusion. Improvement, then, consisting largely in such processes as will make man more merciful and more comprehending of his fellow man, it follows that, if we desire to improve our fellows, we, with our special subject of

2 [William Roscoe (1753–1831), best known for his *Life of Lorenzo de' Medici*, 1795.]

study, shall most certainly arrive at that goal by making man happy through writing.

Herbert thought to bring about an earthly millennium by writing

> A servant with this clause
> Makes drudgery divine;
> Who sweeps a room as for thy cause
> Makes that and the action fine.[3]

On the other hand you may hear – I have heard! – Trade Union Leaders denouncing that very verse as the devil's charter of the capitalist employer – and relatively conservative Trade Unionists at that... And so it is! But that is really none of our business. What *we* have to remember is that in all the welter of conflicting opinions the Philosopher has lost his hold on the world nearly as completely as the priest and though the Newspaper has come amazingly into its own the Newspaper has done that only since it abandoned the great moral tone and the sustained political purpose. Indeed we may say that, paradoxically, the newspaper loses influence as it gains subscribers; or to put it more exactly that the periodicals with the smaller circulations are those that still exercise relatively lasting influences on the minds of their readers. I should say that in England such a paper as the *Morning Post* had in the end a great deal more influence than the London *Daily Mail*; and that still in America periodicals of the class of the *North American Review* are more likely to 'get things done' – large things – than daily papers with large circulations like the *New York American*.

That only means that in Anglo-Saxondom the Instructed Class – the More Select Classes with the more refined poetic imaginations! – have, still, greater political aptitudes and knowledges of how wires are pulled than has the immense welter of *hommes moyen sensuels*. The immense popular paper is the serious book of this class; and, whilst it has the advantage of being infinitely better done than the immense body of portentous-minded volumes it suffers from the same weaknesses the moment it leaves the rendering of minute human vicissitudes in skilful language and takes to being moralist. It can cause immense popular landslides by crying out 'Scandal! Scandal! Treachery! Treachery!'; it can make a whole population take to eating boiled rhubarb leaves. But they do not do so for long. On the moral side of things it exactly resembles the Serious Book, its effects being only more rapid and sooner over.

The fields remain. That is not only a profound political truth – the profoundest political truth of all but a metaphor useful to ourselves. It is a way of saying that Aristotle, the supreme naturalist, has outlasted a wilder-

3 [Herbert's 'The Elixir', slightly misquoted]

ness of generalizers – including the generalizer Aristotle himself; it is a way of saying that the minute observers, Herbert, who wrote 'The man that looks on glass', Herrick who wrote: 'Ponder this when I am gone; by my clock, tis almost one'; and Walton who during showers gave instructions in fly-fishing and after they were over quoted holy Mr Herbert – all these writers of serious books that were yet pure literature have survived a boundless wilderness of sermons from bishops, non-jurors and tinkers! And they have survived themselves when their preachers' gowns were on.

In other words humanity – such humanity as reads Herrick, Herbert and Walton reads them for the passages in which, their beautiful minds and pious powers of patiently observing aiding them, they have rendered beautiful, small humanisms. The mind – even the mind of the sceptic – will pass over Thomas Edward's saying: 'the incomparable works of our adorable Creator'. And for myself I like it, assonance and all; it seems to me a beautiful and a touching phrase. And indeed there is in humanity a passion for moralizing: it is impossible to write without it: you may suppress it from your text, but at bottom it will be there. And, as long as your morality is your own instinctive morality, humanity will tolerate it, though it be as old as Solomon's. No one would be 'choked off' reading the works of Law if all Law's sermons were compact of passages like that about the unjust mother-in-law.

But the point about the field naturalist is that he provides, really, the newspaper of the earth – the chronicles of the little murders, the little escapes, the little fashions in dress, the little loves, courtships, births marriages and deaths of the beasts of the fields, or of the workers on the soil!

transatlantic review, 2:4 (October 1924), 394–404.

X. The Reader

Let it be granted that a re-valuation of English – of all Anglo-Saxon – Literature is a thing eminently to be desired; and few indeed are those who will deny that it is desirable. Their point of view, their reasons for the desire would differ widely, some, amongst whom would be the Reader, I hope, and certainly the Writer, desiring that, so re-valued and trumpeted with enthusiasm by great nations, English letters may take their place again amongst the literatures of the world; some desiring to insulate still further the printed matter of Anglo-Saxondom, restoring it to the 'English' tradition of writers like De Quincey, Oliver Wendell Holmes,

Henry Wadsworth Longfellow, James Russell Lowell, Charles Lamb, Alexander Montgomery, Lords Macaulay, Tennyson and Lytton, whom the European will not very willingly read; and others again – and they the great majority perhaps amongst Deans – being determined to the best of their abilities, since writing has been exhausted in the practices of the long line of Anglican Divines from Archbishop Cranmer to the late Mr Spurgeon, – being determined then to abolish the reading of all works of the imagination... In short there are an infinite number of reasons for desiring a re-estimation of our literary values....

I was sitting in the dusk, last Spring, in a hardly defined London room, awaiting the return from business of the master of the house. It was truly what is called the owlight! But with a book upon his knee, in a window-seat, his back to the dusky panes was a young boy – say he was sixteen. He did not stir; I did not speak for a long time.

I had asked him what was the name of the book and he had answered: 'Oh, Goldsmith... *The Deserted Village*.' and I had got from him, rather painfully, the information that he being waiting for a scholarship exam had got up the names and dates of Oliver Goldsmith amongst a list of English Writers of the Eighteenth Century. Seeing Goldsmith's *Deserted Village* on his father's bookshelves he had taken it down – for the first time in how many years?

I pestered him with no more questions: I was the casual adult in the house, say a not very esteemed uncle; he was the master of all us writers. He was the Reader!

I had nearly written: He was the Only Reader. For there is no reading like that of a boy in the long dusks: it is the deepest abandonment of the soul that we know on this earth... But his father came in after a long time and began to chide him for wasting his time when he should be reading for his examination and he took up a German dictionary and a manual of biology and went into another room. The father said that if the boy would only read something useful he would be less worried. And then he began to upbraid *me* for writing disrespectfully of Shelley, an English Classic. He said he had been told that I was hurting my reputation. Truly the ways of both writers and Readers are thorny ways!

All the same I should not have chosen *The Deserted Village* in the days when I ruined my eyes with those long, twilight readings. My authors were Marryat; Scott, a little; Defoe, Lope de Vega; [Mateo Alemán] – *Guzmán de Alfarache, Lazarillo de Tormes, Lorna Doone, Melmoth the Wanderer*, Gibbon's *Decline and Fall*, Robertson's *History of Charles V*, an odd volume of North's *Plutarch*, an odd volume of Landor's *Imaginary Conversations* containing the conversation between Leofric and Godiva; naturally also *Hark-Away Dick, Sweeney Todd, the Demon Barber; The Scalp-Hunters; Westward Ho* which upon consideration seems to me to be the most wicked book ever written, and Dean Farrar's *Eric* which is perhaps the next most wicked – or less, or more.

I suppose almost every human being could compile a similar list and the exercise is a fascinating one. But I am not writing biography – or only concealedly! – so I will leave the matter there, harping merely on the fact that those were the books I found engrossing. I could read most of them over and over again and indeed often enough I would turn straight back to the first leaf as soon as I had come to the last. I remember making a note in a schoolboy's pocket book that on such a date – I fancy it was the 17/12/(18)86 – I had read *Lorna Doone* thirteen times: I can still relate whole passages of it by heart. But I *will* delay a moment to pay a tribute to what I thought then – and I think it still – *sui generis* the most beautiful book in the world: Samuel Smiles' *Life of a Scottish Naturalist*. I found this book by chance a year ago, bought it for sixpence and recognized at once that my intimate cadence, the typical sentence that I try all my life to create, that I hear all the while in my ear and only once in a blue moon am aided to write, is to be found always in the recorded speeches of Thomas Edward. His sentences have a dying fall, a cadence of resignation. He will write of dotterels on the wet sands, of spoonbills labouring in the immense engineering feat of turning over a great dead fish, of foxes in their homes on the faces of the sea-cliffs – and it is as if you were hearing a *nunc dimittis* spoken without pomp or self-consciousness. Only once did he – as far as Smiles' records go – did he utter a *Jubilate*: he had fallen over a precipice and, caught by a projecting shelf, with his ribs smashed, unable to move and with no apparent prospect of succour, he was enabled to observe an osprey devouring a partridge on a near-by crag. He utters a paean of praise at sight of the beauty, the noble ferocity and address of the bird, and then, thanking the Creator for permitting him to see what perhaps no other man had ever been permitted to witness, this journeyman cobbler who never in his life earned more than eighteen shillings a week, addresses himself to descending the crags…

But I cannot imagine myself, as a young boy, reading *The Deserted Village*, and that must have been a matter of choice for almost certainly it fell under my attention. I was permitted the run of one – of several! – extensive if heterogeneous collections of books and I had most of my dusks to myself. And I remember the proprietor of the first private school to which I was sent at the age of eight or ten telling me that, he having written to my father to ask whether at home I was really permitted to read all the books I seemed to have read, my father had answered that he wished me to have the run of all the books in the schoolmaster's house but would prefer me not to read 'Byron'.

I naturally dipped into Byron: what boy would not have? But I never read more than a line or two and I can remember now with exactitude the sensations that that line or two then caused me. It was at once a weariness, a sort of reluctant dread and a sense as of intense repletion as if after an already too heavy meal I had been confronted with a large quantity of something sweet. And indeed I have the foreshadowings of all those sensations still whenever I look at an opened volume with the columns or verse that seem to have come already many weary miles beyond the left hand page and to be going on for leagues and leagues after the bottom of the right hand page has been reached. I believe that the greater part of humanity feels like that and that that is why the Epic is no longer very fashionable. The reason, I daresay, lies in the personality one ascribes to the writers of immense poems: one imagines them to have uncontemplatable industries, seriousnesses that appal, minatory features – every kind of portentousness. And since the greater part of life is passed, whether one like it or no, in being overborne by one portentousness or another, one will not very willingly let oneself be similarly overwhelmed in the course of an operation which should be a matter of freewill at least, if not of pleasure. I do not mean that I was assailed by those thoughts when as a boy I opened the *Deserted Village*. It was probably something else that stopped me when I had read no more than (I quote from memory)

Dear lovely bow'rs of Innocence and Ease,
Seats of my Youth when every sport could please,
How often have I loitered o'er thy green
Where humble happiness endeared each scene!
How often have I gazed on every charm,
The sheltered cot, the cultivated farm,
The never-failing brook, the busy mill,
The decent Church that topped the neighb'ring Hill!

I remember to this day saying to myself:

'Why couldn't the fellow have written: *I have loitered on thy green: I have gazed upon thy charm*, instead of asking with a note of exclamation questions that can have no possible answer and can be meant to have none.' And 'Innocence and Ease' made me feel impatient at once. And that was not because I had not patience. I owe it to the long London twilights of those years that I can say I have read every word of *Artaxerxes*, every word of *Guzmán de Alfarache*, every word of the *Castle of Otranto*, every word of the *Man of Feeling*. For the matter of that, even in later years I have read every word of Mr Doughty's *Dawn in Britain* – and that with enthusiasm![4] I do not imagine that any living soul other than myself can claim *all* those endurances.

So I will not confess to any abnormal lack of patience: nevertheless I could not do, and I never could have done what that young boy was doing for his own pleasure and with such engrossment. Anyhow, there we have the Readers; I am tempted to say the Two Readers. For

4 [See p. 53 above.]

humanity seems to divide itself into two types when it comes to reading: those who like particularizations and shun allegories and those who reverse the processes of liking and avoiding. There will, that is to say, be those who will desire to read of Villages distinguished by bow'rs of Innocence and Ease; there will be those who, comfortably and with engrossment, can only read of such a village as:

> The village of Selborne and large hamlet of Oakhanger, with the single farms, and many scattered houses along the verge of the forest, contain upwards of six hundred and seventy inhabitants. We abound with poor; many of whom are sober and industrious, and live comfortably (Oh bow'rs of Inocence and Ease!) in good stone or brick cottages which are glazed and have chambers above stairs: mud buildings we have none... The inhabitants enjoy a good share of health and longevity: and the parish swarms with children.

One is tempted to say that it is the eighteenth century against the twentieth were it not for the fact that the letters which make up the *Natural History of Selborne* were being written long before and were continued long after the 'composition' of the *Deserted Village*. Still it is fair to put it that White's *Selborne* attracted very little attention in the eighteenth century and is very much read nowadays whereas the *Deserted Village* must have found very few to read it for pleasure or interest during the last fifty years. It may have been 'set' for examinations or eighteenth-century-minded pastors and masters may have enjoined its perusal as a virtue and so it may have found readers who desired to improve themselves. But it can hardly have been much read either as part of the literature of escape or as a work to which nineteenth-to-twentieth century writers have gone for a model.

But about these things there is no finality and the very fact that that boy, like myself, at his age a boy normal enough, should find engrossment in Goldsmith's poem may well be a sign of a re-action towards the Allegory of the eighteenth, or even towards the Great Moral Purpose of the mid-nineteenth, centuries. Quite apart from the fashionable taste in literatures being a matter of endless reactions, the Literature of Escape itself, the beloved and engrossing printed matter that we read at dusk, is probably in the nature of a re-action against our surroundings. Indeed it is assuredly that and nothing else, the typewriting-girl desiring to read works in which typewriting girls all marry their employers or the merchant seaman in the fo'csle – and they are the most avid readers of all – desiring only books in which, please God, there shall be no more sea. We want to get away from our debts.

So the Allegory may well come into its own again and flourish even as it does on the base of the Albert Memorial where a gentleman in a frock-coat carrying a test-tube typefies Science; a nude figure leading a zebrubull [*sic*] the Colonies; a lady with a nondescriptly rigged ship beneath her arm, the Dominion of the Seas; and the gilt figure of Albert the Good, the Prince of Peace. There may well be conditions in our time to make the weary soul desire to get away into that sort of thing. And indeed the portents are not lacking!

In the more official school of literary Company Promoter of today the tendency is avowedly to bring back the 'English tradition' and indeed the tendency is not limited to the official school which in England is purely Whig. Only today, looking through the pages of a fashionable Tory organ I came upon a review of a volume of poems that still leaves me wondering whether it is not meant to pull the leg of someone or other. It purports to

> bring to the notice of our readers one of the most extraordinary volumes of poems published for a generation.... Alone among the younger poets Mr ... restores to English poetry the larger virtues, the grand manner...
>
> He swings his boat away
> Even as a lonely thinker who has run
> The gamut of great lore and found the Inane...
>
> Philosophy influences his blood like a sensuous excitement, the exalted, impersonal business of States is more his theme than any personal pre-occupation.

Another quotation ends with the singular line: 'England arisen, bared for the battle, blows!' I suppose Macaulay's review of Satan Montgomery contains citations of lines more comic, but then Macaulay did not regard Montgomery as a saviour of society.

Perhaps however it is all a joke. Or perhaps it isn't: there may be Readers – there may be thousands, whole millions of Readers to whom the figure of England blowing may indeed be sublime. The thought opens out for contemplation an immense vista. At the end of it, as through the small end of a prophetic telescope, the Man of Business at the railway bookstall as he goes down town. He wears a full wig, a purple velvet coat, ruffles and a sword and with a gesture of horror he says to the bookstall clerk:

'Take away that Daily... Bring to me, boy, the last sublime epic of the immortal So and So!'

That is not fanciful: it is a perfectly logical projection supposing that the official critic of today should have his way – or supposing merely that the swing of the pendulum should still, as it always has, prevail. Nor is it one half so fanciful as a faithful projection of ourselves, going down town today and faced on the book stall with the incredible rubbish that is all that there you will find – would have seemed to Dr Johnson! For, if there is a pendulum to swing – and almost certainly there is! – it goes to and fro between the awful state of the Full Wig and the sceptical mobility of the Rag Time Army that today we are. Or that yesterday we were!

For, certainly, between 1914 and 1919 such a line as: 'England bared for the battle, blows' would have excited little enthusiasm: would have cut no ice anywhere at all! Indeed it is hardly likely that in those days we were even moved by the remembrance of the great precursor of that sort of thing:

> So when an angel by divine command
> With rising tempests shakes a guilty land,
> Such as of late o'er pale Britannia past,
> Calm and serene he drives the furious blast;
> And pleased th'Almighty's orders to perform
> Rides in the whirlwind and directs the storm!

In a Division with which I was acquainted we used to say: 'Pore b......y old Plumer's got 'em on the run!' And it meant the same as was meant by Addison, but it took less time to say. Indeed, viewed philosophically, you may put it that the whole of the late Armageddon was caused by antagonism between the one point of view and the other: it was the pip-squeak not 'arf against the Shining Sword; Mr Kipling's banjo against the Addisonian lyre. And inasmuch as most of our Academic-Official criticism is and must of necessity be produced by gentlemen temperamentally and ingrainedly pro-German it stands to reason that the object of their work will be to restore the Allegory and with it the dreadful Lives of Poets, the annotated editions, kai panta tauta.[5] I deplore the prospect, for, as the Reader will no doubt have divined I am for the banjo against the lyre all the time; for that is to say the natural man with appetites, desires, physical aptitudes, carelessnesses and interests in life; as against the Professorial Figure that stands for uninspired industry, career-makings and circumspection: I desire that is to say that things should be written, not written about. I deplore then the state into which it is hoped to push this country; but I cannot help seeing that it is extremely likely that into it she will be pushed...

Between Realism and the Allegoric stands however the Romantic: between, that is to say, Pope and Flaubert stands Victor Hugo; between the eighteenth and the twentieth, another century! And it is quite possible that in Anglo-Saxondom a cleavage will come and that, whilst England returns to its diet of half-cold fish – at any rate on the surface, the United States may produce and immensely consume an immense, hybrid Romantic-Realist literature. For it is obvious that the United States with its mixed populations is not going to be limited or turned back to the diet provided by the Concord Group which represents the last activities of the

5 ['and all the same such things'.]

'English' muse in America: ever since the days of Mark Twain and Whitman, and still more of Stephen Crane, it was quite obvious that America was going to have a literature of her own – and a literature nearer in spirit to the literature of the Continent than to the literature of the 'Mother Country'.

transatlantic review, 2:5 (November 1924), 502–10.

From a Paris Quay (II)

★★★

The best writer in America at this moment (though for the moment he happens to be in Paris) the most conscientious, the most master of his craft, the most consummate, is my young friend, Ernest Hemingway. The two worst writers that I have met in Paris (I don't, of course, meet any banal ones!) are Waldo Frank and Robert McAlmon).[1] Mr Hemingway, with immense labour and excruciating thought and knowledge, turns out a short paragraph. Mr McAlmon pours out streams of written matter that will result in three or five volumes of the Contact Publishing Company. How Mr Frank works I do not know.

★★★

And the great need of our modern world is just knowledge.

★★★

So the great need of our time being the saving of time, any soul that can give us very quick, irrefutable and consummate pictures confers a great boon on humanity.

Joseph Conrad gave you Malaysia, South American republics; the Secret Service, the pre-Soviet efforts of Russian revolutionaries, the Congo, the Sea – and above all the English public school frame of mind. Hudson gave you La Plata, London through its birds, the Sussex Downs by way of thistle-down. Doughty has given you Arabia of the Desert; Clarendon the Great Rebellion; Defoe, the Plague of London; Cervantes, the death of altruism – of Christianity itself. It is up to the writer of today to give us today.

To that extent fierce young writers of the type of Mr McAlmon with his admirably photographic gift of observation, his torrential flow of barbaric and harsh words, and his belief that what is wanted is the Document, compiled just anyhow – to that extent these violent ignorers of the past are justified. It is an admirable thing that the atmosphere of the Middle West, that mysterious Prester John's land, should be given to the world. For the incalculable Vote of the unknown Middle West probably sways the United States and regulates her intercourse with the world at large. So a documented picture of this region is at least as important as a

1 [Robert McAlmon (1896–1956), expatriate American 'lost generation' writer living and publishing in France.]

documented compilation of the history of Rome under the Caesars.

The passionately egotistic young writer of these broad fields may then be right in harshly shouting, 'I am Me!' and in setting down without thought any sort of old rendering of any sort of old happening to himself, mental or physical. Having suffered from not very wise parental controls he is subconsciously passionate not so much to grab his parents' possessions and powers as to bash his parents' knowledges. So, before writing books he will determinedly refuse to read the books his parents read.

He is in such a hurry to be doing that not only will he not take time to observe the rules of the game; he will shout as a doctrine that the game has no rules, language no laws, books no structural necessities, sentences no necessary cadences. He will lose thus a great deal of time. For what we have learned in the past has been mainly how to shorten. All the self-disciplining to which my generation of writers subjected itself had that for its sole object – the getting of what our Egos had to say as expeditiously as possible into the mind of a reader who wants to see as little of you as possible. Any man *can* get a gun from his shoulder to the ground beside him, but a long way the quickest way is the three motions of the 'Order Arms' of the drill instructor.

You come with that to the eternal problem that faces Youth – and that in the end causes the passing of Youth. That is the selection of those rules of the Past that are really practical. For Youth cannot get through on mere volition, on mere energy – or cannot get very far though. And the problems of Art – the problems of not being a bore – are so very complex that one is very foolish if one ignores all the pointers that all the dead have found into the labyrinth that the thing is. The problem of not being a Bore....

It is all really in that. Youth undisciplined will, truly, get through a certain way on the strength of its charm and of its necessary newness. But Time is a long thing and after the youngest man has been talking to you prolixly for several hours you will find yourself wishing that he could be a little shorter. But that time has not yet come for my Middle Western writers and the consoling thing to think is that there does exist a whole band, a whole school, a whole swift-footed posse of young, rude, wild, impracticable but impassioned practitioners on paper.

How far up the sands this tide will get heaven knows. Far enough, I imagine, or I should not be here extolling it. And it has this striking characteristic in its favour. The Egotistic Document has been common enough in the past. Every man, proverbially, has it in him to write one book: about himself. But these Middle Westerners continue and their Egotism is objective. Mr McAlmon does not for ever write about the inner processes of Mr McAlmon; he turns his fiercely didactic Me to the rendering of his Middle Western surroundings. About, say, Dr Carlos Williams there is very little of the introspective; about Mr Hemingway there is none at all; young women like Miss Djuna Barnes are no diary writers of the type of the European Marie Bashkirtseff. Their egotism takes the form of making them insist on writing in their own way.

That is all right: it is a Method, like another. It implies no doubt a lack of the sense of proportion; but I take it that a sense of proportion would in the Middle West be destructive to its possessor. In the face of those vastnesses of territory and population if one realized one's own minuteness, one would never attempt the gigantic task of a realization of it all. And the European young writer – the English young writer, in particular – has probably much too much of that sense. He realizes proportions – of Class, of Achievement, of Venerability, of remote Time – to such an extent that he is apt to attack nothing and to fall back on the little, fiddling, Peter Pannishnesses that are the negation of effort. From that dismal form of modesty the young American is preserved from suffering. He has all the luck....

★★★

New York Evening Post Literary Review, 3 January 1925, 1–2.

The Other House

When I was half-way through reading this long-awaited compilation[1] I found myself springing, with my right hand extended, towards my bookshelves. It was an action purely reflex for when I stood before the backs of those volumes I had no idea why I was there. You feel like that when you find yourself out of bed in a black, unfamiliar room. So, my left hand, as it were unknowing, I let the other do what it wanted. It fell on the back of a book called *The Shadow Line* and when the book opened and my eye read the first two or three chance words I found myself saying: 'Thank God!'

I really found myself saying: 'Thank God!' with a feeling of deep, of grateful, relief. Truly, I do not mean to be ungenerous to Monsieur Jean-Aubry, it is only that he is of a different school – so absolutely of the other house. He has done his allotted task with industry, application, conscience, erudition; it betrays every attribute that the official biography of a man of letters lately deceased, can possibly display. If the fact that Monsieur Jean-Aubry is an industrious Frenchman set wandering in the thorny, if not tropical, undergrowth of British literary life – if that fact causes the appearance in his pages of certain minor inaccuracies or unfamiliarities with British conditions they are so minor as to amount to little more than a row of pins.

Because there is true truth – and truth.

Which was Conrad? The bothered, battered person who wrote innumerable, woeful, tactful, timid letters that are here connected by a string of properly noncommittal prose, or the amazing being that I remember? With a spoken word or two he could create a whole world and give to himself the aspect of a returned Sir Francis Drake emerging from the territory of the Anthropophagi and the darkness of the Land of Fire. Or with two sentences of *The Shadow Line* he could make you say: 'Thank God!'

For it is hardly rhetoric to say that one ought to thank one's creator for letting one read 'Youth' or *Heart of Darkness* or *The Nigger of the Narcissus*. Or even *The Shadow Line*. Pure sensation, pure emotion – pure poetry – are so rare in life; and so necessary to the sweetening – the disinfection! – of the soul, that probably the world would be better lacking the telephone which is anyhow a maddening instrument than without.... This sentence

1 [G. Jean-Aubry's *Joseph Conrad: Life and Letters* (Garden City, 1927)]

is, however, so controversial that I had better not finish it, my controversy here being on another line.

The public then, apparently demands the Official Biography, and the greater part of my life, as the greater part of Conrad's whilst vigour remained to him, has been given to combatting the Official Biography – at any rate for men of letters. Or perhaps for anyone. I used to know a diplomat and proconsul who had a rather pompous name, but who was one of the most entertaining of after-dinner speakers and raconteurs that it was possible to imagine. He had besides done the state a great deal of service. He died, in due course, his official *Life and Letters* appeared: well, because he was a pretty poor letter writer and because, for reasons of politics the material facts of his world-transactions had to be omitted, his *Life and Letters* presented him to the world as being infinitely more pompous and ridiculous than his name. The public nevertheless devoured the book.

And in the end the public decides – so no doubt I am playing a losing game in thus fighting, not this alone, but all official biographies and the frame of mind that produces them. Well, I who am about to die salute you.

Conrad, then, was not only an incomparable fingerer of the lute of words, he was an unrivalled autobiographer – not only in his records and reminiscences but in all his writings for publication. Consider Marlow! Consider *Heart of Darkness*. Or consider his remembrances of childhood in Poland.

Well, sentence by sentence, line by line, with scissors, paste and dactylography Monsieur Jean-Aubry – *his* text, as is proper; in large type and Conrad's in small, connects up passages in these works, comments that So and So's name was really This and That or that the city of Coronograd was really the District of Palinzona. The result, at any rate for me, is the exasperation that made me spring for my bookshelf and read just one or two words of Conrad's own writing in a type that did not try the eyes, and in the context where it was meant to lie. (And I am bound to say that, once started, I read the whole of that book through, far into the night before returning to the *Life and Letters* – I simply could not put it down.)

Again I am not attacking Monsieur Jean-Aubry. This book was ordered of him; his conscience, he being of the other house, permits him to compile it, and according to the canons of the followers of Boswell he has performed his work. (Alas, Boswell killed Johnson. Who reads *Rasselas* or even the *Life of Drake*?) And he has done it quite decently and becomingly. Living much in contact with the more official type of British litterateur, he has avoided knocking on the head more writers of other persuasions than he was absolutely forced to. For what a bloody battlefield the book might have been – or have occasioned! But Official Lives and Letters suffer and must always suffer from lack of proportion. The persons most intimate with a man are seldom the recipients of the majority of his letters simply because they are constantly in his society. Or letters are not preserved, or go astray. Or the Official Biographer is ordered to ignore this or that person!

Thus in the world of letters Henry James was almost the only figure in England who constantly perturbed, intrigued and exasperated Conrad. I don't mean to imply that other writers' names did not occur in his conversation or that he did not speak frequently and with generosity of the work of, say, Mr Galsworthy. But James was about the only living figure writing in English and Conrad regarded as at all his equal or whose work presented to him technical problems that he could not solve. Yet as far as I have been able to discover (there is, alas, no index in the copy of the book with which I have been provided), Henry James is hardly mentioned in the work, which contains only two of the several score letters that Conrad wrote to James. And as his letters were frequently in acknowledgment of James's work, they had a peculiar interest as showing what type of praise Conrad thought would please the Old Man.

Or, again, as regards that peculiar type of relationship that is indicated by the English phrase, 'cook, slut and bottle-washer' – as regards two men who were peculiarly intimate with and useful to Conrad – Krieger and the late Arthur Marwood – these again are hardly mentioned in the volumes; to Krieger there is no letter at all, to Marwood only one. Yet I have heard Conrad speak over and over again in terms of the deepest emotion of the services Krieger rendered him in the days when he was attempting to be a financier in the city; Marwood, in the days after those of *The English Review*, was of unfailing solace and support to this author. And Marwood was a man of encyclopaedic knowledge and of clear English Tory common sense such as I at least have never known the like of. So that, until the time of his death he really was, as it were, the measuring stick by which Conrad got his sense of proportion. But how was poor Monsieur Jean-Aubry to obtain letters of Conrad to Marwood? The two men met so constantly that there were none.

If then the official Biography of necessity omits the greatest literary influence and two of the greatest personal influences of its subject's life it must needs be an almost Hamletless Hamlet! It would be going too far to say as much of Monsieur Jean-Aubry's so conscientious pages. They contain an infinite number of details, and little quips of phrase in letters and of such things as the public obviously delights in.

But in the end I remain in the other house. I still prefer the Shelley of Trelawney to the Shelley of the infinite number of Shelleyographers down to my Uncle William and beyond him. I prefer indeed the Shelley of *Ariel*.[2] Monsieur Jean-Aubry falls politely foul of myself for representing Conrad as in his young days '*lieutenant de torpilleurs de la marine militaire Francaise*' (sic) Monsieur adds. And he backs himself up and floors me with

2 [André Maurois' biography of Shelley, 1923.]

a great number of dates, extracts from marine records of Marseilles and the like. I, however, remain impenitent.

I have again and again heard Conrad say that he served on a French naval vessel called the *Ville d'Ompiteda* – I present Monsieur Jean-Aubry with the name so that he may search the naval records – and that he passed the examination for lieutenant – sometimes he would say ensign – in the French torpedo service. During a valedictory interview in 1916 he said quite specifically: 'I, too, have been under fire on service!'

Now Monsieur Jean-Aubry may be quite right and Conrad may have seen all his French sea service in merchant bottoms. But my Conrad is more truly true… Do you mean to tell me that that dark magnetic, devil of a young fellow did not get cashiered from the French navy for going to Marseilles races on an unvarnished four-in-hand covered like a flower garden with all the corps de ballet of Marseilles? If you do, you lie!

For the only alternative would be to say that Conrad lied and that I will never do. Whether he ever sat in his flesh and bones, even, on that unpainted coach with a ballerina in each physical arm I don't know. And I don't care… But that he could have been the dear Conrad that he afterwards was – the Conrad of the flashing eyes, the caressing voice and the infinite Oriental tact that, also, was like a caress; – that he could have been the man he was and done the things with words that he did, that he could have achieved so much and so much suffered without that reminiscence at the back of the inward soul, is impossible. The Poet – and particularly the poor devil so harried as was Conrad – must have escape from the world, anodynes, and drugs of which the lay public has neither need or knowledge. One of these is to *Poetiser un peu* – to romance a little when he talks of himself. Then that romance becomes part of himself and is the true truth. But, once he must have been a glorious fellow – for *respice finem*![3] Look at the miserable end – not of this book but of the true ambition that was in the bottom of his heart! I confess that there are letters of Conrad's that I cannot read without the tears in my eyes – and they are not the ones that you think.

That man's material purpose in life was one, beautiful and single. By the greatness of his labours to that one end he had made of his house a true house of prayer. What have they made of it? What would he say today? The harpies!

That has nothing to do with Monsieur Jean-Aubry: he has done his best. The translation, both in text and letters, is very well and unassumingly done.

New York Herald Tribune Books, 2 October 1927, 2.

3 [Look to the end!]

Cambridge on the Caboodle

All the world is said to love a lover and I am sure that the greater proportion of it loves Mr E.M. Forster. I do myself – Mr Forster as novelist. He has for so long occupied so peculiar a position in Hampstead which is a suburb of London singularly like Beacon Hill; I have for so many years gone in awe of him that I approach this [*Aspects of the Novel*], his exegesis of the products of his art, with the feelings of a naughty schoolboy about to rob his headmaster's apple trees.

Hampstead to the north of London is a very singular place. It is Beacon Hill – but you could tuck Beacon Hill away in the corner of it and never find it again. It is with its rarefied atmosphere, its cold breezes coming from the north, its frosty inaccessibility, the Mecca of our intelligentsia. And, for many years Mr E.M. Forster has been its prophet. Before him it was Mr Henry James. In my young youth I was browbeaten into detesting Shelley by its inhabitants; just after adolescence I was nearly browbeaten into never reading James and my young manhood balked at the mention of Mr E.M. Forster as the pony I used to have in those days balked at the sight of a perambulator.

So that, when *A Room With a View* was published, or a year or so after, happening to be shut up alone with it, and no other book, I took it up with trepidation. I remained, if not to pray, then at least to read all of Mr Forster's earlier work. And, since then, I have ranged myself amongst his warmest admirers. He has retained for me, nevertheless, his aspect of aloofness, awfulness, chaste reason, tenuity, sobriety. I have tiptoed past his windows as the true believer used to do outside the tent of the Prophet – for fear of disturbing his reveries. I even printed him in *The English Review*.

Alas, what was my bewilderment as I read through the pages of *Aspects of the Novel* to find that Mr Forster's attitude towards the art and craft that has given him honour and fame is practically that of the periodical called *Punch* towards the graver problems of life. He admires virtue, all the virtues, 'O dear yes', but how he pokes fun at them! He cites an immense number of second-class English novelists and jests over them for all the world like a contributor to *Punch* making fun of his own children for the benefit of the public. Thus childhood with all its beauty is for the English eternally sullied – and thus for Mr Forster's hearers is the novel kept in its place.

This volume is made up of the Clark lectures delivered for Trinity College, Cambridge, in 1927. I have no means of knowing what Mr Forster's audience was like. I have no doubt that it was young, sober, intellectual, chaste.... Or it may have been old and all that too. But it cannot have contained one novelist who was also an artist. Otherwise Mr Forster would not now be alive.

I hesitated to arrive at this conclusion. I remained incredulous until halfway through the book. I find the language in which it is written extremely difficult to understand. I have had to read sentence after sentence two or three times over. I suppose I am too Americanized – but I daresay I never could have understood the persiflage of the Cambridge don when speaking of serious subjects – religion, love, poverty, or the arts. What the English call Things! You mustn't talk seriously about Things in good English society.

But a university – at any rate an English one – exists to have the aspect at least of talking about Things. Yet it mustn't. The English youth goes to his university with the mentality of a Continental child of fourteen and the province of the university is to maintain him in the same mental status. Because, if the Englishman ever passed the stage of mental puberty the Empire would break up and there could be no more tea parties, club smoking-rooms, Ranelaghs, Colonies, Anglican clergy, or Cabinet ministers. We could not keep on carrying the white man's burden if some god or some don conferred upon us the gift of the seeing eye.

So Mr Forster deserves infinitely well of his college, his university, his country, and his Empire. As I have said, it was only when halfway through the book that I arrived at this, to me, amazing conclusion. Our present day national anthem runs:

> Land of hope and glory, mother of the free,
> How can we extol thee, who are born of thee?

And I can assure you that when in foreign lands with Sir Edward Elgar's music I hear that modest query, tears of nostalgia bedew my lids. We are all right. We really are. But when the same question is addressed by a novelist to his art it becomes quite a different matter. It is no doubt the reason why Mr Forster has to begin his lectures with the assertion that there is no first-class English novelist and, presumably, that a first-class novel never has and never will be written in England, at any rate by an Englishman – for all the first-class novels that were written in England during the last quarter of a century were the products of one sort of dago or another. So at least says Mr Forster, premising in the mouths of the English reader the immortal words of my great Aunt Eliza – 'Sooner than be idle I'd take a book and read.'

This cry from the soul – this whole cry from the soul – was wrung from me by the following words, which occur on page 146 of Mr Forster's book: *He (M. André Gide) is a little more solemn than an author should be about the whole caboodle.* And there you have the whole attitude of the British don-critic towards our art. The novel, novel writing, form, language, construction, ancestry – all these things which are the object of serious study outside England in places from which come the first-class novels – all these things are 'the whole caboodle' which, if you take seriously, you will never make fun of your children in the pages of *Punch*. You will be un-English.

Now I wonder how seriously Mr Forster takes his own novels, and with how much passion – how much *saeva indignatio* – he writes them. For, for a novelist to be great in the sense that Turgenev, or Stendhal, or Flaubert, or Conrad were formally and stylistically great, or in the sense that Dostoevsky was great epilepto-romantically, or even Balzac, pantingly, spouting like a whale, fountains of fairy tales disguised as a *comédie humaine* ... Or even Tolstoy, or Chekhov, or Maupassant, or Daudet... Or great as were undoubtedly Thackeray, Dickens, Smollet, Richardson, and Defoe ... or great as was Henry James and are, if you will, Mr Joyce and Theodore Dreiser – for the production of each of these forms of greatness there is necessary a fierce indignation, if not of necessity against external oppositions or institutions, then at least against that nature of things that will not let one write better than one does. A novelist must know despair, bitterness, passion, and must wear upon his forehead the sweat of agony that distinguishes his Craft and Mystery. It is out of those depths that he must call. Hang it all, this world that has known a million, million thinking souls has produced, let us say, twenty great novelists from the day when the first word of *The Golden Ass* was penned, down to the last word of *Ulysses*. And is this terrific immortality of twenty over a million million to be earned by the facile or lethargically optimistic inhabitant of Cambridge common rooms?

Mind, I am not suggesting that that is what Mr Forster is; I am merely complaining that instead of telling us how *A Passage to India* was conceived, touched in, retouched, smoothed down, or here and there, heightened, he gives us these tea cup clattering disquisitions upon the Sir Willoughby Patterne of George Meredith. I would bet my hat that Mr Forster's novels were not written out of his complacencies but during sedulous and rather dreadful days. Why is it not those that he has given us rather than these heartless disquisitions upon English amateurs with which any one of the readers of his novels could just as well have provided him? It is probably because Mr Forster is too modest to write about himself. English gentlemen do not do this but modesty and novelists have nothing to do with each other and it is impossible for a novelist to be an English gentleman. No can do.

Heaven knows I would not fall foul of Professor Forster if he were not also the author of *A Passage to India* and certainly I would never fall foul of any novel of Mr Forster's. Dog ought not to eat dog and the lowest of all crimes is the crabbing of another fellow's benefit. But, in as much as Mr Forster is a novelist he is a priest and in this work it is as if with the one hand he elevated the Host whilst with the other he writes donnish witticisms about how the sacred wafers are baked. So I shed these tears.

Starting out and finishing with a half-true assertion and ending with the same, Mr Forster includes between those statements a vast number of ingenious tropes, metaphors, similes, figures, quips, and pawkinesses that as I have said make me have to read most of his sentences twice – as one has to read French verse twice, once for the sense and once for the rhythm. But it is no more than a half-truth to say that there are no first-class English novelists when by that you mean that we have no novelists as great as Dostoevsky, and Tolstoy. We have Defoe, Smollett, Dickens, Thackeray, each one as amateurishly great a storyteller and moralist as either of the Russians who are in no sense artists. For it is merely quarrelling with a man's temperament or subject matter to say that *Vanity Fair* is not as great as *War and Peace* or *Humphrey Clinker* as great as *Crime and Punishment*. But the Continental, not English, sense of the word 'greatness' connotes, along with a great seriousness of approach to life, a certain consummate mastery over form, phase, and inevitable progression, and it is perfectly true to say that Anglo-Saxondom has no first-rate novelist in the sense that Turgenev, Chekhov, Stendhal, and Flaubert were first rate. One may make a reservation in favour of Conrad and Henry James to whom we are too near to judge with any certainty. But I am pretty certain that if we ever do prove to have any first-class novelists it is those two writers and their lineage that will produce them. Mr Forster, very symptomatically, does not mention Conrad at all in his list of main references though he does mention Mr Asquith. But neither does he mention Stendhal, Flaubert, Turgenev, or Chekhov. He devotes, however, some rather patronizing attention, as we have seen to M. André Gide, and though he does not mention Anatole France he cites M. Abel Chevalley. These omissions and inclusions are not queer; they are merely characteristic of Cambridge intelligentsia to whom Mr Asquith must be more important than Joseph Conrad and Mr Max Beerbohm than, let us say, Gogol. And so, introducing himself with a half-truth, the Cambridge professor must set out from an impossible projection. He insists that you must think of all the novelists in the world, from Apuleius to Miss Elizabeth Madox Roberts, seated together under a vast dome, all writing away simultaneously whilst you are to peer over their shoulders and perceive that they all write much in the same way, or with not such great differences as all that.

This is to inculcate at once the English doctrine that all art is just a 'caboodle'. The novel, you are to believe, has neither form nor craftsmanship; in the past it has exhibited no development nor will it in the future in any way develop. It is the handmaiden of society and the arts and, unlike Topsy, it has never even growed. Now that doctrine is a profound necessity to the British Empire for as I have said, if we ever took the arts seriously – which is synonymous with thinking – we could not continue to bear up the white man's burden. That I dare say would be a tragedy for the world. I really quite believe it.

But the novel has a perfectly definite history and has developed as traceably as the pterodactyl from amoeba, or the Japanese child's flying toy of twisted rubber, into the Handley-Page. The modern novel began picaresquely with the contemporaries of Lope de Vega and passed to England with John Mabbe's translation of [Mateo Alémán's] *Guzmán de Alfarache* or *The History of a Rogue*, a picaresque but horribly moralizing work.

Guzmán de Alfarache begot Defoe; Defoe, Richardson; Richardson, Diderot; Diderot and the Encyclopaedists, Stendhal, Flaubert, and Turgenev; those three begot Conrad and Henry James and Stephen Crane, and those three again the modern American novelist. During all that time the novel progressed from being the merely barbarous stringing together of piquant rogueries and hypocritical moralizing to be the tremendous social engine that, with its rendering of our times it is today. If the novel as teacher, counsellor, and guide to life has replaced the priest, the historian, the newspaper, and even Dr Sigmund Freud – for the newspaper never was much trusted and according to observers is today not trusted at all, at least in this country and Dr Freud has become nearly as obsolete as Darwin – if the novel has taken the place of all those formidable coercers of the past it is, be sure, because it has developed in its rendering of the live and emotions of humanity.

This the Cambridge don will have none of; should he utter such heresies to Anglicans he would be false to his pious founders and the donors of his stipend. He lets the legions thunder past, utters a few quips, and goes to sleep again till next spring brings its new Clarkian lecturer.

As I have attacked Mr Forster – though only as a don – with a great deal of violence, I hope somebody will ask me to review his next novel so that I may handsomely redress the balance. His book, indeed, is a very good book if you wish to acquire the point of view of a don upon literature. It contains fewer slips of grammar than is usual in collections of lectures and several pleasant little jokes. I dare say that if I had been present at the Clarkian lecture of 1927, given Mr Forster's pleasant voice, cultured appearance, and personal magnetism I might have giggled like any girl graduate, though after that pink pottage there might have come the exceeding bitter cry. But the moral of the whole thing as far as

England is concerned, and Mr Forster is only a symbol of England, is this:

The blacksmith says: 'By hammer and hand all art doth stand'; the baker thinks he is indispensable to society and so he learns his job. Yesterday I was having my shoes scientifically and industriously shined in the Grand Central railway station by some sort of perspiring dago. I said that shining a shoe seemed to be a skilled and complicated affair. He said it was and he added that he guessed New York could not go on without him and his fellows for no one would walk the street without shiny shoes. Well the novelist – the great novelist – must have the same conviction with regard to his own art. Then to the measure of the light vouchsafed him he may shine in his place and be content.[1] But Cambridge won't like him.

Saturday Review of Literature, 4 (17 December 1927), 449–50.

1 [Alludes to Wordsworth's sonnet, 'If thou indeed derive thy light from Heaven'.]

Thomas Hardy, OM
Obiit 11 January 1928

★★★

A little later, in response to some spiritualist anecdote of, I think, Professor Murray's, as if to prove that one sort of ghost story was as good as another, Thomas Hardy told the story of Wild Darrell. It was the most memorable tale-telling that I have ever attended.

In those days he was still sturdy, grizzled rather than white, rather small in stature, a little military in aspect and gifted by God with a naïveté that was at once the source of his talent and the secret of his immense charm. He suggested to me more than anything – as I have already said somewhere or other – one of those uncovered roots of mighty oak-trees that you will see, half bedded in deep moss in the glades of his own New Forest. Something steadfast, rough-grained, retiring, kindly – and eternal. For, surely, there is something kind and eternal about those woodlands, and woodlanders are inspired to tolerant and lasting thoughts. At any rate, in his peasant way he was the most charming man I have ever met – and I have met many. And do not believe that when I use the word 'peasant' I mean anything socially derogatory. There used to be a print that was very popular in English country ale-houses half a century ago. It represents a number of men in scarlet uniforms, robes and periwigs, all supported on the shoulders of one russet-clad fellow. From the respective mouths of king, priest, soldier, peer, issue labels bearing the words 'I pray for all!' 'I fight for all!' 'I make laws for all!' 'I govern all!' and the like. But from the mouth of the bearer who carries a spade issues the groan: 'I support all!' He is the peasant, and that is no doubt the truth of it. And he is unchanging – and so was Thomas Hardy, who might well have taken for his boast the words: 'I think for all!' For deep in the heart of England he kept going that sombre strain of almost Sophoclean thought that is the most English characteristic of all. Fatalistic, gloomy, darkling and determined, it accepts the dictates of fate and faces the universe erect, with the determination to keep all on going, as says the Kentish peasant, and then to keep all on. So, Thomas Hardy, poet! I am frequently told here that England is disappointing to the American visitors because it is so rapidly becoming Americanized. Well, you may Americanize me and the Tower of London, and the advertisements on the buses in London streets, and the

Chancellor of the Exchequer and the Archbishop of Canterbury, and the birthplace, and the city of Stratford on Avon. But you never could have Americanized Thomas Hardy or Gallicized him, or Scotticized or Celtically influenced him. He was as unchanging as the twisted oak-roots.

The story of Wild Darrell is as follows:

Wild Darrell was the owner of Littlecote Manor House, which is the manor house of all England for ghosts, nightriders, evil deeds, treachery and ruin... Well, far from Littlecote lived a midwife who one night was retiring to bed when there came wild thunderings on her door. Without stood a great dark man holding the bridle of a huge, coalblack charger. By menaces and force he made the midwife mount before him on his horse and, having blindfolded her, galloped away through the night. They came to the postern door of an immense house and here the midwife was introduced up a priest's staircase that was in the thick of the wall. They came into an immense chamber where there roared a great log fire, and in the chamber was a great state bed with velvet curtains, and in the bed a lady in labour. As soon as the midwife had delivered the lady Wild Darrell took the child and threw it into the middle of the blazing logs. He then conducted the midwife home again, but during her operations she had contrived to snip a small piece out of the velvet bed curtain, and this was the cause of Wild Darrell's downfall. The midwife talked: the story came up to London, and justice, scenting a rich booty, was finally able to place the fragment into its place in the curtain. Wild Darrell lay long in jail, the Lord Chief Justice Popham tempting him with the offer of his life if Darrell would surrender his land to himself. Darrell at last consented, but he put upon Popham the curse that no eldest son of the Popham family should ever die a natural death. And that has proved the case. Wild Darrell, meanwhile, on his coalblack charger, with fire flashing from its eyes and smoke pouring from its nostrils, rides in the black nights with great bounds up and down the road leading from Littlecote to the place where the midwife's cottage has fallen down.

That was the story, but those were, of course, not Thomas Hardy's words. He told it as he did everything, shyly, almost deprecatingly, but he told it with a force that made it seem extraordinarily real ... the house, the great raftered chamber, the immense fire, the great bed! I see it at this moment superimposed over the room that surrounds me. And when he had finished it was truly as if we had heard how the silence surged softly backward after the plunging hoofs were gone – the last words are Mr de la Mare's. He made his ghosts in truth more visible than any spiritualistic manifestations can ever have been.

I talked a great deal with him afterwards, and the talks always seemed very long – not because of either their duration or their want of interest, but simply because of his minute attention to little things that were also essentials to whatever was the matter in hand. He seemed to have in his mind none of what I would call the 'roughage' of conversation by means of which most men render their conversation tiresome. In common, indeed, with most men of genius whom I have known, he seemed to view life with the fascinated interest of a bird that is on the ground and inspects minute objects, and I have often thought that genius is, in fact, a sort of fountain of youth in that its possessor retains an almost naïve interest in the simplest little things of life as well as in larger generalizations and causes.

★★★

New York Herald Tribune Books, 22 January 1928, 1–3.

Elizabeth Madox Roberts by Ford Madox Ford

There appear now and then for most people – for nearly all people who are of a seriously bookish turn of mind – a book and then an author who change, who render more satisfactory, the whole citadel of books. I remember very well my feelings with the first words of Conrad's that I ever read. They were, I think, 'It has set at last!' And immediately the world seemed to grow larger. That was the aspect it had for me. For the world of letters is a world, a territory, and when a new writer appears, and appears to be trustworthy, certain to go on, an actual region is available over which your mind may for ever travel. As if a new province had added itself to the globe. So it has been for me, at least, ever since. I have come across a great many new writers since Conrad corrected his first proof sheets and I have seldom had to change my mind about them after the first two or three words. And though, alas, many of those writers once new are now dead, their words remain. Just before I sat down to write this I was reading in *A Shepherd's Life* the passage about the ploughman's lad who ran down a great stretch of downs just to see Hudson pass. And just before that a passage about syrens by Norman Douglas, which was, I think, the first essay of his to be published and which I printed in *The English Review*. And both struck me as exquisitely beautiful passages and I was as glad of them as when I first read them. So my world has grown far larger than it was in, say, 1895.

But never between the first words of Conrad's and the first of *The Time of Man* has so extraordinary and so great an enlargement taken place for me – and *My Heart and My Flesh* has enormously enhanced that growth of space. In the case of Miss Roberts as was formerly the case with the author of *Almayer*, it is not so much that a new writer or two new books of singular skill in workmanship had made their appearance, it is as if a whole quality had been added to literature itself – as if literature itself had a new purpose given to it, as if what literature could do had been extended in its scope, as if the number of emotions that literature could convey had been added to, and as if the permanent change that every book must work upon you had been given a new region in which to exercise itself. Of course, to read the book of any new author is to make the acquaintance of a new character, but the quality of each author's isolation is very various, most authors coming out to fall in the ranks in a place fairly obviously awaiting them. Thus to read Mr Joyce for the first time is to see him almost without predecessors, whereas Mr Galsworthy, say, has added a very honourable column to the honourable façade of the British novel.

And for me Miss Roberts stands almost supremely alone. I am fairly acquainted – I daresay that I am better acquainted than most people – with the very striking literature that, since the war, the Middle West of the United States has presented to us. But although that tide of books is autochthonous enough and as redolent of its soil as any regional literature could possibly be, it is to be remembered that Miss Roberts is not a Middle Western writer, but a Southerner. She is, in fact, almost the only writer that the South has given the world. For it is a curious fact that though for long European traditions of formality in manners and a quite astonishing acquaintance with the humaner letters of classical tradition distinguished the Southern populations from the North, and then the Middle West and the West, hardly any writer of any considerable mark was ever born south of the Mason-Dixie [*sic*] line. Or, at any rate, that region of suavities, gallantries and refinements completely lacked a literature which could by any stretch of the imagination be called regional to the South.

Nor have the writings of Miss Roberts any kinship with the work of the Middle Westerners. They are never restless, hurried, broken up – or even, I am tempted to say, arresting. They hold you rather with the sort of possession of you that will be taken by the English lyric writers of the seventeenth century. Reading her is a little like reading Herbert or Donne. Mr Glenway Westcott, who like Miss Roberts was for a time educated in Chicago, has something of the quality, but he is so essentially a poet, whereas Miss Roberts is so essentially a novelist, that a comparison between their works is rather profitless. And all the other Middle Western writers, so many of whom passed together through Chicago University, are completely different, so that I have been tempted to say that if the Middle Westerners are indeed Americans then Miss Roberts is European. Certainly if you consider the faces that seem to look up from their pages as you read them, that of, say, Mr Ernest Hemingway is so extravagantly dissimilar from that of Miss Roberts that, by sheer reaction, you are driven to thinking of Jane Austen.

So Miss Roberts stands solitary. She does in truth a little resemble Jane Austen; if you read them one after the other in the same frame of mind, you will feel a somewhat similar tempo in the unfolding of their stories. They are, in fact, both English ladies – but Miss Roberts's farms are so different, so infinitely, infinitely poorer that the resemblance has to be sought for.

The American Press, whose intelligence goes far, but not quite all the way, received *The Time of Man* with paeans of praise that did it infinite credit, and I believe that even our own reviewers were a little aroused from their lethargy by the earlier book. But the American Press could not quite rise as far as *My Heart and My Flesh*. Nevertheless, the time for that will come, for the latter book is of infinitely greater significance and of cohesion. *The Time of Man* was, in effect, a string of human anecdotes written with extreme beauty, not so much in the matter of writing as in the handling of episode after episode. *My Heart and My Flesh* is written with no less beauty and, indeed, with no less anecdotal luxuriance, but it has an architecture, a building up of effect that was wanting in the earlier book. So that gradually as the psychological *choses données* arrive, are developed and numbered, the mental pressure becomes almost insupportable. I have never in my life read anything that so immensely held me, that so interfered with my own life, as the later hunger-passages of this tremendous book. I know nothing like it in literature and I have never heard of anything that resembled it in life. That is what I mean when I say that a book may enlarge the sphere in which your mind may work. I shall never after this think of heavy toil, sparse living and starvation as I used to think of them in their effects on human psychology. One has been added to.

After that I had better myself add that Miss Roberts is no relation of my own: nepotism has no share in my admiration.

Now & Then: A Periodical of Books & Personalities Published Occasionally from Thirty Bedford Square by Jonathan Cape Ltd, no. 28 (Summer 1928), 18–20.

On Conrad's Vocabulary

★★★

But the main fact is that we worked together – like two navvies digging at a job of work. And what we worked at was not so much specific books as at the formulation of a literary theory, Conrad seeking most of all a new form for the novel and I a limpidity of expression that should make prose seem like the sound of some one talking in rather a low voice into the ear of a person that he liked. Of what took place during those endless conversations I am the sole living witness and my word must be taken for what I say. And they may be taken as going this way, those colloquies: I would ask, 'How would you render such and such a concrete object in words?' Or he would ask, 'Don't you think we have made that rather obvious?' Or even, 'Don't you think we ought to tone that passage down a little?' by the introduction of an obvious word or so, in order that the passage might not read like 'fine writing'.

Our literary friendship, I beg leave to say, was for its lack of jealousy a very beautiful thing. It is a thousand pities that a number of gentlemen who could not, in the nature of things, know anything about that friendship should have attempted to make it look mean and ugly, for whole-hearted friendships that have no other aim than the perfection of a literary method are rare things in this world.

Having said that, I will set down what occurred to me in looking over the manuscript of 'The Sisters' which I was permitted to do by the executors of the late Mr John Quinn.

The manuscript, then, opens up again the question that has always tormented me – and I dare say plenty of other people! – where *did* Conrad get his English? I am accustomed to be told – I was told only yesterday – that he certainly got it from me. He certainly did not. When I am disposed to consider the nature of my interference with his work I think sometimes that I acted for him merely as a sort of thesaurus, a handy dictionary of synonyms. I don't mean to say that his vocabulary was not as large as mine; I dare say it was even larger on the lines of more orthodox English, for he had a marvellous gift for assimilating the printed word and, before I knew him, could have written an article for, say, *The Edinburgh Review*, far, far more easily than I, either then or today. And my function as assistant at his labours was more than anything that of directing him towards an easy use of the vernacular.

It is necessary to labour this point a little. With, then, his marvellous gift of assimilating the printed word, Conrad was just a little obtuse to the spoken one as soon as conversation got outside the stage of *argot*. I suppose that, eager talker as he was, he was not a very minute listener. He could catch, that is to say, a man's characteristic turns of phrase and idiosyncrasies of speaking. That accounts for the wonderful way in which he managed conversation in his novels. But when talk between himself and others grew into conversation and went, as it were, over the country, his attention would wander.

There are three English languages – that of *The Edinburgh Review* which has no relation to life, that of the streets which is full of slang and daily neologisms and that third one which is fairly fluid and fairly expressive – the dialect of the drawing-room or the study, the really living language. It was at this last that Conrad aimed, and which he found difficult to render on paper. That aspiration made his writing life a matter of much torture. Whereas he could have written in the language of *The Edinburgh Review* – I mean no disrespect to that respectable, that even august, organ of a light that never was, since 1820, on land or sea![1] – whereas, then, Conrad could have written that sort of thing with ease and success at any moment, the more fluid language in which words assimilate themselves to each other with delicacy and tenuity tended constantly to escape him. He knew, nevertheless, what he wanted and if any one were at hand to suggest that 'wire' was a more colloquial word than 'telegram' he would accept that word if it would fit into the cadence of his paragraph. Or he would even change the cadence of his paragraph. I daresay that living constantly with a person like myself whose normal conversation is compounded of polite slang words may have influenced his style a little. Indeed I am sure that it did, but he continued his development in that direction long after I had any finger at all in his work, so that it has always seemed to me that *The Rover*, for the limpidity of its style, was almost unapproached.

That would no doubt have happened had Conrad been in daily contact with any other moderately cultivated Englishman who expressed himself in the politer shades of *argot*. I dare say indeed that the slightly stilted nature of Conrad's earliest prose was due to the fact that he consciously guarded himself against the rougher ship's lingo that he had been accustomed to hear. He used to say that he had acquired English by reading in the forecastle the works of Miss Braddon, the *Family Herald* and Bulwer-Lytton's *Pelham*. Indeed the passage in *The Nigger* in which Conrad writes about the frame of mind of the aged seaman, hermetically sealed up as it

1 [Alludes to Wordsworth's 'Elegaic Stanzas' on Peele Castle.]

were between the pages of the book, whilst Donkin and the rest showered expletives all about him – that exposition of a reader's mind may well have gained something from Conrad's own experience. And indeed his own reading of *Pelham* in the forecastle may well account for Conrad's barbarously inaccurate rendering of the cockney's dialect. He must have recognized that the words that exploded around him whilst he read of the tribulations of Miss Braddon's Lady Audley differed enormously from the words that were under his eye on the printed page, dim in the smoky light of the oil lamp. And so he acquired the more stilted style that is most easily recapturable nowadays in his letters of that date. He was not a very good letter-writer, even as novelists go. The prose of his novels was a very carefully calculated affair, its one aim being to be interesting and to be interesting because of the quality of surprise. He avoided the obvious turn of phrase with ferocity – with true ferocity! But when he wrote letters he nearly always just sailed ahead and the result was a certain monotony, even a certain turgidness. I well remember the feeling almost of dismay that I had when during the war I read in a South Wales city a great body of correspondence addressed by Conrad to a compatriot in that port and I well remember the silent petition I put up that those letters might never see the light. But returning to the question of from whom Conrad had his own English I may say that for long I used to think that Mr Edward Garnett must have been largely responsible. But, judging from Mr Garnett's profuse annotations of the actual handwritten copy of 'The Sisters' that can hardly have been the case. Mr Garnett criticizes the work with a minuteness that must have cost him infinite pains, but I cannot discern, in any of the notes that he made, any suggestion of verbal alterations or the corrections of syntax and the like.

The most interesting suggested emendation by Mr Garnett on the margin of this manuscript attaches to the words, 'He made up his mind to try Paris – and started at once'. Mr Garnett comments that this is too abrupt. And indeed to a reader in 1897 it may well have seemed too abrupt, coming as it does at the end of a long passage of psychologizing and completely without preparation.

But the whole, the whole, the whole secret of Conrad's attractiveness as a writer lies in that particular device, that particular form of jolting the reader's attention and if you read Conrad sentence by sentence with minute care you will see that each sentence is a mosaic of little crepitations of surprise and that practically every paragraph contains its little jolt. I must in the old days have accompanied his mind through at least a million written words, and no doubt through as many more that never even got onto paper, and no sound is even today more familiar to me than the voice of Conrad saying, 'No, that's too obvious!' Every two or three minutes the words would come, in a sort of rhythm. And today when I write – at this minute whilst I am writing – my subconscious mind is saying to me, 'Isn't it time to put in a little jolt?' It has become indeed a second nature.

What Conrad got from me as writer I don't know for I never thought about it, but I am perfectly certain that I – and the Anglo-Saxon world – got that particular form of scrupulosity from Conrad. For it is a form – the highest form – of scrupulosity in a writer unceasingly to study how he may interest his reader. And do not let yourself be misled by the orthodox Anglo-Saxon critic into believing that the evolution of such a method is trickery, or a mere device, or merely mechanical. It is the training, as it were, of special muscles for your task. I have seen two quite weedy little furniture removers trot up some narrow stairs carrying a piano that fifteen beefy privates of my command had only succeeded in wedging hopelessly into that orifice. In the same way a really trained writer such as was Conrad can interest you in a washing list or a catalogue of ships whilst the amateur puts you to sleep with an account of the battle of Marathon.

The erasures and alterations in the manuscript of 'The Sisters' are full of interest from this point of view but a disquisition on them would be too technical to be here appropriate. I will however just glance at one or two to show you how Conrad's mind worked:

Thus he changes 'natural aptitude for that sort of thing', which is vague and enforces on the reader the trouble of an effort of the imagination, into 'revelling in a charming occupation', which hints at the charm of the personality and throws on it a certain psychological illumination. Or he changes 'to assert herself' into 'to assert her personality against José' as more precisely establishing the range of the character's self-assertion – as much as to say, 'This character is not of necessity and always self-assertive but one individual calls for a certain measure of self-assertion'. Or, in the interests of precision he changes 'ancient' into 'medieval', the word 'ancient' to some extent connoting classical antiquity: as the phrase 'the world known to the ancients' implies the tract of land round the Mediterranean known to the Greeks and Romans. For the connotations of words must always be considered, a word with double, or vague, meanings causing the reader to pause for a moment, to choose one or the other, and thus taking his mind off the story and slowing down the interest of the passage. Or he transposes, in the interests of his cadence the two phrases, 'of the old people, of the dead', because the short 'e' sound of the monosyllable has the effect of a full stop, whilst the two-syllabled word carries on the continuing cadence. That in effect was how Conrad wrote, at any rate in his early days.

★★★

Bookman (New York), 67 (June 1928), 405–8.

A Distinguished First Novel

Josephine Herbst's novel, *Nothing is Sacred*, which will be issued in September by Coward, McCann, took command of my intelligence with its first sentence when I read it in manuscript and it continued to exercise its singular quality of impressive interest until now it has found its publisher and I have read it right through again in proofs. That is due not to the interest of the subject but to the sheer skill of its narrator. There is no reason – no reason in the world – why I, hardened European as I am – should be interested in and should be kept reading far into the night twice running by the affairs of a quite undistinguished family in a quite indistinguishable American small town – but that is what has happened to me.

You see if a book begins: '"Can I talk to you a minute!" said Harry Norland to his mother-in-law. He stood in the kitchen doorway with his hat on', you are given at once a sense of interest as strong as you receive at the opening of a good detective story and the person who so begins a book will have the sense to carry it on at the same pitch of interest. There is no reason why the story of a small-town family should not be as interesting as any detective-romance – the trouble usually is that the narrators of such tales begin with the thesis that the life described has by them been found uninteresting and that they must therefore make an uninteresting story out of it. But the actual livers of such lives seldom find them uninteresting *per se* – or it might be truer to say that the dwellers in small towns seldom find small-town life as such other than thrilling with its struggles for precedence, local renown, prosperity and the rest. They may of course have intervals of dullness – but who has not? But the fact that they continue to live in small towns and that small towns continue to exist is the proof that their inhabitants find there an interest in life that is not apparent to the outsider.

That really is the problem that is before the modern novelist. If the novel in the future as in the past can only exist with the unusual, the hero, the type, or the demi-god for its sole pabulum, it must in a more and more standardizing world end by losing all contact with life – and by dying as a form of art. And that is the problem that Mrs Herbst has attacked and triumphantly overthrown. For me at least she has done this, and I do not believe that as reader I differ much from the ordinary reader of light fiction: I mean that when I do surrender to reading a book I surrender just as fully as any child reading Hans Andersen or any commuter reading *Sherlock Holmes.*

I have been, twice, just as thrilled to know whether Harry Norland made good the club-money that he had embezzled as to know who committed any murder anywhere – just as thrilled, twice, to know, how his mother-in-law was going, once again, to get the resulting mortgage off her house; and I have twice been left speculating as to how Mr Winter, after his wife's death, liked living by turns with his daughters and their families, and saying to myself: 'Perhaps he will – because in the end they are very decent, dutiful girls – or perhaps he won't because he is an old man of strong character and they are all rather nervous people...' The problems of these quite commonplace people become, in short, one's own problems during the reading of the book, and one leaves them, with a pang of regret – for the destroyed contents of the ragbags of a lifetime in the attic, and of regret as if one were moving into another town and leaving people whom on the whole one liked and respected. In short this is the sort of novel that I want to see make its mark – for the sake of the art of the novel, which is an art I love. I hope it may *faire école,* find thousands of readers, and earn for its writer glory enough to make her continue to go on doing this. And I don't know that, if I wanted to impress a foreign audience with what the native American really is – a normal, honest, wrong-headed, rightly-inspired, undulled – above all undulled! – American that I really like, I don't know that it isn't *Nothing Is Sacred* that I would give to those Dagos. For there stands out in this book a quality of family solidarity, of family dutifulness and above all of family consideration between sensitive individuals such as rarely swims to the surface in the more tumultuously manifest features of life here. I know, I mean, that it exists and is touching and beautiful, but I don't know where – if it isn't in *Nothing Is Sacred* – I should put my finger on the expression of it.

Bookman (New York), 68 (September 1928), 87–8.

Dodsworth, by Sinclair Lewis

I wonder if one could not start a literary journal that should be contributed to solely by the unspoiled readers of books, since, from the standpoint of the novelist, it seems wholly inappropriate that he should criticize the work of his brothers who are, also, inevitably his rivals! However, since the critics are usually too lordly to bother their heads about anything so humble as the inside problems of mere novel-writing, it is difficult to see who is to do that rather necessary job. The most, therefore, that one ought to permit oneself is a friendly hail across space, using the press as it were as a sort of broadcasting apparatus. Then, one may give forth an exposition!

I shall, thus, permit myself to say that I like *Dodsworth* much better than *Elmer Gantry* and that I like Mr Dodsworth much better than Mr Babbitt as being the more convincing, the more human and, I daresay, more 'felt' by his creator. With an immense admiration for *Babbitt* as a book, I always had behind me the dim feeling that Mr Babbitt himself was a little of a Robot, moved here and there by his creator in an unimaginably real projection of Main Streets – the landscape, as it were, being in the major chord. Humanly speaking (I am not here attempting literary criticism), this is a relatively wrong way to look at a landscape. The fact is, if you go to look at a landscape or to observe a country you won't much do so, your impressions being too self-conscious; whereas, if you live and are your normal self and, above all, suffer in any given environment, that environment will eat itself into your mind and come back to you in moments of emotion and you will be part of that environment and you will know it. It is because Mr Dodsworth suffers and endures in odd places all over the European and semi-European world that both he, as a person, and the settings in which he suffers, as settings, seem to me to be very real. Perhaps that is only saying that *Dodsworth* is a poem which *Babbit* isn't.

Indeed, the title might just as well have been 'Europa, an Epic'. For Mr Lewis presents to you practically all of Europe that counts in our civilization, including New York which isn't America. He also poetizes these places so admirably through the emotions of the sympathetic Mr Dodsworth that when you have finished the book you, too, will have suffered and had your own emotions in the rue de la Paix – genuine emotions and not limited to the fact that in a shoe-shop they tried to charge you one hundred and fifteen francs for paste shoe-buckles instead of one hundred francs which is the price on the label. Indeed, I lately heard a lady say that Egypt was a rotten country because you could not get shredded wheat biscuits in Shepherd's Hotel, which was not true at that. I learn from another that Corsica is a bum island because the New York papers could not be had in an obscure mountain village, whereas it is a known fact that the birthplace of Napoleon might as well be sunk beneath the sea, but for American money.

That is the sociological value of *Dodsworth* and the benefit it may do to civilization. Indeed, I think it is safe to say that the superiority of Mr Lewis as a sociological writer far in advance of others lies in the fact that he has a remarkable gift for rendering and the restraint which keeps him from pointing morals. Of course, his characters do indulge themselves in a great number of expository disquisitions but Mr Lewis makes it sufficiently clear that he backs neither set of views when they do discourse. Thus, things remain very much as they were at the beginning and the final impression is one of a sort of solidarity of mankind from Altoona to the Adriatic and back.

That is a great achievement and I hope that *Dodsworth* will diffuse itself by the million on both sides of the Atlantic. It will do more to spread a knowledge of the world and its friendlinesses and freshness and attractions than a wilderness of Baedekers. Besides, it is a good novel, a good story. I found myself towards the end of the book really hoping that the hero might get his young woman – hoping against hope and turning to the last page to make sure. This is the real test – more particularly for a book that is going to do good: for it must be read for itself and the moral must sink in unperceived as do the morals that we draw from life itself. To that end, we must identify ourselves with the characters and live in the scenes.

I found myself, as I have said, hoping that Mr Dodsworth might have his luck because, subconsciously, I regarded it as an omen that I might have mine; and that is to read a book as one read in the old good days before fifty or so winters and half a century or so of books had besieged these brows. That is the real, unconscious tribute and the real, true, friendly hail!

Bookman (New York), 69 (April 1929), 191–2.

Mediterranean Reverie

The warm winter sun falls on my back as I sit writing. There is an orange on a tree that never yet bore. That is consolation. One once had friends. The cities swarmed with them. One could go towards any of the cardinal points or between them in any direction to find joyous discussion of things worthy the attention of proper men. That is all done. The world's arguments are grim – and profitless. It is to me great consolation to let my mind wander along the pink corrugations of these Mediterranean beaches. Their rocks hardly fret at all the blue water, and, when the thoughts have sufficiently but not too far pursued the shore, they shall come on where Ezra sits plucking – in the name of the poets – figs from the dusty thistles of this world. So all in our civilization is not lost. All that is civilized in our time comes from these shores by one bye-road or another. Their winds enjoin reason, moderation, frugality and, in due measure, saturnalia. If our civilization is to continue or even to be remembered, we must have our outposts not only in torrid or boreal wildernesses, but beneath these tempered and undying suns. We must have, too, our spies into the Past that inexorably governs us and that changes constantly its aspect. The giant Atlas to refresh his strength must constantly retouch the earth of these Mediterranean shores. So must we.

Mr Pound[1] learned all that he knows of life and letters from, in the first place, Flaubert. Tactics he learned at Altaforte at the feet of the Bertran de Born who incensed the whole world with his libels. Of strategy Mr Pound never heard, nor yet, though he sits in the shadow of the statue of Columbus, has he permitted his mind to be opened by travel. Of infinite mental tenacity he reclines in a remote fragment of Coney Island that has dropped from the skies near Porto Fino. There he pursues what Flaubert pursued in his solitudes under the Norman cliffs of Croisset – the just, the 'charged' word in just and even more charged cadences. That is his constant pursuit. But at times he throws down the pen, grasps any tool, from chisel to sword, and springs, ululating, into any ballyhooly that may be going on anywhere. With these activities he keeps his muscles keyed up. Very likely without them he could not support the strain of his pursuit of the intangible. These, his minor passions, have been innumerable and boundless in scope. Always writing poetry, from the age of ten, he has

1 *Cantos*. By Ezra Pound.

been by turns professor of the Romance languages, cattle-hand in liners, Cook's guide to Spain, founder of movements in London. He has taken chunks of rock, hit them with hammers and produced eggs or golden birds *à la* Brancusi; he has hammered tennis balls with rackets and become champion of Southern countries; he has taken *fleurets* and *épées de combat* and challenged with them admirers of Milton; he has hammered, tickled and blasted pianos, bassoons, spinets and ophicleids and has produced operas that have been broadcast by the BBC. He has been at once the last survivor of Murger's *Vie de Bohème*, censor of world morals and Professor of Economics for the Province of Genoa.

These activities would be bad for his work if he pursued them *en amateur*. But not a bit of it. He has acquired his fantastic erudition by really being in turn all these things. He was professional Professor of the Romance Languages, professional cattle-hand, professional sculptor, duellist, bassoonist and composer of operas. Yesterday he was Professor of Economics at Rapallo. Today, to my relief, he is head impresario of his Ligurian Academe. His Mozart week rivalled that of Salzburg, and he is at the moment organizing concerts of chamber music that should make all proper men desire to go to the Gran Sala Del Municipio di Rapallo. It gives me at least a feeling of, let us say, *Sehnsucht* to think that, if I could exchange the sunlight in which I am sitting for that other sunlight, I could this very afternoon listen to this programme of Ezra's Concoction:

1. From the Collezione Chilesotti:	
Canzone degli uccelli	Francesco da Milano
Suite da Ballo	Giovanni Terzi
2. *Sonata per due violini e pianoforte*	Corelli
3. *Golden Sonata per* do. do.	Purcell
[4.] *Sonata, violino e pianoforte*	Debussy

Olga Rudge, *Violinista*; Gerhard Munch, *pianofortista*; Luigi Sansoni, *violinista*;

Professor Marco Ottone, *cellista invitato*.

I wonder where in London I could hear the Purcell, or where in Paris the Debussy. Or, in either, such players! And all the while Ezra pursues the writing of his cantos on his fifth floor over the Mediterranean.

Nor is it to be imagined that all his other activities are merely devices for passing the time, getting rid of uric acid or emulating the wasp. The war put an end to his remarkable activities in London of the '13s and '14s. Without that, London might well today be the literary, plastic and musical centre of at least Anglo-Saxondom. As it was, the spirit passed to West Eighth Street between Fifth and Sixth, and from there spread throughout the United States, so that the whole American approach to the Arts resembles today very nearly that of the exciting times that we witnessed round Holland and Church Streets when Vorticists and Cubists and

Imagistes and Futurists and the morning stars and Mr Wyndham Lewis (Percy) and Signor Marinetti sang all together in their glory.... *Tempi Passati! Tempi Passati!*

I do not mean that that gay, iconoclastic spirit passed entirely to transatlantic *parages*. Of the contributors to the remarkable, spontaneous tribute to the cantos and their writer that sprang up last year at their first publication in the United Stales, six at least of the fifteen are European by birth – Hugh Walpole, Francesco Menotti, Paul Morand, James Joyce, Basil Bunting and another; and two more, T.S. Eliot and H.D., have become British subjects, the Old World having thus the majority, the seven, dyed in the wool – and Anglo-Saxon – sons of Old Glory being Ernest Hemingway, Elizabeth Madox Roberts, John Peale Bishop, Archibald MacLeish, Allen Tate, Edmund Wilson and William Carlos Williams. So this Poet's Progress has not wanted for observers either in the New or the Old Worlds. And the tributes were as remarkable to his activities as to the cantos themselves. Mr Walpole says that Ezra stirs both his appetite for beauty and his creative zest; Mr Hemingway that any poet in this century or in the last ten years of the preceding century who can honestly say that he has not been influenced by or learned greatly from the work of Ezra Pound deserves to be pitied rather than rebuked; Mr Joyce that 'but for him I should still probably be the unknown drudge that he discovered' – and so on through the whole gamut of admiration or gratitude....

The reason is that Mr Pound has a genius for words that no one – not excluding Shakespeare in England or Heine in Germany – has ever in modern times much surpassed. Almost any line of his: *'Here we are picking the first fern-leaves'*, *'You who lean from amber lattices upon the cobalt night'*, *'And dawn comes, like a silver-sandalled Pavlova'*, *'Kung walked by the silver temple and into the dynastic grove'* – any line of his, in a hundred moods – *'Sleep thou no more, I see the star upleaping that hath the dawn in keeping'* – without context or support, any such line is like the trumpet-call awakening of a good novel. Mr Pound has, of course, learned a great deal from the novelists – perhaps more from Flaubert than from any other individual, though obviously the Romance and Italian poets of before 1500 and seventeenth-century English – and the Yellow Press and railway time-tables – have all played their parts with his rhythms. So that the range of tones and rhythms of his lyre-bassoon-ukalele-kettledrum-klaxon verse music is almost incredible, and he can turn on this or that stop with the ease and certainty of the consummate organist who plays the double toccata of Bach and at the same time fourteen games of chess at once. I do not recall anyone – not even Pierre Vidal – who ever had the rhythmic virtuosity of the poet of Rapallo – or, indeed, his scholarship, erudition in fantastic human instances and invention.

The *XXX Cantos* make up part of an immense epic history of the world as it centres round the Mediterranean. It is also the divine comedy of the twentieth century. It differs from most other epics in the fact that it is interesting. Mr Pound has learnt what there is to know of form from his long apprenticeship to novelists, and the result is a permanent advance of the poetic art. That is what Mr Hemingway means when he says that the modern poet who has not learned from Mr Pound is to be pitied. The day is over for the solemn individual who augustly specialized in nothing but archaic verbiage, sham medievalism, florists' catalogues and the habits of birds – all things that no human being can much care about. Mr Pound's words are singularly alive, his medievalism is infinitely modern, his subjects infallibly chosen; but his great characteristic is his power to awaken and to hold the interest – a power that is in part the result of training but much more that of his native gift of words – his genius in the strictest sense of the term.

He uses his erudition with extreme boldness, and because Artemis, Sigismund Malatesta, Poggio – and Picasso – all equally live for him, so they and their times and the times between live in his pages. Obviously in so immense a work there will be inequalities. Here and there half a page or half a canto will be given up to humorousnesses that might well have delighted us when we were in the fourth form – and to devote a whole canto of his inferno to human excrement and natural processes is to be prodigal of the inessential. That is no doubt a relic of Americanism. You must have some unpleasantnesses in a hell for financiers, and, for a son of Philadelphia, defective plumbing may well have a hypnotizing dreadfulness. I mention these characteristics so that, should, say, the keeperess of the public lavatories in Charing Cross Station be induced by these lines to purchase a copy of *XXX Cantos* she may not upbraid me. Other adults may well support with equanimity Mr Pound's boisterousnesses.

Boisterousness – which is also vitality – is, of course, necessary to getting Mr Pound through his labours. No person of correctitude of views or nicety of expression could have compassed them. In any case here is a work of vast scope, extending from the heights of Olympus to the bottom of the Cloaca Maxima, and one of which our age may well be proud. Banks may break, sterling sink into bottomless pits, and great financial figures know disgrace, and yet the Age need not hang its head. But an Age that does not produce at least one huge, vital and Joviainly laughing epic must stand for ever shamed in the endless ranks of her sisters. From that Mr Pound's great work may well save us. There seems to be very little else that will.

Week-End Review, 8 (11 November 1933), 495–6.

Hands Off the Arts

[I.]

We are about to consider the eternal – and eternally vexed – question of propaganda by means of the Arts, whether literary, plastic, polyphonic or applied. For myself I hold so profoundly the view that the moment an artist introduces propaganda of whatever kind into his works of art he ceases to be an artist; and I have so many reasons for holding that belief that I do not propose to waste time on doing any more than make the assertion. It is the merest common sense.

No sane member of the USSR would ask of the blacksmith that he should make all his ploughshares look like sickles or bid the baker form all his loaves in the shape of hammers; neither would any sane supporter of MM. Hitler or Mussolini insist that the wheelwright should build all his wheels untrue to the greater glory of fascist government. The baker, the blacksmith, the wheelwright would be told to reserve their political activities for the marketplace, the rostrum or the ballot box. And a propagandist work of art is as dangerous a vehicle as one that should have all its wheels untrue. It will exaggerate, and the reaction from exaggeration is nausea; it will over-stimulate, and the reaction from over-stimulation is indifference. The result of all the artists in Anglo-Saxondom from Mr Kipling downward thundering or cat-calling for the late World War has been a resultant and complete indifference to the aims of that War or even a rapprochement with the late Enemy Countries. The wise leader of states or of political movements is he who leaves his propaganda in the hands of pamphleteers, political journalists, caricaturists, military song-writers – and the more temperate, documented and moderate he can persuade them to make their statements, the more lasting will be the effects that they will produce. That again is the merest common sense.

It is unfortunately a common sense that is shared in only by the very few.

The imaginative artist like every other proper man owes a twofold duty – to his art, his craft, his vocation, and then to his State. His duty to himself and to his art is the distillation of emotions from his own time, whether he deal in words, in instrumental or vocal music or in plastic materials. Whilst he is in his workroom, his study or his studio he has no other duty.

Outside his workshop he may be a citizen like the blacksmith, the baker or the wheelwright; he may vote, persuade others to vote in his sense; he may enlist in the armies of his state; he may sail the seas or what he will. But whilst he is at work his mind must be set solely on the production of pretty pictures, enthralling narratives, music that shall move you to tears, armchairs whose very lines suggest repose of the mind, gardens that shall make the day seem brighter, horse-trappings that shall on the highroads delight the eye. His work must first please himself; then it must arouse emotions in his fellow-citizens. He may there rest his case.... Obviously, like other men, he must sell his products so as to live.

But how should the Republic regard these, its citizens? How shall it most benefit from their labours?

The body politic needs proper men. They used to say – as I am never tired of recording – that the proper man was one who had built a house, planted a tree, written a book and begotten a child. Figuratively that is good enough. That proper man has written a book, so he is literate; he has built a house, so he is a man of action; he has planted a tree, contributing thus to lessening the cost of living; he has begotten a child and to that extent has contributed to the perpetuation of his State without causing over-population. You could obviously change his activities. He might have painted a house, written a fugue, laid down a tennis court or advanced the study of birth-control. But as long as he is well educated, to some extent instructed and physically efficient he is good stuff out of which to build up a state. For in statecraft three things abide – Education, Instruction and Physical Efficiency.

The greatest of these is education since only the educated man is capable of so developing the other attributes that he shall not be a danger to the State. Without education the instructed colossus is a mere blond beast. His sole social or cultural expedients will consist in the burning of books and standing up against a wall all who mock at him or diminish his profits.

Your only educators are the Arts. The biologist, the technocrat, the encyclopaedist, the mathematician, the philatelist – all these may instruct; priests and moralists may inculcate their varying and conflicting codes; the statistician may indoctrinate you with the economic theory that is for the moment the mode. But whereas instruction is a pumping in of records of facts, education consists in the opening of men's minds to the perception of fitnesses. That can only come from the consumption, from subjection to the influences, of the arts. The humaner letters are so called because gradually their assimilation differentiates man from the beast that perishes and causes to perish.

A man may be a very proper man, a good citizen, neighbour, father or small producer and may yet know nothing of any science whatever or have had only the most rudimentary mechanico-technical instruction. But without contacts with one or the other of the arts his ideals will be those of the savage who dines off the thighbones of those he has preallably set up against walls and decorates with trophies of their skulls his public galleries or ancestral tombs. Of such you can build no lasting bodies politic.

The function of the arts in the Republic is then educational and they have there no other functions.

II.

I am aware that I am sending forth on behalf of the artist a manifesto that will, as to every word of it, be contested by auto- and technocrats, by the priest, the business man, the American – not the Russian – communist and by the immense majority of the painters, sculptors, architects, writers, composers, painter-etchers, executant musicians and fine printers of Anglo-Saxondom. The autocrat considers that the musician is born to compose and execute marches that shall quicken the step of his troops; the business man, if he considers the arts at all, considers that the function of writer, designer and – over the radio – of the musician, is to aid him in putting over his goods. The priest calls on all three to do nothing but celebrate the glories of his merchandise by promoting the spread of his particular form of bogey-worship: the American communist who is before all things sacerdotal, thinks like the priest. The technocrat proclaims that the artist, along with all the other small producers whom he finds detrimental, shall be set up against walls, five deep and blown out of the world by his latest explosives. And of their bones and flesh he shall manufacture further high explosives that shall finally lead to the world-empire of the twenty to thirty technocrats who alone shall be permitted to survive that Armageddon.

We come then to the hardest knot of all. It is that of the Anglo-Saxon artist himself. That poor fellow can never be brought to see that the mere practice of his art will make him be regarded as any thing but a social *castrato*. In the English branch he mishandles his work forever in order to be acknowledged a country gentleman, a member of the Fabian society, a philanthropist, a Tory member of parliament, a reformer, or in the last resort a vestryman or member of a parish council. He will profess to be what you will so only he may be relieved of the names of inkslinger, dauber or catgut tormentor.

The American artist, on the other hand, tended till lately to aspire to the state of the he-man baring his breast to the Arctic tempest. He would hitchhike, break clinkers, shoot mountain lions, fight bulls, live with Indians.... There would be no end to his semi-public, male exacerbations or derivatives and if you should whisper to him *ne sutor ultra crepidam*[1] he

1 [A variant on the footnote from Pliny, 'sutor, ne supra crepidam indicabet', let the cobbler stick to his last.]

would strike you to the ground with the jawbone of a bull moose.

It is hard for the Anglo-Saxon artist to stick to his mahlstick or his portable typewriter. The climate is against it. And, of late the social revolution has seemed to give him the chance of male-ly opening his lungs and advocating the setting against walls and massacring of innumerable fellow-citizens. To do that renders you all one, at least, with army officers. You may command troops to shed blood. Uniforms and decorations and the adoration accorded to heroes shall follow. The American Communist Party on the other hand, for whom the American artist is almost too willing to propagandize, distrusts the workings of the imaginative parts of artists. At any moment they may go off the handle and lead the party into the arms of the small producer. So you have the spectacle of practitioners of the arts standing on party platforms, spouting propaganda and afterwards constrained publicly to confess that they are not members of the party because the party will not let them be.

I am no politician – or I am a member of a party that never was on land or sea[2] but that may rule the world when Arthur shall come again. And, if I were dictator of the world tomorrow I do not think that I should decree that all gubernatorial and administrative posts must be filled by artists. The artist is needed for other things. Nevertheless the spectacle of the artist thus blinking timidly on the platforms of the ingrate is one to make the blood boil and to cause the ironic cachinnations of the gods to shake the welkin.... There was never a time when humanity so needed the inculcation of the gift of sympathetic insight; yet, Rome being already a-burning, the artist is to become the platform protagonist of any bloodthirsty party in the State.

France before all others is the country of the small producer and the artist, he being the only member of the human comity who cannot mass-produce and France was the first amongst the nations to declare that her books were her best ambassadors. And we have just been confronted with the spectacle of France being represented at the White House by the most elegantly distinguished of her poets[3] whilst this country was represented at the Quai d'Orsay by the most elegantly distinguished of her department store proprietors.[4] This country nevertheless is represented at the Kremlin by a novelist – and between Franklin, Hawthorne and Mr Bullitt as many American writers have diplomatically represented this country abroad as has been the case with France.[5] And these artist-ambassadors have been as

2 [Alludes to Wordsworth's 'Elegaic Stanzas' on Peele Castle.]

3 [Paul Claudel (1868–1955), diplomat, poet and dramatist, was ambassador to the USA from 1927 to 1933.]

4 [The US ambassador to France from 1933 to 1936 was Jesse Isidor Straus. His father, Isidor Straus, was one of the owners of the R.H. Macy & Co. department store in New York.]

5 [Benjamin Franklin was sent on diplomatic missions to England and France. Hawthorne was consul at Liverpool. Ford's friend William C. Bullitt was the first US ambassador to the Soviet Union, and later to France.]

successful as the career-diplomatists of other countries.... And even England, in the person of Bulwer Lytton[6] once had a novelist for ambassador – without fatal results, though the work of Lytton made a queer appearance at the turning point of the history of the modern world.

That turning point when the blond-beast tradition of applied sciences and mechanics registered its first immense victory over the Latin tradition of the humaner letters occurred at the battle of Sedan. And, on the night after that battle, when he had surrendered his person, but had not yet formally abdicated his power into the hands of the Prussians, Napoleon III passed his sleepless hours reading *The Last of the Barons* by Bulwer Lytton.... You may read allegories into that – the Latin tradition, culture and civilization failing in the dawnlight of the slaughterhouse-materialism that today reigns almost unchallenged in the chancelleries of nearly all the nations the world over.

An allegory indeed – the spectacle of that poor champion of an old faith – for that was how Napoleon saw himself and no doubt was – lying, racked with the pains of gallstones and the despair of his lost cause, on the ground of a hut on the battlefield whilst outside tramped the footsteps of his Prussian gaolers. And he reading one of the worst novels that even official Britain ever produced from the pen-end of a British novelist-diplomat.

The moral is perhaps that if you wish to retain your Empire you should not read bad novels. But that is not the main deduction that I wish here to make. Artist-diplomatists make no worse representatives of their countries than trained diplomats – and no better. That being the case it is useless to waste them on jobs that anyone can perform and it is better to concentrate on the educative function of the artist in the Republic and to accentuate the fact that the educative function has in it nothing of the instructional.

Instruction consists in the introduction of always more facts into the memory of a man and facts are of no educative value. That the new Ecuador stamp is magenta in colour and, when it is of the face value of twenty pesetas shows a streamlined wing as a device; that, according to Dr Whitney, electricity may be called a flow of electrons; that from the pheno-phenyl ring an infinite number of synthetic products may be obtained... all these statements and an infinite number of others gathered from the biologist and the rest are of no educative value. They have of course an applied usefulness as often destructive as constructional, but the human imagination got on very well without them for millions of years and will one day have to get on without them again.

But education provides not for the stuffing but for the enlarging of the

6 [Actually his son, Lord Lytton, who wrote under the name of 'Owen Meredith', and was Viceroy of India and French ambassador. Bulwer Lytton was an MP, but not a diplomat.]

human perception. It acts on the mind of man as the light of the sun on the petals of an unclosing water-lily and, since the arts of our day can refresh their traditions from the arts of empires that fell in ruins thousands of years ago, the stream of the arts is for ever broadening. And, most urgent of all, whereas instruction sets barriers between the races of mankind, education alone conduces to their union. Your nation of ideally instructed human beings would be one whose chief executive could exterminate all the other races of the globe by the touching of a button so that all those races of the globe should become the helots of that ideal race – for fear the button should be touched.... But as against that your ideally educated world would be one in which a ubiquitously heard and perfect performance of the Matthew Passion[7] would carry humanity a little further towards mutual benevolence, comprehension and union.... Those are the alternatives.

The ideally educated citizen of an ideal Republic is one whose emotions have been sufficiently often stirred to let him control them in face of outbursts of public passion – and merely passing your time amongst the manifestations of the arts by so much puts off the approach of Armageddon. That is what education is and that its purpose. A day devoted to the reading of the Greek Anthology in the shadow of the wings of the Victory of Samothrace will be a day saved from the promptings to bloodshed that are the most distinctive feature of the psychology of today. That at least is time gained. On the other hand, if you spend, as I did lately, a whole day listening to the sadist objurgations of a technocrat leader who desired to see the massacre of all Belgians, the sterilization of all Frenchwomen, the razing from the earth of all such Italian buildings as contained works of ancient art – who called for the expulsion from the United States, or the standing-up against a wall of all Jews, Catholics, Communists, Slavs, Wallachs, Mongols and Englishmen – if you pass a day listening to such doctrine you may be the mildest of men but the odds are that, as you retire to bed, you will be wondering what throats you yourself might order to be cut... to show your manhood! And it is today difficult to go anywhere in the world – I do not mean merely in these United States – without hearing similarly frenetic outpourings of hate... for hate's sake.

In face of that are you really going to advocate the enlistment of the imaginative arts which can forge weapons terrible enough for incitement to short madnesses ... are you really going to advocate their enlistment in this struggle of sadist maniacs?

7 [Bach's *St Matthew Passion*.]

III.

Let us recapitulate.... The duty of the artist towards himself is once more, to produce pretty pictures, lovely music, thrilling stories, golden spires, horse-trappings that, on roads, shall delight the eye. The duty of the State is so to utilize such products of the arts of escape that its citizens may not have before them forever promptings to gain by butchery.

Education by the arts proceeds in this way. They do not instruct: they sensitize. Let your mind dwell for a moment on the recollection of the passage in literature that most permanently has impressed itself on your personality; go to see the picture you esteem the most beautiful in the world or the building that seems to you the most tranquil of mighty things and spend some time in front of them. Or merely examine for a long time a curious and beautiful piece of craftsmanship. You will ensure in yourself a certain change. You will ensure for yourself a moment of silence and in that your perceptions of human values will become more clear in your subconsciouness. For the immediate effect of the contemplation of matchless things is a marking time of the spirit, a deep oblivion of the material passions of the world surrounding you. Read *Lear*; come suddenly upon the Winged Victory on the top of her staircase on the Louvre; upon the Maison Carrée amongst the turmoil of the streets at Nimes; on the *Déjeuner sur l'herbe* of Manet.... And there is nothing to say. There is no comment. The leaven of education is at work; the mind is unclosing a little. Liszt records that after he had one day made what he considered to be a matchless rendering of the Appassionata, for two minutes there was not a movement in all his audience, till they went away in silence; and when King René of Provence first threw back the wings of Fromentin's triptych of the Adoration of the Shepherds no man of his court spoke for a long time.

It makes no odds to what school your masterpiece belongs. The lines of verse that most search my own person are these:

> Less than a God they said there could not dwell
> Within the hollow of that shell
> That spoke so sweetly and so well ...[8]

and the four lines of Catullus that begin *Te spectem suprema mihi quum venerit hora.*[9] The single clause of prose that to me has been most surprising and most educative is from the passage about the hat of Charles Bovary ... *une de ces pauvres choses dont la laideur muette a des profondeurs d'expression comme le visage d'un imbécile.* Or if I want to remember a magic verbal projection of the concrete there is the picture of the boy Alyusha and the

8 [Dryden, 'Song for St Cecilia's Day'.]

9 [In fact Tibullus, I.i.59: 'te spectem, suprema mihi cum venerit hora' – let me see you when my last hour comes.]

rushes and the horses in the firelight of Turgenev's Byelshin Prairie which, in its entirety seems and has always seemed to me to be the most marvellous poem in the world. Or for simplicity or direct statement there is Conrad's '"It has set at last," said Nina', or James's 'We were alone with the quiet day and his little heart, dispossessed, had stopped', or poor Stevie's: 'The waves were barbarous and abrupt.' ... oh, and the Coronation of the Virgin in Heaven of Enguerrand Quarton at Villeneuve les Avignon and the Baigneur of Cézanne. And I hope that when I am dying someone may be playing the second movement of the Concerto for Two Violins....[10]

But it makes no odds what it is. You may – and some very good people do – prefer the livelier first part of the Bach piece; or the paintings of Correggio, or 'Ulalume'; or passages of Stendhal or Dostoevsky, or the projection of the river at night from the Mississippi Pilot or Cavalry Crossing a Ford or Simone Martini's Annunciation or something written yesterday or composed four years ago. It is all one. You will know the magic of such remembrances and they will have opened, to the measure of the light vouchsafed,[11] your feelings of perception of the harmonies of the universe. There is hardly a human being so low as has not experienced that change. I met one day a man who was one of the business autocrats of this country. He said that, he being one night a guest on a dahabeah on the Nile, his host who was going ashore had given him one of his matchless cigars and one of my novels. He said he had never known such pleasure as in that smoking and that reading. He said he had never read a novel before or since but he distinctly remembered that it had made him feel a better man.

I could not explain why a phrase about Charles Bovary's hat should so profoundly move me – though the phrase is very famous and has similarly moved many thousands of people, mostly writers. And neither could you explain what it is that moves you in the pictures or symphonies that your subconsciousness chooses shall remain for ever in your memory. It has nothing to do with context, subject, ethics. It has nothing to do with reason or the idea of immortality. It is the rake-off that Providence vouchsafes to mankind in order that, in a world that is a maze of murderous walls, he may maintain within his heart a faint glimmer of sanity.

The preservation of that Promethean spark is, it must be evident, more precious to man than the prevalence of any one creed, of any single party,

10 [Flaubert, *Madame Bovary*, Part 1, ch. 1; Turgenev, *Sportsman's Sketches*; Conrad, *Almayer's Folly*, opening of ch. 10; James, conclusion of *The Turn of the Screw*; Stephen Crane, 'The Open Boat'; Bach's Concerto for two violins.]

11 [Another allusion to Wordsworth's sonnet 'If thou indeed derive thy light from Heaven'.]

of any disputed economic doctrine. And it is equally evident that if mankind is to be preserved, the note of sadist slaughter that underlies the doctrines of all the parties of all the states of today must be qualified by the spirit that has inspired the humaner letters and the finer arts.

It would be a good thing therefore if the leaders of temporal parties would adopt the doctrine: Hands off the Arts.

American Mercury, 34 (April 1935), 402–8.

Men and Books

Edward Crankshaw, *Joseph Conrad: Some Aspects of the Art of the Novel* (London: John Lane, 1936)

What most strikes me on reading Mr Crankshaw's admirable and unusual monograph about my late friend is astonishment at the way in which his speculations into the art of the novel re-cast Conrad's own wandering into that endless maze. The resemblance of the mental attack is at times startling. Reading the book I seem to be a third of a century back, sprawling in a deep chair as I used to do in the smallest hours of the mornings, listening whilst Conrad stormed up and down the long, low parlour of the Pent, in his endless search after the New Form… for the Novel. Hour after hour, for night after night, for year after year…. For, next to his family solicitudes, or before them, even, that was the one stable and for ever unsatisfied longing of his life.

And, with Conrad's books to help him – which poor Conrad hadn't – Mr Crankshaw comes amazingly near to working out the pattern on that carpet. He gets indeed everything that he could get out of Conrad's books; to get more he would have had to know Conrad – to know the really extraordinarily Promethean quality of Conrad's mind… of his very passions.

For really to know Conrad you had to realize that he was always acting a part – except in the matter of the two passions I have mentioned. And one of those was a dual affair. He desired passionately to find a New Form for the Novel because he desired with every fibre of his being that the Novel should be honoured. Novel-writing was to be regarded as – as indeed it is – the only pursuit worthy of the proper man. It was to present a picture of life so that humanity might appreciate its own nature; it was to solve all human problems because it would present all human problems in a steady, clear light and thus they should become assimilable. It was to be the Gospel; the Stay; the Light; the Paraclete. It could, he used to repeat over and over again, do anything. As who should say: 'With God all things are possible!'

The Novel was, in fact, his religion, his country, his unchanging home and his only real means of communication with his fellow beings. So that really to know Conrad you had to read all his books and then to fuse the innumerable Conrads that are in all of them into what used to be called a composite photograph.... You could know him in fact only as you know Shakespeare who was at once Iago and Othello. In the same way Conrad *was* Marlow; but he was also Stein and the French naval lieutenant – and Nostromo and Lord Jim and Haldin – and Mr Verloc – and tried desparately to be all the Anarchists of *The Secret Agent*.

He hated the necessity to be all these things. He became unwell whilst he was being Haldin. He tells you himself in the preface to *The Secret Agent* how he groaned over the necessity to become for three weeks what he imagined Anarchists to be. But he could be Verloc with pleasure because what he liked best to be was what in their leases the French call *bon père de famille*, in a blue melton cloth overcoat with velvet collar and billycock to match, in the endless rattle of dominoes in a City Mecca playing interminable games of matador, a game at which he displayed real genius. I must have played a thousand games with him and never won more than four. When he was sleepy! ... But he was so seldom sleepy over his darling pursuit.

His central, his unbuttoned, self was in fact just you and me ... And the grocer of the corner shop. And the policeman, a little.... And of course any dago of mysterious avocation... A commission agent making large profits, with lots of leisure.... He had to make his desperate sorties into the wearisome and disreputable pursuit of weaving innumerable lies... but didn't he groan over it! And didn't he at times in sheer exasperation of boredom throw, like Cézanne, his mahlstick at his canvas and shout:

'I can't go on with these damn masterpieces. A daub's a daub. Damn aesthetic consistency.'

I like to consider Conrad as a painter because it was about the only thing he never was.... Unfortunately he was not, like Cézanne, a rich man. So he could not afford, like Cézanne, to slit his canvases to pieces with his palette knife and throw them into the tops of trees. He was *bon père de famille* and they had to go to make fortunes for the parasites who prey upon us novelists.

It is because he does not take into account all these characteristics of the author of *Under Western Eyes* that Mr Crankshaw's book is not a complete, an exhaustive, résumé of the methods of Conrad. But that was not his purpose as is shown by his sub-title. His sensitive probings would eventually have brought him to all these conclusions ... perhaps only after he shall have written as many novels as Conrad himself will he really have arrived at that conclusion. For I suppose it is only the weary novelist who can really tell you how novels are written.

But his sub-title Mr Crankshaw does exactly fill out. Some aspects of the Novel he comments on exhaustively, using some aspects of Conrad for his *corpus vile*. His book is all the more valuable because of that. Conrad was an individual with wilfulnesses, private characteristics, *défaillances*. But the Novel is something clear, hard, unchanging.... Merciless even.

And because, in his search for the New Form, Conrad brought the Novel to its present stage, Mr Crankshaw could have used no one else for the purpose of his dissection. No one else, at any rate, has since Conrad made any new excursions into the Form of the Method of the novel. The temper of the times has changed. We have evolved prose cadences more suited to our passing moods. But as far as form, construction, *charpente* and *progression d'effet* go,[1] if you want to progress beyond him you will have yourself to make the difficult explorations into the minds of men.

All that Mr Crankshaw finely brings out. I do not know of any book like his in English-English or any better one in either American or French … or indeed any one nearly so complete. It should thus prove extremely valuable; for the poor Novelist – and the poorer Public – should have someone to go to for light on the Difficult Art of conveying vicarious experience. And with Mr Crankshaw they will be safe.

His chief defect is that he writes so admirably that the soothed mind glides over his phrases missing at times the content. To get home to our bemused intelligences criticism should he written crudely and with the brutality of the up-state crime reporter. This trick Mr Crankshaw has not yet learned. And I don't know that we ought not to hope that he never will.

Because, if we had many writers who wrote such sensitized matter in a manner so unobtrusive and rhythmed, we might become civilized beings.

Time and Tide, 17:21 (23 May 1936), 761–2.

1 [*charpente:* framework or construction; *progression d'effet:* a central Fordian technical term, connoting a calculated progressive increase in tension. See pp. 147, 186 above.]

Observations on Technique

Notes on a lecture given by Ford at Olivet College in June 1938.

Conversation is the best means by which a 'character' in a piece of fiction may be indicated. This is the only purpose for which direct quotation should be used. Conversation should never be employed to carry the story along, develop the plot, or to indicate action. If the author uses his characters' speech to develop his story, the reader will wonder whether or not the character who speaks is being allowed to tell the truth. Therefore, the author should never let this doubt enter.

All the narration of the story should be done by the author himself.

The first speech of a character is important inasmuch as it serves to 'fix' or typify or indicate the kind of character we may expect.

Never let characters remain static throughout the course of the story – each important character must be altered by the circumstances touching him and surrounding him or the story may easily fail.

My method to make conversation seem more natural and to imitate the continual breaks, unfinished sentences and undeveloped thoughts of ordinary converse is to use the pause …. before the speech. The reader loves what he takes to be 'real' conversation not 'speech' and not some artificial exchange of neat sentences that has been concocted by the author.

Usually in a conversation neither speaker cares very much what the other is talking about. Each will go along following his own theme of thought and quite oblivious to the interruptions of the other.

Conversations must be realistic, not 'real'. There must be just enough normal-sounding breaks, pauses, catch-phrases and well-worn expressions in a long speech to make it convincingly human and not literary.

Example of Projection: 'The glass had bubbles.' Example of Narration: 'He looked and he saw that the glass had bubbles.' Projection: the author telling the story and moving the character about with his hands. Narration: a character moving through the action of the story and the author simply on hand to record what happens, what is thought or felt.

In narration the author may conceal his literary idiosyncrasies. In first-person narration, by filtering the story through a carefully concerned set of prejudices, ideas, habits of thinking and observation owned by his chief character, the author may avoid the difficulty of too personal and too autobiographical a style. De Maupassant never bothered to conceal his method in this way. (Reference: 'The Field of Olives.')

Edited by Robie Macauley, *Shenandoah*, 4 (Spring 1953), 49–50.

Ralston Crawford's Pictures[1]

Li Po says somewhere: 'By the stirring of the emotions and their expression the heart is set free'... And since the Arts both express and stir the emotions the Republic is benefited since a Republic of men with free hearts is the best sort of republic. The Artist is not concerned with these matters. His task is to make you see[2] – to make you see what he either sees or remembers having seen or has felt whilst seeing. He may be looking at the leaning tower of Pisa and be reminded of a wave of the sea, mnemonic suggestions being queer affairs.

The beholder on the other hand may see only what is on the canvas – only the colours and the texture of the paint. Or he may see only the wave of the sea painted by the painter on seeing the leaning tower at Pisa. Or – the Artist cannot help this; it is not what he paints for but it is what happens – the beholder in turn, on seeing a picture, may feel a breeze on his forehead or smell the scent of new-mown hay or remember the walks he used to take with his grandmother. At any rate, on seeing a good, authentic piece of painting he will have his emotions stirred and, since the civilized man is one who is habituated to the stirrings of his emotion he is, that beholder, rendered more civilized... Yes, you will go out of Mr Crawford's exhibition more civilized than when you went in.

And again, when you see a picture, you make a new acquaintance, a picture conveying a sense of the personality of the man or woman who has painted... And, still more, when you buy a picture – which is YOUR chief duty, you will take into your household for good a valued and soothing or stimulating fireside friend who will always be there. For I take it that if you do not like the personality expressed by a painting you will not buy it ... That would be carrying a sense of duty too far.

1 [American Precisionist artist and photographer, 1906–78. Ford's note was written for an exhibition of Crawford's paintings held at the Boyer Galleries, Philadelphia, March 10–30, 1937. There have been retrospectives of his work in New York at the Whitney Museum in 1985 (see the *New York Times*,11 October) and the Salander-O'Reilly Galleries in 2001 (see *New York Times*, 11 May).]

2 [Ford frequently alluded to Conrad's preface to *The Nigger of the 'Narcissus'*: 'My task which I am trying to achieve is, by the power of the written word to make you hear, to make you feel – it is, before all, to make you *see*.']

The personality of Mr Crawford – I don't mean the gentleman on two legs who has gone about to see the scenes presented on these canvases, I mean the personality that seems to look out at you, as if through a mirror, from behind the colours – that personality, then, is male, vigorous, honest, perceptive. It would make a good friend to have in the house. His colours have an infectious gaiety because they are clear and juxtaposed with knowledge the one beside the other. His composition is good, in the sense that the eye cunningly directed, has no difficulty in finding the place where the gaze should alight. It alights without shock and moves from place to place on the canvas, as the colours and forms direct it, until they have exhausted the picture. That again makes you gay, because what makes much of the world distressing and most pictures bad – what in fact the artist is there to cure – is that the eye is uncertain where the gaze should alight or where it should go when it has got there. That is all, in the domain of aesthetics, that you can ask of the artist and since Mr Crawford's work possesses and gives out those qualities and vibrations of the sense, Mr Crawford has the right to assert that his labours give us that finest of all things… Fine Art.

***

The Flame in Stone

The Sleeping Fury, by Louise Bogan[1]

There is one word singularly useful that will one day no doubt be worn out. But that day I hope is not yet. It is the word 'authentic'. It expresses the feeling that one has at seeing something intimately sympathetic and satisfactory. I had the feeling acutely the other day when slipping along the east side of the Horseshoe Bend, in the long broad valley that runs down to Philadelphia. I saw sunlight, and almost in the same moment a snake fence wriggling its black spikedness over the shoulder of what in England we should call a down, and then the familiar overhanging roof of a Pennsylvania Dutch barn. It would take too long and it would perhaps be impolite to the regions in which these words will be printed to say exactly why I felt so much emotion at seeing those objects. Let it go at the fact that I felt as if, having travelled for a very long time amongst misty objects that conveyed almost nothing to my inner self – nothing, that is to say, in the way of association or remembrance – I had suddenly come upon something that was an integral part of my past. I had once gone heavily over just such fields, stopping to fix a rail or so on just such a fence, and then around the corner of just such a barn onto a wet dirt road where I would find, hitched up, the couple of nearly thoroughbred roans who should spiritedly draw over sand and boulders my buck-board to the post office at the cross-roads. I had come, that is to say, on something that had been the real part of my real life when I was strong, and the blood went more swiftly to my veins, and the keen air more deeply into my lungs. In a world that has become too fluid, they were something authentic.

I had precisely the same sense and wanted to use that same word when I opened Miss Bogan's book and read the three or four first words. They ran:

> Henceforth, from the mind,
> For your whole joy …

Nothing more.

I am not any kind of a critic of verse poetry. I don't understand the

1 [Bogan was poetry editor of the *New Yorker*.]

claims that verse poets make to be (compared with us prosateurs) beings set apart and mystically revered. Indeed if one could explain that, one could define what has never been defined by either poet or pedestrian: one could define what poetry is.

But one can't. No one ever has. No one ever will be able to. You might almost think that the real poet, whether he write in prose or verse, taking up his pen, causes with the scratching on the paper such a vibration that that same vibration continues through the stages of being typed, set up in print, printed in magazine, and then in a book – that that same vibration continues right through the series of processes till it communicates itself at last to the reader and makes him say as I said when I read those words of Miss Bogan's: 'This is authentic.' I have read Miss Bogan for a number of years now, and always with a feeling that I can't exactly define. More than anything, it was, as it were, a sort of polite something more than interest. Perhaps it was really expectation. But the moment I read those words I felt perfectly sure that what would follow would be something stable, restrained, never harrowing, never what the French call *chargé* – those being attributes of what one most avoids reading. And that was what followed – a series of words, of cadences, thought and disciplined expression that brought to the mental eye and ear, in a kind of television, the image of Miss Bogan writing at the other end of all those processes all the words that go to make up this book.

There are bitter words. But they are not harassingly bitter:

> And you will see your lifetime yet
> Come to their terms, your plans unmade –
> And be belied, and be betrayed.

There are parallel series of antithetical thoughts, but the antithesis is never exaggerated:

> Bend to the chart, in the extinguished night
> Mariners! Make way slowly; stay from sleep;
> That we may have short respite from such light
> And learn with joy, the gulf, the vast, the deep.

There are passages that are just beautiful words rendering objects of beauty:

> … The hour wags
> Deliberate and great arches bend
>
> In long perspective past our eye.
> Mutable body, and brief name,
> Confront, against an early sky,
> This marble herb, and this stone flame.

And there are passages of thought as static and as tranquil as a solitary candle-shaped-flame of the black yew tree that you see against Italian heavens:

> Beautiful now as a child whose hair, wet with rage and tears
> Clings to its face. And now I may look upon you,
> Having once met your eyes. You lie in sleep and forget me.
> Alone and strong in my peace, I look upon you in yours.

There is, in fact, everything that goes to the making of one of those more pensive seventeenth-century, usually ecclesiastical English poets who are the real glory of our twofold lyre. Miss Bogan may – and probably will – stand somewhere in a quiet landscape that contains George Herbert, and Donne and Vaughan, and why not even Herrick? This is not to be taken as appraisement. It is neither the time nor the place to say that Miss Bogan ranks with Marvell. But it is a statement of gratification – and a statement that from now on, when we think of poetry, we must think of Miss Bogan as occupying a definite niche in the great stony façade of the temple to our Muse. She may well shine in her place and be content.[2]

Poetry, 50 (June 1937), 158–61.

2 [Another allusion to Wordsworth's 'If thou indeed derive thy light from Heaven'.]

None Shall Look Back

Mrs Tate is for me the most mysterious of writers.[1] Others no doubt could explain her by her patriotism, her Southern days, her studies. But not these attributes alone can explain where she gets her calm self – the calm self that gets itself into her writings. Her outside-the-study activities are on the side of what the French call *bruyant* – a portmanteau word implying at once vivid, brilliant, clamorous, with a slight soupçon of exaggeration in all three attributes.... How much of the present predominance of Southern Literature in the Western World may not be due to Caroline Gordon's public activities there is no knowing. Certainly she was early in the field. She must have been the first lady in New York to pull down her blinds and declare a public fast on Lincoln's birthday.

All that is to the good. It can be of nothing but benefit to the world to have its attention called to a locality, provincial in itself, in which during five years of obscure mud-fighting, the fate of the whole world for seventy later years was coloured and decided – as certainly as it was at Thermopylae. But *bruyant* championing of Southern charm, manners, dialects, vegetation, landscapes, dog-run architecture, will, if left to itself, merely ensure the reaction usual to our age and situation. To have a permanent effect the Movement must be based on solid, on convincing, on erudite groundings. It must have its classical side.

And that is what is mysterious about Mrs Tate. Her writing is as quiet as Tibullus'. Her Southern mansions are burned by unimpassioned men from Michigan with no more outcry than will attend upon a Westchester public funeral. It is only when you have finished the reading that you realize that you have been present at a very horrid affair and one that you will not soon forget.

None Shall Look Back is most of all a landscape ... as is the *Iliad*. Whilst you read you are suspended above a great territory of champaign, rivers, forests, marshes, monticules. Below you run men in grey or blue, goring the gentle bosom of the earth, or, by turns milking the cows and watching the weather. The men run, the bosom is gentle, you are suspended.

Then gradually you realize that what is going on beneath you is most horrible, the predestined passing of a civilization, the vain mirror of

1 [The novelist Caroline Gordon, and her husband, the poet and novelist Allen Tate, were both friends of Ford.]

unavailing chivalries.... And beside you, as if herself watching, Mrs Tate remains mysterious, unimpassioned, almost impartial as the tragic destiny unrolls itself beneath you both. She writes with the knowledge of a man about the intimate details of men's occupations. Yet you cannot say that she writes like a man – or, for the matter of that, like a woman. It is as if she were Pallas Athene, suspended above the Grecian hosts, knowing what destiny decrees, only at moments of agonized uncertainty intervening on behalf of a hero ... watching.

In its method of attack Mrs Tate's book resembles Tolstoy's *War and Peace*, but lacking Tolstoy's moral point of view and his rather transparent military solecisms it is really a better book against War as well as painting the Civil War with a sufficient military exactness to make you see that war as a numb and horrible thing. It has a peculiar quality of tranquillity; there is no single harrowing scene in Mrs Tate's book, yet when you have read it your impression is that you have attended at an event that is mournful, monstrous, catastrophic, stupid, brutal ... that is all of the gamut of the tragic futilities of Life and its attendant, Death.

I do not know of any other book that so vitally renders the useless madness of human contests ending in mass murder that is called war. There may be such books but I have read a great deal and have not come across them. But I am pretty sure that there is hardly any other book that so enforces the great lesson that all artists must learn before they can write tragedies – that if your approach to horror is not that of the quiet and collected observer and renderer you will fail in attaining to the real height of tragedy. I do not suppose that the book will find any great, hurried troops of readers but I am pretty sure that eventually it will have the support of a tenacious body of great admirers such as will not readily let it fall unnoticed to the ground.

Scribner's *Bookbuyer*, 3:2, new series (April 1937), 5–6.

Statement on the Spanish War

Printed in the section 'FOR' the government:

I am unhesitatingly for the existing Spanish Government and against Franco's attempt – on every ground of feeling and reason. In addition, as the merest commonsense, the Government of the Spanish, as of any other nation, should be settled and defined by the inhabitants of that nation. Mr Franco seeks to establish a government resting on the arms of Moors, Germans, Italians. Its success *must* be contrary to world conscience.

Authors Take Sides on the Spanish War (London: Left Review, 1937), 11.

Index

Abbey Theatre, 143, 164
Acton, Lord, 10, 11, 50
aestheticism, xii, 30, 48, 82
Aldington, Richard, 152–3, 180
Alemán, Mateo, 262, 264, 280
Allegory, 29, 144, 171, 265–6, 304
Aloofness, 22, 26
American Mercury, 300–8
Anabaptists, 13
Andersen, Hans Christian, 293
Anglicanism, 16
Apuleius, 137, 186, 208, 242, 247, 278–9
Aragon, Katharine of, 5, 6, 8
Aristotle, 258, 260–1
Arnold, Matthew, xii, 223, 245
Artzibashef, Michale, 173–7
Asquith, Herbert Henry, 99
Athenaeum, 198, 203–5, 213
Austen, Jane, 286

Bach, J. S., 231, 242, 298, 305, 307
Bailey, ['Festus'], Philip James, 28
Balfour, A. J., 80, 102–5
Balzac, Honoré de, 278
Barnes, Djuna, 270
Barrett, Elizabeth, 193
Barrie, J. M., 109, 235, 251
  WORK
  Peter Pan, 58, 106, 109, 271
Bashkirtseff, Marie, 270
Beerbohm, Max, 56, 192–7, 214, 279
Belloc, Hilaire, 251
Bennett, Arnold, x, 109, 110, 111, 118, 119, 191, 208
Benson, Monsignor, 129–33
Bertran de Born, 47, 242, 296
biography, 93–6, 197–200, 263, 272–5
Bion, 137
Bishop, John Peale, 298
Bismarck, Karl Otto von 103
Blast, 182–5
Boccaccio, 46, 47, 242
Bogan, Louise, 316–18
Boleyn, Anne, 5, 6, 7, 8, 45
Bonar Law, Andrew, 106, 137
Bookman, 288–91, 292–3, 294–5
Boswell, James, 259, 273
Braddon, Mary Elizabeth, 289–90
Brancusi, Constantine, 297
Brough, Fanny, 106–7, 109
Browne, Sir Thomas, 137, 184
Browning, Robert, 73, 163, 194, 237
Bucer, Martin, 13
Bullitt, William C., 303
Bunting, Basil, 298
Bunyan, John, 246, 250–1
Butler, Samuel, 187, 191, 197–200, 241
Byron, Lord, 72, 128, 221, 246, 263
Bystander, 98–109

Caine, Hall, x, 91, 93, 97
Calthrop, Dion Clayton, 43–6
Cannan, Gilbert, 175, 186–9
Carlyle, Thomas, 50, 73, 141, 256–7, 259
'Carroll, Lewis', 251
Carson, Sir Edward, 102, 105
Catholicism, 4–14, 16, 92, 103, 130–2, 150
Catullus, 242, 247, 306
Cervantes, 186–7, 211, 269
Cézanne, Paul, 201, 307, 310
Chamberlain, Joseph, 101
Chapbook, 206–7
Charles V, 5, 6, 9, 12
Chateaubriand, vicomte de, 179, 186, 190, 242
Chaucer, Geoffrey, 31, 46, 150
Chekhov, Anton, 176, 209, 242, 278–9
Chesterfield, Lord, 98, 99, 104
Chesterton, G. K., 251
Chicago Tribune, 232–40
Clarendon, Lord, 193, 269
class, 31, 35, 38, 42, 48, 59–62, 74, 101–2, 134–6, 161–2,

224, 260, 282
Claudel, Paul, 303
Cleves, Anne of, 7
Coleridge, Samuel Taylor, 185, 221
Conrad, Joseph, ix, x, 36–9, 51, 76–90, 110, 111, 187, 190, 208, 210–11, 213, 220, 228–31, 239, 269, 272–5, 278–80, 285, 288–91, 309–11
WORKS
Almayer's Folly, 229, 285, 307
Chance, 229
Heart of Darkness, 77, 114, 229–30, 272
'The End of the Tether', 80, 89
'Falk', 80, 82
Lord Jim, 78, 80, 82, 85, 235, 310
The Mirror of the Sea, 231
The Nigger of the 'Narcissus', 272, 289, 314
Nostromo, 82, 229
The Rescue, 230
Romance (with Ford), 86–7
The Rover, 289
The Secret Agent, 38–9, 51, 82, 310
The Shadow Line, 272
'The Sisters', 288–91
Typhoon, 228–9
Under Western Eyes, 78–82, 310
Victory, 229
Youth, 88–9, 272
conversation, 23, 38, 108–9, 130, 140, 157, 283–4, 288, 312
Corregio, Antonio Allegri da, 307
Cournos, John, 173, 176–7
Court Theatre, 35
Crabbe, George, 194
Craig, Edward Gordon, 109
Cranach, Lucas, 230
Crane, Stephen, 113, 147, 180, 191, 268, 280, 307
Crankshaw, Edward, 309–11
Cranmer, Thomas, 262
Crashaw, Richard, 130
Crawford, Ralston, 314–15
Cromwell, Oliver, 98, 100, 159–60
Cromwell, Thomas, 6, 7, 8, 12
Cubism, 145, 150, 155–6, 297
Cunninghame Graham, Robert Bontine, 10
culture, xii, 44, 61, 72, 124, 304

Daily Mail, x, 260
Dane, Clemence, 208, 212–13, 220
Dante, 38, 242
Darwin, Charles, 150, 199, 280
Daudet, Alphonse, 114, 190, 278
Davies, W. H., 60
Debussy, Claude, 297
Defoe, Daniel, 111, 186, 190, 262, 269, 278–80
Delacroix, Ferdinand-Victor-Eugène, 16
De Morgan, William, 51, 110
De Quincey, Thomas, 261
Dickens, Charles, 42, 72, 91, 114, 162, 220–1, 237, 243, 250–1, 278–9
Diderot, Denis, 186–7, 190, 280
Disraeli, Benjamin, 160
Donne, John, 194, 318
Doolittle, Hilda (H.D.), 152, 158, 180–1, 298
Dostoevsky, Fyodor, x, 40, 126–9, 176, 190–2, 201, 234–5, 279, 307
WORKS
An Honest Thief, 190–2
The Brothers Karamazov, 126–7, 187, 219
The Idiot, 126–9
Douglas, Norman, 208, 213–14, 285
Doughty, Charles, x, 52–5, 193, 264, 269
Drake, Sir Francis, 272–3
drama, 35
Drayton, Michael, 62
Dreiser, Theodore, 278
Dryden, John, 243–4, 306
Dumas, Alexander, 11, 166
Dunsany, Lord, x, 142–6
Dürer, Albrecht, 242

Edgeworth, Maria, 239–40
Edinburgh Review, 288–9
Edward, Thomas, 254–61
'Eliot, George', 188–9
Eliot, T.S., 182, 298
Elgar, Sir Edward, 277
Emerson, Ralph Waldo, 258–9
English Review, ix, 59–90, 98, 164–5, 186, 218–27, 274, 276, 285
Englishness, 33–4, 76, 85, 134, 139, 159, 246–7, 277–8
Epstein, Jacob, 156

Fabian Society, 108, 133, 135, 145–6, 302

Fielding, Henry, 36, 162, 186–7
WORK
Tom Jones, 36, 221, 250–3
First World War, xii
Fitzgerald, Edward, 91
Flaubert, Gustave, 4, 34, 118, 155, 186, 190, 201, 210–11, 216, 219, 242, 247, 267, 278–80, 296
WORKS
Bouvard et Pécuchet, 4
Education sentimentale, 11, 114, 119, 187, 213, 219
Madame Bovary, 147, 187, 210, 250, 306–7
Salammbô, 11, 47, 111, 235
Trois contes, 13, 47, 119, 228
Fletcher, John Gould, 180
Flint, F. S., 151, 154, 156, 180–1, 203–5
Ford, Ford Madox
WORKS
Ancient Lights, 118
A Call, ix
Collected Poems, xv
The Critical Attitude, 98
The English Novel, ix, x, xi
The Fifth Queen, ix
The Good Soldier, ix
Henry James, ix
It was the Nightingale, xii
Joseph Conrad, ix
The March of Literature, ix, xii
The New Humpty-Dumpty, 118
Parade's End, ix, 192
Portraits from Life, ix, xi
Provence, xi
Return to Yesterday, 222
Thus to Revisit, ix, xii, 186
Women & Men, 232
Form, 29, 52, 187, 190–2, 194–5, 278, 292, 309
Forster, E. M., 276–81
WORKS
Aspects of the Novel, 276–81
A Passage to India, 278–9
A Room With a View, 276
France, Anatole, x, 36, 69, 213, 279
WORK
Thaïs, 47
Francis, Saint, 65
Franco, Francisco, 321
Franklin, Benjamin, 303
Freud, Sigmund, 223, 225, 280
Froissart, Jean, 46
Frost, Robert, x, 167–70
Froude, J. A., 4, 5, 6, 7, 10, 12, 259
Futurism, 145, 155–6, 165, 298

Gairdner, James, 11
Galsworthy, John, x, 33–6, 74, 110, 111, 114–18, 274, 286
WORKS
The Country House, 35, 51
The Dark Flower, 114–18
The Fugitive, 115–17
The Island Pharisees, 35
Joy, 113, 115
The Man of Property, 35
The Pigeon, 115
The Silver Box, 35, 115, 116
Villa Rubein, 34
Garnett, Constance, 128–9
Garnett, Edward, 290
Garnett, Dr Richard, 259
Gaudier-Brzeska, Henri, 182–5
Gaugin, Paul, 201
Genée, Adeline, 44
Gibbon, Edward, 10, 262
Gibbon, Percival, 118–22
Gide, André, 278–9
Gissing, George, 111, 137–9, 141, 191, 211–13, 216
Gladstone, William, 100
Goethe, Johann Wolfgang von, 26, 242
Gogol, Nikolai Vasilievich, 279
Goldsmith, Oliver, 262–5
Goncourt brothers, 118, 189, 190
Gordon, Caroline, 319–20
Gorky, Maxim, x, 39–42, 43, 108, 176
Goschen, Sir William, 101, 110
Gosse, Edmund, 50
Granville Barker, Harley, 108, 125
Grimm, Brothers, 247, 251
Guzmán de Alfarache, 262, 264, 280

Hannibal, 41
Hardy, Thomas, x, 110, 190, 208, 237, 282–4
Harte, Bret, 41, 42, 170
Hawthorne, Nathaniel, 303
Hazlitt, William, 196

Heine, Heinrich, 44, 45, 122, 166, 242–3, 298
Hemingway, Ernest, xi, 233, 269–70, 286, 298–9
Henley, W. E., 91, 158
Henry VII, 8
Henry VIII, 4–14, 190
Herbert, George, 130, 260–1, 286, 318
Herbst, Josephine, 292–3
Herrick, Robert, 55, 73, 261, 318
Hewlett, Maurice, x, 46–8, 119
Heywood, Thomas, 78
history, 4–14, 47, 130, 257
Hitler, Adolf, 300
Holbein, Hans, the Younger, 6, 73, 123, 242
Holmes, Oliver Wendell, 261
Holmes, Sherlock, 85, 293
Homer, 4, 247, 319
Howard, Katharine, 5, 8, 9
Hroswitha, 23
Hudson, W. H., 51, 65–71, 187, 192–6, 205, 208, 258–9, 269
  WORKS
  Birds in London, 66, 68
  Birds in Town and Village, 192–6
  Green Mansions, 66, 187
  Hampshire Days, 68
  Idle Days in Patagonia, 68, 70, 193
  The Land's End, 67, 70
  A Little Boy Lost, 70
  A Naturalist in La Plata, 68
  Nature in Downland, 67–8, 193
  The Purple Land, 66, 114, 187
  A Shepherd's Life, 285
Hugo, Victor, 250, 267
Hume, Martin, 10
Hunt, William Holman, 220
Huxley, Aldous, 234–5
Huxley, Thomas Henry, 141

Ibsen, Henrik, 38, 115, 116
Imagism, x, 150–8, 178–82, 298
Impressionism, x, 155, 163, 233
Ireland, 73, 98–105, 107, 134–5, 142–6, 159, 164–5, 208

Jacobs, W. W., 146, 209
James, Henry, 48, 51, 110, 111, 147, 187, 190, 210–13, 274, 276, 278–80
  WORKS
  'The Aspern Papers', 213
  The American Scene, 50
  'The Real Thing', 213
  'The Turn of the Screw', 307
Jane Eyre, 212
Jean-Aubry, G., 272–5
Johnson, Samuel, 53, 91, 193, 197, 200, 259, 266, 273
Jones, Henry Festing, 197–200
Joyce, James, x, 208, 210, 215–17, 218–27, 236–40, 278, 286, 298
  WORKS
  A Portrait of the Artist as a Young Man, 215, 217
  Ulysses, 217, 218–27, 239–40

Keats, John, 107, 163, 193–4, 197, 206, 237, 259
Kingsley, Charles, 249, 262
Kipling, Rudyard, 30, 86, 122, 139, 146–7, 191, 206, 208–9, 245, 267, 300
Kyd, Thomas, 78, 207

Lamb, Charles, 245, 251, 262
Landor, Walter Savage, 218, 262
language, 52–4, 63, 73, 122–5, 170–3, 224–5, 288–91
Law, William, 261
Lawrence, D.H., xi, 110, 180–1, 208, 210, 214–15
Lazarillo de Tormes, 77, 262
Lear, Edward, 239
Leighton, Lord, 184
Leopardi, Giacomo, 242
Lewis, Percy Wyndham, 182–3, 197–202, 208, 210, 214, 220, 298
Lewis, Sinclair, 294–5
Liberal Party, 98–105
Lilly, W. S., 4
Liszt, Franz, 306
Lloyd George, David, 80, 101
Longfellow, Henry Wadsworth, 262
Lope da Vega, 190, 242, 262, 280
Lorna Doone, 208, 252, 262–3
Lowell, Amy, 152, 181
Lowell, James Russell, 262
Luther, Martin, 13, 171
Lytton, Bulwer, 262, 289, 304
Lytton, Lord, 304

McAlmon, Robert, 269–70
Macaulay, Lord, 10, 262, 266
MacColl, Norman, 203–4
Mackenzie, Compton, 110–14, 118
Mackenzie, Henry, 264
MacLeish, Archibald, 298
Maeterlinck, Maurice, 109
Mallarmé, Stéphane, 242
Mallock, W. H., x, 159–63
Manet, Edouard, 306
Mann, Mary E., x, 191
Mann, Thomas, 123
Mansfield, Katherine, 208–10
Marinetti, Filippo, 150, 155, 158, 298
Marlowe, Christopher, 64, 77–8, 230
Marryat, Captain, 28, 208, 252, 262
Marvell, Andrew, 318
Marwood, Arthur, 129, 192–4, 274
Mary Tudor, 7
Marx, Karl, 161–2
Masefield, John, 206
Massinger, Philip, 78
Masterman, C.F.G., 73–5, 160
Matisse, Henri, 201
Maugham, Somerset, 191
Maupassant, Guy de, 29, 118, 123, 146–7, 155, 189, 190, 209, 213, 242, 278
WORKS
'Boule de suif', 120
'The Field of Olives', 29, 313
Fort comme la mort, 127–8, 187
La Maison tellier, 120
Yvette, 120, 209, 250
Mazarin, Cardinal, 11
medieval, 30, 45, 47
Melmoth the Wanderer, 262
Mencken, H. L., 251
Meredith, George, 48, 53, 72–3, 110, 149, 209, 278
metre, 24–5
Michelangelo, 16
Millais, John Everett, 184
Milton, John, 206, 221, 297
modern, 28–32, 46, 52, 141, 184
modernism, x
Montaigne, Michel de, 218
Montgomery, Alexander, 262
Montgomery, ['Satan'], Robert, 28, 266
Moore, George, 187, 208
Moore, Marianne, ix
Moore, T. Sturge, 28–32, 143
morals, xii, 13, 19, 35, 37, 39, 44, 46, 52, 53, 77, 78, 80, 82–3, 84–5, 95, 249–50, 252, 265, 295, 320
Morand, Paul, 234–5, 298
More, Sir Thomas, 8, 141
Morning Post, 260
Morris, William, 46, 53, 115, 155, 163
Moschus, 137
Murger, Henri, 297
music, 24, 25, 60, 63, 140, 297
Musset, Alfred de, 242
Mussolini, Benito, 300

Napoleon, 101, 247
Napoleon III, 304
Nation, 35
Nero, 40
New York Herald Tribune, 272–5, 282–4
Northcliffe, Lord, 104–5
novel, 13, 33, 36, 112, 153, 186–9, 190–2, 193–4, 208–17, 276–81, 292, 309–11

Ompteda, Freiherr von, 123
'Ouida', 194, 213
Outlook, ix, x, 1–3, 110–85
Ovid, 112

Paradise Lost, 30
Pater, Walter, 229
Paul, Saint, 243
Pepys, Samuel, 243–4
personality, 37, 45, 48, 57, 66, 67, 84, 91, 92, 157–8, 164, 214, 264
Petronius Arbiter, 242
phonetic syzgy, 25, 63, 229
Picasso, Pablo, 201, 299
Piccadilly Review, 186–202
Piers Plowman, 150
Plautus, 44, 45
Pliny, 302
Plutarch, 262
Poe, Edgar Allen, 307
poetry, 15–27, 28–32, 49, 62–4, 71–3, 150–8, 163–70, 178–82, 203–7, 230–1, 316–18
Poetry, 316–18
Pole, Cardinal, 5, 6, 8, 12
Pollard, A.F., 4, 7

Pope, Alexander, 44, 45, 243–5, 267
Pound, Ezra, ix, x, 110, 151, 153, 232, 296–9
Pre-Raphaelite, 16, 30, 69, 237
progression d'effet, 147, 186, 311
Protestantism, 4–14
Prussia, xi, 94, 96, 100, 101, 183
psychology, 5, 8–9, 18, 113, 123, 192, 207, 211–12, 217, 219, 220
Pugh, Edwin, 51, 191
Punch, 144, 251, 276, 278
Purcell, Henry, 297
Pushkin, Alexander Sergevich, 128, 208

Quinn, John, 288

Rabelais, François, 218
Racine, Jean, 242
reader, xi, 12, 49, 91, 126, 145, 147, 149, 156, 185, 195, 218, 226, 236–8, 240, 241, 248, 257, 258, 261–8, 270, 285, 287, 292, 294–5, 312, 317
realism, 41, 119, 123, 128, 139, 143–6, 156, 190–2, 201, 267
Reeves, Amber, 133–7
republic, xii, 27, 35, 38, 39, 42, 43–4, 46, 49, 50, 54, 85, 206, 209, 300–2, 304–5, 314
Reynolds, Stephen, 59–62, 74, 110
Richardson, Dorothy, 208, 210, 215–16, 220
Richardson, Samuel, 111, 186, 190, 278, 280
Roberts, Elizabeth Madox, 279, 285–7, 298
Roberts, Morley, 137–42
Robertson, William, 10, 262
Roby, Henry John, 11
romance, 71, 186–8, 201, 267, 275
Rome, 40
Ronsard, Pierre de, 242
Rossetti, Christina, xii, xiii, 15–27, 64, 69
Rossetti, Dante Gabriel, xii, xiii, 20, 91–7, 220, 237
Rossetti, William Michael, 15, 17, 26, 91, 93, 138, 197, 203, 274
Round, John Horace, 10–11
Rousseau, Jean-Jacques, 66, 115, 161
Ruskin, John, xi, 16, 46, 73, 141, 189, 200, 242, 256
'Rutherford, Mark', 111, 139, 191

Saintsbury, George, 62–4
Sappho, 163
satire, 114–8, 148
Saturday Review of Literature, 276–81
Satyricon (Petronius), 186–7, 211
Schnitzler, Arthur, x, 122–5, 209
Schopenhauer, Artur, 8
Scott, Sir Walter, 252, 262
Seccombe, Thomas, 137
serious books, 50, 74, 192–7, 254–61
Shakespeare, William, 4, 31, 36, 40, 43, 73, 78, 92, 96, 150, 197, 207, 211, 242, 245, 246, 251, 298
WORKS
The Comedy of Errors, 64
Hamlet, 31, 32, 191–2, 235, 274
Julius Caesar, 47, 111
King Lear, 40, 138, 207, 306
Love's Labour's Lost, 64
Macbeth, 47, 77, 144
The Merchant of Venice, 40, 56–8
The Merry Wives of Windsor, 40
Othello, 189, 310
Romeo and Juliet, 58
The Tempest, 15
Troilus and Cressida, 253
Two Gentlemen of Verona, 64
Shaw, George Bernard, x, 106–9, 119, 124–5, 142, 246, 251
WORKS
Arms and the Man, 107
Getting Married, 108
How He Lied to Her Husband, 107
John Bull's Other Island, 108
Major Barbara, 108
Man and Superman, 108
Shelley, Percy Bysshe, 95, 163, 193–4, 197, 206–7, 221, 237, 243, 262, 274
short story, 146–9, 209
Sidney, Sir Philip, 98
Sinclair, May, 51, 146–9
Smiles, Samuel, 150, 249, 254–6, 263
Smith, Goldwin, 4, 5, 6, 7, 8, 10, 12
Smollett, Tobias, 111, 186–7, 190, 278–9
Sologub, Feodor, 173–7
Soupault, Philippe, 234–5
The Spanish Tragedy, 77

Spectator, 228–31
Spencer, Herbert, 189, 247
Spenser, Edmund, 31, 53, 241
Stang, Sondra J., ix, xii, xiii, 14
Stendhal, 138, 186–7, 190, 201, 235, 278–80, 307
Stevenson, Robert Louis, 69, 112, 252
WORK
Treasure Island, 208
style, 4, 34, 53–4, 69, 77, 126, 140, 194–5, 222, 228–31, 257
suppression, 23–4
Surtees, R.S., 85, 120
Swift, Jonathan, 243
Swinburne, Algernon Charles, 71–2, 73, 110, 203
Swinnerton, Frank, 127, 208, 211–13, 216
Symons, Arthur, 208

Tate, Allen, 298, 319
Tate, Caroline, *see* Gordon
technique, 21, 22, 23, 50, 62–4, 83–4, 86–90, 94, 118, 121, 139–40, 143, 166, 189, 212, 219, 228–31, 242, 270, 288–91, 311, 312–13
Tennyson, Alfred, 53, 73, 159, 163, 184, 220, 237, 244, 262
Thackeray, W. M., 84, 86, 91, 114, 187, 211, 243, 253, 278–9
Theocritus, 137
Thoreau, Henry David, 258
Throgmorton, Sir Nicholas, 7
Tibullus, 306, 319
Time and Tide, 309–11
Times, 38, 151, 202
Tolstoy, Leo, 39, 40, 176, 278–9, 320
Tory, 70, 80, 98–105, 159–63, 193–4, 244–5, 266, 274, 302
transatlantic review, ix, xii, 241–68
Tree, Herbert Beerbohm, 56–8
Trelawney, Edward John, 274
Tribune, x, 33–55, 110, 111
Trollope, Anthony, 51, 246
Turgenev, Ivan, 34, 39, 40, 118, 128, 155, 174, 176, 186–7, 190, 242, 247, 278–80
WORKS
Fathers and Children, 40, 114
The House of Gentlefolk, 40, 174
'Lisa', 118, 138
A Sportsman's Letters, 40, 174, 176, 306–7
Torrents of Spring, 174
'Twain, Mark', 251–2, 258, 268

Van Eyck, Jan, 16, 242
Vaughan, Father Bernard, 38
Vaughan, Henry, 130, 318
vers libre, 153–4, 157–8, 169, 179, 182, 203–5
[vicarious] experience, 38, 54, 83, 85, 293
Vidal, Pierre, 298
Villon, François, 242
Vorticism, x, 182–5, 297

Wagner, Richard, 203–4
Walpole, Horace, 264
Walpole, Hugh, 298
Walton, Izaak, 261
Wardour Street, 29, 69
Watson, William, 30
Watts-Dunton, Theodore, 91, 93, 97, 203, 213
Webster, John, 31, 77–8
Wells, H. G., x, 51, 110, 111, 118, 191, 209, 245
WORKS
Ann Veronica, 245
The Country of the Blind, 209, 245
The Invisible Man, 245
Kipps, 51, 74
Tono-Bungay, 51, 74
Wharton, Edith, 51
Whistler, James Abbott McNeill, 200, 242
White, Gilbert, 65, 265
Whitman, Walt, 158, 169–70, 203–4, 268
Wilde, Oscar, 229
Williams, William Carlos, 232–3, 270, 298
Wilson, Edmund, 298
Wister, Owen, 51
Wolsey, Cardinal, 8
Woolf, Virginia, 186–9
Wordsworth, William, xi, 250, 281, 303, 307
Wyatt, Thomas, 6, 12

Yeats, W. B., x, 143, 163–7

Zangwill, Israel, 191
Zola, Emile, 123, 211, 250

THE FORD MADOX FORD SOCIETY

Ford c. 1915 ©Alfred Cohen, 2000 Registered Charity No. 1084040

This international society was founded in 1997 to promote knowledge of and interest in Ford. Honorary Members include Julian Barnes, A.S. Byatt, Samuel Hynes, Alan Judd, Sir Frank Kermode, Ruth Rendell, Michael Schmidt, John Sutherland, and Gore Vidal. There are currently over one hundred members, from more than ten countries. The Society organizes an active programme of events. Besides regular meetings in Britain, it has held major international conferences in Italy, Germany, and the U.S.A. In 2002 it launched the annual series, International Ford Madox Ford Studies, which is distributed free to members. If you are an admirer, an enthusiast, a reader, a scholar, or a student of anything Fordian, then this Society wants to hear from you, and welcomes your participation in its activities.

The Society aims to organise at least two events each year, and to publish one or two Newsletters. It has also inaugurated a series of Ford Lectures, which have been given by Martin Stannard, Alan Judd, David Crane, Sergio Perosa, and Oliver Soskice.

To join, please send your name and address (including an e-mail address if possible), and a cheque made payable to 'The Ford Madox Ford Society', to:

Sara Haslam, Department of Literature, Open University, Walton Hall, Milton Keynes, MK7 6AA.

Annual rates: **Pounds sterling:** Individuals: £12; Concessions £6;
Member Organisations £25

US Dollars: Any category: $25

For further information, either contact Sara Haslam (Treasurer) at the above address, or Max Saunders (Chairman) on e-mail at: **max.saunders@kcl.ac.uk**
The Society's Website is at: **www.rialto.com/fordmadoxford_society**

CHESTER COLLEGE LIBRARY